PRIVATE RENTING IN THE ADVANCED ECONOMIES

Growth and Change in a Financialised World

Edited by
Peter A. Kemp

First published in Great Britain in 2023 by

Policy Press, an imprint of
Bristol University Press
University of Bristol
1–9 Old Park Hill
Bristol
BS2 8BB
UK
t: +44 (0)117 374 6645
e: bup-info@bristol.ac.uk

Details of international sales and distribution partners are available at policy.bristoluniversitypress.co.uk

British Library Cataloguing in Publication Data
A catalogue record for this book is available from the British Library

ISBN 978-1-4473-6208-1 hardcover
ISBN 978-1-4473-6210-4 ePub
ISBN 978-1-4473-6211-1 ePdf

Cover design: Liam Roberts Design
Front cover image: Unsplash/@victor_g
Bristol University Press and Policy Press use environmentally responsible print partners.
Printed and bound in Great Britain by CPI Group (UK) Ltd, Croydon, CR0 4YY

FSC
www.fsc.org
MIX
Paper | Supporting responsible forestry
FSC® C013604

Contents

List of figures, tables and boxes

Figures

Tables

Boxes

List of abbreviations

ABS	Australian Bureau of Statistics
AC	Autonomous Community
AE	advanced economy
AMI	Area Median Family Income
BTL	buy-to-let
BTR	build-to-rent
DLV	*det lejedes værdi* (notional market clearing rent)
GDP	gross domestic product
GFC	global financial crisis
HAP	Housing Assistance Payment
HB	housing benefit
ICPFs	insurance companies and pension funds
LCL	large corporate landlord
LLC	Limited Liability Corporation
LLP	Limited Liability Partnership
LP	Limited Partnership
LRR	local reference rent
OECD	Organisation for Economic Co-operation and Development
OMK	*omkostningsbestemt husleje* (running cost system of rent regulation)
PBSA	purpose-built student accommodation
PRS	private rental sector
REA	Real Estate Australia (REA Group Ltd.)
REIT	Real Estate Investment Trust
RPZ	Rent Pressure Zone
RTB	Residential Tenancies Board

Notes on contributors

Michael Byrne is Lecturer in Political Economy, School of Social Policy, Social Work and Social Justice, University College Dublin, Ireland.

A.D.H. (Tony) Crook is Emeritus Professor of Town and Regional Planning, University of Sheffield, UK.

Marietta E.A. Haffner is Assistant Professor, Faculty of Architecture and the Built Environment, Delft University of Technology, the Netherlands.

Kath Hulse is Emeritus Professor of Housing Studies at Swinburne University of Technology, Australia.

Peter A. Kemp is Professor of Public Policy, Blavatnik School of Government, University of Oxford, UK.

Stefan Kofner is Professor of Housing and Real Estate Management, University of Applied Sciences, Zittau/Görlitz University, Germany.

Montserrat Pareja-Eastaway is Associate Professor, Department of Economics, University of Barcelona, Spain.

Teresa Sánchez-Martínez is Associate Professor, Department of Applied Economics, University of Granada, Spain.

Kath Scanlon is Distinguished Policy Fellow, LSE London, London School of Economics and Political Science, UK.

Alex Schwartz is Professor of Public and Urban Policy, The New School, USA.

Mary Ann Stamsø is Associate Professor, Inland Norway University of Applied Sciences, Norway.

Preface

I would like to pay tribute in this Preface to the distinguished contribution that Tony Crook, Emeritus Professor of Town and Regional Planning at the University of Sheffield, and one of the authors of this book, has made over the past four decades.

Tony is one of the world's leading academic experts on private rental housing. He was awarded his first research grant on the topic in 1979, to study the impact of changes in the private rented sector on Sheffield's inner city. This was followed up, among other projects, with a pioneering study in the mid-1980s of the changing ownership structure of the private rented sector in Sheffield. More than three decades later, he continues to research and publish on the supply side of the privately rented housing market.

I have been very fortunate to work with Tony on some of that research. He is a wonderful person with whom to collaborate: an outstanding team worker, always willing to do his share of the work, utterly reliable, meticulous attention to detail, and a rare ability to see both the wood and the trees; absolute commitment to robust research methods and to drawing conclusions and policy implications that are firmly rooted in research findings; and a deep understanding and knowledge of how private rental markets work in practice.

As well as his research on the private rented sector, Tony is one of the world's leading academic experts on planning gain: the use of planning permission obligations to fund new affordable housing and infrastructure (land value capture). Since 2000, in collaboration with academics at Sheffield, Cambridge and the London School of Economics and Political Science, and as a sole investigator, Tony has worked on 17 research grants and commissions on planning gain. This has resulted in a prodigious volume of publications on the topic, including *Planning Gain: Providing Infrastructure and Affordable Housing* (2016) written jointly with the late John Henneberry and Christine Whitehead. Tony authored or co-authored six of the ten chapters in the book. It won the Royal Town Planning Institute (RTPI) Research Excellence Award in 2016. In 2020, Tony and Christine Whitehead won the Sir Peter Hall prize for the impact of their work on policy and practice.

One of the defining characteristics of Tony's academic life is his career-long commitment to what these days is referred to as 'research impact'. That is, research that informs, and ideally underpins, public policy and practice. This is reflected in the countless presentations to, and discussions with, senior public officials that he has given; the numerous government consultations to which he has submitted written evidence; the times he has been invited to give oral evidence to parliamentary and other policy-related inquiries on housing and town planning issues; and the many occasions where senior officials have consulted with him for policy advice.

Tony is not only a distinguished scholar. He has also contributed extensively to academic service. At Sheffield, the university to which he devoted his entire academic career, Tony served for eight years as an outstanding Head of the Department of Town and Regional Planning. It was no surprise that he was then appointed Pro-Vice Chancellor at Sheffield, and subsequently the Senior Pro-Vice Chancellor with responsibility for academic planning, human resources and capital projects. Even after his formal retirement, Tony continued to serve the university in a variety of ways, including acting as its Public Orator.

Throughout his career, Tony – who is a chartered planner – has contributed to his professional body: the RTPI. This includes being a member – and very often, the chair – of various committees and working groups; as well as serving on visitation panels to assess whether university departments should be awarded, or continue to receive, professional accreditation by the RTPI. He also serves on the Architects Registration Board, the statutory regulator of architects in the UK.

Tony has also contributed with high distinction to public service. He has served, and often acted as chair, of countless management boards, committees, working parties and public inquiries. There are far too many to mention here. But, to name just a few, they include: Chair of the Board of Trustees of Shelter, the national housing and homelessness charity; Deputy Chair of the Construction Industry Council (and Chair of its housing panel); founding Chair of Sheffield Homes, which took over responsibility for Sheffield City's 48,000 council housing stock; Deputy Chair of the Orbit Group, one of the largest housing associations in England; and a board member of the National Housing Federation, the representative body of all housing associations in England.

In short, throughout his stellar career Tony has made countless contributions to housing and town planning research, to academic service, to his professional institute; to engagement with policy makers at local, national and international levels; and to public service. The remarkable thing is that, somehow, Tony managed to undertake these very many activities concurrently. And, what's more, was able to fit them all into his life without ever seeming flustered, overworked or anything other than his normal calm, patient, friendly and reassuring self.

Not surprisingly, Tony has been the recipient of awards in recognition of the countless contributions that he has made during his long and distinguished career. In 2001 he was elected a Fellow of the Royal Town Planning Institute. In 2004, he was elected as Fellow of the Academy of Social Sciences (and subsequently served in various roles for the Academy of Social Sciences). In 2013, the university conferred on Tony the honorary degree of DLitt in recognition of his outstanding research and public service. And in 2014, Tony was appointed CBE in the New Year's Honours List, for services to housing and the governance of charities.

I am delighted Tony agreed to co-author with me the chapter on England in this book; and that he also agreed to write the chapter on the short-run impact of the COVID-19 pandemic on the private rented sector.

Peter A. Kemp
Oxford, July 2022

New trajectories in private rental housing

Peter A. Kemp

This book explores recent developments in private rental housing in the advanced economies since the turn of the century and especially since the global financial crisis (GFC). It does so through case studies of nine countries in all of which, to a greater or less extent, the private rental sector (PRS) has either grown, begun to change in fundamental ways or both. These countries are Australia, Denmark, England, Germany, Ireland, the Netherlands, Norway, Spain and the United States. Other advanced economies have experienced similar developments. As we shall see, the timing, pace and extent of these trends have varied between the nine countries in this book. But they are sufficiently pronounced and important in all of them that private rental housing is now receiving a level of attention in public debate and government policy that it has not experienced for many decades. And the same is true for academic research and scholarship on private renting: it is no exaggeration to say that private renting has become a 'hot topic' in academic debates in housing studies after many years on the backburner.

It seems unlikely that many observers in the late 20th century would have foreseen these new trajectories of change in private renting or the revival of interest in the sector that has subsequently occurred. That is hardly surprising. For many decades after 1945, private renting in many, but not all, of the advanced economies was a story of long-term decline (Harloe, 1985) and one from which few commentators expected it to recover. In some countries, including Britain and Spain, it was also a story of decay as rigid forms of rent control inhibited investment, not only in new private rental construction, but also in the refurbishment and repair of the existing stock of dwellings in the sector. After 1945, many advanced economies (AEs) introduced or expanded social rental housing provision; and in some it became an attractive alternative to private renting and thereby a competitor to private landlords (Harloe, 1995). Meanwhile, homeownership grew apace and eventually came to dominate housing provision in most of the AEs; and especially so in what Richard Ronald (2008) called the Anglo-Saxon 'homeowner societies'.

The growth in the owner-occupied market in the AEs during the second half of the 20th century was the result of a highly favourable and unpreceded conjunction of trends. These included: full male employment for the three decades up to the early 1970s; the more recent rise in female participation in the labour market, which increased the income of two-adult households; improvements in social safety nets after 1945, thereby providing increased income protection against 'social risks' such as unemployment, divorce/separation, bereavement, sickness and disability; rising real incomes, enabling more households to save or save more; increasing availability of mortgages for home purchase, especially after financial market deregulation in the 1970s and 1980s; and, not least, the promotion of homeownership by governments in the AEs (Forrest and Hirayama, 2015; Kohl, 2017; 2020).

By the end of the 20th century – with the notable exceptions of Austria, Germany and Switzerland – owner-occupation was the dominant housing tenure across the AEs. It was very popular with the public; and for that reason, among others, was subsidised by most governments in the AEs via market interventions such as low-cost mortgages, tax relief and first-time buyer grants (Whitehead and Williams, 2020). Meanwhile, the housing industry – land developers, house builders, mortgage lenders and real estate agents – had become primarily focused on and organised around owner-occupation (Merrett, 1982; Ball, 1983). When the mass media discussed 'the housing market' it was the owner-occupied sector they usually had in mind, rather than private rental housing. And the prevailing assumption, at least in the classic homeowner societies, was that the owner-occupation rate would continue to increase, primarily at the expense of private renting, as real incomes rose.

In that context, it is hardly surprisingly that owner-occupation, and to a lesser extent social housing, received the lion's share of attention in academic research and debates during the last third of the 20th century. By contrast, private renting – which was either declining or not expanding as a sector of housing provision – was relatively neglected in the scholarly literature. However, because of recent developments since the turn of the century, private rental housing is now firmly in both the research and the public policy spotlight. And very often, that gaze is a critical one, reflecting growing concerns about declining rental affordability, insecurity of tenure, property conditions at the lower end of the rental market, and the investment strategies of landlords, to name just a few topics.

The remainder of this chapter outlines key trends in private renting that have been taking place over the past two decades and the policy concerns that they have prompted (compare Rugg and Rhodes, 2018; Hick *et al*, 2022). Chapters 2–10 then explore the particularities of these trends, policy concerns and the impact of the COVID-19 pandemic, in each of the nine countries considered in this book: Australia, Denmark, England, Germany,

Ireland, the Netherlands, Norway, Spain and the United States. Chapter 11 examines the short-run impacts of the COVID-19 pandemic on the PRS, focusing especially but not exclusively on the nine country case studies. The final chapter draws conclusions about the ways in which the PRS has changed over the past two decades.

Trends in private renting

The developments that have taken place in private rental markets have been the subject of a rapidly growing and impressive body of scholarly research. Most of the attention has focused on the post-GFC period, though some of the developments had been taking place since at least the turn of the century, if not earlier. To set the scene for the subsequent country chapters, this section summarises the main trends that have emerged, many of which are ongoing. However, it is impossible within the space available to discuss these trends in depth, or to review all of the rapidly growing academic literature on the topic. It is also important to note that the ways in which, and the extent to which, these trends have emerged and evolved has varied between countries.

Re-growth

Given the context sketched out previously, perhaps the most unexpected development in many AEs is the relatively recent growth in the proportion of households living in the PRS of the housing market. Hick *et al* (2022) found that 23 out of the 28 European countries they studied had experienced a decline in owner-occupation and growth in private renting between 2005/7 and 2016/18. Likewise, Martin *et al* (2018) found that seven of the ten countries – including Australia, New Zealand and the United States – in their comparative study had seen growth in the PRS. In most AEs this partial re-growth, important though it is, has been relatively modest. But in Britain, Denmark, Ireland, Spain (Hick *et al*, 2022) and New Zealand the growth in the market share of private renting has been substantial. It has been mainly at the expense of owner-occupation, though in some countries – including England, Scotland and Ireland – it also reflects a decline in social housing (Crook and Kemp, 2014).

Because of the decline in owner-occupation, some households that might previously have expected to buy their home are now living in the PRS for the foreseeable future; or are doing so for longer than was the case for their parents' generation. In the UK, the mass media coined the term 'Generation Rent' to describe the growing numbers of young adults who, unlike their parents, are unable to buy their home (Halifax, 2015). Meanwhile, households that in the past would have had a realistic prospect of renting from a social housing landlord are now renting from private landlords. Instead of their preferred tenure, increasing numbers of households are living in the PRS, for the time being at least. Although some may be renting privately from choice, most are doing so through necessity (Clapham *et al*, 2012; McKee, 2012; Byrne, 2020).

The causes of the decline in owner-occupation – and by implication, the accompanying re-growth of private renting – are complex and contested. However, the marked rise in real house prices in many AEs since the late 1990s has clearly been an important factor, not least because it has outpaced the growth in average incomes over the same period. As a result, it generally takes longer for young households to save up for a down payment, thereby reducing their ability to buy a home. While there is broad consensus about this effect on owner-occupation, there is considerable debate about why home prices have risen so much relative to earnings since the late 1990s. There is not the space to discuss this debate here, though Chapter 5 summarises the key issues in relation to England, many of which are applicable more generally.

Growth in buy-to-let landlordism

Private individual investors – often referred to as 'buy-to-let' (BTL) or 'mom and pop' landlords (Scanlon and Whitehead, 2005; Rhodes, 2007; Bierre *et al*, 2010; Martin, 2018; Hulse *et al*, 2020) – comprise a cottage industry of landlords most of whom operate on a very small scale individually but who collectively account for a substantial share of the private rental housing market (Crook and Kemp, 1996; 2011). Wind *et al* (2020) found that a small but significant share of households in the Eurozone countries owned rental housing. In most AEs, BTL landlords are by far the most common type of landlord. Reliable, cross-national data on the proportion of private rental dwellings owned by different types of landlords is patchy. However, drawing on a range of sources and country experts, Kath Scanlon (2011) found that individuals and couples accounted for the ownership of least three-quarters of private rental dwellings in Australia, Belgium, England, France, Ireland, Norway, Spain and the United States. And in Finland, Germany and Switzerland, they accounted for about three-fifths of private rental homes. Private individual landlords also dominate the ownership of private rental housing in New Zealand (Bierre *et al*, 2010).

With a long-established tradition of private individual landlords in most of the AEs, it is hardly surprising that a non-trivial share of the growth in private rental supply has come either from existing private individual landlords expanding their portfolios or from new ones entering the market (Crook and Kemp, 2011; Arundel, 2017; Morris *et al*, 2021). For example,

Aalbers *et al* (2021) found that BTL landlords, and especially small-scale operators, constituted a growing share of purchases in the Dutch housing market. This growth was particularly exhibited in larger and university cities. They argued that, across the financialised homeowner societies, 'changing housing policies and realities have fed the demand for PRS as an investment class and as a place to live' (Aalbers *et al*, 2021, 542). Analysis of British Household Panel Study data by Ronald and Kadi (2018 found that the absolute number of individual private landlords in Britain increased from 558,000 in 1991 to 2.12 million in 2012. They concluded that 'it is overwhelmingly households with small portfolio sizes and little experience, rather than professional institutional investors who have driven increases in landlordism' (Ronald and Kadi, 2018: 798), a finding that is consistent with analysis by Crook and Kemp (2011).

Growth in large corporate landlords

Among the 15 countries for which Scanlon (2011) had information, only in two – Austria and Sweden – did financial institutions and other forms of large-scale corporate landlords dominate the market. Meanwhile, in Finland, the Netherlands and Norway institutional landlords accounted for a substantial share of rental homes. Corporate landlords were present to a greater or lesser extent in the other countries but for very few rental homes in Australia, England and Ireland (Scanlon, 2011).

However, in the wake of the GFC there has been an upsurge in the number of residential property companies including large corporate landlords (LCLs) investing in new construction and existing rental portfolios (Kemp, 2015). Much of this new wave of investment has been in rental apartments; though there has been a surge of investment in single-family rental homes in the United States (Christophers, 2022). The construction, purchase and management of rental apartment blocks is not new. As Martin *et al* (2018: 48) pointed out, in the United States, 'large real estate companies have been in operation for decades, particularly in the "multifamily" or apartment sector' – as they also have in Canada (August, 2020). But over the past decade, LCLs have become more evident in other advanced economies, including those where supply is dominated by BTL landlords.

Martin *et al* (2018) highlighted two important developments that precipitated growth in LCL investment in Germany and the United States (see also Aalbors, 2016). The first was the privatisation of municipal housing companies in Germany from the 1990s. As Kofner (2006; 2014 explained, this privatisation enabled what he termed 'financial investor' property companies to make opportunistic acquisitions of large portfolios of apartments in Berlin (Fields and Uffer, 2016) and other large German cities (Kemp and Kofner, 2014). These companies included Deutsche Annington and Gagfah, which are now among the largest private landlords in Germany (Wijburg and Aalbers, 2017).

The second development highlighted by Martin *et al* (2018) and other researchers (Mills *et al*, 2019) is the acquisition by about half a dozen companies of large numbers of single-family dwellings being sold at auction by mortgage lenders in the wake of the post-GFC evictions crisis in the United States. As Schwartz notes in Chapter 3, many of these homes were in neighbourhoods with high numbers of vacant and often rundown homes in the 'sunshine states' such as Las Vegas where house prices had risen sharply before the GFC and then fallen sharply in its aftermath. The most active buyer of these 'distressed' dwellings was Invitation Homes, a new company set up for this purpose by private equity firm Blackstone (Fields, 2018: Christophers, 2022). On a smaller scale, substantial acquisitions of stocks of repossessed homes were also made in Ireland and Spain, countries that were badly affected by the GFC and that have relatively limited mortgage social safety nets (Byrne, 2016; 2020).

In the remainder of this section, we highlight several important components of the rise of LCLs in the private rental market. They are overlapping developments, but nonetheless merit highlighting individually. These are residential property funds, build-to-rent (BTR) and purpose-built student accommodation (PBSA) blocks.

Residential property funds

One important component of the rise of LCLs has been the growth in residential property funds (Fuller, 2021). Insurance companies and pension funds (ICPFs) have been among the major investors in such funds. ICPFs have long invested in real estate, and especially in *commercial* property including offices, factories and shopping centres. But *residential* property has typically accounted for a very small share of their real estate portfolios or none. Real estate accounts for a small proportion of ICPF assets. Instead, their primary investments have been government bonds and equities. However, while bonds and equities will continue to be the largest ICPF asset classes – not least because of regulatory requirements – the 'search for yield' since the GFC has encouraged ICPFs to invest (more) in residential property (Kemp, 2015) among other assets classes such as logistics distribution centres and infrastructure.

Build-to-rent

In England and (as Byrne points out in Chapter 4) Ireland, a further important component of the rise of LCLs has been the emergence and rapid growth since the mid-2010s in the construction of purpose-built private rental housing. The construction of purpose-built private rental housing has waxed and waned over time but has been present to a greater or lesser degree in most AEs since 1945. But important exceptions include Australia, Ireland and New Zealand. In England, new construction of private rental housing has barely featured since 1945 but has re-emerged over the last decade; and that explains why it is referred to as BTR and regarded as a new market segment.

A rapidly growing number of new private residential companies have entered the BTR market in England, many of them set up by private equity firms and ICPFs. According to the British Property Federation, over 200,000 BTR homes had been completed, started, or were going through the land planning system for approval by the first quarter of 2022 (BPF, 2022). In 2021, an estimated £4.1 billion was invested in BTR schemes by institutional investors. In addition, Lloyds Bank has invested in the BTR market via its new Citra Living subsidiary company set up for the purpose. Meanwhile, a small group of the largest non-profit housing associations in England have set up *for-profit* subsidiary companies to develop, own and manage portfolios of private rental housing. Instead of their traditional clientele of low-income and disadvantaged tenants, these for-profit portfolios have mainly been let to young professionals and other middle-income households (Crook and Kemp, 2019).

In addition, the decline in high street retail shopping has created the opportunity for the existing owners to sell redundant department stores to developers for conversion into rental apartment blocks: 'convert-to-rent' rather than BTR. The high-profile John Lewis department store chain has gone one step further and decided to enter the private rental market. In response to the growth in online shopping and to diversify its business, John Lewis plans to remodel some of its city centre department stores into rental housing and build new ones on other sites that it owns. The company has announced a £500 million investment in 1,000 new homes in partnership with listed investment company Abrdn (formerly Standard Life Aberdeen) which is based in Scotland. A BTR subsector may also be emerging in Australia, a country dominated by BTL landlords (Nethercote, 2020; Morris *et al*, 2021).

Student accommodation blocks

Since the GFC, there has also been rapid growth in private, PBSA blocks. Companies specialising in PBSA have long existed in the United States. Unite Group plc – established in 1991 and the largest owner of PBSA in Britain – was listed on the London Stock Exchange in 2000. It has a property portfolio of over 170 properties, housing more than 70,000 students, across 25 university towns. The PBSA market is rapidly expanding elsewhere in

Europe and elsewhere including Australia. Much of this activity has involved cross-national investment by insurance companies and pension funds in both new and existing PBSA portfolios, as well as by long-established US property companies such as Greystar Real Estate. In short, PBSA blocks have become a new international asset investment class.

Property management

With some exceptions – including Australia (Hulse *et al*, 2018), England and Scotland – in most AEs, the great majority of private individual landlords self-manage the rental homes they own, with only a minority making use of a managing agent. This is important because, for better or worse, landlord–tenant relations are inevitably more personal when the landlord is managing the properties than when an intermediary – a managing agent – is doing so. Among other things, that introduces a higher degree of emotion into the landlord–tenant relationship and hence the possibility of less dispassionate or even irrational behaviour than might be seen when a managing agent is involved.

Research on landlords in England (Crook and Kemp, 1996) and in Scotland (Kemp and Rhodes, 1997; Crook *et al*, 2009) has found that a substantial minority of private individual landlords were ignorant or ill-informed about landlord–tenant law. This inevitably increases the possibility that such landlords use procedures (such as issuing a notice to quit) that are not legally compliant. Many BTL landlords manage their properties in their spare time and (at least in England and Scotland) do not belong to landlords' associations or professional bodies. To that extent, they could be described as 'amateur landlords' (Crook and Kemp, 1996).

In England, letting and managing agents have historically comprised a mix of small, locally based firms and larger, regional chains. However, recent years have seen increasing mergers and acquisitions of letting agents, led by ambitious firms acquiring local competitors and entering other markets within or beyond their region. As Hulse explains in Chapter 2, a similar trend is taken place in Australia, in part to achieve economies of scale. Meanwhile, across the AEs, internet property platforms have become a ubiquitous tool for advertising homes to let and, correspondingly, a virtual shop window for tenants seeking to move home (Rogers, 2017; Hulse *et al*, 2018, Fields and Rogers, 2021; Fields, 2022). This has opened access for landlords and letting agents to a larger pool of prospective tenants; and access for tenants to a larger pool of potential homes than is found in letting agent shop windows or notice boards in the windows of small convenience stores. The emergence and rapid growth of these 'PropTech' platforms has virtually wiped out the 'To Let' columns in local newspapers and shop windows. For tenants, PropTech platforms reduce property search 'transaction costs' (Williamson, 1985) and especially so for those seeking to move from one housing market to another, interregionally, or internationally. The use of internet PropTech platforms have also facilitated cross-international investment in rental property and Airbnb (Fields and Rogers, 2021). As Ho and Atkinson (2018) show, an ecosystem of 'property transaction professionals' – including marketing executives, estate agents, mortgage brokers and solicitors – has developed to facilitate and thereby benefit from the desire of private individuals to invest in rental housing in other countries. These intermediaries 'connect global investors with local markets' (Cocola-Gant and Gago, 2021).

Airbnb

The rise of the internet and digital technologies has also facilitated the emergence and rapid growth of Airbnb and other accommodation providers catering primarily for tourists and people on business trips (Rogers, 2017; Fields, 2022). Since it was founded in 2008 Airbnb has grown exponentially and by 2019 over 'six million, rooms, flats and houses in more than 81,000 cities' were listed on Airbnb (Sherwood, 2019). The company is now listed on the Nasdaq – the second largest stock exchange in the world – and as of March 2022 was worth over US$100 billion. Airbnb forms part of the hotel industry but is discussed here and in the chapters that follow because it has had important impacts on the private rental housing market.

Professional Airbnb hosts letting an entire property to short-stay guests account for a substantial share of all listings on Airbnb. For example, Simcock (2021) found that entire properties accounted for 56 per cent of all Airbnb listings in London during 2019. He also found there had been substantial growth over the previous five years in the proportion of listings by hosts with more than one listing. By 2019, these 'multi-hosts' accounted for 44 per cent of the entire property listings in London (Simcock, 2021). The rise of multi-hosts on Airbnb is common across the AEs (Cocola-Gant and Gago, 2021). Letting accommodation to a succession of tourists and business travellers is typically more profitable than letting it to a single household living there as their home (Yrigoy, 2019). That enables Airbnb hosts to outbid residential landlords and owner-occupiers in the local housing market; and in areas with high concentrations of Airbnb properties, this could potentially drive up house prices and residential rents (Yrigoy, 2019; Cocola-Gant and Gago, 2021).

A growing number of empirical studies has found that Airbnb has had an upward effect on residential rents and house prices, and displaced residents, in areas with a high density of listings. Garay-Tamajon et al (2022), for example, concluded that rents in Barcelona had increased significantly in 'highly touristified', 'trendy' and more affluent neighbourhoods where Airbnb listings were more concentrated. Meanwhile, an analysis of the private rental market in eight French cities by Ayouba *et al* (2020), using data for 2014/ 15, found that Airbnb raised rents in Paris, Lyon and Montpellier, though not in the other five cities analysed. In the United States, Barron *et al* (2021) used a dataset of listings at postcode level to assess the impact of Airbnb on the housing market. They found that Airbnb had increased both rents and house prices. They also found that, while Airbnb did not increase the supply of housing, it did increase the supply of short-stay accommodation and hence reduced the supply of long-term rental homes. Not surprisingly, local authorities in very popular tourist cities such as Amsterdam, Barcelona and Edinburgh are increasingly concerned about the impact of Airbnb on house prices, rents and supply in local housing markets (Cocola-Gant and Gago, 2021).

Policy concerns

Many of these trends have raised public awareness of, and concern about, the nature and role of private renting. This in part reflects greater mass media coverage of private renting than in the recent past, perhaps further fuelling public concerns. For these reasons, in some AEs political parties seeking to maintain or increase their attractiveness to voters have turned their attention to these concerns. In the previous section, we discussed concern about the impact of Airbnb on local housing markets and neighbourhoods. In this section, we highlight more general concerns about private renting: rental affordability; insecurity of tenure; and international investors. In some AEs, the extent of public concern around these issues is such that there is growing antipathy to private rental landlords (Roberts and Satsangi, 2021; Jones and Mostafab, 2022). As described in the country chapters, anti-landlord sentiment has grown in England, Denmark, Ireland and Germany. But whereas in England anti-landlord sentiment is mainly focused on BTL landlords, in the latter three countries it is mainly focused on private equity firms based in other countries, such as the United States.

Since the GFC, housing affordability has become an increasingly important topic of public concern in many AEs. Especially in the Anglophone homeowner societies (Ronald, 2008) the inability of many young households to buy their first home has been the primary focus of public and policy-maker concern (McKee, 2012; Byrne, 2020). But across the AEs more generally, rental affordability has also featured prominently in public discourse, mostly in relation to low-income households, but also with respect to young professionals living in 'world cities' such as Amsterdam, Berlin, London, New York, Paris, Sydney and Toronto (Wetzstein, 2017). Not surprisingly, this 'new housing affordability crisis' has attracted growing attention in recent years from academic researchers, think tanks and policy analysts (Colburn and Allen, 2018; Desmond, 2018; Anacker, 2019; Galster and Lee, 2021;

Haffner and Hulse, 2021). Public concerns about rising rents have in turn prompted calls for the introduction of rent controls and for making existing rent controls stricter (Wetzstein, 2017: 7; Marsh *et al*, 2022).

A further policy concern arising from the regrowth of private renting is about tenant insecurity (Byrne and McArdle, 2022). In part, this relates to lettings that are for fixed terms – rather than of indefinite duration – which is the norm in the Anglophone liberal market economies (Hulse and Milligan, 2014; Morris *et al*, 2021). Unless prohibited from doing so by law, landlords can decline to renew a tenancy at the end of the lease, even where the tenant has paid the rent on time and adhered to the other conditions in their contract. One consequence of these 'no-fault evictions' is that 'making a rental house a home' (Easthope, 2014; Morris *et al*, 2021) is less easy to achieve in liberal market economies than in countries like Germany where leases are mostly for indefinite terms and tenants know that they can stay for the long term. Indeed, Morris *et al* (2021) found that the sense of insecurity at the back of their minds was pervasive among the private renters they interviewed in Australia. Tellingly, the subtitle of Morris *et al*'s (2021) book on the private rental sector in Australia is 'Living with uncertainty'.

And yet even in countries with long-term or indefinite rental leases, tenant insecurity can be pervasive. As Hulse and Milligan (2014) have pointed out, it is not only short-term tenancies that make rental housing insecure. Low-income tenants who are struggling to afford their rent are insecure because they risk being evicted if they get into non-trivial rent arrears and cannot repay the outstanding debt. In theory, such tenants could look for a cheaper place to live, but there are barriers to moving home, such as a chequered rent payment history, the need to pay a rental bond along with rent in advance, and landlord reluctance to let to tenants in receipt of rent allowances. These barriers are particularly difficult in tight rental markets where demand is significantly greater than supply. It follows that, in practice, tenant insecurity is greater in high-demand than in low-demand localities. And this is especially likely to be true in markets where rents are racing ahead of incomes. Meanwhile, in their discussion of the Irish private rental market, Byrne and McArdle (2022) argue that the power asymmetry between landlords and tenants is integral to the lived experience of tenant insecurity and cannot be divorced from it.

The COVID-19 pandemic

The context within which these policy concerns are discussed was transformed almost overnight, in the short term and perhaps the longer term as well, by the unexpected arrival of the SARS-CoV-2 virus (COVID-19) in late 2019 in China and its subsequent rapid transmission across the globe. As we know, the virus has had a terrible impact on population health in most countries around the world and placed health systems and social care provision under almost intolerable strain in the early stages of the pandemic. To contain the health emergency caused by the pandemic, governments around the globe responded by imposing unprecedented lockdowns on economic activity including housing markets. These pandemic-induced lockdowns acted as a massive exogeneous shock to the economies across the developed and the less developed nations (Tooze, 2021). Housing markets, including private rental housing, constitute an important component of the economy and have therefore also been profoundly impacted by COVID-19 and the lockdowns that were introduced in the early stages of the pandemic.

This book

This book explores these recent developments and accompanying policy concerns in private rental housing in the AEs since the turn of the century. It does so through case studies of nine countries in all of which, to a greater or less extent, the PRS has either grown, begun to change in fundamental ways, or both. In some respects, the book could be seen as a sequel to an earlier book that Tony Crook and I edited (Crook and Kemp, 2014). Eight of the nine countries in this volume were also covered in that book – the difference this time being the chapter on Ireland by Michael Byrne – and many of the authors are the same. The current volume, however, is rather different in its focus from the previous one, which was essentially cross-sectional, examining the PRS at a point in time (circa 2012). In contrast, this book is devoted to an examination of change and continuity in the private rental housing over the last two decades. In doing so, it considers transformations in private rental housing that were less apparent when the previous book was written.

In the two decades covered by this book, private rental housing, and the political economies within which they are situated, have experienced two major, historically important macroeconomic shocks. The GFC of 2007–2009, and the recession the followed in its wake, was the largest economic crisis since the Great Depression of the interwar period; and it was one in which the preceding housing boom and subsequent bust played a central role (Mian and Sufi, 2014; Turner, 2016; Tooze, 2018). It has had important ramifications for housing across the AEs, as well as for macroeconomic policy that have in turn affected housing markets. As the country chapters in this volume show, the GFC and its aftermath have had important impacts on private rental housing markets, albeit in varying ways and to different degrees in each country.

More recently, the COVID-19 pandemic resulted in the biggest economic downturn for centuries, as governments took unprecedented measures to lock down their economies and societies to contain the virus and limit infections, deaths and the impact on healthcare systems (Tooze, 2021). The country chapters in this book all examine the short-term impact of COVID-19 on private rental markets and the penultimate chapter explore the impacts in more depth.

This book was completed before the longer-term impact of the pandemic-induced economic shock had time to become apparent. And in any case the waters have been greatly muddied by the Russian invasion of Ukraine in February 2022. This invasion has caused the third major economic shock to the global economy since the turn of the century. One consequence of the invasion was a sharp increase in inflation, which lead to a partial reversal of the 'cheap money' era that existed over the previous two decades. Another has been the exodus of millions of refugees from Ukraine to other countries including over a million to Germany. The Russian invasion of Ukraine occurred too recently for its possible impacts on private rental markets to be covered in this book. It is arguably premature to do so, but the final chapter offers some brief pointers as to some of the potential implications of the war on private rental housing in the AEs over the next few years.

References

Aalbers, M.B. (2016) *The Financialisation of Housing: A Political Economy Approach*, New York, Routledge.

Aalbers, M.B., Hochstenbach, C., Bosma, J. and Fernandez, R. (2021) 'The death and life of private landlordism: how financialized homeownership gave birth to the buy-to-let market', *Housing, Theory and Society*, 38(5), 541–563.

Anacker, K.B. (2019) 'Introduction: housing affordability and affordable housing', *International Journal of Housing Policy*, 19(1), 1–16.

Arundel, R. (2017) 'Equity inequity: housing wealth inequality, inter and intra-generational divergences, and the rise of private landlordism', *Housing, Theory and Society*, 34(2), 176–200.

August, M. (2020) 'The financialization of Canadian multi-family rental housing', *Journal of Urban Affairs*, 42(7), 975–997.

Ayouba, K., Breuillé, M.-L., Grivault, C. and Le Gallo, J. (2020) 'Does Airbnb disrupt the private rental market? An empirical analysis for French cities', *International Regional Science Review*, 43(1–2), 76–104.

Ball, M. (1983) *Housing Policy and Economic Power*, London, Methuen.

Barron, K., Kung, E. and Proserpio, D. (2021) 'The effect of home-sharing on house prices and rents: evidence from Airbnb', *Marketing Science*, 40(1), 23–47.

Bierre, S., Howden-Chapman, P. and Signal, L. (2010) '"Ma and Pa" landlords and the "risky" tenant: discourses in the New Zealand private rental sector', *Housing Studies*, 25(1), 21–38.

British Property Federation (2022) *Build to Rent Map of the UK*, London, BPF.

Byrne, M. (2016) '"Asset price urbanism" and financialisation after the crisis: Ireland's National Asset Management Agency', *International Journal of Urban and Regional Research*, 40(1), 31–45.

Byrne, M. (2020) 'Generation rent and the financialization of housing: a comparative exploration of the growth of the private rental sector in Ireland, the UK and Spain', *Housing Studies*, 35(4), 743–765.

Byrne, M. and McArdle, R. (2022) 'Secure occupancy, power and the landlord-tenant relation: a qualitative exploration of the Irish private rental sector', *Housing Studies*, 37(1), 124–142.

Christophers, B. (2022) 'Mind the gap: Blackstone, housing investment and the reordering of urban rent surfaces', *Urban Studies*, 59(4), 698–716.

Clapham, D., Mackie, P., Orford, S., Buckley, K., Thomas, I., Atherton, I. and McNulty, U. (2012) *Housing Options and Solutions for Young People in 2020*, York, Joseph Rowntree Foundation.

Cocola-Gant, A. and Gago, A. (2021) 'Airbnb, buy-to-let investment and tourism-driven displacement: a case study in Lisbon', *Environment & Planning A*, 53(7), 1671–1688.

Colburn, G. and Allen, R. (2018) 'Rent burden and the Great Recession in the USA', *Urban Studies*, 55(1), 226–243.

Crook, A.D.H. and Kemp, P.A. (1996) *Private Landlords in England*, London, HMSO.

Crook, A.D.H. and Kemp, P.A. (2011) *Transforming Private Landlords: Housing, Markets and Public Policy*, Oxford, Wiley-Blackwell.

Crook, A.D.H. and Kemp, P.A. (eds) (2014) *Private Rental Housing: Comparative Perspectives*, Cheltenham, Edward Elgar.

Crook, T. and Kemp, P.A. (2019) 'In search of profit: housing association investment in private rental housing', *Housing Studies*, 34(4), 666–687.

Crook, A.D.H., Kemp, P.A. and Ferrari, E.T. (2009) *Views and Experiences of Landlords in the Private Rented Sector in Scotland: Scottish Government Review of the Private Rented Sector*, vol 3, Edinburgh, Scottish Government.

Desmond, M. (2018) 'Heavy is the house: rent burden among the American urban poor', *International Journal of Urban & Regional Research*, 42(1), 160–170.

Fields, D. (2018) 'Constructing a new asset class: property-led financial accumulation after the crisis', *Economic Geography*, 94(2), 118–140.

Fields, D. (2022) 'Automated landlord: digital technologies and post-crisis financial accumulation', *Environment and Planning A: Economy and Space*, 54(1), 160–181.

Fields, D. and Rogers, D. (2021) 'Towards a critical housing studies research agenda on platform real estate', *Housing, Theory & Society*, 38(1), 794.

Fields, D. and Uffer, S. (2016) 'The financialisation of rented housing: a comparative analysis of New York City and Berlin', *Urban Studies*, 53(7), 1486–1502.

Forrest, R. and Hirayama, Y. (2015) 'The financialisation of the social project: embedded liberalism, neoliberalism and homeownership', *Urban Studies*, 52(2), 233–244.

Fuller, G.W. (2021) 'The financialization of rented homes: continuity and change in housing financialization', *Review of Revolutionary Political Economy*, 2(3), 551–570.

Galster, G. and Lee, K.O. (2021) 'Introduction to the special issue of the global crisis in housing affordability', *International Journal of Urban Sciences*, 25, 1–6.

Garay-Tamajón, L., Lladós-Masllorens, J., Meseguer-Artola, A. and Morales-Pérez, S. (2022) 'Analysing the influence of short-term rental platforms on housing affordability in global urban destination neighbourhoods', *Tourism and Hospitality Research*, 22(4), 444–461.

Haffner, M.E.A. and Hulse, K. (2021) 'A fresh look at contemporary perspectives on urban housing affordability', *International Journal of Urban Sciences*, 25, 59–79.

Halifax (2015) *Five years of Generation Rent: Perceptions of the First-Time Buyer Housing Market 2015*, Halifax, Halifax Bank.

Harloe, M. (1985) *Private Rented Housing in the United States and Europe*, London, Croom Helm.

Harloe, M. (1995) *The People's Home: Social Rented Housing in Europe and America*, Oxford, Wiley-Blackwell.

Hick, R., Pomati, M. and Stephens, M. (2022) *Housing and Poverty in Europe*, Cardiff, Cardiff University.

Hulse, K. and Milligan, V. (2014) 'Secure occupancy: a new framework for analysing security in rental housing, *Housing Studies*, 29(5), 638–656.

Hulse, K., Martin, C., James, A. and Stone, W. (2018) *Private Rental in Transition: Institutional Change, Technology and Innovation*, Melbourne, Australian Housing and Urban Research Institute.

Hulse, K., Reynolds, M. and Martin, C. (2020) 'The Everyman stereotype: discursive reframing of private landlords in the financialization of rental housing', *Housing Studies*, 35(6), 981–1003.

Jones, C. and Mostafab, A. (2022) 'The revival of private residential landlordism in Britain through the prism of changing returns', *Journal of Property Research*, 39(1), 56–76.

Kemp, P.A. (2015) 'Private renting after the global financial crisis', *Housing Studies*, 30(4), 601–620.

Kemp, P.A. and Rhodes, D. (1997) 'The motivations and attitudes to letting of private landlords in Scotland', *Journal of Property Research*, 14(2), 117–132.

Kemp, P.A. and Kofner, S. (2014) 'Germany', in A.D.H. Crook and P.A. Kemp (eds) *Private Rental Housing: Comparative Perspectives*, Cheltenham, Edward Elgar, pp 27–47.

Kofner, S. (2006) 'Private equity investment in housing: the case of Germany', paper for the European Network of Housing Research International Housing Conference, Ljubljana, Slovenia, 2–5 July.

Kofner, S. (2014) *The Private Rented Sector in Germany*, CreateSpace Independent Publishing Platform.

Kohl, S. (2017) *Homeownership, Renting and Society*, London, Routledge.

Kohl, S. (2020) 'The political economy of homeownership', *Socio-Economic Review*, 18(4), 913–940.

Marsh, A., Gibb, K. and Soaita, A.M. (2022) 'Rent regulation: unpacking the debates', *International Journal of Housing Policy*. DOI: 10.1080/19491247.2022.2089079.

Martin, C. (2018) 'Clever Odysseus: narratives and strategies of rental property investor subjectivity in Australia', *Housing Studies*, 33(7), 1060–1084.

Martin, C., Hulse, K. and Pawson, H. (2018) *The Changing Institutions of Private Rental Housing: An International Review*, Melbourne, Australian Housing and Urban Research.

McKee, K. (2012) 'Young people, homeownership and future welfare', *Housing Studies*, 27(6), 853–862.

Merrett, S. (1982) *Owner Occupation in Britain*, London, Routledge and Kegan & Paul.

Mian, A. and Sufi, A. (2014) *House of Debt: How They (and You) Caused the Great Recession, and How We Can Prevent It From Happening Again*, Chicago, University of Chicago Press.

Mills, J., Molloy, R. and Zarutskie, R. (2019) 'Large-scale buy-to-rent investors in the single-family housing market: the emergence of a new asset class', *Real Estate Economics*, 47(2), 399–430.

Morris, A., Hulse, K. and Pawson, H. (2021) *The Private Rental Sector in Australia: Living with Uncertainty*, Singapore, Springer.

Nethercote, M. (2020) 'Build-to-rent and the financialization of rental housing', *Housing Studies*, 35(5), 839–874.

Rhodes, D. (2007) 'Buy-to-let landlords', in D. Hughes and S. Lowe (eds) *The Private Rented Housing Market: Regulation or Deregulation?* Aldershot, Ashgate, pp 37–50.

Roberts, S. and Satsangi, M. (2021) 'The "bad landlord": origins and significance in contemporary housing policy and practice', *Housing, Theory and Society*, 38(4), 496–511.

Rogers, D. (2017) *Geopolitics of Real Estate: Reconfiguring Property, Capital, and Rights*, London, Rowman & Littlefield.

Ronald, R. (2008) *The Ideology of Home Ownership*, Basingstoke, Palgrave Macmillan.

Ronald, R. and Kadi, J. (2018) 'The revival of private landlords in Britain's post-homeownership society', *New Political Economy*, 23(6), 786–803.

Rugg, J. and Rhodes, J. (2018) *The Evolving Role of the Private Rented Sector: Its Contribution and Potential*, York, Centre for Housing Policy.

Scanlon, K. (2011) 'Private renting in other countries', in K. Scanlon and B. Kochan (eds) *Towards a Sustainable Private Rented Sector: The Lessons From Other Countries*, London, London School of Economics and Political Science, pp 15–44.

Scanlon, K. and Whitehead, C. (2005) *The Profile and Intentions of Buy to Let Investors*, London, Council of Mortgage Lenders.

Sherwood, H. (2019) 'How Airbnb took over the world', *The Guardian*, 5 May, https://www.theguardian.com/technology/2019/may/05/airbnb-homelessness-renting-housing-accommodation-social-policy-cities-travel-leisure

Simcock, T. (2021) 'Home or hotel? A contemporary challenge in the use of housing stock', *Housing Studies*, https://doi.org/10.1080/02673037.2021.1988063

Tooze, A. (2018) *Crashed: How a Decade of Financial Crises Changed the World*, London, Penguin Books.

Tooze, A. (2021) *Shutdown: How Covid Shook the World's Economy*, London, Viking.

Turner, A. (2016) *Between Debt and the Devil*, Princeton, Princeton University Press.

Wetzstein, S. (2017) 'The global urban housing affordability crisis', *Urban Studies*, 54(14), 3159–3177.

Whitehead, C. and Williams, P. (2017) *Changes in the Regulation and Control of Mortgage Markets and Access to Owner-occupation Among Younger Households*, Working Paper 196, Paris, OECD.

Whitehead, C. and Williams, P. (2020) *Thinking Outside the Box: Exploring Innovations in Affordable Homeownership*, Glasgow, UK Collaborative Centre for Housing Evidence.

Wijburg, G. and Aalbers, M.B. (2017) 'The alternative financialisation of the German housing market', *Housing Studies*, 32(7), 968–989.

Williamson, O.E. (1985) *The Economic Institutions of Capitalism*, New York, Macmillan.

Wind, B., Dewilde, C. and Doling, J. (2020) 'Secondary property ownership in Europe: contributing to asset-based welfare strategies and the "really big trade-off"', *International Journal of Housing Policy*, 20(1), 25–52.

Yrigoy, I. (2019) 'Rent gap reloaded: Airbnb and the shift from residential to touristic rental housing in the Palma old quarter in Mallorca, Spain', *Urban Studies*, 56(13), 2709–2726.

2

Growth and change: private renting in Australia in the 21st century

Kath Hulse

Introduction

An important feature of the Australian housing system in the 2000s has been the sustained growth of private renting. This development denotes a change in what has long been characterised as a classic homeownership society. In the decades after the Second World War, private renting declined as homeownership increased to the early 1970s, followed by a period of relative stability in the housing system until the 1990s. From that time, private renting began to increase again as homeownership rates fell modestly (Burke *et al*, 2014). In the 2000s the private rental sector began to grow more strongly, with changes in the profile of tenants, landlord investment and more professional management of properties.

Definitions of private renting vary between countries (Haffner *et al*, 2010). In Australia, private renting refers to households who live in private properties who pay rent to either a real estate agent or a private landlord who does not live with the tenant. This definition excludes households paying rent to residential park operators and employers (government and other) and social landlords (public and not-for-profit landlords). Rents are set according to the market and vary between accommodation types/sizes and by area and lettings are based on ability to pay market rent not administrative criteria. Private rental housing is not a distinct stock that has been purpose built and managed for rental; properties move between ownership and private rental, either on sale or simply change of use (Hulse and Yates, 2017). For this reason, rented accommodation is not usually let furnished nor do rents usually include utility costs as is the case in some other countries. There are other rental niches with purpose-built accommodation which are let to specific groups, often furnished, and including utilities, including short-term lets like Airbnb, rooming houses and purpose-built student accommodation (Pawson *et al*, 2020: 181). This chapter examines growth and change in the private rental sector in the 2000s.

Changes in the size and role of the Australian private rental sector

More than a quarter of all Australian households rent privately, up from just over one in five at the start of the 21st century.[1] This increase has occurred in the context of historically high levels of household growth in the 2000s (37.7 per cent household growth between 2001 and 2021). There were 1,023,000 more private renter households in 2021 compared to 2001, a 76 per cent increase, and more than twice the increase in overall household growth.[2]

This disproportionate increase in private renting suggests structural change within the Australian housing system which has been termed a 'quiet revolution' (Wood and Ong, 2017) and is illustrated in Figure 2.1. The steady increase in private rental in the 2000s reflects some decline in the rate of homeownership (from 68.6 per cent in 2001 to 65.9 per cent in 2021), which has been attributed to increasing problems of 'housing affordability' in the 2000s (Burke *et al*, 2020). A further factor is that the percentage of social renters, already low by international standards (Martin *et al*, 2018), declined further during this period. The increase in private renting together with an increased percentage of households purchasing with a mortgage rather than owning outright (see Figure 2.1) indicates increased exposure of Australian households to volatility in the real estate and finance markets since the start of the 21st century.

Figure 2.1: Australian households by main housing tenure type, 2001–2021 (%)

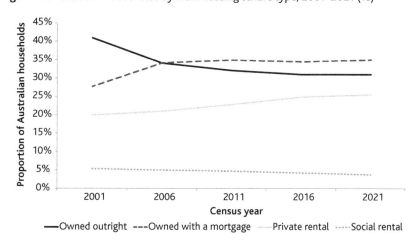

Note: Does not sum to 100 per cent as 'renting from other landlord' (including employers), renter with landlord type 'not stated'; 'other tenure' and tenure type 'not stated' are excluded (a total of 4.8 per cent of all households in 2021).

Source: Calculated from ABS Census of Population and Housing, Community Profiles, various years (ABS 2022).

Factors outside of the housing system underpin the increase in private renting in Australia in the 2000s, most notably changes to the level and type of migration and in employment and incomes. On the first of these, the increased volume of net overseas migration (in-migration minus out-migration) averaged 212,308 people per annum between 2011 and 2016 and 247,000 people per annum between 2017 and 2019 (prior to the COVID-19 pandemic), compared to an annual average of 79,000 per annum in the 1990s (1990–1999) (Hulse *et al*, 2019: 18). Importantly, in the 21st century the composition of migrants changed from predominantly permanent migration to include higher levels of temporary migration such as international students and those on temporary work visas (Phillips and Simon-Davies, 2017). Although many migrants rent privately on arrival in Australia, temporary visa holders are less likely to buy and more likely to remain in the private rental market than permanent migrants (Khoo *et al*, 2012), clustering in large cities with tertiary education institutions and high skill employment.

Second, while unemployment rates have been relatively low in the 2000s compared to the 1990s, particularly in the years before the global financial crisis (GFC) of 2008, there has been an increase in casual, contract and part-time work, and in underemployment with higher rates among young people and women (Campbell *et al*, 2014; Parkinson *et al*, 2019) whereas mortgage repayment typically requires stable and predictable earnings over a long period. At the same time, escalating real housing prices, particularly in capital cities, have required larger deposits and bigger loan sizes such that more middle-income households are renting for longer periods (Pawson *et al*, 2020).

Changes in the profile of private renters

The types of households renting in the private rental sector have changed over the 2000s, as shown in Table 2.1.

There are fewer young renters, indicating the difficulty in young people leaving home when they are students or first entering the workforce. While the key age group of private renters remains the 25–44 age cohort, there has been an increase in the percentage of private renters aged 45 years and over. These changes suggest the growth in private rental is driven mainly by mid-life and older households who are unable to leave the private rental sector for homeownership (or social rental housing) as occurred in previous decades, rather than by the entry of new, younger households into private renting (Pawson *et al*, 2017).

Households increasingly rely on two incomes to rent housing in the 2000s, whether purchasing housing (Burke *et al*, 2020) or renting privately. Table 2.1 shows an increase in the percentage of couple households renting privately

Table 2.1: Profile of private renter households, 2000–2001 and 2019–2020

	2000–2001	2019–2020	Percentage point change
Age of reference person			
15–24	15.0%	9.1%	−5.9
25–34	36.5%	31.2%	−5.3
35–44	24.3%	27.0%	2.7
45–54	13.7%	15.3%	1.7
55–64	5.5%	9.4%	3.8
65+	4.9%	7.9%	3.0
Household type			
Couple only	15.5%	21.9%	6.4
Couple with children	22.3%	26.7%	4.3
Lone parent	14.3%	11.0%	−3.3
Other family types and multi-families	6.6%	6.5%	−0.2
Lone person	30.3%	26.5%	−3.7
Group	11.0%	7.5%	−3.5
Gross household income quintile			
Q1 (lowest)	18.2%	15.9%	−2.3
Q2	22.5%	22.5%	0.0
Q3	24.9%	26.1%	1.2
Q4	20.2%	21.8%	1.5
Q5 (highest)	14.3%	13.8%	−0.5
Total	**100.0%**	**100.0%**	

Source: Calculated from the ABS Survey of Income and Housing, 2000–2001 and 2019–2020.

and a decrease in single parents and lone persons on one income. Four in ten private renter households have children, a percentage which has been relatively constant in the 2000s, although the share of such households who are lone parents has declined. An estimated 1.6 million dependent children lived in private renter households in 2019–2020, constituting 26 per cent of Australian children.[3] Notwithstanding these changes in the profile of private renters, it is important to note that the private rental sector continues to play a disproportionate role for some household types. For example, 47.7 per cent of all lone-parent households in Australia in 2019–2020 were private renters (compared to 40.7 per cent in 2000–2001).

A key feature of the private rental sector in Australia throughout the 2000s is the increased diversity of household incomes of those living in the sector.

In 2019–2020, just over seven in ten private renter households had gross incomes in the three middle quintiles, many of whom faced affordability challenges in buying housing in areas that they want to live in, particularly in view of rapidly escalating housing prices in large cities such as Sydney and Melbourne. They had a greater choice of properties to rent in such areas reflecting both sector growth and less differentiation in rents by location than in house prices (Hulse *et al*, 2019). The percentage of households with very low incomes (bottom 20 per cent) declined slightly over the same period while the share of those private renters in the highest quintile incomes has remained much the same, as shown in Table 2.1.

Changes in the profile of private renter household incomes should not obscure the increasing *numbers* of lower-income private renter households in the 2000s due to the substantial sector growth discussed previously. In 2019–2020, just under a million private renters were in the bottom two quintiles of household income.[4] There is a strong association between low income and various types of vulnerability, such as at least one Indigenous person, a person aged over 65 years, or a person with a disability or long-term health condition (Productivity Commission, 2019: 4).[5]

In Australia's homeownership society, private renting was long viewed as a transitional tenure for younger households between leaving the parental home and buying their first property. The phenomenon of long-term renting (renting for ten or more years although not necessarily in the same dwelling) was first identified in Australia in the mid-1990s and estimated at 27 per cent of all private renters by Wulff and Maher (1998). A later estimate was that this had increased to 33 per cent by 2007–2008 (Stone *et al*, 2013: 2). As homeownership has declined further it is likely that more than one in ten of all Australian households are now long-term renters (Pawson *et al*, 2017: 1067).

Perhaps surprisingly, long-term private renting has been relatively little studied but recent research (Pawson *et al*, 2017; Morris *et al*, 2021) suggests that long-term renters are a diverse cohort ranging from those who value the flexibility, typically households with a considerable financial buffer, to lower-income households (mainly those on pensions and benefits) who face many problems in Australia's lightly regulated private rental sector including not only considerable financial stress but also the cumulative effects of long-term insecurity in their living arrangements.

Rental affordability trends and government responses

There are several measures of rental affordability in use in Australia as elsewhere including ratios (simple and adjusted), residual income and after housing poverty measures (see Pawson *et al*, 2020: chapter 3, for a recent review). Using one very broad-brush approach, the median rent to median household income ratio, rental affordability has not changed substantially nationally since the mid to late 1990s, with the ratio ranging between 23 per cent and 27 per cent, the highest percentage being in 2007–2008 just before the GFC (Productivity Commission, 2019: 60). It is important, however, to examine changes in the distribution of household incomes and rents for a more nuanced approach.

The overall rate of increase in real rents was particularly high between 2006 and 2011, stabilised and then declined by 2016 and thereafter, however, rents still increased after 2011 but the rate of increase was smaller than earlier in the first decade of the 21st century (Hulse *et al*, 2019: 25). In 2001, rental properties were concentrated at the low rent end of the market, but from 2006 and beyond, as the sector increased in size, the supply of lower-rent properties has declined in both absolute and relative terms while the supply of mid-market rentals has increased markedly, as shown in Figure 2.2.

This change in the distribution of real rents may not matter if real household incomes have also changed and/or the distribution of private renter household incomes has followed a similar pattern to rents. Gross household incomes have risen slightly in real terms since 2003–2004, but mainly to the benefit of households in the top two quintiles (Hulse *et al*, 2019: 19 and Figure 2.2). Significant increases in private rental supply in the 2000s may have maintained affordability for middle- to higher-income households who have a plentiful supply of affordable rentals but have not led to improved rental affordability for lower-income (bottom 40 per cent) households. In 2017–2018, two-thirds of lower-income private rental households spent more than 30 per cent of their income on rent and almost

Figure 2.2: Distribution of private rental dwellings by weekly rent, Australia, 2001–2016

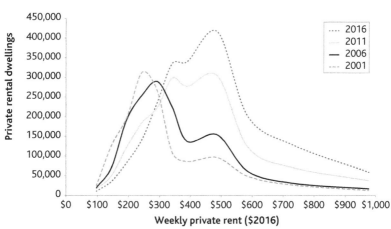

Source: Used with permission from the Australian Housing and Urban Research Institute Limited. First published in Hulse *et al* (2019).

a quarter spent more than 50 per cent of their income on rent (Productivity Commission, 2019: 58).[6]

This calculation of rental affordability only takes into account those who have been able to access and remain in private rental; others on lower household incomes have been squeezed out of the mainstream private rental market due to unaffordability of rents and competition from middle- and higher-income households who are more attractive to landlords. The main avenues for accommodating people in this situation are moving home to live with family, living in secondary accommodation types, residential parks, rooming houses, other sharing arrangements, and homelessness (Parkinson et al, 2018).

These are broad national aggregate trends; rental affordability varies by area and is significantly worse in capital cities than in other areas of the Australian states/territories. The Australian Institute of Health and Welfare (AIHW, 2020) reports on rental stress using the so-called 30/40 rule,[7] finding that the percentage of lower-income households in rental stress increased from 35.0 per cent in 2007–2008 to 43.1 per cent in 2017–2018. In capital cities, however, the increase in rental stress was greater (from 38.5 per cent in 2007–2008 to 47.8 per cent in 2017–2018). In the major metropolitan housing markets of Sydney (population 5.3 million) and Melbourne (population 5.1 million), lower-income renters are increasingly found in lower-rent outer suburban areas and regional centres with fewer jobs and poorer public transport (Pawson et al, 2020).

In Australia's system of government (with a federal government, six states and two territories) the federal government sees its role as contributing to improved affordability for private renters via demand subsidies called Rent Assistance. Rent Assistance is a cash transfer directly to private renters as part of the nation's income support system rather than a housing programme and as such is not rationed; there is no regional variation to the formula to take into account variation in rents between different housing markets (Ong et al, 2020). Federal governments have consistently argued that this type of payment improves rental affordability and that the private market will supply the necessary accommodation. In 2018–2019, the federal government reported the payment reduced the percentage of recipients paying more than a benchmark 30 per cent of income on rent from just under 70 per cent to 41 per cent after rent assistance (DSS, 2020: 46). This calculation deducts rent assistance from rent paid and produces a more favourable result than if rental affordability was calculated as rent as a percentage of all income including rent assistance. Singles and couples without children who are on low wages and outside of the income support/family payment system are not eligible for the payment. There are no requirements on landlords in terms of housing outcomes (affordability, appropriateness, quality), notwithstanding the AU$4.4 billion the rent assistance scheme cost in 2018–2019 (DSS, 2020: 87), unlike funding of social housing where the modus operandi and outcomes are tightly prescribed and regulated. Federal governments have resisted calls to increase or restructure Rent Assistance since the mid-1990s (see Ong *et al*, 2020 for the latest review).

Landlord investors: financing and market segments

At the start of the 21st century, the Australian private rental sector was characterised as a sector of petty landlords who mostly saw private rental housing as 'a long-term investment' (Berry, 2000: 665). Research conducted just prior to the GFC of 2008–2009 also portrayed most landlords as conservative, seeing residential property as 'a good (long-term) investment, with a sense of "low risk" and "guaranteed" return' (Seelig *et al*, 2009: 2). Since then, there appears to have been some change with more emphasis on purposive investment to achieve financial returns, echoing research in other advanced economies (for example, Soaita *et al*, 2017).

It is difficult to provide an accurate overview of the ownership of private rental *properties* across the sector due to a lack of data. Of 2.3 million privately rented properties in 2015–2016, 80 per cent were held by households holding four or fewer properties with just under half of these (38 per cent) owned by single property landlords (Hulse et al 2020), as shown in Table 2.2. An estimated 20 per cent of rental properties comprised a range of other landlords including corporate and institutional owners as well as households with larger portfolios (Hulse *et al*, 2020: 991; Pawson *et al*, 2020: 183).

Almost all the data on rental property ownership is about the household sector. In 2018–2019, just over one in five Australian households (20.7 per cent) owned residential property other than the one they live in (up

Table 2.2: Private rental sector ownership by landlord type and portfolio size, Australia, 2015/16

Landlord type/portfolio size	Number of private rental properties	% of private rental properties
HH with 1 rental property	870,998	38.4
HH with 2 rental property	451,371	19.9
HH with 3 rental property	224,552	9.9
HH with 4 rental property	260,843	11.5
Other	460,444	20.3
Total	2,268,97	100

Note: Other is a residual which includes households with five or more properties, real estate and property companies, overseas individuals/companies and trusts including Self-Managed Superannuation Funds. HH refers to household.

Source: Calculated from customised data from the ABS Survey of Income and Housing, 2015–2016.

from 16.1 per cent in 2003–2004). While seven in ten of these households own one rental property, the percentage of households with three or more properties has increased slowly since 2009–2010, the first year for which comparable data on portfolio size is available. The typical household owning rental property is 'an owner occupier, at midlife, in a household with two incomes' (Hulse *et al*, 2018: 4). Four in five of these landlords have taken out a loan to buy their properties and one in five are cash buyers.

In the 2000s an increasing number and percentage of taxpayers with an interest in rental property reported making a loss on their rental property, compared to the late 1990s when roughly half of individual taxpaying landlords said that they made a profit and half a loss. This coincides with greater public awareness of long-standing 'negative gearing' provisions in which rental losses can be offset against general taxable income, discussed further in the context of tax, subsidies and regulation later in this chapter. While the percentage making a loss has plateaued since 2011–2012, the percentage of taxpayers declaring a loss on their rental properties in 2018–2019 was just under 60 per cent, as shown in Figure 2.3.

This trend is important for private renters in the light of research which found that landlords who were negatively geared were more likely to terminate leases and sell their properties at any stage (Wood and Ong, 2013: 3256), indicating a less conservative and long-term approach to holding property than previously. Financially driven landlord activity has been observed in disadvantaged areas of Sydney and Melbourne where

Figure 2.3: Individual taxpayers declaring a net profit or loss on private rental property

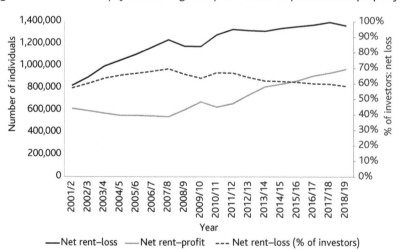

Note: Data for 2018–2019 may be subject to amendment in subsequent years.

Source: Calculated from Australian Taxation Office (ATO) Taxation statistics 2019–20 Individuals, Table 1: Selected items for 2001–02 to 2019–20 income years.

capital values are lower but rents nearer to city median, a process which has been termed 'investification' (Hulse and Reynolds, 2018). A survey of landlords owning properties in disadvantaged areas of western Sydney found that most landlords were experienced investors already owning multiple properties, who expected to get capital gain as well as good rental income, although a significant minority were first-time landlords (Pawson and Martin, 2020).

In making decisions about rental properties, landlords can access a wealth of property and financial information via digital media, including property price histories and likely rental returns, enabling landlords to operate outside of their local areas, including in other states. There has also been a growth in property/wealth advisors acting as intermediaries for rental property purchase and highly visible property investment 'spruikers' who run seminars and other events for people who want to build a rental portfolio, often valorising buying and trading rental property as a way to get rich (Martin, 2018).

In contrast, little is known about landlords of the other 20 per cent of privately rented properties since they are not picked up in Australian Census collections nor domestic household surveys. In the 2000s, there has been public and media concern about the extent of investment by foreign nationals and companies in the private rental market, notably the inner-city apartment market in Sydney and Melbourne (Rogers *et al*, 2017). In May 2017, the federal government announced stronger rules about foreign investment in Australian housing to tackle affordability issues[8] to be administered by the Foreign Investment Review Board, whose guidelines generally prohibit purchase of established dwellings by 'non-resident foreign persons' but allow them to purchase newly constructed dwellings. There are no data on compliance with, or the impact of, these changes although the development industry claims that these changes have the effect of dampening pre-sales of apartment complexes which are required to get finance (Hulse *et al*, 2018).

Likewise, there is little data on the extent to which real estate and property companies who have traditionally operated on a 'develop and sell' model have moved to a 'develop and hold' model. The one sector for which data are available is the growing purpose-built student accommodation market in Australia, notably in Sydney and Melbourne, which indicates at least 90,000 bed spaces are available (Pawson *et al*, 2019: 37). There has been active lobbying by the property/development sector for a broader Build to Rent (BTR) sector influenced by the UK model and the multi-family US model. The BTR lobby argues that this approach provides a more professional approach to private rental housing with purpose-built stock, better quality accommodation, provision for long-term tenancies and better management (Pawson *et al*, 2019; Nethercote, 2020). A review of the potential for BTR, however, concluded that the sector will not generate rental at scale, nor a more affordable rental product without 'a strategic national framework that integrates tax reform, revenue support, land, and planning levers' (Pawson *et al*, 2019: 10).

There has been surprisingly little change in the types of properties in the private rental sector during the 2000s. Just under a half (48.2 per cent) of all private rentals nationally are single detached dwellings since landlords typically buy established not new dwellings and just under seven in ten (69.1 per cent) of all Australian housing is of this type (2019–2020). A third (34.4 per cent) of private rental properties in 2019–2020 are apartments or units,[9] unlike the situation in many countries where renting is strongly associated with apartment living (Martin *et al*, 2018). Detached dwellings are relatively attractive to small-scale landlords who are reluctant to hold strata title properties with consequent fees and potential management issues, since most such complexes have a mixture of owners and renters. Since liquidity to realise capital gain is a big factor, landlords buy and sell typical properties in a thick market where there are most home purchasers and other investors; this is most likely in the single dwelling market (Hulse and Yates, 2017). This is the national picture. In Sydney, just over half of all private rental dwellings were apartments or units, reflecting higher land values and denser built form (Hulse *et al*, 2018: 30, figure 2.9).

Letting and management in an era of digital technology

Although attracting less attention, letting and management have undergone substantial change in the 2000s due to the application of digital technology, although the extent of take up of digital technology varies across the sector.

Traditionally, rental properties were advertised in local newspapers and in the windows of real estate agents and were a major revenue source for print publications. It was only in 1999 that Fairfax Media, a traditional Australian print media company, put its first newspaper advertisements online. Fast-forward to 2020 and most properties are advertised, and most rental property searches take place, online. The dominant players are the big online property portals, realestate.com.au (Real Estate Australia) and Domain.com.au (Domain) (Hulse *et al*, 2018: 56) in which major media companies have controlling interests.[10] Put simply, property sales and rentals are big media business in terms of regular and predictable revenue generation. There are some specialist rental property portals, such as rent.com.au, which promotes its services to self-managing landlords as well as agents, and other models that promote 'rent without agents'. Niche sites such as flatmates.com.au advertise vacancies in shared rental housing as well as general online classified sites, such as Gumtree, which has a lot of share housing advertisements (Hulse *et al*, 2018: 57). The 2000s have seen a range of start-up businesses entering the rental sector utilising new digital technology. Successful start-ups are sometimes acquired by the big online property portals, for example, the successful flatmates.com.au application for shared properties was bought by REA in 2016.

The advantages of advertising properties in this way are that prospective landlords (or as discussed later in this chapter, mainly real estate agents acting on their behalf) can reach a greater range of potential tenants and prospective tenants get more information about properties including photos, floor plans and other 'add ons' such as access to transport and facilities to screen for suitable properties. The potential risks lie in the accumulation of data which may assist landlords/agents in assessing property demand but also lead to targeted marketing to those who have viewed properties and potential for on-selling data to other data purchasers. Property advertisement is very lightly regulated, for example, not all states/territories require that advertisements specify the amount of rent sought, though most advertisements do this.

Digital technology has been applied to facilitate contact between landlords/agents and prospective tenants including online platforms for organising the property search and booking and managing initial inspections, which can be more efficient for both parties. Landlords/agents can also vet tenants' prior tenancy history through their subscription to specialist digital residential tenancies databases. For many years unregulated, and notorious for operating 'blacklists' of tenants, residential tenancies databases are now subject to state/territory residential tenancies regulation under national privacy provisions. This regulation covers matters such as the accuracy of information, tenant access and time limits on listing (Hulse *et al*, 2018: 55). There are new business models such as 'rent resumes' to make rental applications more 'competitive' and 'rent bidding' which is not prohibited by legislation in three states and are of concern in high-demand rental markets. There is also the potential to use digital technology to rank renters in ways that could discriminate against marginalised groups and breach anti-discrimination legislation.

Offer and acceptance of a property is generally better covered by state/territory residential tenancies legislation than advertising and tenant selection. Specific provisions vary by jurisdiction but generally cover the amount of rent, payment of rent in advance, and payment of a bond and where the bond monies must be lodged. Nevertheless, there have been recent developments in this area including bond loans products, including by residential tenancies databases, and alternative bond products which provide a non-cash surety or guarantee instead of a cash bond. The surety costs the tenant less up front, but it is not refundable at the end of the tenancy as is the case with the bond (Hulse *et al*, 2018: 61).

These types of developments have implications not only for regulators who struggle to keep pace with new businesses based on digital technology, as highlighted previously, but also for the real estate industry. The 2000s have seen an increase in the numbers and percentages of private rental properties managed by real estate agents. In 2016, three-quarters of private renters paid rent to real estate agents (74.8 per cent up from 58.5 per cent in 2001) while the percentage of private renters paying rent directly to their private landlords had a commensurate decline. In line with more financially driven landlordism in rental property, including owning property in non-local areas, landlords became increasingly likely to use real estate agents to manage their investments. For the most part, such agents also sell property, but a small number of specialist property management agencies have also developed in large cities. Real estate agents themselves have become more aware of the importance of regular income from real estate management fees compared to the vagaries of commissions on house sales.

In consequence, the real estate industry has undergone restructuring in the 2000s to achieve economies of scale through growing rental portfolios either through acquisitions or through buying existing rent rolls from other agents, including those going out of the business. The latter often involves specialist rent roll brokers who assess the quality of the rent roll and its strategic value and facilitate the sale (Hulse *et al*, 2018: 69). There appears to be little transparency in these transactions; landlords must sign up to the new management arrangements, but tenants are simply informed about the change of agent.

Management of rental properties involves multiple repetitions of the same tasks and there has been gradual application of digital technology in the bigger independent real estate agents and franchises to achieve greater efficiencies using rental property management software. These provide portals for tenants and landlords for matters such as invoices, rental statements and inspections. REA, the online portal and associated businesses discussed previously, has moved into the technology side of the business selling integrated software for rental property management. This includes 'virtual property manager' functions for back-office functions such as data entry, maintaining client databases, creating letters, research, and managing social media accounts. In some cases, the search for greater efficiencies involves outsourcing of these types of functions to third parties including in offshore locations such as the Philippines where wages are lower (Hulse *et al*, 2018: 71–72). These strategies enable real estate agents to keep costs down so that rental property managers can handle more properties. The effect of these changes on service to tenants is unknown.

Tax, subsidies and regulation

There has been little change to the tax and subsidy systems which support landlord investment in the 2000s and attempts to introduce reforms at the federal level have been very controversial and ultimately unsuccessful. In brief, there is a 50 per cent discount on nominal capital gains tax if properties are sold after more than 12 months and rental losses can be offset against general income tax (negative gearing). Removing the capital gains tax discount is off the political agenda largely because this is seen as the 'thin edge of the wedge' in applying capital gains tax to personal property (framed discursively as 'the family home'). Negative gearing has been subject to more sustained criticism since it provides more financial benefit to individual taxpayers with high marginal tax rates (Hulse *et al*, 2020). Federal governments[11] have consistently argued that landlords are 'ordinary' Australians who are 'rental investors' helping their families become self-sufficient as a form of asset-based welfare and, further, that rental affordability would worsen if changes to taxation settings prompted landlords to on-sell their properties (Hulse *et al*, 2020). While it is the case that there has been a substantial increase in private rental supply of mid-market rentals in the 2000s under these settings, the latest in a series of research projects examining changes in supply for very low-income households (bottom 20 per cent) has found that the private rental market 'has not provided, does not provide and cannot provide enough rental dwellings at this level' under current policy settings (Hulse *et al*, 2019: 80).

There was one attempt in the 2000s for policy innovation to provide more affordable supply targeted at low- to moderate-income households and to encourage some investment by mid-sized and large organisations via the National Rental Affordability Scheme, 2008–2026. Loosely modelled on Low Income Housing Tax Credits in the United States, the National Rental Affordability Scheme offered an index-linked annual financial incentive to the owners of new rental housing let to eligible low- to moderate-income households with rents at least 20 per cent below market. The incentives are funded mainly by the federal government and supplemented by the states/territories, and it was intended that these would become a recognised and continuing asset class.[12] Originally intended to offer 50,000 incentives, the federal government announced in its 2014–2015 Budget that no new allocations would be made, and the scheme was capped at 38,000 allocations. The ten-year cap on incentives means that the scheme will be finalised by the end of 2026.

The federal government did change its policy on managed investment trusts, including Real Estate Investment Trusts, in a way which deters foreign institutional ownership of Australian real estate. Managed investment trusts can invest in residential property but income from residential property (other than affordable rental housing) is regarded as non-concessional and distributions to foreign investors are subject to a 30 per cent withholding tax (Pawson *et al*, 2019: 16). This has been viewed as a deterrent to overseas based companies looking to develop the nascent BTR sector discussed earlier.

The main instrument used by the federal government in respect of rental housing investment has been macro-prudential regulation. The key agency is the Australian Prudential Regulatory Authority which is funded by Approved

Deposit-taking Institutions (such as banks and building societies) with a remit to protect depositors' funds. The Australian Prudential Regulatory Authority has been active since 2011 in assessing lending, particularly in view of the high volume of lending to landlords on interest-only terms. In late 2014 and early 2017, the Australian Prudential Regulatory Authority issued guidance on lending to investors, including: the permitted rate of increase in lending to landlords; loan serviceability buffers; prudent lending standards; loan to valuation ratios; limits on interest-only lending; and lending to higher-risk segments (Hulse *et al*, 2018: 34). It appears that these measures have had mainly short-term effects.

Finally, reform to states and territories' regulation of residential tenancies moves at a very slow pace. Most state/territories have recently reviewed their legislation or are currently reviewing it. There are some common themes in these reviews such as responses to domestic/family violence, safety/security and minimum standards but there is no uniformity between jurisdictions and most still permit eviction without a specified reason. The COVID-19 pandemic has highlighted some challenging issues in current residential tenancies legislation, as discussed later in the chapter.

Global financial crisis

The GFC had a lesser effect on the Australian private rental market than in some other countries due in part to contemporaneous resources investment boom which lasted until 2011–2012. The country did not enter recession and enjoyed a period of continuous economic growth from 1991 (until the onset of the COVID-19 pandemic in March 2020) and there were few of the austerity policies that were introduced elsewhere. However, viewed more than ten years after the event, it seems that the GFC was a stimulus to investment in residential property which was seen as a safer investment than other assets and the surge in activity by landlord investors, particularly from the GFC to 2017, was a major contributing factor to the increase in private rental supply, which was discussed earlier. This contributed to increases in house prices, particularly in large cities, which made purchase unaffordable for an increasing number of middle-income households, thereby increasing demand for private rental. In other words, the GFC was not a major catalyst for change in the private rental market but may have contributed to changes that were already taking place.

The impact of the COVID-19 pandemic

The COVID-19 pandemic has had a significant effect on the private rental market notwithstanding that Australia was arguably less affected than many other advanced economies in Europe and North America. Case numbers, hospitalisations and deaths from COVID-19 were low in 2020–2021, however, all states/territories had restrictions and lockdowns of varying lengths while pursuing a COVID-19 elimination or suppression strategy. While the public health response has been primarily a state/territory responsibility, the federal government played two important roles in the response to COVID-19 with direct implications for the private rental market: closing the borders and provision of income support to individuals and businesses that were affected by the pandemic. The states/territories have made direct interventions in the private rental market.

The first federal government response was to ban entry to all foreign nationals coming from China on 1 February 2020 in response to COVID-19 in that country, followed by the closure of Australia's border early in the pandemic on 20 March 2020, except for returning citizens and permanent residents, all of whom were required to enter quarantine for 14 days after arrival. Temporary and permanent international migration virtually stopped and net overseas migration was marginally negative for the first time in decades. The ban on migration meant that in the early stages of the pandemic demand for private rental fell, rents decreased and vacancy rates increased, although this was offset to some extent later by Australians returning from overseas. This affected some housing markets more than others, for example, private rental accommodation near tertiary education institutions had high vacancy rates. The borders were re-opened in stages beginning 1 November 2021.

The second federal government measure was to introduce a new flat rate payment per eligible staff member paid to businesses which had experienced a large drop in turnover (such as hospitality and tourism) so that they could retain staff even if the businesses were closed temporarily (called Job Keeper). The government also, surprisingly, temporarily doubled the then rate of unemployment benefit after years of refusing to increase the payment (renamed Job Seeker). These measures were intended to last from March to September 2020 but were extended at a reduced rate from September 2020 to March 2021 when they ceased. The income support measures were expensive (an estimated AU$90 billion for Job Keeper) but appear to have been successful in keeping unemployment lower than would otherwise have been the case and enabling the economy to rebound as COVID-19 restrictions were eased in the second half of 2020 in most states/territories[13] although lockdowns were re-imposed in some jurisdictions in mid-2021.

Although these measures benefited many private renters, the plight of residential (and commercial) tenants and landlords in the pandemic was a significant political issue. In the early period of the pandemic, a new 'national cabinet' was formed comprising the prime minister and all state and territory premiers. The national cabinet agreed to harmonisation of state/territory laws to protect private tenants through eviction moratoria and suspension of rental increases for six months (Mason *et al*, 2020); changes to state/territory legislation were required to implement the moratoria. States were also encouraged to provide temporary land tax relief for landlords and landlords were encouraged to negotiate with tenants to reduce or defer some rent payments until tenants' situation improved. Other targeted measures included getting homeless people off the streets and into hotels and other accommodation and provision of more crisis accommodation to victims of domestic violence so that they did not have to stay in unsafe situations. Some states, such as Victoria, also provided supplementary rent relief for tenants experiencing financial hardship through its Rental Relief Grant programme. The moratoria on rent increases and evictions were subsequently extended beyond the initial six months, albeit on a temporary basis.

Early attempts to assess these measures have produced varied results. Baker *et al* (2020) undertook a survey of private renters conducted in July–August 2020 which identified a range of concerns. These included the disproportionate effects on lower-income and younger people, the latter facing reduced hours of work; whether tenants had been able to negotiate rent reductions or deferrals with their landlords; and a range of issues including the suitability of rental premises for working from home and for sustaining mental health in these circumstances. Oswald *et al* (2020) in further empirical research found that tenants were affected by the pandemic but so too were landlords who relied on rent to pay the mortgage, arguing for a protective negotiation framework for tenants and better training in landlord–tenant relationships. It appears, however, that lower-income private renters were particularly affected by possible rent arrears and the threat of eviction, despite the moratoria on rent increases and evictions (Horne *et al*, 2020). The attempts to get landlords and tenants to negotiate even with support from fast-track mediation processes have highlighted the disparity in bargaining power between the two which already existed prior to COVID-19.

The tentative conclusion is that the rental market interventions were successful in the short term but the medium- and longer-term implications are harder to assess due to the long-term strain on the private rental sector (Mason *et al*, 2020: 53). Further, Horne *et al* (2020: 6) conclude that 'the rent and mortgage support measures have been less successful [than Job Seeker and Job Keeper] and should be reviewed in the light of the "soft power" relations' they revealed, including the householders' reticence and lack of willingness to engage with landlords and banks in what they view as uneven power relations.

As the prospect of adverse public health and economic effects dwindled in late 2021, the effect of border closures and lack of international travel for Australians has boosted savings which have flowed through into the housing market. House prices have risen across the board; not only in major cities but also in regional locations around these cities. There is an acute shortage

Figure 2.4: Housing finance (household sector), investors by purpose, Australia, July 2019 to December 2021

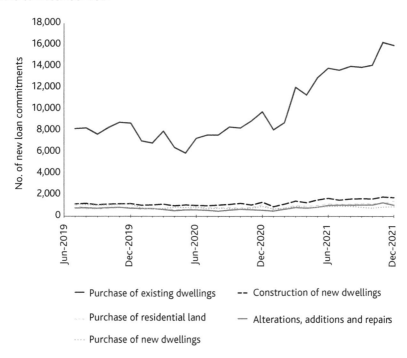

Note: Number of loans from Approved Deposit-taking Institutions and excludes refinancing.

Source: Calculated from ABS (2022) Lending Indicators, Cat No 5601.0, Table 13 Households; housing finance; By detailed purpose; New loan commitments; Numbers and values.

of rentals in these locations at any price as many people have relocated either temporarily or permanently from large cities as they can work from home, pricing out local households. Further, investor landlords have returned to the market (see Figure 2.4), bidding against home purchasers and putting additional pressure on house prices which has increased demand for private rental by those who are priced out of the purchase market.

Conclusion

The Australian private rental sector has become a more important and more visible part of the housing system in the 2000s. Its growth can be attributed to increased demand from migrants, particularly temporary migrants, and middle-income households who are unable, or do not wish, to purchase housing in an era of rapidly escalating house prices particularly in large cities. As a result, the profile of private renters has become more diverse in terms of age, household type and household income. The implications of these changes, including a growth in mid-life and older households and long-term renters, on Australia's housing, welfare, retirement and other policies are yet to be worked through.

As private rents became increasingly concentrated at mid-market levels during the 2000s, lower-income households have experienced declining affordability, which is particularly acute for those on very low incomes. However, the lack of policy to address these issues reflects path dependence and a laissez-faire attitude to the operation of rental markets. Rather, the focus has been on difficulties in accessing homeownership on one hand and homelessness on the other; private rental remains somewhat of a 'policy orphan' despite the large numbers of lower-income households dependent on the sector, many of whom experience rental stress.

Investment in private rental has become wider and deeper in the 2000s. There are still many small-scale landlords but also some indications of more financially driven activity, including debt-financed purchases, strategic investment in disadvantaged areas of large cities, a gradual increase in properties owned by landlords with multiple properties and emerging activity by some corporate and institutional landlords. There has been policy inertia on tax settings and subsidies for rental investment with a reliance on prudential supervision to dampen down excessive and risky lending.

Most private rental properties are now managed by real estate agents and there have been many changes in property advertising/search and matching properties to potential tenants due to the widespread development and application of digital technology. It has often proved difficult for regulators to keep apace of these developments. The real estate sector has been undergoing restructuring to increase efficiencies through the adoption of digital technology, in some cases outsourcing functions to third parties, to keep costs down in a high volume and repetitive business. Regulation of residential tenancies remains a state/territory matter and varies by jurisdiction, with changes occurring generally at a slow pace.

While Australia was relatively unaffected by the GFC, a medium-term effect has been increased investment in rental property as a safe asset. The COVID-19 pandemic, in contrast, has affected the economy notwithstanding lesser public health effects than in many other advanced economies. Federal government policies on closing Australia's borders and pumping billions of dollars into income support have shored up the economy which has started to rebound. What is clear, is that, notwithstanding emergency interventions in the private rental market, COVID-19 has highlighted the existing power imbalance between landlords/agents and tenants.

Acknowledgements

The author would like to acknowledge Margaret Reynolds for assistance with the tables and figures.

Notes

[1]   The last Census of Population and Housing undertaken by the Australian Bureau of Statistics (ABS) in 2021 found 25.5 per cent of households were private renters, up from 20 per cent in 2001. Due to a definitional change by the ABS relating to rent-free households, this figure is estimated to be approximately 0.4 per cent lower than if the definition applied in previous Censuses had been used. An ABS biennial sample survey, the Survey of Income and Housing, estimates 26.2 per cent of households were private renters in 2019–2020, up from 21 per cent in 2000–2001.

[2]   Calculated from the ABS Census of Population and Housing, 2001 and 2021.

[3]   Author's calculation from the ABS Survey of Income and Housing, 2019–2020.

[4]   The numbers of private renters in the bottom two quintiles combined in 2019–20 is similar whether gross or equivalised disposable income is used (979,000 using gross household income and 952,000 using equivalised disposable income) but the household composition is different. There are more single-person households using the former and more couples and families with children using the latter.

[5]   The Productivity Commission defines low-income households as those in the 3rd to the 40th percentiles of the equivalised disposable household income distribution (Productivity Commission, 2019: 44).

[6]   Using the so-called 30/40 rule – households in the bottom 40 per cent of equivalised disposable income spending more than 30 per cent of income on rent.

[7]   In this case, households in the lowest two gross income quintiles paying more than 30 per cent of gross household income on rent.

[8]   These included limiting foreign ownership to a 50 per cent cap in new multi-storey developments with at least 50 dwellings; provide for an annual charge on properties owned by foreign investors that are not occupied or available to rent for at least six months of the year; and increase the withholding tax for capital gains made by foreign residents.

[9]   The ABS groups together 'flats, units and apartments' referring to dwellings that do not have their own private grounds and usually share a common entrance foyer or stairwell. Since apartments have replaced flats in common usage, the chapter refers to apartments or units.

[10] REA is majority-owned by News Corp Australia. Domain is now majority owned by Channel 9 Entertainment. Both have major interests across traditional and digital media.

[11] The Liberal/National Party Coalition Government has been in power federally since 1996 except for 2007–2013 when the Australian Labor Party formed the federal government.

[12] Fifty-three per cent of allocations were held by 'for profit and other organisations', some managed by not-for-profit organisations, and 47 per cent by 'endorsed charities' (DSS, 2021).

[13] After decreases in gross domestic product (GDP) in the first half of 2020, the economy rebounded with a GDP growth of more than 3 per cent in Q3 and Q4 2020, the first time in the 60-year history of National Accounts that GDP has grown by more than 3 per cent in consecutive quarters (Hutchens *et al*, 2021). Further lockdowns in major cities in mid-2021 saw one more quarter of GDP decline but a rebound to a 3.9 per cent increase in GDP 2021–2022.

References

ABS (2022) Australia 2021 Census Community Profiles, https://www.abs.gov.au/census/find-census-data/community-profiles/2021/AUS, accessed 28 May 2023.

AIHW (Australian Institute of Health and Welfare) (2020) 'Housing affordability, snapshot', Australia's Welfare 2019, Canberra, AIHW, https://www.aihw.gov.au/reports/australias-welfare/housing-affordability

ATO (Australian Taxation Office) (2021) Taxation Statistics 2017-18, Individuals Detailed Tables, https://www.ato.gov.au/About-ATO/Research-and-statistics/In-detail/Taxation-statistics/Taxation-statistics---previous-editions/Taxation-statistics-2017-18/

Baker, E., Bentley, R., Beer, A. and Daniel, L. (2020) *Renting in the Time of COVID-19: Understanding the Impacts*, AHURI Final Report No. 340, Melbourne, Australian Housing and Urban Research Institute Limited, https://www.ahuri.edu.au/research/final-reports/340

Berry, M. (2000) 'Investment in rental housing in Australia: small landlords and institutional investors', *Housing Studies*, 15(5), 661–681.

Burke, T., Stone, W. and Ralston, L. (2014) *Generational Change in Home Purchase Opportunity in Australia*, AHURI Final Report No. 232, Melbourne, Australian Housing and Urban Research Institute Limited, https://www.ahuri.edu.au/research/final-reports/232

Burke, T., Nygaard, C. and Ralston, L. (2020) *Australian Home Ownership: Past Reflections, Future Directions*, AHURI Final Report No. 328, Melbourne, Australian Housing and Urban Research Institute Limited, https://www.ahuri.edu.au/research/final-reports/328

Campbell, I., Parkinson, S. and Wood, G. (2014) *Underemployment and Housing Insecurity: An Empirical Analysis of HILDA Data*, AHURI Final Report No. 230, Australian Housing and AHURI Final Report No. 230, Melbourne, Australian Housing and Urban Research Institute Limited, http://www.ahuri.edu.au/research/finalreports/230

DSS (Department of Social Services) (2020) *Annual Report 2019–2020*, Canberra, Australian Government.

DSS (Department of Social Services) (2021) *National Rental Affordability Scheme Quarterly Performance Report*, Canberra, Australian Government, https://www.dss.gov.au/sites/default/files/documents/02_2021/nras-quarterly-report-31-dec-2020.pdf

Haffner, M.E.A., Hoekstra, J., Oxley, M. and van der Heijden, H. (2010) 'Universalistic, particularistic and middle way approaches to comparing the private rental sector', *International Journal of Housing Policy*, 10(4), 357–377.

Horne, R., Willand, N., Dorignon, L. and Middha, B. (2020) *The Lived Experience of COVID-19: Housing and Household Resilience*, AHURI Final Report No. 345, Melbourne, Australian Housing and Urban Research Institute Limited, https://www.ahuri.edu.au/research/final-reports/345

Hulse, K. and Yates, J. (2017) 'A private rental sector paradox: unpacking the effects of urban restructuring on housing market dynamics', *Housing Studies*, 32(3), 253–270.

Hulse, K. and Reynolds, M. (2018) 'Investification: housing market dynamics in metropolitan areas of persistent socio-economic disadvantage', *Urban Studies*, 55(8), 1655–1671.

Hulse, K., Martin, C., James, A. and Stone, W. (2018) *Private Rental in Transition: Institutional Change, Technology and Innovation in Australia*, AHURI Final Report No. 296, Melbourne, Australian Housing and Urban Research Institute Limited, https://www.ahuri.edu.au/research/final-reports/296

Hulse, K., Reynolds, M., Nygaard, C., Parkinson, S. and Yates, J. (2019) *The Supply of Affordable Private Rental Housing in Australian Cities: Short-Term and Longer-Term Changes*, AHURI Final Report 323, Melbourne, Australian Housing and Urban Research Institute Limited, http://www.ahuri.edu.au/research/final-reports/323

Hulse, K., Reynolds, M. and Martin, C. (2020) 'The Everyman archetype: discursive reframing of private landlords in the financialization of rental housing', *Housing Studies*, 35(6), 981–1003.

Hutchens, G., Chalmers, S. and Janda, M. (2021) 'GDP figures show economy shrank in 2020 by 11 per cent with a record drop in Q2 but grew 3.1 per cent in the December quarter', *ABC Online*, 3 March.

Khoo, S.-E., McDonald, P., Temple, J. and Edgar, B. (2012) *Scoping Study of Migration and Housing Needs*, Report for National Housing Supply Council Unit, Canberra, Department of the Treasury, https://treasury.gov.au/sites/default/files/2019–03/migration_and_housing_needs.pdf

Martin, C. (2018) 'Clever Odysseus: narratives and strategies of rental property investor subjectivity in Australia', *Housing Studies*, 33(7), 1060–1084.

Martin, C., Hulse, K. and Pawson, H. (2018) *The Changing Institutions of Private Rental Housing: An International Review*, AHURI Final Report No. 292, Melbourne, Australian Housing and Urban Research Institute Limited, https://www.ahuri.edu.au/research/final-reports/292

Mason, C., Moran, M. and Earles, A. (2020) *Policy Coordination and Housing Outcomes during COVID-19*, AHURI Final Report No. 343, Melbourne, Australian Housing and Urban Research Institute Limited, https://www.ahuri.edu.au/research/final-reports/343

Morris, A., Hulse, K. and Pawson, H. (2021) *The Private Rental Sector in Australia: Living with Uncertainty*, Singapore, Springer.

Nethercote, M. (2020) 'Build-to-rent and the financialization of rental housing: future research directions', *Housing Studies*, 35(5), 839–874.

Ong, R., Pawson, H., Singh, R. and Martin, C. (2020) *Demand Side Assistance in Australia's Rental Housing Market: Exploring Reform Option*, AHURI Final Report No. 342, Melbourne, Australian Housing and Urban Research Institute Limited, https://www.ahuri.edu.au/research/finalreports/342

Oswald, D., Moore, T. and Baker, E. (2020) *Post Pandemic Landlord–Renter Relationships in Australia*, AHURI Final Report No. 344, Melbourne, Australian Housing and Urban Research Institute Limited, https://www.ahuri.edu.au/research/final-reports/344

Parkinson, S., James, A. and Liu, E. (2018) *Navigating a Changing Private Rental Sector: Opportunities and Challenges for Low-Income Renters*, AHURI Final Report No. 302, Melbourne, Australian Housing and Urban Research Institute, http://www.ahuri.edu.au/research/final-reports/302

Parkinson, S., Rowley, S., Stone, W., Amity, K., Spinney, A. and Reynolds, M. (2019) *Young Australians and the Housing Aspirations Gap*, AHURI Final Report No. 318, Melbourne, Australian Housing and Urban Research Institute Limited, https://www.ahuri.edu.au/research/final-reports/318

Pawson, H. and Martin, C. (2021) 'Rental property investment in disadvantaged areas: the means and motivations of Western Sydney's new landlords', *Housing Studies*, 36(5), 621–643, DOI: 10.1080/02673037.2019.1709806

Pawson, H., Hulse, K. and Morris, A. (2017) 'Interpreting the rise of long-term private renting in a liberal welfare regime context', *Housing Studies*, 32(8), 1062–1084.

Pawson, H., Martin, C., van den Nouwelant, R., Milligan, V., Ruming, K. and Melo, M. (2019) *Build-to-Rent in Australia: Product Feasibility and Potential Affordable Housing Contribution*, Sydney, Landcom.

Pawson, H., Milligan, V. and Yates, J. (2020) *Housing Policy in Australia*, Singapore, Palgrave Macmillan.

Phillips, J. and Simon-Davies, J. (2017) *Migration to Australia: A Quick Guide to the Statistics*, Research Paper Series, Canberra, Parliamentary Library.

Productivity Commission (2019) *Vulnerable Private Renters: Evidence and Options*, Canberra, Commission Research Paper.

Rogers, D., Wong, A. and Nelson, J. (2017) 'Public perceptions of foreign and Chinese real estate investment: intercultural relations in global Sydney', *Australian Geographer*, 48(4), 437–455.

Seelig, T., Thompson, A., Burke, T., Pinnegar, S., McNelis, S. and Morris, A. (2009) *Understanding What Motivates Households to Become and Remain Investors in the Private Rental Market*, AHURI Final Report No. 130, Melbourne, Australian Housing and Urban Research Institute, https://www.ahuri.edu.au/research/final-reports/130

Soaita, A.M., Searle, B.A., McKee, K. and Moore, T. (2017) 'Becoming a landlord: strategies of property-based welfare in the private rental sector in Great Britain', *Housing Studies*, 32(5), 613–637.

Stone, W., Burke, T., Hulse, K. and Ralston, L. (2013) *Long-Term Private Rental in a Changing Australian Private Rental Sector*, AHURI Final Report No. 209, Melbourne, Australian Housing and Urban Research Institute Limited, https://www.ahuri.edu.au/research/final-reports/209

Wood, G. and Ong, R. (2013) 'When and why do landlords retain property investments?', *Urban Studies*, 50(16), 3243–3261.

Wood, G. and Ong, R. (2017) 'The Australian housing system: a quiet revolution?', *Australian Economic Review*, 50(2), 197–204.

Wulff, M. and Maher, C. (1998) 'Long-term renters in the Australian housing market', *Housing Studies*, 13(1), 83–98.

3

Rental housing dynamics and their affordability impact in the United States

Alex Schwartz

Introduction

In the United States, the term 'private rental housing' is seldom, if ever, used. This is because most rented housing in the United States – unlike the UK and other European countries – is under private, for-profit ownership. Nearly all market-rate rental housing is privately owned, as is most subsidised low-income housing. This chapter provides an overview of rental housing in the United States, focusing on key changes that have occurred since 2000, especially in the wake of the foreclosure crisis that began in 2007 and extended to around 2012. The chapter begins with an overview of the rental housing stock, its ownership and management, and its inhabitants, followed by an examination of rental housing affordability. It then turns to key changes in rental housing since 2000. These include relative and absolute growth in renter households; the increasing presence of relatively affluent renters; and the growth of single-family rental housing, which is driven in part by institutional investors. The chapter concludes with a preliminary assessment of how COVID-19 has affected tenants and owners of rental housing.

As of 2021, there were 50.7 million rental housing units in the United States, accounting for 36 per cent of the nation's total housing stock of 139.8 million units. Ninety-one per cent of the nation's rental housing is occupied, and 9 per cent is vacant and available for rent. Nearly 90 per cent of all occupied rental housing is privately owned. The rest consists of various forms of social housing. This includes less than one million units of public housing owned by local housing authorities, and about four million units owned by various types of non-profit organisations, cooperatives and community land trusts (Bratt, 2020). While social housing overwhelmingly consists of subsidised housing for low- and moderate-income households, subsidised low-income housing is not confined to social housing. Well over two million units of subsidised low-income housing units are under private, for-profit ownership. In addition, more than 2.5 million low-income households receive tenant-based rental subsidies (Housing Choice Vouchers); most of them reside in privately owned housing. Perhaps because most rental housing is privately owned, nearly all statistical surveys of rental housing do not distinguish between housing under different forms of ownership.

Physical characteristics

Although many people may assume that rental housing is largely synonymous with apartment buildings and other forms of multi-family housing, more than one-quarter of all rental housing in 2021 consisted of detached single-family buildings. Furthermore, as discussed later in this chapter, much of the growth in rental housing since the mortgage crisis of 2007 has been driven by single-family rentals. Table 3.1 shows that detached single-family

Table 3.1: Physical characteristics of renter and owner-occupied housing, 2021

	Owner	Renter
Total units (000s)	82,513	45,991
Units in structure		
1, detached	84.2%	26.6%
1, attached	5.4%	8.0%
2–4	1.6%	15.7%
5–9	0.6%	11.0%
10–19	0.5%	14.1%
20–49	0.6%	8.8%
50 or more	1.0%	11.9%
Manufactured/mobile home or trailer/other	6.1%	3.8%
Condominium or cooperative	6%	8%
Year constructed		
2010–2021	9.1%	9.9%
2000–2009	15.0%	12.1%
1990–1999	13.6%	10.1%
1980–1989	12.8%	13.7%
1970–1979	13.9%	15.1%
1950–1969	20.2%	19.4%
Pre-1950	15.4%	19.6%
Median	**1980**	**1977**

(continued)

Table 3.1: Physical characteristics of renter and owner-occupied housing, 2021 (continued)

	Owner	Renter
Number of bedrooms		
None	0.1%	2.1%
1	2.2%	26.5%
2	15.8%	40.2%
3	49.1%	23.9%
4 or more	32.8%	7.3%
Median square footage	1,800	969
Units with physical problems		
Per cent severely inadequate	0.9%	2.4%
Per cent moderately inadequate	2.5%	6.0%

Source: US Census Bureau (2022a).

structures account for 27 per cent of all occupied rental units and attached single-family dwellings for an additional 8 per cent. Buildings with 2–4 units make up 16 per cent of the rental stock, and buildings with 5–9 units 11 per cent. Larger residential buildings with 10 or more units account for 35 per cent of all rental housing, including buildings with 50 or more units, which constitute 12 per cent of all rental housing. Whereas substantial amounts of rental housing can be found in buildings of various sizes, more than 95 per cent of all owner-occupied housing involves some form of single-unit structure (detached, attached or manufactured/mobile home).

Rental housing tends to be slightly older than owner-occupied housing, with a median year of construction of 1977 compared to 1980. Rental housing is usually smaller than owner-occupied housing. While 82 per cent of all owner-occupied housing contains three or more bedrooms, the same is true for just 31 per cent of all rentals. Whereas studio and one-bedroom units account for only 2 per cent of all owner-occupied units, they constitute 29 per cent of all rentals. The median owner-occupied unit, at 1,800 square feet, is nearly twice as large as the median rental unit at 969 square feet.

Finally, Table 3.1 shows that while most owner- and renter-occupied housing is physically sound, rental housing is more than twice as likely as owner-occupied housing to be severely or moderately inadequate.[1]

Ownership, debt and management

Table 3.2 provides an overview of the ownership, mortgage debt and management of rental housing in the United States as of 2018. The

Table 3.2: Ownership and management of rental housing by property size in 2018

	All	1 unit	2–4 units	5–24 units	25–49 units	50–99 units	100–149 units	150 units or more
Total units (in 000s)	48,248	17,106	6,251	4,746	2,801	1,111	1,600	14,633
Per cent distribution	100	35	13	10	6	2	3	30
Current ownership entity of property (per cent distribution)								
Individual investor	41	73	72	30	12	16	11	6
Trustee for estate	2	4	4	5	2	2	1	0
LLP, LP or LLC	37	16	15	46	59	53	55	62
Tenant in common	0	0	1	0	0	0	0	0
General partnership	2	0	1	6	4	3	6	4
Real Estate Investment Trust (REIT)	2	1	0	1	0	1	2	6
Real estate corporation	3	1	0	3	5	5	5	5
Housing cooperative organisation	0	0	0	1	1	1	1	0
Non-profit organisation	3	1	1	5	9	9	6	4
Other	2	1	1	1	4	3	4	2
Not reported	6	3	4	4	5	8	8	11
Mortgage status								
With mortgage or similar debt	59	39	52	63	67	69	71	81
No mortgage or similar debt	41	61	48	37	33	31	30	19
Day-to-day management								
Property owner or unpaid agent of owner	42	72	77	36	22	8	7	5
Management agent directly employed by owner	25	11	10	26	36	46	44	42
Management company	29	12	11	33	39	42	44	51
Other	2	4	1	3	2	2	2	1
Not reported	2	2	1	1	1	1	3	2

Note: LLP = Limited Liability Partnership; LP = Limited Partnership; LLC = Limited Liability Corporation.

Source: US Census Bureau (2021a).

source is the US Census Bureau's Rental Housing Finance Survey, a statistically representative sample of the nation's privately owned rental housing (excluded is public housing). The top panel of Table 3.2 shows the distribution of rental units across various ownership categories by property size. It is important to note that a single property can vary in size from a single dwelling unit to a multi-family apartment building, to an assemblage of numerous buildings – buildings that need not be in close proximity. Properties containing only one unit (presumably single-family houses and individual condominium units) form the largest property category, accounting for 35 per cent of total units. Properties with 150 or more units is the next largest category with 30 per cent of all units, followed by properties with 2–4 units (13 per cent) and 5–24 units (10 per cent).

Overall, Table 3.2 shows that more than 40 per cent of all rental units (excluding public housing) are owned by an individual investor and more than 37 per cent are owned by a Limited Liability Partnership (LLP), Limited Partnership (LP) or Limited Liability Corporation (LLC). However, ownership patterns vary by property size. Nearly three-quarters of all units in properties with one unit or with 2–4 units are owned by individual investors, compared to just 11 per cent in properties with 100–149 units and 6 per cent in properties with 150 units or more. Conversely, LLPs, LPs and LLCs account for 16 per cent or fewer units in properties with fewer than five units, and about half or more of the units in all larger properties. Real Estate Investment Trusts (REITs) account for fewer than 1 per cent of all units in properties with less than 100 units but constitute almost 6 per cent of the units in properties with 150 or more units. Non-profit and cooperative organisations own 6–10 per cent of all housing units in properties with 5–99 units, but substantially fewer in smaller and larger properties. Other, smaller ownership categories include trustees of estates and general partnerships.

In addition to ownership type, Table 3.2 shows the percentage of units in properties that have one or more mortgage in effect (or a similar debt). Not surprisingly, given their higher acquisition and development costs, larger properties are more likely to carry a mortgage than smaller ones. Whereas 39 per cent of single-unit properties and 52 per cent of units in 2–4-unit properties are in properties with a mortgage, the same is true for 81 per cent of units in properties with 150 or more units, and about 70 per cent of units in properties with 50–149 units.

Table 3.2 also shows major differences across property size in management responsibility. Overall, 42 per cent of all units are managed by the property owner or by an unpaid agent of the owner. However, this is true for about three-quarters of all units in properties with fewer than five units, 30 per cent of units in properties with 5–24 units, and a smaller percentage in larger properties, including less than 6 per cent of units in properties with 150 or more units. Conversely, less than one-quarter of units in properties with fewer than five units are managed by a management agency directly employed by the owner or by a management company, compared to 90 per cent of units in the largest property size category.

Most rental housing is leased for periods of six months or longer. This includes 87 per cent of all single-family rentals, and 96 per cent of all units in multi-family buildings. Nearly three-quarters of all multi-family units available for daily or weekly leases are found in properties with 150 units or more. Few cities or states regulate the rents that can be charged. For many years New York City, New Jersey, Washington, DC and a few cities in California were the only jurisdictions with some form of rent regulation. However, in 2018, California and Oregon adopted state-wide regulations that cap the maximum allowable rent increase (Schwartz, 2021).

Household characteristics

Renters differ from homeowners in numerous ways. Table 3.3 compares the two groups regarding race and ethnicity, age, household type, education, income and other respects. In general, compared to homeowners, renters are more likely to be from a minority group, to be younger, less likely to be married, more likely to live alone, more likely to have a disability, and to be poorer. Table 3.3 shows that non-Hispanic Whites comprise 73 per cent of all homeowning households, but 50 per cent of all renter households. Blacks and Hispanics each account for about 20 per cent of all renters but only 9 and 11 per cent, respectively, of all homeowners.

Renters are younger than owners, with a median age of 43 years compared to 57 among owners. Thirty-three per cent of all homeowners are at least 65 years of age, compared to 9 per cent of all renters. Almost one-third (29 per cent) of both homeowners and renters have children under 18, but married couples constitute 60 per cent of homeowners compared to 27 per cent of renters, and female-headed households make up 11 per cent of all homeowners as opposed to 22 per cent of all renters. Renters are almost twice as likely to live alone as homeowners: 38 per cent versus 23 per cent.

Renters are also much more mobile than homeowners, moving far more frequently. As of 2021, 76 per cent of all renters had moved into their current unit after 2015 compared to 35 per cent of all homeowners. Less than 3 per cent had moved in before 2000, compared to 29 per cent of all homeowners. While the median year in which renters moved into their unit was 2018, for homeowners it was nine years earlier, in 2009.

Table 3.3: Profile of renters and homeowners in 2021

	Owners	Renters
Total (000s)	82,513	45,991
% non-Hispanic White	73.0	49.6
% non-Hispanic Black	9.1	20.8
% Hispanic	10.5	20.0
% Asian	5.1	5.9
% 65 years or older	32.8	9.3
Median age	57	43
% households with children under 18	29.2	29.5
% married couple families	59.6	26.3
% female-headed households	10.8	22.4
% one-person households	22.9	38.3
% bachelor's degree or higher	41.6	28.7
% citizen of US	96.0	87.6
% moved into unit after 2015	35.0	76.0
% moved into unit before 2000	29.0	2.4
Median year moved into unit	2009	2018
% with a disabled person	22.5	23.2
Median household income in 2019	US$78,000	US$41,000
% in poverty	9.0	22.6
Median net wealth	US$255,000	US$6,300
% with more than 1 person per room	1.2	2.0

Source: US Census Bureau (2022a) and Bhutta *et al* (2020).

Fewer renters have attained a college or graduate degree than homeowners (29 per cent versus 42 per cent). Renters and homeowners are about equally likely to include a person with disabilities in their households (23 per cent). Whereas 96 per cent of all homeowners are US citizens, the same is true of 88 per cent of all renters.

Renters also earn less income than homeowners and are far less wealthy. The median household income for renters, at US$41,000, was barely half that of homeowners (US$78,000). Nearly one-quarter of all renters are in poverty, compared to 9 per cent of all homeowners. The median net wealth of renters, at US$6,300, is less than 3 per cent of that of homeowners (US$255,000).

Although few renters and homeowners live in overcrowded conditions, defined as more than one person per room – the incidence of overcrowding among renters at 2 per cent is nearly twice that of homeowners.

Rental affordability

In the United States, the standard of housing affordability is usually set at 30 per cent of income. If a household spends more than 30 per cent of its pre-tax income on housing costs, it is 'cost burdened'; and its cost burden is 'severe' if housing–related expenditures exceed 50 per cent of its income. Table 3.4 shows the extent of housing cost burden in the United States, for all renters and for renters in different income groups. On average, renters paid US$1,184 in rent (including utilities) in 2021. Only 9 per cent spent less than US$500 on rent and an additional 27 per cent spent between US$500 and US$999. At the other extreme, 16 per cent paid US$2,000 or more.

Nearly half of all renters in 2021 were cost burdened, spending more than 30 per cent of their income on rent and related expenses. These renters were about evenly divided between those paying 30 per cent to 50 per cent of their income on rent, and those paying more than 50 per cent (that is, severely cost burdened). The bottom panel of Table 3.4 shows the incidence of housing cost burden in 2019[2] among renters in different income groups. The income categories are defined in relation to the median family income in the renters' metropolitan area or nonmetropolitan county i.e., Area Median Family Income (AMI).

Not surprisingly, the incidence of rental cost burden is inversely correlated with income. This is especially true for severe rent burdens of more than 50 per cent of income. Table 3.4 shows that 78 per cent of all renters in the lowest income group earning up to 30 per cent of AMI spent more than 30 per cent of their income on rent, including nearly 63 per cent who spent more than 50 per cent of their income. In the next highest income group comprising renters earning between 30 and 50 per cent of AMI, 77 per cent are cost burdened, but the majority spent 30 to 50 per cent of their income on rent as opposed to 50 per cent or more. Among renters earning more than 50 per cent of AMI, relatively few experienced severe cost burdens, and the incidence of moderate cost burdens diminish sharply when income exceeds 80 per cent of AMI.

The pervasiveness of housing affordability problems among renters is due primarily to their low incomes, the growing shortage of appropriately priced housing, and the lack of rental subsidies. Most fundamentally, they reflect the nation's widening economic inequality, with most of the income growth flowing to the highest income households (Tilly, 2006; Petach, 2022). After

Table 3.4: Rental affordability in the United States

Monthly gross rent (including utilities) in 2021

Less than US$500	9%
US$500–999	27%
US$1,000–1,499	28%
US$1,500–1999	16%
US$2,000 or more	16%
No cash rent	4%
Median (excluding no cash rent)	1,184

Rent burden in 2021

Less than 30%	43%
30–49%	24%
50% or more	25%
Median	31%

(excludes no cash rent and households with zero or negative income)

Rent burden by income group (% of AMI in 2019)

	% total renters	% with cost burden of 30–50%	% with cost burden of 50%+	% with cost burden more than 30%
Less than 30% of AMI	26.3	15.2	62.8	78.0
30–50% of AMI	14.9	45.4	31.1	76.5
50–80% of AMI	19.7	39.9	10.0	50.0
80 to 100% of AMI	17.0	17.9	3.8	21.7
More than 100% of AMI	22.2	6.2	1.3	7.6
Total	100	23.0	24.0	47.1

Source: US Census Bureau (2022a) and HUD (2021).

adjusting for inflation, median renter incomes increased by only 0.5 per cent from 2000 to 2018, while the median gross rent (which includes utilities) increased by 17 per cent (Schwartz, 2021: 38).

Whereas the number of renters with extremely low incomes increased by more than three million from 2001 to 2019, the number of units potentially affordable to these households increased by less than half as much (1.4 million). And the number that were both affordable and available – that is, either vacant or occupied by an extremely low-income household – increased by only 929,000. The gap between the number of extremely

Table 3.5: Demand and supply of affordable rental housing by income group, 2019 (in 000s)

Income range (as per cent area median family income)	Renter households	Affordable units	Shortage or surplus in income range	Cumulative units per 100 renters	Affordable and available units	Shortage or surplus in income range	Cumulative units per 100 renters
0–30%	11,748	8,256	-3,492	70	4,732	-7,016	40
30–50%	6,640	9,393	2,753	96	6,700	60	62
50–80%	8,786	19,112	10,326	135	15,009	6,223	97
80% +	17,486	12,574	-4,912	110	22,894	5,408	110
Total	44,660	49,335	4,675	110	49,335	4,675	110

Source: HUD (2021: Table A-13).

low-income households and the number of units affordable and available to them increased from 4.9 million in 2001 to 7.0 million in 2019 (US Department of Housing and Urban Development, 2021: 75).

Table 3.5 shows the number of renter households in 2019 by income group and the corresponding number of units that were affordable and available to rent. Looking first at units that were affordable (but not necessarily available) the table shows a deficit of units at the two ends of the income distribution. There was a shortfall of 3.5 million units affordable to renters with incomes up to 30 per cent of the AMI. It also shows an additional deficit for tenants with incomes above 80 per cent of median. This latter shortfall, however, is more apparent than real. It shows that more affluent renters often rent homes that cost less than 30 per cent of their incomes, thus reducing the number of units affordable and available to lower-income renters.

Table 3.5 also shows that there is a more severe shortage of units that are affordable and available to the lowest-income renters. Of the 8.26 million rental units that were affordable (at 30 per cent of income or less) to extremely low-income renters, 3.5 million were occupied by higher-income households, leaving only 4.7 million that were available. As a result, the 11.7 million extremely low-income renters faced a shortfall of seven million affordable and available units in 2019. Expressed differently, only 40 units were affordable and available for every 100 extremely low-income renters; and only 62 units were affordable and available for every 100 renters with incomes up to 50 per cent of the AMI (that is, extremely low and very low income combined). Going further up the income ladder, only 97 units were affordable and available to every 100 renters earning up to 80 per cent of the AMI. With affordable housing in short supply, low-income renters have little choice but to occupy housing that costs more than they can afford.

Most fundamentally, the lack of housing affordable to the lowest income renters reflects the inability of the private housing market to produce and maintain low-cost housing without public subsidy. The rents collected from housing affordable to the lowest income households are often simply too low to cover the cost of maintenance, debt service and taxes, to say nothing of profit for the investors (Mallach, 2019; Urban Institute, 2020). For example, 12 per cent of all rental buildings in 2001 with average rents of US$400 or less posted negative net operating income: their rents were insufficient to cover operating costs (Joint Center for Housing Studies, 2006: 24). Similarly, Garboden and Newman, in an analysis of 1–4-unit rental properties in the United States with units renting for less than the regional median rent, found that 22 per cent of the properties had negative net operating incomes in 2001 (rent revenues were less than maintenance, taxes and other operating costs). Moreover, of the properties with positive net operating income, 23 per cent lacked sufficient cash flow to cover their debt service costs. The authors concluded that only 5 per cent of these rental properties were financially stable, 65 per cent were salvageable but at risk, and about 30 per cent were not salvageable (Garboden and Newman, 2012).

As a result, almost all new unsubsidised rental housing is built for upscale markets. Owners of the affordable low-income housing that does exist are all too frequently left with two choices: gradually disinvest until the property becomes uninhabitable or reposition the property for higher-income tenants. When rental revenue fails to keep up with operating costs, conditions will frequently deteriorate as owners cut back on maintenance and upkeep. Eventually, the gap between revenue and expenses reaches the point at which owners decide to disinvest altogether and vacate the property. An alternative to this dynamic of disinvestment, when market conditions allow, is to raise rents to levels above what low-income households can afford or to convert rentals into condominiums for higher-income occupancy. These responses, most common in gentrifying neighbourhoods (Leonard and Kennedy, 2001), preserve the property as a physical asset but remove it from the affordable inventory. Furthermore, when market conditions permit, most owners of unsubsidised housing affordable to low-income households are free to increase their rents. Reflecting these dynamics, the number of units renting for less than US$600 a month (affordable to households earning up to US$24,000) fell, after adjusting for inflation, by nearly 2.5 million from 2004 to 2019, a drop of 20.2 per cent. These low-cost units accounted for 21 per cent of all rental housing in 2019, down from 31 per cent in 2004 (Joint Center for Housing Studies, 2020).

In some places, popular tourist destinations especially, significant portions of the rental housing stock have been converted for short-term occupancy, further exacerbating affordability pressures. Airbnb and other internet-based platforms for renting out rooms and entire dwelling units can generate more income for property owners than they would obtain through long-term rental leases (Horn and Merante, 2017; Hoffman and Heisler, 2021). The New York City Comptroller's Office, for example, estimates Airbnb was responsible for 9.2 per cent of the city's total increase in rents between 2009 and 2016 (Hoffman and Heisler, 2021: 57). In a study of Airbnb's impact on Boston's housing market, Horn and Merante (2017) found that an increase of one standard deviation in Airbnb listings relative to total housing units led to an increase of 0.4 per cent in the mean asking rent, or US$93 per month.

A more widespread and perhaps more fundamental cause of the shortage of rental housing affordable to low- and moderate-income households lies in the land-use regulations of local government. Numerous cities and especially suburbs restrict, if not prohibit, the construction of multi-family housing, or single-family housing built at relatively high densities, thereby limiting the supply of such housing that is available (Downs, 1994; Pendall, 2000; Glaeser and Gyourko, 2008). In Connecticut, for example, only 2 per cent of the state's three million zoned acres allow for 'as of right' (without requiring zoning variances or public hearings) construction of residential buildings with four or more units, and only 2.3 per cent allowed for the construction of buildings with three units. Eight jurisdictions prohibit all forms of multi-family housing (Prevost, 2021).

Also contributing to the shortage of affordable housing for low-income renters are reductions in the federally subsidised housing stock. The public housing inventory decreased by nearly 394,000 units (28 per cent) from 1994 (when the public housing stock was at its peak) to 2019, partially reflecting the widespread demolition of distressed projects.[3] Many of these projects have been replaced with much nicer, often mixed-income developments, but the result is a net loss of subsidised units. In addition, more than 429,000 units of privately owned but federally subsidised housing were lost from 1998 through 2014 because owners did not renew their subsidy contracts, opted out of their federally insured mortgages, or forfeited the property because of foreclosure or other reasons (Finkel et al, 2006; Ray et al, 2015). Finally, the number of rental housing vouchers available to low-income households increased by less than 10,000 annually on average from 2010 to 2019 (Schwartz, 2021). Overall, only about one-in-four eligible low-income households receive federal housing subsidies, whether in the form of public housing, project-based rental assistance or Housing Choice Vouchers.

Key changes in rental housing

The mortgage crisis that began in 2007 marked an inflection point in the growth and composition of rental housing. Prior to the crisis, homeownership rates were rising across nearly all population groups and rental housing was increasingly dominated by people with low incomes. Of course, the surge in risky, subprime lending proved to be unsustainable, and the resulting collapse sparked a global financial crisis and economic recession that caused millions of homeowners to lose their homes to foreclosure (Immergluck, 2015). From 2007 through 2012, more than eight million homeowners lost their homes to foreclosure, short sales and other related means. At first, most victims of foreclosure had taken out risky subprime mortgages, but the Great Recession caused millions of people with conventional, lower-interest mortgages to go into default starting around 2009 due to unemployment and income loss (Immergluck, 2015).

Growth in renter households

The most immediate way by which the housing crisis and subsequent recession propelled the rental sector to grow was through mortgage foreclosure and related transactions. Most households who lost their homes to foreclosure and related causes became renters. Some were able to purchase other homes, and some ended up moving in with relatives and friends, but most ended up renting. In some cases, families rented the very homes they had previously owned. Foreclosures probably account for an increase of several million renters since the onset of the housing crisis.

The second way by which the housing crisis triggered growth in the rental sector is less direct. Whereas mortgage foreclosures, short sales and the like displaced millions of homeowners into renting, post-crisis changes in mortgage underwriting prevented millions of other households who would previously have qualified for a mortgage from acquiring one. Stricter underwriting standards including down-payment requirements, minimum credit scores and maximum income-to-debt ratios, have made it much more difficult for people to qualify for mortgages and have thus required them to remain as renters. In 2019, the median credit rating (FICO score) for a home-purchase mortgage was 40 points higher than before the crisis. The 10th percentile of credit scores for home buyers in 2019, representing 'the lower bound of creditworthiness to qualify for a mortgage', was nearly 50 points higher (Housing Finance Policy Center, 2020: 15).

Figure 3.1 charts the homeownership rate in the United States from 2000 through 2021 along with the annual change in the total number of renter and homeowner households. The homeownership rate in 2000 stood at 67.5 per cent. It peaked at 69 per cent in 2004 and plateaued near that level through 2006. It then declined continuously through 2016 when it reached a low of 63.4 per cent (the lowest level since 1965). Homeownership rates subsequently moved up for several years, reaching 66.6 per cent in 2020, but then dropped back in 2021 during the COVID-19 pandemic. Figure 3.1 also shows that the total number of renter households increased in all but two years from 2005 through 2021. Conversely, not only did the homeownership

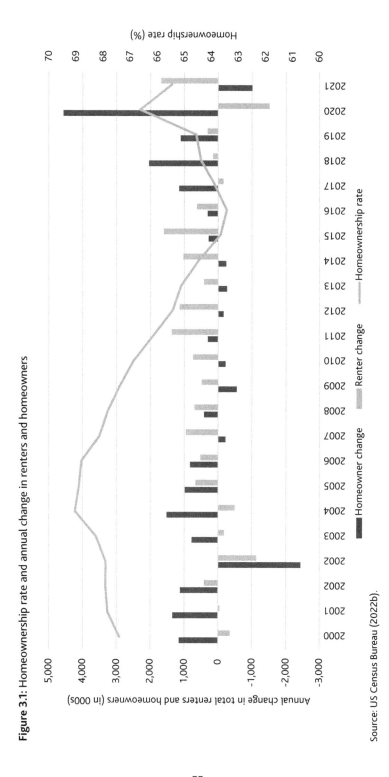

Figure 3.1: Homeownership rate and annual change in renters and homeowners

Source: US Census Bureau (2022b).

Figure 3.2: Total renters (000s) by income group (% of AMI) in 1999, 2009 and 2019

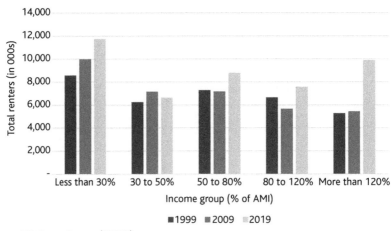

Source: US Census Bureau (2022b).

rate decline after 2006, so did the total number of homeowners. From 2007 through 2016 renters accounted for the entire net household growth in the United States. It has only been since 2017 that homeownership began to register any growth in absolute and relative terms.

Growth among higher-income renters

In addition to effectuating an increase in the number and percentage of renters, the mortgage crisis also led to an increase among higher income renters. Figure 3.2 shows the number of renter households in various income groups in 1999, 2009 and 2019. It shows that the lowest-income households, earning up to 30 per cent of AMI, consistently comprised the largest group of renters. In 1999 they represented 25 per cent of all renters. Their share of total renters peaked at 28 per cent in 2009, and then fell back to 26 per cent by 2019. In absolute terms, the lowest-income group included more than 11.7 million renters in 2019, up more than three million from 1999.

The second largest income group among renters in 2019 consisted of households earning more than 120 per cent of AMI. This group numbered nearly ten million. Previously, this highest-income group usually claimed the fewest renters, with its share generally hovering around 15 per cent. From 2009 to 2019 the total number of renters in the highest income category rose by more than five million, or 82 per cent. Most of this increase occurred between 2009 and 2017. Unlike renters in the lowest and highest income groups, those earning between 50 per cent and 120 per cent of AMI saw relatively little change in number over the 1999–2019 period. An obvious consequence of these changes is that low-income renters have faced increasing competition for rental housing from more affluent households.

The growth among higher-income renters is not fully understood. It partly reflects stricter mortgage underwriting standards that make it more difficult even for households with relatively high incomes to qualify for a mortgage. Relatedly, it may reflect the fact that many renters lack the savings necessary for the down payment on a home; and it may also reflect the rapid growth in student debt among younger adults. Millions of people took out loans to finance the increasingly high cost of college and graduate school, and it can take more than a decade to pay back these loans, which reduce the amount of income available to spend on a mortgage. A Federal Reserve study estimated that increased student debt was responsible for 20 per cent of the decline in homeownership from 2005 to 2014 among young adults 24 to 32 years of age (Mezza *et al*, 2019). Some relatively affluent renters may also favour renting over homeownership for the flexibility it affords and the opportunity to reside in popular urban neighbourhoods (Ghorbani, 2017; Warnock, 2019). Many of these renters eventually purchase homes, but they delay doing so relative to their age cohort in previous years (Ghorbani, 2017).

Growth in single-family rentals

A third change triggered by the foreclosure crisis is the recent growth in the number and share of rental detached single-family houses. Overwhelmingly associated in the popular imagination with homeownership, detached single-family houses have always comprised a large portion of the rental housing stock. In 2005, they accounted for 24 per cent of all occupied rental housing units. However, the supply of single-family rental housing increased sharply in the wake of the mortgage crisis. From 2005 through 2021 detached single family units accounted for 33 per cent of the total growth in occupied rental housing, rising by more than 3.9 million units, with attached single-family rental units accounting for an additional 12 per cent of the total growth (see Table 3.6). The next largest growth category consisted of units in buildings with 10 to 19 units, which increased by 2.3 million units. Buildings with 50 or more units ranked a close fourth. As of 2019, detached single-family houses comprised 27 per cent of all occupied rental housing.

Most of the growth in rental housing since 2005 reflects the transfer of previously owner-occupied single-family homes to renters. Whereas the total number of renter-occupied units increased by more than 12 million units from 2005 to 2021, the number of newly constructed multi-family housing units[4] (not all of which are for renter occupancy) increased by fewer than

Table 3.6: Rental housing by structure size (in 000s)

Structure size	2005		2019		2021		Change 2005–21		Change 2019–21	
	Total	Per cent	Total	Per cent	Total	Per cent	Total	Per cent Share	Total	Per cent Share
1, detached	8,297	24.4	12,554	28.1	12,236	26.6	3,939	32.8	-318	-24.0
1, attached	2,182	6.4	2,520	5.6	3,669	8.0	1,487	12.4	1,149	86.7
2–4	6,829	20.1	7,814	17.5	7,234	15.7	405	3.4	-580	-43.8
5–9	4,607	13.6	5,465	12.2	5,070	11.0	463	3.8	-395	-29.8
10–19	4,175	12.3	4,730	10.6	6,482	14.1	2,307	19.2	1,752	132.2
20–49	3,203	9.4	4,231	9.5	4,031	8.8	828	6.9	-200	-15.1
50 or more	3,222	9.5	5,632	12.6	5,489	11.9	2,267	18.9	-143	-10.8
Manufactured/mobile home or trailer	1,424	4.2	1,694	3.8	1,754	3.8	330	2.7	60	4.5
Total	33,939	100.0	44,640	100.0	45,965	100.0	12,026	100.0	1,325	100.0

Source: US Census Bureau (2022a).

five million units (US Census Bureau, 2022c). Given that most homeowners reside in single-family properties, it follows that most victims of mortgage foreclosure also lived in single-family homes. When they vacated their homes because of foreclosure many of these properties became rentals.

In addition, some of the increase in single-family rentals, especially before the onset of the mortgage crisis, reflected an increase in the acquisition of houses for investment. An increasing share of properties financed with home mortgages were not acquired for owner-occupancy but rather as a speculative investment for capital gains from the quick sale of the property to another buyer ('flipping') or as a rental property (Schwartz, 2021).

Recent trends suggest that the growth of single-family rental homes may have plateaued. Table 3.6 shows that the number of detached single-family rental homes decreased by 318,000 from 2019 to 2021 (-2.5 per cent), although the number of townhouses and other attached single-family rentals continued to grow. Buildings with 10 to 49 units were the only other category see meaningful growth in rental units during this period. One reason for the recent flatlining of single-family rentals may be the resurgent demand for homeownership fuelled in part by historically low mortgage interest rates (until 2022, when the Federal Reserve ratcheted up interest rates to combat inflation) and low amounts of homes available for sale. As a result, single-family rentals were sold off to home buyers. As many as two million (16 per cent) of the single-family homes that were rented in 2014 were owner-occupied in 2019 (Joint Center for Housing Studies, 2022).

Emergence of large-scale owners of single-family rentals

Single-family rentals had typically been owned by 'mom and pop' investors, that is, individuals and families owning one to 20 or so rental dwellings (Dill, 2012; Immergluck and Law, 2014). However, in the wake of the mortgage foreclosure crisis several institutional investors, among them Blackstone and other private-equity firms, acquired thousands of houses at deeply discounted prices to rent out. They frequently acquired foreclosed properties at steep discounts in bulk sales from banks and other lenders, as well as from Fannie Mae and Freddie Mac. From the spring of 2012 to the spring of 2014 these firms had invested more than US$20 billion to acquire about 200,000 homes to rent. The Blackstone Group alone spent more than US$8 billion in this period to acquire 43,000 homes in 14 metro areas (Gittlelsohn and Perlberg, 2014). At one point in 2013 Blackstone was spending US$100 million every week to acquire single-family houses (Gittlelsohn and Perlberg, 2014). Most of the firms that had accumulated large portfolios of single-family homes became publicly traded REITs or spun off their portfolios into a REIT. At the end of 2017, about two-thirds of all institutionally owned single-family rentals were owned by REITs and the rest were under private ownership (Colburn *et al*, 2021). As of 2019, REITs alone owned more than 200,000 homes, valued at more than US$30 billion (Colburn *et al*, 2021). By 2016, single-family rental housing had become a distinct 'asset class' (Amherst Capital Management, 2016; Colburn et al, 2021).

Notwithstanding the rapid growth of institutional investment in single-family rental property in the wake of the mortgage crisis, institutional portfolios constitute only about 2 per cent of all single-family rentals. However, in some areas, they account for a larger share. For example, Colburn *et al* (2021) found that three of the largest institutional investors owned 10 per cent of all single-family rentals in the Tampa, Florida, metropolitan area; over 7 per cent in the Atlanta area; and nearly 6 per cent in the Phoenix area. In general, institutional investors have targeted their acquisitions 'in fast-growing regions hardest hit by the foreclosure crisis and economic recession where price declines and increases in rental demand were steepest' (Colburn *et al*, 2021). Most of these regions were in Sunbelt states. Furthermore, investors favoured 'middle and working-class suburban neighbourhoods that are racially and ethnically diverse but remain credit-challenged' (Colburn *et al*, 2021). They were particularly attracted to areas with 'lower-price to rent ratios and low poverty, crime, and tax rates, and higher proportions of college graduates and households with children' (Colburn *et al*, 2021). Institutional investors have also preferred certain types of housing over others. They are especially inclined to acquire units with three to four bedrooms and that were built after 1978 (Colburn *et al*, 2021).

The growth of single-family rentals under institutional ownership was initially fuelled through the bulk purchase of foreclosed properties, often at low prices. In recent years, as the availability of foreclosed property dwindled, institutional investors pursued other acquisition strategies. These include acquisition of property portfolios from other institutional investors, purchases of existing single-family homes available for sale from their owner, and, in some cases, construction of new single-family homes for the rental market (Colburn *et al*, 2021; Fields and Vergerio, 2022).

Researchers have documented several negative consequences of institutional investment in single-family homes for both renters and home buyers. Compared to other, smaller-scale owners of single-family rentals, institutional investors have raised rents and pursued evictions more aggressively (Fields and Vergerio, 2022; Raymond, 2022). Moreover, the growth of institutional investors has been detrimental to first-time and other home buyers who typically require a mortgage. Because institutional investors almost always purchase properties with cash, they can close on the transaction far more quickly than home buyers who must apply for a mortgage (Lambie-Hanson and Slonkosky, 2018; Raymond, 2022).

COVID-19 and rental housing

COVID-19 arrived in the United States in February 2020. By the end of October 2022, it had infected more than 97.6 million Americans, killing more than one million (Centers for Disease Control, 2022). Globally, more than 628 million people had contracted the virus, and more than 6.5 million had died from it (World Health Organization, 2022). The United States, which contains 4.25 per cent of the world's population, accounted for 16 per cent of all COVID-19-related deaths.

The virus forced much of the US economy to shut down in the spring of 2020, causing millions of people to lose jobs and income for months on end, if not permanently. COVID-19 and the economic calamity it engendered put millions of Americans at risk of losing their homes; it was by far the most daunting challenge for US housing policy since the Great Depression of the 1930s.

Total non-farm employment in the United States fell by more than 22 million from February to April 2020, plummeting by 15 per cent in just two months. By the end of January 2021, total employment remained down by nearly ten million jobs (US Bureau of Labor Statistics, 2021a). The nation's unemployment rate stood at 6.3 per cent at the end of January, compared to 3.8 per cent in February 2020 (US Bureau of Labor Statistics, 2021b). This was down from a high of 14.4 per cent in April, but part of the decrease reflected the fact that several million people had left the workforce (that is, stopped looking for jobs) and were no longer counted among the unemployed (Guilford and Cambon, 2020).

The economic fallout of COVID-19 hit some occupations and industries much harder than others. The people most prone to be laid off worked in travel and tourism, retail, entertainment, restaurants, bars, and other fields that involve public gatherings and/or extensive person-to person contact. Many of these workers earned low wages and were disproportionately people of colour. On the other hand, much less job loss occurred within higher-paid occupations and industries where, thanks to the internet, employees could work remotely from home.

The loss of jobs and income put millions of renters and homeowners at risk of losing their homes. Relatively few Americans had sufficient savings to cover their housing costs for more than a few months. Indeed, prior to COVID-19, the Federal Reserve found that 37 per cent of all adults lacked the funds to cover an unexpected US$400 expense. The same study found that nearly three in ten adults 'were either unable to pay their monthly bills or were one modest financial setback away from failing to pay monthly bills in full' (Board of Governors of the Federal Reserve System, 2020: 21).

As of February 2021, the US Census Bureau found that 18 per cent of all renters, more than 9.2 million in total, were behind on their rent, including 29 per cent of all Black renters, 21 per cent of all Hispanic renters, and 23 per cent of all renters in households that had experienced a loss of employment income. Nearly one-third (29 per cent) of all renters reported that they had no or slight confidence that they would be able to pay the next month's rent (US Census, 2021b). According to Moody's Analytics, more than ten million renters owed back-rent in January 2021. On average, these renters were 3.8 months late in paying rent, and owed an average of US$1,130 plus utilities and late fees (Parrott and Zandi, 2021).

Far more renters would have been in arrears, and millions of renters would have been evicted from their homes, were it not for government intervention. From March 2020 through March 2021, Congress passed three COVID-19 relief bills totalling nearly US$5 trillion. In addition, the federal Centers for Disease Control issued a moratorium on eviction in August 2020, which was subsequently extended to 30 June 2021. Numerous state and local governments also imposed eviction moratoria and provided emergency rent payments and other forms of relief (Schwartz, 2021).

Among other things, the federal COVID-19 relief 'packages' included one-time payments to households earning below a specific amount, enhanced unemployed insurance benefits (including benefits for contractors and gig economy workers who are generally not eligible or traditional unemployment insurance), support for small businesses, loan forbearance for homeowners and landlords with federally backed mortgages, emergency rental assistance, and funding for homeless programmes. The US$1.9 trillion American Rescue Plan Act, passed in March 2021, for example, included US$1,400 for adults and dependents in households earning up to US$150,000, an increase in the childcare tax credit, US$27.4 billion in emergency rental assistance and US$5 billion for homeless housing.

Federal, state and local eviction moratoria prevented most renters from being forced out of their homes if they fell behind on their rent. However, moratorium enforcement was uneven, and not all renters knew about or understood the steps they needed to take to qualify for the moratoria (Goldstein, 2020). Also, eviction moratoria by themselves do not absolve renters of the need to pay rent; they allow back-rent to accumulate, often along with late fees and other charges. Many renters are barely able to pay a single month's rent, much less several months' rent at once.[5] Fortunately, the final two COVID-19 relief bills passed by Congress included a combined total of US$52 billion in emergency rental assistance, covering most but not all the accumulated rental arrears to date.

Eviction moratoria can also put stress on the finances of rental housing. If a substantial portion of a property's tenants fall behind on their rent, it obviously becomes more difficult for the landlord to cover operating and debt-service costs. Unless the property has substantial reserves, or the owner has access to additional resources, owners may cut back on essential repairs and upkeep and fall behind on mortgage and property tax payments. Smaller-scale owners were hit hardest by rental arrears. According to the National Multi Housing Council (2021) – a trade association of owners and managers of large, professionally managed rental properties – only about 5 per cent of tenants had not paid their rent by the end of the month during the pandemic, compared to about 4 per cent before (and 21 per cent had not paid it by the 6th of the month, compared to 19 per cent before). Smaller-scale owners of rental property, on the other hand, reported higher levels of rent arrears, especially Black and Hispanic landlords (Goodman, 2020; National Association of Hispanic Real Estate Professionals and Terner Center for Housing Innovation, 2020).

In addition to undermining the ability of millions of households to pay their rent, COVID-19 also changed the dynamics of the rental housing market. Initially, rents decreased sharply in the face of income loss and reduced demand – especially in cities where many households fled to the suburbs and to rural areas for larger homes and more open space (Badger and Bui, 2021). This decrease in rental price proved to be short lived. By 2021, reflecting a combination of increasing demand and constrained supply, rents had reversed direction and began to increase markedly (Bhattarai, 2022; Joint Center for Housing Studies, 2022). By 2022, they had become a key driver of the nation's high inflation rate, the highest in over 40 years (Smialek, 2022).

Conclusion

The rental housing sector in the United States has undergone significant changes in the wake of the mortgage crisis of 2007. Prior to the crisis, the number of renters was diminishing as a share of total households, and registered little absolute gain. From 2006 to 2017, in contrast, they accounted for 70 per cent of total household growth, and increased both in number and as a proportion of total households. Underlying this growth was the slow recovery from the Great Recession triggered by the mortgage crisis and the more stringent underwriting standards adopted by mortgage lenders in the wake of the crisis.

Not only did the rental sector grow, but it also became more diverse economically. Relatively affluent households earning more than 120 per cent of AMI accounted for 43 per cent of the growth in renters from 1999 to 2019. As a proportion of all renter households, the highest income group rose from 16 per cent in 1999 to 22 per cent in 2019.

A third change in rental housing to emerge from the mortgage crisis is the growth in rental single-family homes, driven in part by institutional investors. Although single-family dwelling units have always comprised a large portion of the rental housing stock in the United States, they along with attached single-family homes accounted for nearly half of the total growth in rental housing from 2005 to 2021.

One area of constancy is the problem of housing affordability. For decades, most renters have spent more than 30 per cent of their income on housing costs, and many spent more than half of their income on housing – including most renters with very low incomes. When renters confront these affordability burdens, they have less money available to cover other needs, and are often at heightened risk of becoming homeless.

Finally, COVID-19 underscored the precarious financial position of many renters. The loss of employment and income triggered by the pandemic forced millions of households to fall behind on their rent. Were it not for enhanced unemployment insurance, rental assistance and eviction moratoria, and other forms of government assistance, millions of renters would have been evicted.

Notes

[1] The most widely used measures of the physical adequacy of housing in the United States are two composites derived from the American Housing Survey, a biannual study of the nation's housing. Units are categorised as having 'severe' or 'moderate' housing problems if they have one or more designated deficiencies regarding plumbing, heating, hallways, upkeep, electric service and kitchen equipment (Schwartz, 2021: 24).

[2] Cost-burden data by income group, as defined by the percentage of area median family income, were not yet available for 2021.

[3] Roughly one-third of this decrease in public housing stemmed from the transfer of properties from the public housing programme to another subsidy programme (project-based Section 8) under the Rental Assistance Demonstration programme. Households in these properties continued to pay the same rents as before, and the number of subsidised units remained unchanged (Schwartz, 2021: 157–159).

[4] Multifamily housing refers to structures with two or more housing units.

[5] In a report conducted for the National Council of State Housing Agencies, the consulting firm Stout estimated that between 9.7 million and 14.2 million renter households – *roughly one-quarter to one-third of all renters* – would be unable to pay their rent and be at risk of eviction when the Centers for Disease Control moratorium was set to expire at expire at the end of 2020 (Stout, 2020). The Centers for Disease Control subsequently extended the moratorium and Congress authorised emergency rental assistance to help renters avoid eviction when the moratorium does end.

References

Amherst Capital Management (2016) *U.S. Single-Family Rental: An Emerging Institutional Asset Class*, New York, Amherst Capital Management, https://www.amherstcapital.com/documents/20649/22737/US+SFR+Emerging+Asset+Class/9d84e0da-4a9f-4665-9880-88a4515d9d2b

Badger, E. and Bui, Q. (2021) 'Where have all the houses gone?', *New York Times*, 26 February, https://www.nytimes.com/2021/02/26/upshot/where-have-all-the-houses-gone.html

Bhattaria, A. (2022) 'Four reasons your rent is going up', *Washington Post*, 10 February, https://www.washingtonpost.com/business/2022/02/10/rent-rising-inflation-housing/

Bhutta, N., Bricker, J., Chang, A.C., Dettling, L.J., Goodman, S., and Hsu, J.W. et al (2020) 'Changes in U.S. family finances from 2016 to 2019: evidence from the Survey of Consumer Finances', *Federal Reserve Bulletin*, 106(5), 1–42, https://www.federalreserve.gov/publications/files/scf20.pdf

Board of Governors of the Federal Reserve System (2020) *Report on the Economic Well-Being of U.S. Households in 2019*, Washington, DC, Board of Governors of the Federal Reserve System.

Bratt, R. (2020) 'The U.S. approach to social housing', in K.B. Anacker, M.T. Nguyen and D.P. Varady (eds) *The Routledge Handbook of Housing Policy & Planning*, New York, Routledge, pp 173–188.

Centers for Disease Control (2022) 'Covid data tracker', 4 November, https://covid.cdc.gov/covid-data-tracker/#datatracker-home

Colburn, G., Walter, R.J. and Pfeiffer, D. (2021) 'Capitalizing on collapse: an analysis of institutional single-family rental investors', *Urban Affairs Review*, 57(6), 1590–1625.

Dill, J. (2012) Investor Participation in the Home-Buying Market, Atlanta, Federal Reserve Bank of Atlanta macroblog, 19 October, http://macroblog.typepad.com/macroblog/2012/10/investor-participation-home-buying-market.html

Downs, A. (1994) 'Reducing regulatory barriers to affordable housing erected by local governments', in G.T. Kingsley and M.A. Turner (eds) *Housing Markets and Residential Mobility*, Washington, DC, Urban Institute Press, pp 255–281.

Fields, D. and Vergerio, M. (2022) 'Corporate landlords and market power: what does the single family rental boom mean for our housing future?', https://escholarship.org/content/qt07d6445s/qt07d6445s.pdf

Finkel, M., Hanson, C., Hilton, R., Lam, K. and Vandawalker, M. (2006) *Multifamily Properties: Opting In, Opting Out and Remaining Affordable*, Washington, DC, Econometrica, Inc. and Abt Associates for the US Department of Housing and Urban Development, www.huduser.org/Publications/pdf/opting_in.pdf

Garboden, P.M.E. and Newman, S. (2012) 'Is preserving small, low-end rental housing feasible?', *Housing Policy Debate*, 22(4), 507–526.

Ghorbani, P. (2017) 'Homeownership after the Great Recession: essays on "owner-ready" families', doctoral dissertation, Public and Urban Policy, The New School.

Gittelsohn, J. and Perlberg, H. (2014) 'Blackstone's buying binge ends as prices surge: mortgages', *Bloomberg.com*, 14 March, http://www.bloomberg.com/news/2014-03-14/blackstone-s-home-buying-binge-ends-as-prices-surge-mortgages.html

Glaeser, E. and Gyourko, J. (2008) *Rethinking Federal Housing Policy: How to Make Housing Plentiful and Affordable*, Washington, DC, American Enterprise Institute.

Goldstein, M. (2020) 'How does the federal eviction moratorium work? It depends where you live', *New York Times*, 16 September, https://www.ny times.com/2020/09/16/business/eviction-moratorium-renters-landlords.html

Goodman, L. (2020) 'Black and Hispanic landlords are facing great financial struggles because of the COVID-19 pandemic. They also support their tenants at higher rates', *Urban Institute*, 4 September, Washington, DC, https://www.urban.org/urban-wire/black-and-hispanic-landlords-are-facing-great-financial-struggles-because-covid-19-pandemic-they-also-support-their-tenants-higher-rates

Guilford, G. and Cambon, S.C. (2020) 'Covid shrinks the labor market, pushing out women and baby boomers', *Wall Street Journal*, 3 December, https://www.wsj.com/articles/covid-shrinks-the-labor-market-pushing-out-women-and-baby-boomers-11607022074#comments_sector

Hoffman, L. and Heisler, B.S. (2021) *Airbnb, Short-Term Rentals, and the Future of Housing*, New York, Routledge.

Horn, K. and Merante, M. (2017) 'Is home sharing driving up rents? Evidence from Airbnb in Boston', *Journal of Housing Economics*, 38, 14–24.

Housing Finance Policy Center (2020) 'Housing finance at a glance: a monthly chartbook', *Urban Institute*, January, Washington, DC, https://www.urban.org/sites/default/files/publication/101611/january_chartbook_2020.pdf

Immergluck, D. (2015) *Preventing the Next Mortgage Crisis*, Lanham, Rowman & Littlefield.

Immergluck, D. and Law, J. (2014) 'Investing in crisis: the methods, strategies, and expectations as investors in single-family foreclosed homes in distressed neighborhoods', *Housing Policy Debate*, 24(3), 568–593.

Joint Center for Housing Studies (2006) *State of the Nation's Housing 2006*, https://www.jchs.harvard.edu/sites/default/files/media/imp/son2006.pdf

Joint Center for Housing Studies (2020) *State of the Nation's Housing 2020*, https://www.jchs.harvard.edu/sites/default/files/reports/files/Harvard_JCHS_The_State_of_the_Nations_Housing_2020_Report_Revised_120720.pdf

Joint Center for Housing Studies (2022) *America's Rental Housing 2022*, https://www.jchs.harvard.edu/sites/default/files/reports/files/Harvard_JCHS_Americas_Rental_Housing_2022.pdf

Lambie-Hanson, L., Li, W. and Slonkosky, M. (2018) 'Investing in Elm Street: what happens when firms buy up houses?', *Economic Insights*, Federal Reserve Bank of Philadelphia, pp 9–14, https://www.philadelphiafed.org/the-economy/investing-in-elm-street-whathappens-when-firms-buy-up-houses

Leonard, P. and Kennedy, M. (2001) *Dealing with Neighborhood Change: A Primer on Gentrification and Policy Choices*, Washington, DC, Brookings Institution Center on Metropolitan and Urban Policy, www.brookings.org/es/urban/gentrification/gentrification.pdf

Mallach, A. (2019) 'Rents will go only so far no matter how much we build', *Shelterforce*, 13 December, https://shelterforce.org/2019/12/13/rents-will-only-go-so-low-no-matter-how-much-we-build/

Mezza, A., Ringo, D. and Sommer, K. (2019) 'Can student loan debt explain low homeownership rates for young adults?', *Consumer and Community Context*, 1(1), 2–14, https://www.federalreserve.gov/publications/files/consumer-community-context-201901.pdf

National Association of Hispanic Real Estate Professionals and Terner Center for Housing Innovation (2020) 'How are smaller landlords weathering the COVID-19 pandemic?', https://ternercenter.berkeley.edu/wp-content/uploads/pdfs/NAHREP-Terner-Center-Survey-Factsheet-July-2020.pdf

National Multi Housing Council (2021) 'NMHC rent tracker', 1–6 February, https://www.nmhc.org/research-insight/nmhc-rent-payment-tracker/

Parrott, J. and Zandi, M. (2021) *Averting an Eviction Crisis*, New York, Moody's Analytics, https://www.moodysanalytics.com/-/media/article/2021/averting-an-eviction-crisis.pdf

Pendall, R. (2000) 'Local land use regulation and the chain of exclusion', *Journal of the American Planning Association*, 66(2), 125–142.

Petach, L. (2020) 'Income stagnation and housing affordability in the United States', *Review of Social Economy*, DOI: 10.1080/ 00346764.2020.1762914

Petach, L. (2022) 'Income stagnation and housing affordability in the United States', *Review of Social Economy*, 80(3), 359–386.

Prevost, L. (2021) 'A push for zoning reform in Connecticut', *New York Times*, 26 February, https://www.nytimes.com/2021/02/26/realestate/connecticut-zoning-reform.html

Ray, A., Kim, J., Nguyen, D. and Choi, J. (2015) 'Opting in, opting out a decade later', report prepared for the US Department of Housing and Urban Development, Office of Policy Development and Research by Economic Systems, Inc., 8 May, https://www.huduser.gov/portal/sites/default/files/pdf/508_MDRT_Opting%20In_Opting%20Out.pdf

Raymond, E. (2022) Testimony before the House Committee on Financial Services Oversight and Investigations Subcommittee, 28 June, https://www.congress.gov/117/meeting/house/114969/witnesses/HHRG-117-BA09-Wstate-RaymondE-20220628.pdf

Schwartz, A. (2021) *Housing Policy in the United States*, 4th edn, New York, Routledge.

Smialek, J. (2022) 'Inflation explained: the good, the bad, and the uncertain', *New York Times*, 13 September, https://www.nytimes.com/2022/09/13/business/cpi-inflation-explained.html

Stout (2020) 'Analysis of current and expected rental shortfall and potential evictions in the U.S.', report prepared for the National Council of State Housing Agencies, 25 September, https://www.ncsha.org/wp-content/uploads/Analysis-of-Current-and-Expected-Rental-Shortfall-and-Potential-Evictions-in-the-US_Stout_FINAL.pdf

Tilly, C. (2006) 'The economic environment of housing: income inequality and insecurity', in R.G. Bratt, M.E. Stone and C. Hartman (eds) *A Right to Housing: Foundation for a New Social Agenda*, Philadelphia, Temple University Press, pp 20–37.

Urban Institute (2020) *The Cost of Affordable Housing: Does It Pencil Out?*, https:// apps.urban.org/ features/cost-of-affordable-housing/

US Bureau of Labor Statistics (2021a) *Current Employment Statistics*, https://www.bls.gov/ces/a

US Bureau of Labor Statistics (2021b) *Labor Force Statistics From the Current Population Survey*, https://www.bls.gov/cps/

US Census Bureau (2021a) *Rental Housing Finance Survey*, https://www.census.gov/programs-surveys/rhfs.html

US Census Bureau (2021b) *Week 24 Household Pulse Survey: February 3 – February 15*, https://www.census.gov/programs-surveys/household-pulse-survey/data.html

US Census Bureau (2022a) *American Housing Survey*, https://www.census.gov/programs-surveys/ahs.html

US Census Bureau (2022b) *Housing Vacancies and Homeownership. Historical Tables. Table 7a. Annual Estimates of the Housing Inventory*, census.gov/housing/hvs/data/histtabs.html

US Census Bureau (2022c) *New Residential Construction: Historical Data, Housing Units Completed*, https://www.census.gov/construction/nrc/historical_data/index.html

US Department of Housing and Urban Development (HUD) (2021) *Worst Case Housing Needs*, report to Congress 2021, https://www.huduser.gov/portal/sites/default/files/pdf/Worst-Case-Housing-Needs-2021.pdf

Warnock, R. (2019) 'Rich and renting: understanding the surge of high-earning renters', *Apartment List*, 21 February, https://www.apartmentlist.com/research/rich-and-renting-understanding-the-surge-of-high-earning-renters

World Health Organization (2022) *WHO Coronavirus (COVID-19) Dashboard*, 4 November, https://covid19.who.int/

4

The Irish rental sector and the post-homeownership society: issues and challenges

Michael Byrne

Introduction

The Irish housing system has undergone tremendous change over recent decades. In addition to the turmoil of the property boom and bust associated with the global financial crisis (GFC), it has also witnessed a long-term decline of homeownership and social housing, a growing share of households in private rental accommodation, almost a decade of record rent inflation, and a chronic homelessness crisis. Indeed, for many years now housing has rarely been absent from the newspaper headlines and was among the most important issues for voters in the most recent general election. For most of the 20th century housing outcomes improved steadily. In the 21st century this trend appears to have been reversed.

These changes can be conceptualised in terms of the transition from a 'homeownership society' to a 'post-homeownership society' (see Ronald and Kadi, 2017). For most of the post-war era, Ireland was a quintessential homeownership society, reaching some of the highest rates of homeownership in Europe. Homeownership was engrained, not just in housing policy, but also politically and culturally. Homeownership supports throughout this period acted as a social leveller by facilitating access to affordable and secure housing for a wide spectrum of households, including the working class. Because of the central role of the state in housing, Norris (2016) has characterised Ireland during this period as a 'property-based welfare state'.

The transition to a post-homeownership society, characterised by the growth of the private rental sector (PRS), has, in contrast, transformed the housing system into a key driver of inequality for an increasing number of households. Homeownership continues to be the dominant tenure, and roughly half of all homeowners are mortgage-free. Most commentators would agree that homeownership is also the most culturally dominant tenure. According to survey data, for example, the overwhelming majority of PRS tenants continue to aspire to homeownership (Corrigan *et al*,

2019). The term 'post-homeownership', then, should not be taken to mean that homeownership no longer plays a central role within the housing system. Instead, it refers to the erosion of the structures which generated majority homeownership, and consequently the growing difficulty faced by households in accessing homeownership and the related prevalence of the PRS (Ronald and Kadi, 2017; see also Forrest and Hirayama, 2015).

Housing system change across decades is of course a complex process and cannot be reduced to a single causal factor. Nevertheless, by taking the GFC as an inflection point in the transition from a homeownership to a post-homeownership society, we can identify changing patterns of housing investment, demand and policy. Importantly, the transition towards a post-homeownership society has produced a formidable set of policy challenges, with successive governments seeking to respond to the ever-growing affordability challenges and stem the tide of homelessness. In recent years an unprecedented volume of new policy has been introduced, including rent regulation, enhanced security of tenure and strengthened enforcement. These policy reforms have, however, met with mixed success, and the challenges of affordability and security remain. An examination of the Irish case is instructive in understanding the structural changes associated with the transition to post-homeownership, the issues associated with this transition and the challenges in terms of how policy can respond.

As with many other social and economic issues, the COVID-19 pandemic has shone a spotlight on the PRS, revealing the vulnerability of private renters and the relationship between socioeconomic inequality and private renting. It has also resulted in another wave of policy reforms aimed specifically at mitigating the impact of the pandemic on the PRS and related public health concerns. This experience is also addressed in this chapter.

The chapter begins by examining the GFC as a key inflection point in this transition, focusing especially on the investment dynamics and the changing nature of housing demand and tracing the emergence of 'generation rent'. It looks at the underlying structural changes in the Irish housing system that ensure that a growing proportion of households cannot access homeownership and are channelled into the PRS. The chapter than examines policy responses and their effectiveness, exploring the challenges policy makers face in attempting to reform the PRS and create a long-term, secure and affordable tenure of choice. The final section examines the impact of COVID-19 and emergency measures introduced to protect tenants in the context of the pandemic and associated economic disruption.

The transition to a post-homeownership society

In 2019 institutional investment in the PRS represented 44 per cent of all real estate investment in Dublin (Hooke and McDonald, 2020). This is a remarkable figure, particularly given the fact that before 2014 institutional PRS investment had been non-existent in Ireland. What changed to turn the capital of a quintessential homeowner society into one of the hottest PRS markets in Europe? To understand this, we can take the GFC as an inflection point; a lens through which we can glimpse the transition between two housing regimes. The most intense period of housing financialisation (2000–2008) represents both the apex of the Irish homeownership society and its crisis.

However, the process of financialisation was itself built upon Ireland's history of homeownership. Widespread intervention in the housing system emerged in the early 20th century and, as in many jurisdictions, was particularly evident in the post-war period. In the Irish case, this involved a series of supports for homeownership and social housing. These are discussed in detail in Norris (2016) and include public construction of housing for both homeownership and social housing, local authority borrowing for large-scale social housing construction, local authority provided mortgages, and various grants and tax reliefs for mortgage holders.

To a significant extent social housing functioned as a route to homeownership rather than as an alternative to it. This was due to a long-standing tenant purchase programme which existed in various forms since the inception of the state but was fully developed in the Housing Act of 1966. Low- and middle-income households could thus avail of a variety of routes towards homeownership. By the 1990s, homeownership accounted for approximately 80 per cent of households. Despite the tenant purchase programmes, large-scale investment in social housing saw this tenure also grow, representing one in five households at its peak in the 1960s. The extent of homeownership supports was such that Norris (2016) has described owner occupation as a 'socialised tenure' and a part of Ireland's welfare state. Throughout this period, in common with many jurisdictions, the PRS dwindled.

Housing during the 20th century was linked to a number of important political issues. On the one hand, Ireland's highly redistributive approach to residential property reflected the nation's origins in the struggle for land (Norris, 2016).[1] On the other, that redistribution served to incorporate the working class into the Irish national project (McCabe, 2011). The political significance of access to housing, combined with its welfare function, ensured that housing operated as a 'great leveller' during this period.

In the last decade of the 20th century, Ireland's homeownership regime was undermined by the twin processes of neoliberalism and financialisation (Ó Broin, 2018). Most of the supports for homeownership were discontinued or reduced in scale in the 1980s and 1990s (Norris, 2016). Similarly, investment in social housing declined during the same period. Homeownership, however, did not decline during the 1990s as the deregulation of the financial system combined with Ireland's entry into economic and monetary union generated a wave of cheap credit which made continued access to homeownership possible for many households (Ó Riain, 2013). This in turn generated a well-documented mortgage lending and house price bubble which lasted until the GFC of 2008. However, what is sometimes missed is that at the peak of the property bubble homeownership began to *decline*. This contrasts with the comparable cases of Spain and the United States, where homeownership expanded up until the crash of 2008 (Byrne, 2020a).

Irish census data shows that homeownership began to decline in 2002, falling from 79.7 to 77.2 per cent of households between that year and 2006. Moreover, from 2006 to 2011 homeownership fell further, from 77.2 per cent to 70.8 per cent of households, and the PRS grew rapidly from 11 per cent to almost 19 per cent of households (Byrne, 2020a).[2] This shift can be explained by affordability issues as soaring prices excluded a growing number of would-be first-time buyers. The advent of 'buy-to-let' (BTL) mortgage products in the early 2000s also played a role. The BTL sector expanded from 18.8 per cent of the mortgage market in 2004 to 26.9 per cent in 2008 (Norris and Coates, 2014). Indeed, the proportion of outstanding mortgages held by homeowners fell by 6.7 per cent between 2004 and 2006, while the proportion held by landlords expanded by 6.3 per cent concurrently (Norris and Coates, 2014). What this suggests is that BTL investors piled into the housing bubble at its peak, driving house prices beyond the reach of first-time buyers (Byrne, 2020a).

In the years since 2008 there has been a significant reorganisation of the Irish housing system. The trend towards declining homeownership has become embedded, and the PRS now represents roughly one in five households, and one in four in Dublin. In the immediate years after the GFC, an ailing banking sector meant constrained credit for first-time buyers. Subsequently, the Irish Central Bank has introduced macroprudential lending rules that have meant that, even as the financial sector has returned to solvency, access to credit has continued to be a challenge for many low- and middle-income households. Central Bank lending rules cap loan-to-value ratios for first time buyers at 90 per cent and at 80 per cent for existing owners. A loan-to-income ratio of 3.5 applied to first time buyers for most of the last decade, although it has recently been increased to 4. Since 2014, house prices have rebounded,[3] and thus the tightened access to credit has combined with rising prices to exclude many households from access to homeownership.

The post-crash context also saw a marked decline in the availability of social housing. Successive 'austerity budgets' saw the capital spending budget for social housing, which funds most social housing, slashed by 90 per cent and the output of social housing also plummeted. Following the publication of the *Rebuilding Ireland* housing strategy in 2016 (Department of Housing, 2016), subsidised private rental accommodation has to a significant extent replaced social housing as the main plank of government social housing supports, reflecting a shift from supply-side to demand-side subsidies common across many jurisdictions (discussed later in this chapter). Taken together, these factors have driven the transition from a homeownership-based housing regime to a post-homeownership society. In the absence of either government supports or cheap credit, and given high house prices, a significant section of low- and middle-income households struggle to access homeownership. According to Eurostat data, by 2019 homeownership in Ireland had fallen to 66.7 per cent. Having once enjoyed one of the highest levels of homeownership in Europe, Ireland now ranks 21st in Europe.

The Irish private rental sector: issues and challenges

The resurgence of the PRS, since 2014, has been accompanied by a series of entrenched challenges. The issues include inadequate supply, high rents, insecurity of tenure and poor levels of compliance. Private renting has become a significant feature of inequality in Ireland today, with a growing divide between homeowners and private tenants in terms of access to, and experience of, housing. These issues are particularly important given renters are disproportionately made up of low-income households, younger and migrant households.

The already vulnerable nature of private tenants has been exacerbated by the record rent increases which have prevailed from 2014 until the onset of the COVID-19 pandemic (discussed later in this chapter). Between 2010 and 2020, average rents in Dublin increased by a startling 107 per cent (Lyons, 2020). At a national level, Ireland experienced the third largest increase of rents between 2010 and 2019 of any European country.[4] Figure 4.1 shows that annual rent increases have been higher than 5 per cent in Dublin since the fourth quarter of 2013, and close to or above 10 per cent per annum through much of the 2014–2016 period. Constrained supply is a major factor driving rent increases.

In common with many Anglophone countries, the Irish rental sector provides a relatively weak form of security of tenure. The Residential Tenancies Act (2004), the main legislative framework for the PRS, establishes six-year tenancies (known as Part IV tenancies). However, the protections afforded to tenants within the tenancy period are limited. Tenancies can be terminated within the first six months without any grounds at all. After this six-month 'probation', there are a number of grounds according to which the landlord may terminate the tenancy that are beyond the control of the tenant, including intention to sell or refurbish the property, or for family use of the property. These grounds are, moreover, based on landlords' expressed intentions, which in practice make them very difficult for tenants to challenge (Byrne and McArdle, 2022). Finally, there are high levels of non-compliance in the sector and the security of tenure protections that are in place are not

Figure 4.1: Rent inflation annual percentage change

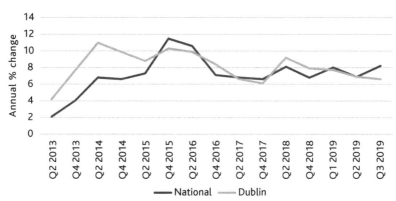

Source: Residential Tenancies Board (2019).

always respected. Consequently, research suggests that many tenants believe that landlords can terminate tenancies at will, a view shared by organisations which provide advice to tenants (see Byrne and McArdle, 2020).

Data on the number of tenancy terminations issued each year is limited. However, data from the Household Budget Survey, capturing duration of residence, suggests that there is a large 'churn' of private rental tenancies: more than 55 per cent of households within the PRS have been resident in their current home for less than three years. This contrasts with just under 15 per cent across all households. For households who own with a mortgage, the figure is just 5.5 per cent, while for local authority tenants it is 11.5 per cent (Byrne and McArdle, 2020). Corrigan *et al*'s (2019) survey of renters found that 48.4 per cent of renters surveyed reported that they were worried that they will not be able to live in their current home for as long as they wish. Another report found that one-third of tenants looking for a property to rent were doing so because they had been evicted from their previous rental home (Knight Frank, 2019). Perhaps most importantly, the majority (68 per cent) of households presenting as homeless identify private rental accommodation as their last stable accommodation and the most reported reasons for becoming homeless are linked to either 'rental properties being withdrawn from the market' (31 per cent) or 'PRS-related issues' (26 per cent) (Gambi *et al*, 2018). These data suggest that frequent moves are the norm, and that a substantial proportion of those moves are landlord-initiated.

Reforming the private rental sector: confronting the challenges of post-homeownership

Le Corbusier (2015: 338) once argued that urban planners confront the city as a 'wild beast'; a set of deep, structural trends driving urbanisation.

Not only do planners, for Le Corbusier, confront a set of forces which are immensely powerful, they do so without a clear vision of the type of city they seek to bring about. This formulation of the urban planner's dilemma perfectly captures the process of policy reform in the Irish PRS since 2015. The 'wild beast' here, however, is not the 'great city', but structural trends that drive the growth of the PRS, ensure inadequate supply and generate intense rent inflation. These structural forces are the neoliberalisation and financialisation of housing policy, discussed previously, as well as the longer run factors of urbanisation (for example, migration into the Dublin region and other cities, related in turn to labour market dynamics) and demographic change (for example, an ageing population and a growing number of one-person households).

Since 2015, policy makers have sought to respond to these challenges and especially their most egregious consequences: rent inflation and homelessness. But the ensuing policy reforms, while in many cases necessary and progressive, have been formulated in a reactive fashion. Policy makers not only confront deep-seated forces associated with the transition to a post-homeownership society, but they do so without a clear vision for the PRS. Consequently, it is fair to say there has been a lack of overall coherence to the changes experienced both in terms of policy objectives and at an ideological level. Despite this lack of coherence, this section attempts to analyse the most important trends that we can identify in this period and draw out lessons for the challenges of reforming housing policy in the transition to the post-homeownership society.

We can identify three major trends, some of which have already been alluded to. First, a 'build-to-rent' (BTR) and institutional landlord sector has been created and is now sufficiently established to be considered a major component of the PRS and urban housing in general. Second, in response to issues of affordability and homelessness, subsidised PRS housing has been integrated into Ireland's social housing system. Third, Ireland has experienced what we might call a 'partial convergence'. Policy makers have attempted to bring about a convergence of PRS policy in Ireland with Western European norms, primarily through greater protections for tenants. The aim, although as noted it falls far short of a fully-fledged vision, is to transform the PRS into a long-term, secure and affordable tenure of choice. This process, however, has been hampered by structural issues within the sector, specifically constrained supply, the informal nature of the sector, and the unequal and asymmetrical nature of the landlord–tenant relationship.

Build-to-rent and institutional investment in the private rental sector

As noted, Ireland has not historically had an institutional landlord sector. However, in the wake of the financial crisis, and as part of a wider effort to

Figure 4.2: Institutional investment, 2010–2018

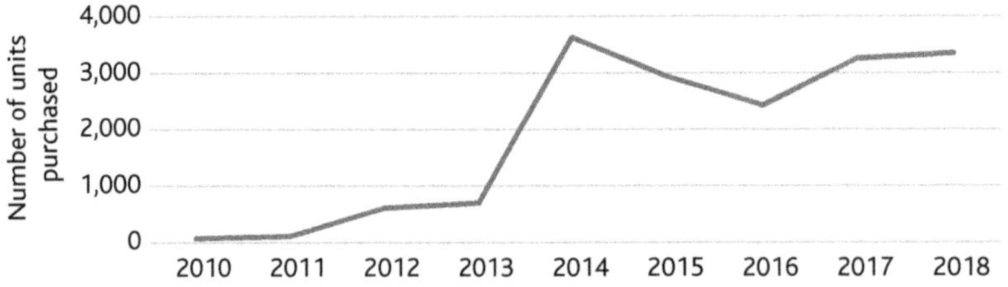

Note: The figures are based on two categories presented in the Property Price Register data: 'real estate' and 'financial'. These include all residential property purchased by real estate and financial companies in Ireland, and thus measure investment of institutional landlords.

Source: Property Price Register.

attract international capital into the Irish PRS (Byrne, 2016; Waldron, 2018), a concerted effort has been made to establish both a specific BTR segment and institutional investment more generally. This has been largely successful and was brought about by the sale of discounted assets to international investors, in particular private equity firms; the establishment of Real Estate Investment Trusts via legislation; and advantageous tax treatment. While small-scale landlords continue to dominate the PRS as whole, institutional landlords now play a major role in the supply of apartments in urban and some suburban areas (Lyons, 2020).

Figure 4.2 shows that institutional investment has dramatically increased from 76 units purchased in 2010 to 3,344 in 2018, representing a 4,300 per cent increase. In 2019, PRS investment accounted for 44 per cent of all transactions in Dublin, growing from just 6 per cent in 2016 (Figure 4.3). This sector of the residential property market is also playing a very significant role in new housing supply, with an estimated 30,000 rental units currently at various stages of development (Lyons, 2020).

There has been much debate on the significance of institutional landlords. The various positions in these debates can be summarised via a series of avian metaphors which, somewhat bizarrely, have become common within media discussions. For critics, institutional landlords are 'vulture funds' who feed off the wreckage of the GFC to accumulate property assets and exploit tenants. This view is aligned with some of the academic literature in the area of financialisation, which has positioned post-crisis institutional landlord investment at the centre of 'financialisation 2.0' (Beswick et al, 2016; Fields, 2018). These critics typically focus on the unaffordable nature of institutional landlord stock. In general, institutional landlords in Ireland have indeed targeted the higher rent segment of the market, often targeting middle- to high-income migrant employees in Dublin's tech sector, for example (Marler, 2019).

Another criticism refers to institutional landlords as 'cuckoo funds'. This term considers that institutional landlords, by purchasing new apartments

Figure 4.3: Private rental sector investment as a proportion of total real estate investment in Dublin

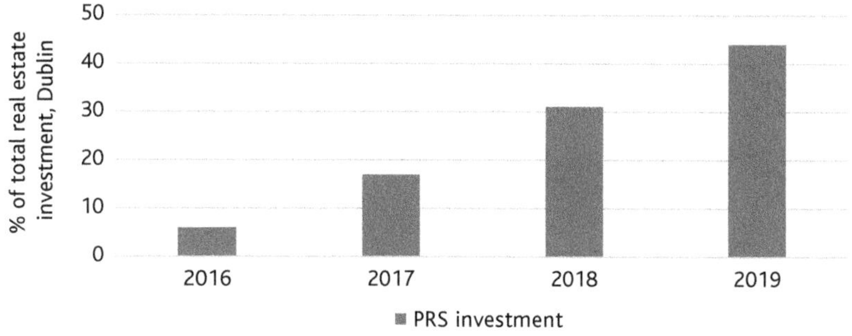

Source: Hooke and McDonald (2020).

en masse, are 'stealing' the possibility of purchasing from would-be first-time buyers (Hennessy, 2019). As purchasers of property, they are outcompeting households, thus fomenting the exclusion of a section of the population from homeownership. Finally, for those who defend the industry, institutional landlords are more reminiscent of 'swallows', whose arrival signals the end of the long winter of the Irish property market following the carnage of 2008–2014, and the revival of much-needed supply (Lyons, 2019). The argument here is that while institutional landlords may be targeting the higher end of the market, all supply is good supply and will filter through to the rest of the market providing much-needed housing and stabilising rents.

There is very limited evidence through which we might assess the merits of these arguments, but it seems likely that they all contain some truth. Certainly, providing new supply of the most in-demand form of PRS housing (one- and two-bedroom apartments located close to major centres of employment) is likely to lead to some improvement across the PRS.[5] On the other hand, well located urban land is of course a finite commodity, and thus the tendency is for institutional investors targeting high rents to reduce the amount of available land for other uses, including affordable housing. This is even more problematic because the rise in PRS investment has been accompanied by an increase in some similar asset classes, specifically student housing and a controversial form of 'co-living'. Institutional investment does pose a challenge, then, in terms of the provision of affordable housing in well located urban areas.

From a government point of view, as well as providing much-needed capital, institutional landlords have the further benefit of having a much greater capacity to cope with regulatory and policy change and are possibly more amenable to longer-term tenancies. The more 'professional' nature of BTR and institutional PRS is indeed something explicitly highlighted in the *Rebuilding Ireland* housing strategy of 2016. On the other hand, Ireland's

PRS has traditionally been dominated by small-scale landlords. Eighty-five per cent of Ireland's approximately 170,000 landlords own between one and two properties (Residential Tenancies Board, 2019). Although we do not have robust investment data, small-scale 'mom and pop' landlords, in contrast to the institutional segment, appear to be declining.

Subsidised private rental sector as a cornerstone of 'social housing'

Perhaps the most controversial development in recent years has been the decision to make subsidised private rental housing a key component of what is considered 'social housing', as articulated in the *Rebuilding Ireland* strategy. This reflects a longterm shift from supply-side to demand-side subsidies evident across many jurisdictions. It is not entirely novel in the Irish context either. Rent supplement, the original PRS rent subsidy, goes back to the 1970s. However, more recently rent subsidy has moved from a short-term support to a form of long-term, quasi-social housing. This has occurred through the establishment of the Housing Assistance Payment (HAP) in 2014. Like Rent Supplement claimants, HAP claimants rent private dwellings and most of their rent is subsidised, but unlike the former the latter continue to receive a subsidy towards rent costs if they enter employment (albeit at a reduced level). But in contrast to traditional social housing, HAP does not provide security of tenure or a guarantee of affordable rents. Therefore, it provides little of the insulation from the market enjoyed by mainstream social housing tenants (Hearne and Murphy, 2018). Notably, the Housing (Miscellaneous Provisions) Act, 2009 defined HAP as legally equivalent to mainstream social housing and recipients are removed from the waiting list for access to mainstream social housing on the grounds that their 'long-term' housing need has been met (Byrne and Norris, 2018).

HAP tenancies are included as part of targets for the provision of social housing, and successive ministers have described HAP tenancies as part of the social housing sector. One-third of all households in private rental accommodation receive a rent subsidy (Doolan *et al*, 2022). For the majority of these, the subsidy covers all or most of their rent. As such, government supports now represent an extremely significant subsidy for demand for private rental housing and is an important source of revenue for landlords.

The establishment of rent subsidy schemes as a cornerstone of social housing provision will impact the future development of the PRS. In addition to increasing demand, it ensures that PRS housing maintains its role as a major source of housing for low-income households. This has led to concern in many quarters, notably among housing charities who point out that HAP tenancies do not provide secure, long-term housing and thus there is a risk of households re-entering homelessness (Hearne and

Murphy, 2018). Many commentators also raise value-for-money concerns as the proportion of total housing spending dedicated to subsidising rents continually increases. Finally, there is evidence of discrimination against HAP and Rent Supplement on the part of landlords, which makes finding accommodation for recipients difficult (Threshold and Saint Vincent de Paul, 2019).

Partial convergence and modernisation

Many researchers have described Ireland's housing policy as neoliberal (McCabe, 2011; Downey, 2014; Ó Broin, 2018), and in many respects it is. However, the changing nature of PRS policy in response to the sector's growing importance cannot be captured by the concept of neoliberalism, at least not in any straightforward form. Although the growing importance of subsidised PRS suggests a turn towards state-supported market provision, most reforms introduced in recent years have strengthened tenants' rights and regulation of the sector, including the regulation of rent prices. The latter was virtually unthinkable as recently as ten years ago. I characterise the transformation of PRS policy in recent years in terms of a 'partial convergence' with Western European norms. The explicit aim has been to transform the PRS into a long-term, secure tenure of choice for Irish households. An array of policy reforms has been introduced to this end, but ultimately the project has been undermined by structural aspects of the PRS and the wider housing system.

The major policy reforms, excluding temporary interventions associated with the COVID-19 pandemic (discussed later in this chapter), are summarised in Table 4.1. They can be summarised as pertaining to three areas: security, rent regulation and enforcement. In relation to security, the period of Part IV tenancies was lengthened from four to six years under the Planning and Development (Housing) and Residential Tenancies Act 2016 (the 2016 Act) (Government of Ireland, 2016). The 2016 Act also established the so-called 'Tyrrelstown clause', which restricts the termination of tenancies where a landlord is seeking to sell ten or more units within a single development in a period of six months. This was introduced to mitigate the tendency of financial investors to purchase distressed rental property assets and undertake mass evictions to 'flip' the properties. More recent amendments also provide for longer notice periods for terminations. Taken together, these reforms represent a significant strengthening of security of tenure. They also reflect a clear change of the underlying understanding of the nature of rental housing among successive ministers and policy makers; it is no longer reduced to a transitory form of tenure dominated by students, migrants and others seeking short-term and flexible housing. However, the fundamental weaknesses of security have not been addressed (Byrne and

Table 4.1: Selected legislative changes, 2015–2019

Legislation	Contents
Residential Tenancies (Amendment) Act 2021	Extension of RPZ designations to 2024; introduction of 2 per cent maximum rent annual rent increases.
Residential Tenancies (Amendment) Act 2019	Extension of the RPZ designations to 2021 and removal of some exemptions.
	Creation of new offences: non-compliance with rent increase limit; knowingly/recklessly furnishing information to RTB which is false/misleading to claim exemption from rent increase; and non-compliance with requirement to notify RTB of exemption from rent increase limit.
	Extension of notice periods for tenancy terminations.
	Strengthening of enforcement via empowerment of RTB to investigate and section landlords.
Planning and Development (Housing) and Residential Tenancies Act 2016	RPZs introduce 4 per cent rent caps in designated areas that experienced annual rent increases of 7 per cent or more in four of the last six quarters.
	Restrictions on terminating tenancies where a landlord is seeking to sell ten or more units within a single development within a period of six months (known as the Tyrrelstown amendment).
	Tenancy period extended from four to six years.
Residential Tenancies (Amendment) Act 2015	Rent review permitted once every 24 months, rather than 12 months as it previously had been (currently applies outside RPZs).
	Notice of rent review period extended from 28 days to 90 days.
	Notice of termination of tenancy periods extended.

Source: This table is partially derived from Byrne and McArdle (2020).

McArdle, 2022). Landlords can still terminate tenancies within the tenancy period on several grounds, which creates uncertainty for tenants.

The regulation of rents represents an even more significant departure in PRS policy. Between 2004 and 2016, there was effectively no regulation of rents. The Residential Tenancies Act 2004 stipulated that rents could only be increased in line with 'market rents'. This of course gave tenants no protection against rising market rents and meant that tenants had no predictability about their rent. The 2016 Act introduced Rent Pressure Zones (RPZs) which are now the central plank of the government's strategy to contain rent inflation. RPZs came into effect in December 2016 and were adopted as an emergency measure with a duration of three years (later extended). An area can be designated as an RPZ if it has experienced annual rent increases of 7 per cent or more in four of the last six quarters. In the initial iteration of the RPZ measures, rent reviews could take place once in a 12-month period and were limited to a maximum increase of 4 per cent. Some exemptions from the 4 per cent cap applied, for example, where a landlord undertakes renovations or refurbishments that constitute 'substantial change' to the dwelling. Given that average rents have continued to grow rapidly, a further reform, introduced in summer 2021 as part of the new government's *Housing for All* strategy (Department of Housing, Planning and Local Government, 2021), capped annual rent increases based on the Harmonized Consumer Price Index or 2 per cent, whichever is the lower. This legislation, while continuing to present rent regulation as a 'temporary measure', once again extended RPZs, this time until 2024. Today, more than 75 per cent of tenancies fall within RPZ areas.

Analysis has shed light on the impact of the RPZ legislation by examining trends in rent price inflation (Ahrens *et al*, 2019). The research finds evidence that the RPZ measures reduced the level of rent inflation by approximately 2.6 percentage points. However, it also found that more than two-fifths of tenancies within the RPZs received rent increases of more than 4 per cent, suggesting significant non-compliance. Since 2020, rent increases have reduced much further.

There have also been significant changes in the area of, compliance and enforcement, and as such to the powers of the Residential Tenancies Board (RTB, the PRS regulator) and the scope of its remit. Under 2019 legislation, the RTB was empowered to cause, of its own volition or in response to a complaint, an investigation to occur in respect of possible improper conduct on the part of a landlord relating to 'certain matters'. Such matters include rent reviews and the provision of false and misleading grounds for the termination of a tenancy. This allows the RTB to proactively monitor and enforce important aspects of the PRS. The introduction of these new measures in part reflects a recognition, although not always explicit, that previous policy reforms have been undermined by significant non-compliance. At the time of writing, these measures have only recently been put into practice and as such future research will be required to understand their impact.

Considering all these policy developments together, we can see that the regulation of the Irish PRS has been substantially strengthened over recent years. However, these measures have been undermined by ongoing structural issues. First, the housing system is characterised by major supply constraints in urban areas. Annual housing output has not recovered since the crash of 2008. Most analysis suggests that Ireland requires in the region of 35,000 new units per year (Housing Agency, 2017; Lyons, 2017), but output in recent years has been woefully short of this. The structural imbalance between supply and demand has exerted significant pressure on rents since 2014. Second, the rental sector continues to be dominated by small-scale landlords, despite the recent growth of the institutional sector. The predominance of small-scale, non-professional landlords, creates several issues that have undermined the effectiveness of recent policy reforms. On the one hand, the non-professional nature of landlords can lead to high levels of non-compliance and informality. On the other, small-scale landlord investors have been buffeted by the volatile housing market of the last two decades, and therefore the churn in the sector appears to be high. For example, landlords terminating tenancies to sell property is one of the most frequently cited reasons for becoming homeless (Gambi *et al*, 2018). Third, qualitative research has identified that tenants feel disempowered within the sector, struggle to advocate for themselves, and experience breaches of their rights and of the legislation on the part of landlords (Threshold, 2019; Byrne and McArdle, 2020). The mixed success of recent reforms must be understood in the context of a systematic asymmetry between landlords and tenants which undermines tenants' agency and fosters a culture of non-compliance (Byrne and McArdle, 2020).

These three factors make for a chaotic and volatile PRS in which the key problems of high rents and weak security can appear intractable, and stubbornly resistant to policy reform. Despite its relatively ambitious nature, policy has failed to tackle the underlying issues and thus the attempt to transform the PRS into secure, long-term and affordable housing has been largely unsuccessful. Instead, on the eve of the COVID-19 pandemic, insecure and unaffordable housing in the PRS represented an increasingly central aspect of inequality in Ireland. For low-income households, the absence of security and predictability, frequent moves, high and volatile rents, and poor quality housing had all become commonplace. These inequalities were even more starkly revealed by the onset of the pandemic.

The COVID-19 pandemic and the Irish private rental sector

The COVID-19 pandemic emerged in the context of a housing system already struggling to come to terms with the transition to post-homeownership and widening inequality between private renters and homeowners. The literature to date on COVID-19 and housing internationally tends to agree that COVID-19 intensified existing issues and inequalities while at the same time generating new ones (Brown *et al*, 2020; Byrne, 2020b; Horne *et al*, 2020; Jones and Grigsby-Toussaint, 2021). This has certainly been the case in Ireland (Byrne and Sassi, 2022). The pandemic's impact on the PRS has manifested at the intersection of two sets of forces: the labour market and housing insecurity. As has been the case internationally, the impact on employment and incomes could hardly have been greater, but was to a large extent offset by an equally unprecedent roll out of government income supports and tenant protections.

Labour market issues are relevant here because private renters are disproportionately concentrated in sectors of employment which have experienced particular impact due to the pandemic and related public health measures. Even before the pandemic, the interaction between precarity in the labour market and in PRS housing had already been noted in Ireland (Pembroke, 2018) and internationally (Arundel and Lennartz, 2020). In the context of the pandemic, we can note that 15 per cent of workers living in the PRS are employed in the accommodation and food sectors. That is three times the figure for mortgaged households (O'Toole *et al*, 2020). Byrne *et al* (2020) estimate that 44 per cent of households working in the sectors of the economy most impacted were private tenants. O'Toole *et al* (2020: 11), in their examination of the impact of the pandemic on rent arrears, note that 'the relatively high proportions of workers in the most at-risk sectors indicate that households in the PRS are likely to be disproportionately affected by the shock to the labour market and the resulting impact on household incomes'.

As has been the case internationally, the concentration of renters in heavily hit sections of the economy, combined with the vulnerability of renters to rent arrears and eviction more generally, led to significant concern from the outset of the pandemic. In the Irish case a series of income supports and tenant protections were rolled out. A Pandemic Unemployment Payment, initially introduced as a flat-rate payment of €350 per week, was made available to workers who became unemployed as a result of the pandemic. A Temporary Wage Subsidy scheme was also set up to subsidise the salaries of employees in firms affected by the pandemic. By May 2020, approximately 46 per cent of the labour force were on some form of income-related support (O'Toole *et al*, 2020).

Protections for renters were also introduced. These were initially blanket protections but were later tailored to focus more specifically on certain categories of tenants. In March 2020, a rent freeze and a prohibition on evictions were introduced for an initial emergency period of three months, later extended until July 2020 (Ahern and Roy, 2020). These measures offered more or less complete protection for tenants, in particular from any form of eviction. Subsequently, in autumn 2020, as Ireland moved out of its first 'lockdown', the initial emergency measures were replaced by a more targeted, if significantly more complex, set of measures. Rather than general protection from rent increases and eviction, a scheme was introduced whereby tenants who declare themselves 'relevant persons' are protected from any rent increase or tenancy termination due to rent arrears. A 'relevant person' was defined as any tenant who was unable to pay rent and in receipt of a COVID-19 related state support, such as the income supports mentioned earlier. It was up to the tenant to make a declaration to the RTB and their landlord. However, the landlord can also declare themselves to be a relevant person, for example if non-payment of rent on the part of their tenant would lead to undue financial hardship, such as being unable to pay a mortgage attached to the rental property in question. Where a landlord declares themselves a 'relevant person', the protections did not apply to the tenant (Ahern and Roy, 2020).

Moreover, legislation was also enacted to tie a complete eviction ban and rent freeze to the introduction of Ireland's highest level of public health restrictions. Blanket tenant protections kicked in automatically once the government introduced a five-kilometre limit on household mobility, which happened at various points over the course of the pandemic.

The measures introduced became more complicated over time. The logic of this evolution can be understood as follows. In the initial emergency period (the first lockdown), the government introduced measures which were universal and simple to ensure that tenants under no circumstances would find themselves in a situation of needing to move out of their home, find another property or become homeless. This was considered a priority in terms of limiting the transmission of COVID-19. However, as Ireland moved out of the initial emergency period and through various degrees of public health restrictions, the government's view was that blanket measures were potentially unconstitutional, and that therefore more tailored measures were required.[6] Whether or not there is any issue of constitutionality has been disputed. In any event, it has meant that PRS reforms have become extremely complex (discussed further later in this chapter).

In terms of the impact of these measures, several observations can be made. First, the 'eviction ban' appears to have been relatively effective. Indeed, this period saw a decrease in homelessness for the first time in many years,[7] which most commentators, including in the homeless charity sector, attribute to the eviction ban. One 'ray of hope' that we might take from this period, then, is that by ending tenancy terminations in the PRS we can reduce homelessness. However, qualitative research suggests that despite additional protections, many tenants felt insecure in their homes, partially because they did not believe their landlords would comply with the eviction ban (Byrne and Sassi, 2022). Second, the initial emergency period also saw an increase in the number of properties available to rent, which some commentators argue arose from short-term lettings in the tourism sector being converted into the mainstream rental market. Within a few short weeks of the pandemic, the number of properties available to rent in urban areas in Ireland jumped by 30 per cent (Lyons, 2020). Half of the increase was in the most badly needed property type in the rental market: one- and two-bed houses in the central Dublin area (Hennessy, 2020).

Third, rent inflation moderated during the COVID-19 pandemic. The year 2020 saw some of the lowest levels of annual rent inflation since 2012 (Residential Tenancies Board, 2021). Indeed, prior to the pandemic, annualised rent increases above 4 per cent had occurred in every quarter since 2014. Nevertheless, the softening of rent inflation was hardly surprising given the catastrophic impact of COVID-19 on the economy and on tenants' incomes. There is so far no evidence as to the level of rent arrears arising out of the turmoil of this period. Modelling by the Economic and Social Research Institute in June 2020 suggested that there was not likely to be a significant increase in rent arrears. This is because the reduction of tenants' incomes was offset by a reduction in expenditure associated with the closure of childcare, the lack of transport expenditure and the general closure of the economy. Government income supports were also identified in this report as crucial.

One important observation is that take up of two important PRS measures was notably low. Ahern and Roy (2020: 17) note that 'by early October 2020, only 159 renters had applied for protection under the [relevant persons] scheme'. Similarly, O'Toole *et al* (2020) point out the number of Rent Supplement claimants increased by just 5,403 between February 2020 (that is, pre-pandemic) and May 2020. These figures suggest that measures which require tenants to advocate for themselves, by declaring themselves a relevant person or by securing the agreement of their landlord to accept rent supplement, may be ineffective. This analysis is supported by existing research in Ireland which shows that tenants are disempowered and their capacity to advocate for themselves is limited (Byrne and McArdle, 2020), a pattern which has also been identified internationally (Chisholm *et al*, 2020; see Brown *et al*, 2020 for a discussion of this in the context of COVID-19).

Conclusion

Since the GFC, the travails of the Irish housing system can best be understood as an attempt to come to terms with the transition to a post-homeownership society. This transition consists of the decline of the traditional model of widespread homeownership supported by reasonably wide access to social housing. In place of this model, we see much greater difficulties for younger households to access homeownership in urban areas, and a consequent growth of the PRS. Homeownership continues to be the dominant tenure, but the housing regime no longer functions in a way which facilitates access to the tenure. The effect of this transformation is much greater volatility within the housing system. From a government perspective, for example, this volatility manifests in consistently high levels of rent inflation and a marked growth in homelessness. From the perspective of renters, it manifests in the difficulty of finding suitable accommodation, high and unpredictable housing costs, an absence of security and the consequent inability to create a genuine home, and frequent involuntary moves. Underneath the volatility, so to speak, structural issues of affordability, insecurity and the disempowerment of tenants can be identified.

Since 2015, successive governments have sought to tackle the issues described in this chapter. Somewhat paradoxically, we have witnessed a series of policy reforms in the PRS which are both sweeping and ambitious and at the same time woefully inadequate. Measures to enhance security of tenure, regulate rents and strengthen enforcement have all been of limited effectiveness. This suggests that the challenges in the sector are deep-seated and require structural reform.

The COVID-19 pandemic unfolded, then, in a housing system already beset by difficulties. It has both intensified existing housing inequalities and generated new ones. What are the likely impacts of this on the Irish housing system and the PRS in particular? There are certainly reasons to be hopeful. The pandemic has exposed the vulnerabilities of the PRS, the absence of security and the precarious nature of tenancies. At the same time, the government response has demonstrated the possibility for robust, determined government action, for example in ending evictions. If it is possible to stop people becoming homeless in a pandemic, the public may well consider that it is possible under normal conditions. The importance and meaning of home as a place of security, certainty and safety have also been highlighted throughout the pandemic and this is likely to have an impact at a cultural level (Brown *et al*, 2020; Byrne, 2020b). Indeed, it may galvanise the growing campaign in Ireland for a referendum which would include a right to housing in the constitution.

This notwithstanding, there is no clear evidence that we will see deep structural reforms in the PRS or the housing system more generally. While we will likely see further reforms in the PRS, it is also likely that concerns with ensuring continuing investment in the sector will limit those reforms. Moreover, most commentators now agree that given the extreme supply shortages and affordability problems in urban areas, what is most needed is an alternative form of non-market housing for renters, which can deliver affordability and security. The debate in Ireland has focused on increased investment in social housing, as well as the development of a new 'Vienna style' cost rental model. Investment in social housing has indeed increased in recent years and a small amount of capital has been made available to launch a cost rental sector in Ireland. To meet the levels of housing demand, however, very substantial investment would likely be required as well as a long-term strategy. At present neither seem likely, and yet, in the wake of the pandemic, they will no doubt be needed more than ever.

Notes

[1] The 'land wars' of the 1870s galvanised the national independence of movements of the early 20th century.

[2] It is worth noting that during this period the proportion of younger households fell and for much of the period, specifically the 'crisis years' between 2010 and 2014, Ireland

experienced net *emigration* (McCartney, 2017). This supports the argument that housing and political economy factors have driven the housing system changes discussed here, as opposed to demographic factors.

[3] Looking at the evolution between 2010 and 2019, Ireland experienced the largest increase in house prices in Europe. See Eurostat data: https://ec.europa.eu/eurostat/cache/dig pub/housing/bloc-2a.html

[4] https://ec.europa.eu/eurostat/cache/digpub/housing/bloc-2a.html

[5] Some recent research in the US context, for example, supports this (Asquith *et al*, 2019; Li, 2019).

[6] See Ahern and Roy (2020) for a review of the issue of constitutionality

[7] See Focus Ireland homelessness date here: https://www.focusireland.ie/homeless-figu res-and-the-impact-of-covid-19/

References

Ahern, D. and Roy, S. (2020) *Law and Policy Responses to COVID-19 in Ireland: Supporting Individuals, Communities, Business and the Economy*, Dublin, COVID-19 Legal Observatory, Trinity College Dublin.

Ahrens, A., Martinez-Cillero, M. and O'Toole, C. (2019) *Trends in Rental Price Inflation and the Introduction of Rent Pressure Zones in Ireland*, Dublin, Economic and Social Research Institute.

Arundel, R. and Lennartz, C. (2020) 'Housing market dualization: linking insider–outsider divides in employment and housing outcomes', *Housing Studies*, 35(8), 1390–1414.

Asquith, B.J., Mast, E. and Reed, D. (2019) *Supply Shock Versus Demand Shock: The Local Effects of New Housing in Low-Income Areas*, https://resea rch.upjohn.org/cgi/viewcontent.cgi?article=1334&context=up_workin gpapers

Beswick, J., Alexandri, G., Byrne, M., Vives-Miró, S., Fields, D., Hodkinson, S. and Janoschka, M. (2016) 'Speculating on London's housing future: the rise of global corporate landlords in "post-crisis" urban landscapes', *City*, 20(2), 321–341.

Brown, P., Newton, D., Armitage, R. and Monchuck, L. (2020) *Lockdown, Rundown, Breakdown*, Sunderland, Northern Housing Consortium.

Byrne, M. (2016) '"Asset price urbanism" and financialization after the crisis: Ireland's National Asset Management Agency', *International Journal of Urban and Regional Research*, 40(1), 31–45.

Byrne, M. (2020a) 'Generation rent and the financialization of housing: a comparative exploration of the growth of the private rental sector in Ireland, the UK and Spain', *Housing Studies*, 35(4), 743–765.

Byrne, M. (2020b) 'Stay home: reflections on the meaning of home and the Covid-19 pandemic', *Irish Journal of Sociology*, 28(3), 351–355.

Byrne, M. and McArdle, R. (2020) *Security and Agency in the Irish Private Rental Sector*, Dublin, Threshold.

Byrne, M. and McArdle, R. (2022) 'Secure occupancy, power and the landlord-tenant relation: a qualitative exploration of the Irish private rental sector', *Housing Studies*, 37(1), 124–142.

Byrne, M. and Norris, M. (2018) 'Procyclical social housing and the crisis of Irish housing policy: marketization, social housing, and the property boom and bust', *Housing Policy Debate*, 28(1), 50–63.

Byrne, M. and Sassi, J. (2022) 'Making and unmaking home in the COVID-19 pandemic: a qualitative research study of the experience of private rental tenants in Ireland', *International Journal of Housing Policy*, 1–20.

Byrne, S., Coates, D., Enda, E., McIndoe-Calder, T. Corcoran, D., Cronin, H. and Brioscú, A. (2020) *The Initial Impacts of the COVID-19 Pandemic on Ireland's Labour Market*. Dublin: Economic and Social Research Institute.

Chisholm, E., Howden-Chapman, P. and Fougere, G. (2020) 'Tenants' responses to substandard housing: hidden and invisible power and the failure of rental housing regulation', *Housing, Theory and Society*, 37(2), 139–161.

Le Corbusier (2015) 'A contemporary city', in R. LeGates and F. Stout (eds) *The City Reader*, Routledge, pp 336–344.

Corrigan, E., Cotter, P. and Hussey, G. (2019) *The Housing Aspirations and Preferences of Renters*, Dublin, Department of Housing, Local Government and Heritage.

Department of Housing, Planning, and Local Government (2016) *Rebuilding Ireland*, Dublin, Department of Housing, Planning and Local Government.

Department of Housing, Planning and Local Government (2021) *Housing for All*, Dublin, Department of Housing, Planning and Local Government.

Doolan, M., Roantree, B. and Slaymaker, R. (2022) *Low Income Renters and Housing Supports*, Dublin, Economic and Social Research Institute.

Downey, D. (2014) 'The financialization of Irish homeownership and the impact of the global financial crisis', in A. MacLaran and S. Kelly (eds) *Neoliberal Urban Policy and the Transformation of the City: Reshaping Dublin*, Basingstoke, Palgrave Macmillan, pp 120–138.

Fields, D. (2018) 'Constructing a new asset class: property-led financial accumulation after the crisis', *Economic Geography*, 94(2), 118–140.

Forrest, R. and Hirayama, Y. (2015) 'The financialization of the social project: embedded liberalism, neoliberalism and homeownership', *Urban Studies*, 52(2), 233–244.

Knight Frank (2019) *Dublin PRS Tenant Survey*, Dublin, Knight Frank.

Gambi, L., Sheridan, S. and Hoey, D. (2018) *Insights into Family Homelessness No. 16: Causes of Family Homelessness in the Dublin Region during 2016 and 2017*, Dublin, Focus Ireland.

Government of Ireland (2016) Planning and Development (Housing) and Residential Tenancies Act, Dublin, Stationary Office.

Hearne, R. and Murphy, M. (2018) 'An absence of rights: homeless families and social housing marketization in Ireland', *Administration*, 66(2), 9–31.

Hennessy, M. (2019) 'What are cuckoo funds and why are people complaining about them?', *Journal.Ie*, https://www.thejournal.ie/cuckoo-funds-explainer-4640142-May2019/

Hennessy, M. (2020) 'Increase in available rental properties in Dublin "likely related to collapse of tourism"', *TheJournal.Ie*, 20 March, https://www.thejournal.ie/rental-properties-coronavirus-5052953-Mar2020/

Hooke and McDonald (2020) *The Dublin Private Rented Sector Investment Report Q4 2019*, Dublin, Hooke and McDonald.

Horne, R., Willand, N., Dorignon, L. and Middha, B. (2020) *The Lived Experience of COVID-19: Housing and Household Resilience*, AHURI Final Report 345, Melbourne, Australian Housing and Urban Research Institute.

Housing Agency (2017) *National Statement of Housing Supply and Demand 2016*, Dublin, Housing Agency.

Jones, A. and Grigsby-Toussaint, D.S. (2021) 'Housing stability and the residential context of the COVID-19 pandemic', *Cities & Health*, 5(1), 159–161.

Li, X. (2019) 'Do new housing units in your backyard raise your rents?', https://blocksandlots.com/wp-content/uploads/2020/02/Do-New-Housing-Units-in-Your-Backyard-Raise-Your-Rents-Xiaodi-Li.pdf

Lyons, R. (2017) 'Ireland in 2040: urbanization, demographics and housing', *Journal of the Statistical and Social Inquiry Society of Ireland*, 47, 122–128.

Lyons, R. (2019) *Daft Rent Report Q1 2019*, Dublin, Daft.

Lyons, R. (2020) *The Daft.ie Rental Price Report: An Analysis of Recent Trends in the Irish Rental Market 2020 Q1*, https://www.daft.ie/report/2020-Q1-rental-daftreport.pdf

Marler, T. (2019) 'Dublin Landings: BTR/multifamily in Dublin', Business Post National Property Summit, Business Post National Property Summit, 4 December 2019, Dublin.

McCabe, C. (2011) *Sins of the Father: Tracing the Decisions that Shaped the Irish Economy*, Dublin, History Press Ireland.

McCartney, J. (2017) *A Rent Forecast Model for the Rental Sector in Ireland*, Dublin, Savills Ireland.

Norris, M. (2016) *Property, Family and the Irish Welfare State*, Basingstoke, Palgrave Macmillan.

Norris, M. and Coates, D. (2014) 'How housing killed the Celtic tiger: anatomy and consequences of Ireland's housing boom and bust', *Journal of Housing and the Built Environment*, 29(2), 299–314.

Ó Broin, E. (2018) *Home: Why Public Housing is the Answer*, Dublin, Merrion Press.

Riain, S.Ó. (2014) *The Rise and Fall of Ireland's Celtic tiger: Liberalism, Boom and Bust*, Cambridge, Cambridge University Press.

O'Toole, C., Slaymaker, R., McQuinn, K., Coffey, C. and Corrigan, E. (2020) *Exploring the Short Run Implications of the COVID-19 Pandemic on Affordability in the Irish Private Rental Market*, Dublin, Economic and Social Research Institute.

Pembroke, S. (2018) *Precarious Work, Precarious Lives: How Can Policy Create More Security*, Dublin, TASC.

Residential Tenancies Board (2019) *Annual Report 2018*, Dublin, Residential Tenancies Board.

Residential Tenancies Board (2021) *Rent Index Q3 2020*, Dublin, Residential Tenancies Board.

Ronald, R. and Kadi, J. (2017) 'The revival of private landlords in Britain's post-homeownership society', *New Political Economy*, 23(6), 786–803.

Threshold (2019) *Topping Up: The Cost of HAP*, Dublin, Threshold.

Threshold and Saint Vincent de Paul (2019) *The Housing Assistance Payment: Making the Right Impact?*, Dublin, Threshold.

Waldron, R. (2018) 'Capitalizing on the state: the political economy of real estate investment trusts and the "resolution" of the crisis', *Geoforum*, 90, 206–218.

5

Private renting in England: growth, change and contestation

Tony Crook and Peter A. Kemp

Introduction

The private rental sector (PRS) in England has undergone profound change since the turn of the century.[1] Its market share has doubled from one in ten households to one in five, a level last seen in the early 1970s. This re-growth of the sector began around the turn of the century and accelerated after the global financial crisis (GFC). It has been at the expense of owner-occupation and social rented housing. As a result, the roles that the sector plays in the housing market have also changed in significant ways. The share of private tenants that are families has increased and that of single-person households has decreased. There are now relatively more middle-aged and fewer young adult private renters than there were before the turn of the century. Meanwhile, both the average length of occupancy in the *current home* and of residence in the *PRS* have increased. Despite this, the great majority of private tenants continue to have short-term leases and private renting in England remains characterised by insecurity of tenure.

The lack of significant change in the terms on which private tenants occupy their accommodation reflects both landlord resistance to longer tenancies and, until recently, the absence of political will to significantly update the laws governing residential leases. The result is that the sector is arguably still in a state of transition from its late 20th-century role as a largely transitional tenure for households who are en route to owner-occupation or social rented housing (Kemp, 2015). Nevertheless, the growth of private renting has given the sector a new political salience and the government has faced growing calls to improve security of tenure. Changes in residential tenancy legislation have been promised several times by Conservative governments since 2018 and seem likely to be introduced.

The nature of private landlordism has also evolved since the turn of the century, with continued decline in property companies and increasing market share by small-scale private individual owners (Crook and Kemp, 2014). In addition, the last decade has witnessed the emergence of a 'build-to-rent' (BTR) subsector, largely owned by large corporate landlords, which could in time partially reshape the profile of private landlordism in England. Meanwhile, since the GFC, private landlords have come under sustained attack in the mass media and from tenants' groups, who have questioned the motives, behaviour and even the existence of private landlords (see Roberts and Satsangi, 2021; Farnood and Jones, 2022). Capitalising on this rising tide of discontent, the 2010–2015 Conservative–Liberal Democrat coalition government introduced a series of tax increases on private landlords. As well as increasing tax revenue and seeking votes from private renters, these tax increases aimed to inhibit investment by buy-to-let (BTL) landlords and thereby reduce their ability to compete with first-time home buyers in the housing market.

The next section examines in more detail these trajectories of change in private renting since the turn of the century. Subsequent sections look at the demand side and the supply side of the private rental market, landlord taxation, rent regulation, housing allowances, trends in rents and rental affordability, and the incidence of rent arrears. The penultimate section explores the short-run impact of the COVID-19 pandemic on the PRS and the final section presents our conclusions.

Growth dynamics

The most obvious change in the private rental housing market since the turn of the century has been its remarkable growth, doubling in size from one in ten to one in five households – a level last seen in the early 1970s. This partial re-growth began around the turn of the century and accelerated in the wake of the GFC (Kemp, 2015). In the ten years from 1998 to 2008 the share of households renting privately grew by four percentage points and in the next seven years by six percentage points. In absolute terms, the number of households renting from private landlords increased from three million in 2008/9 to a peak of 4.7 million in 2016/17.[2] Since then, the number of private renting households has fallen to 4.4 million (Table 5.1). This in part appears to reflect the impact of the tax increases levied on private landlords.

The sharp re-growth of private renting up to 2016/17 was at the expense of owner-occupation and social housing. It reflects changes on both the demand and the supply side of the housing market (Kemp, 2015) many of which are in turn related to a complex array of domestic sociodemographic and employment trends, as well as macroeconomic and finance market developments internationally. In this section, we summarise the key causes of this resurgence of private renting in England.

A key reason why the sector has doubled in size is the inability of new households to afford to buy their home. House prices have doubled since the mid-1990s and at a much faster rate than incomes. As a result, the house price to income ratio has also increased and reached historically

Table 5.1: Trends in households renting privately

Year	000s	Percentage
1988	1,702	9
1998	2,063	10
2008	2,982	14
2008–2009	3,067	14
2009–2010	3,355	16
2010–2011	3,617	17
2011–2012	3,843	17
2012–2013	3,956	18
2013–2014	4,377	19
2014–2015	4,278	19
2015–2016	4,528	20
2016–2017	4,692	20
2017–2018	4,530	20
2018–2019	4,552	19
2019–2020	4,438	19

Note: Calendar year until 2008. The financial year (31 March to 1 April) from 2008–2009 onwards.
Source: Office of National Statistics: English Housing Survey Live Tables, www.ons.gov.uk.

high levels. There is considerable debate about the reasons for this increase in house prices. Some commentators attribute it to *supply*-side factors such as the very strict planning regulations in England; 'not in my back yard' opposition to building houses in their locality; and the resulting low price–elasticity of supply. Other commentators have focused on the *demand* side, citing factors such as the secular decline in interest rates, which (other things being equal) has allowed households to service a larger mortgage from their incomes; the rise in two-earner households; growth in wealth inequality, which has made it possible for better-off households to buy more expensive primary residences, purchase holiday homes and invest in rental housing; BTL investors outbidding first-time buyers; and the acquisition of housing in England by overseas investors, many of whom are believed to be cash buyers. There is not space here to resolve this highly contested and politicised debate, other than to note that the increase in real house prices is almost certainly the result of the interaction of *both* demand- and supply-side factors: increased demand in the context of chronic low elasticity of supply will inevitably cause house prices to rise.

The sharp increase in house price to income ratios means that it takes many more years for prospective first-time buyers to save for a deposit than it did before the mid-1990s when house price inflation began to take off. An additional factor since the GFC is that, like other central banks, the Bank of England introduced macroprudential tools to limit the procyclical nature of mortgage lending to households on the margins of owner-occupation. This includes restrictions on the amount of mortgage lending at very high loan-to-value ratios and requiring lenders to engage in greater scrutiny of prospective buyers' ability to afford the mortgage payments.

However, the reasons for the growth of private renting go well beyond the housing market. Public discourse about the causes of high house prices and the fall in owner-occupation has largely focused on housing-related factors and to a lesser extent wealth inequality. Meanwhile, academic research has also highlighted socioeconomic trends that have impacted upon the ability of prospective first-time buyers to realise their aspiration to become owner-occupiers. For example, Arundel and Doling (2017) argued that the growth of the gig economy, and in particular zero-hours contracts and other forms of insecure employment, has restrained young people's ability to save for a deposit and made them less credit-worthy mortgage borrowers. The growth in higher education has also dampened effective demand among young people in two ways. First, the need to repay student loans has negatively affected graduates' ability to save for a deposit (Andrew, 2010). Second, by extending the number of years before young people leave full-time education, it has delayed independent living and especially the age at which graduates buy a home. For this and other reasons, the age at which young people marry or cohabit, and at which women have their first child, has also risen; and both life events are associated with the decision to buy a home. Many of these private renters will eventually move into owner-occupation, but others are likely to remain in the sector for the long term (Clapham *et al*, 2012).

A second key reason why the PRS has grown is decline in the availability of social rented housing. Although the number of homes provided by not-for-profit housing associations has rapidly grown, this has been more than offset by the fall in the number provided by local authorities; contrasting trends that began well before the turn of the century and continued thereafter. Over the past two decades, the stock of council homes has halved, falling from 13.3 million in 2001 to only 6.6 million in 2020 (Stephens *et al*, 2022). This sharp decline is the outcome of three trends that began well before the turn of the century:

1. the relatively low levels of new construction by local authorities;
2. the transfer of council housing stocks to newly established housing associations by about half of all local authorities in England (Pawson and Mullins, 2010); and
3. the sale of council homes to sitting tenants at very large discounts under the Right to Buy policy introduced by the Conservative government in 1980 (Jones and Murie, 2006; Murie, 2022).

As a result, many low-income households now have little choice but to rent from private landlords.

The reciprocal of increased effective demand for private renting is increased supply of housing to let by private landlords. There has been an important, though partial, transformation in private landlordism since the turn of the century and especially since the GFC (Crook and Kemp, 2011). The number of households that own private rental housing has increased and they account for a larger share of landlords. This growth in private individual landlords was facilitated by the development of a distinct BTL mortgage market from the turn of the century (Ball, 2006). And while corporate landlords have become relatively less important overall, there is an emerging BTR subsector as well as growth in purpose-built student housing blocks. The latter provides strong competition for BTL landlords in the student housing market, though in many cases the high rents are only affordable for better-off students rather than those from lower-income backgrounds.

Private renters

Sociodemographics

Private renting in England has not only increased absolutely and relatively; it has also diversified with respect to the types of households living in the sector. Most strikingly, and despite the extensive media focus in England on young private renters – 'Generation Rent' – growth has been greatest among middle-aged households. The sector has become relatively less young and more middle-aged. As Table 5.2 shows, since the turn of the century, the proportion of privately renting households that are aged under 35 years has fallen by nine percentage points, while the proportion aged from 35 to 54 years has increased by 11 percentage points. The net outcome is that the combined proportion of renters that are either young or middle-aged is the about same as it was two decades ago, but the balance has shifted towards the latter.

The growth in middle-aged private renting since the turn of the century is reflected in the changing composition of the households living in the sector. The proportion of private renters that comprise single-person households has fallen by 12 percentage points. Meanwhile, the share of renters that are couples with children has increased by 11 percentage points, balancing out the decline in single-person households. The proportions accounted for by other household types have remained broadly the same over the last two decades. Taking couples and lone parents together, however, the share of privately renting households with children has risen from one in five to one in three since the turn of the century (Table 5.2). The number of children living in households renting from private landlords has trebled, rising from half a million to one and a half million (Kemp, 2015). This remarkable increase

Table 5.2: Sociodemographic characteristics and ethnicity of privately renting households

Column percentages^	1999–2000	2009–2010	2019–2020
	%	%	%
Age*			
16–24	18	15	11
25–34	34	35	32
35–44	19	22	24
45–54	10	14	16
55–64	7	7	9
65+	13	8	8
Ethnicity*			
White	90	84	82
Black	3	4	4
Indian	1	4	3
Pakistani or Bangladeshi	1	2	3
Other	5	7	8
All ethnic minority	10	16	19
Household type*			
Single person	38	29	26
Couple	24	26	25
Couple with children	13	18	24
Lone parent with children	9	12	11
Multi-person household	16	15	15
Economic status*			
Full-time work	53	60	68
Part-time work	9	9	10
Unemployed	5	7	3
Full-time education	7	6	4
Retired	14	8	8
Other inactive**	12	11	8
Years at current address*			
< 1	40	33	22
1 to 2	26	34	16
3 to 4	11	14	18
5 to 9	7	9	17
10 +	15	10	12
Total	**100**	**100**	**100**

Notes: ^ Data rounded to nearest 1 per cent. * Head of household 1999/2000; household reference person 2009/2010 and 2019/2020. ** Includes people who are economically inactive due to disability, chronic sickness or elder care responsibilities.

Source: Office of National Statistics: English Housing Survey.

in families with children living within the PRS raises important questions about security of tenure and residential stability for tenants (discussed later in this chapter).

The economic status of privately rented households has likewise changed in important ways over the past two decades. Most notably, the proportion of households in full-time paid work has increased, rising from about half at the turn of the century to two-thirds by 2019/20 (Table 5.2). Given the growth in the gig economy, it is perhaps surprising that the proportion of private renters in part-time work has barely increased over the past two decades. It may reflect the fact that lone parents – who are the group most likely to be working part-time as their primary economic status – have not increased much as a share of private renters.

The PRS in England has also become more ethnically diverse since the turn of the century. Private rental housing has long been an important source of accommodation for Black and ethnic minority households (Rex and Moore, 1967) as well as for economic migrants; and over the past two decades it has become even more so. The share of households from minority ethnic groups has doubled, rising from one in ten at the turn of the century to about one in five today. This increase has been mainly among households with Indian, Pakistani and Bangladeshi ethnic backgrounds (Table 5.2).

Residential mobility and insecurity

The 1988 Housing Act freed new lettings from rent regulation and required them to be either fixed-term 'assured shorthold' tenancies or indefinite 'assured' tenancies. Since 1996, assured shorthold tenancies have been the default tenancy. In practice, the vast majority of post-1988 lettings have been assured shortholds; and most of them have had either six-month or one-year terms. In 2019/20, for example, 83 per cent of lettings were assured shortholds and 4 per cent were assured tenancies. The remainder were pre-1989 regulated tenancies (0.7 per cent), lettings by resident landlords (0.9 per cent) and a miscellany of other types of lettings including those tied to a job or business and lettings by universities and other education providers.

The post-1988 letting regime was predicated upon the implicit assumption that most new private tenants would be young, short-term residents who were renting before going on to buy their home or, failing that, eventually moving into social housing. At that time, it largely reflected the lived reality for most new entrants to the sector. Six-month and one-year tenancies remain the strong preference for most landlords because they ensure the liquidity of their investment and reduce the business risk of being stuck with tenants who do not pay the rent (Crook et al, 2012). The relatively high volatility of house prices in England is an important investment reason why BTL landlords much prefer short-term leases to longer ones (Kemp and

Kofner, 2010). In contrast, because their rental model is long-term, BTR corporate landlords let properties on longer leases for those who want them.

The re-growth of private renting, and especially the rise in middle-aged and family renting, has generated a new debate about security of tenure for tenants. The private rental market is no longer so dominated by short-term renting it was at the end of the previous century. As Table 5.2 shows, turnover has significantly reduced over the last two decades. In 1999/2000, two-thirds of private tenants had lived in their current address for two years or less, but by 2019/20 only two-fifths had done so. Meanwhile, the share of households who had lived at their current address for between three and nine years has doubled since the turn of the century. About half of all initial tenancy agreements in the private rental market are 12 months and three out of ten are just six months. And yet the average length of residence at the current address was 4.3 years in 2019/20 – an increase from 3.7 years in 2010/11 – and the average number of years living in the PRS was 8.1 years. A succession of short-term tenancies may well suit young people but is less suitable for families and other households renting for the medium or long-term and for whom security of tenure is especially important. Moreover, the average age of private tenants in 2019/20 was 40 years, an age that seems difficult to label as a 'young person'.

Thus, there is increasingly a sharp contrast between the very short-term initial tenancies and the longer time that private tenants are living in their current home; and even more the length of time for which they are resident in the PRS. Hence tenants are typically required to sign a succession of tenancy renewals in order to continue living in their current home. This regime benefits landlords and their letting agents, but not necessarily the tenants. It may not be a problem for tenants who want to stay in their home for a one year or six months because they can leave at the end of their tenancy without having to give any notice. In fact, the 2019/20 English Housing Survey showed that, among those who had moved in the past year, in three-quarters of cases the previous tenancy had ended because the tenant wanted to leave (Table 5.3). Eight per cent were asked to leave by the landlord and the remainder ended for a variety of other reasons including the fact that the tenancy was for a fixed period (9 per cent). Therefore, most moves within the PRS are voluntary.

In contrast, for tenants who wish to continue living in their present home, the letting regime in place works much less well. Under section 21 of the Housing Act, landlords can require tenants to leave even if they are up to date with their rent payments and have fully adhered to the terms of the tenancy agreement. These 'no fault evictions' are especially a problem for families with children who want to remain in their current home but are forced to leave. They have also become a problem for local authorities who have a statutory duty to rehouse 'unintentionally homeless' applicants who have dependent children or who are deemed to be 'vulnerable'. Indeed, the

Table 5.3: Mean proportion of income spent on rent*

Households paying rent	Private renters	Social renters
Age	%	%
16–24	43	32
25–34	28	25
35–44	30	24
45–64	31	26
65–74	39	27
75 +	48	31
Economic status		
Full-time work	25	19
Part-time work	40	27
Retired	44	29
Unemployed	54	40
Full-time education	65	44
Other inactive	42	30
Household income quintile		
1 (lowest)	56	36
2	35	22
3	26	16
4	22	12
5 (highest)	18	9
All households	32	27

Note: * Figures exclude services but include housing benefit.

Source: Office of National Statistics: English Housing Survey 2019–2020.

single most important reason for the sharp growth in homelessness since 2010 is no fault evictions.

Not surprisingly, there is growing political pressure on the government in England to reform this system to allow tenants who want to stay in their current home to do so without the uncertainty of knowing whether the landlord will renew the tenancy when it comes to an end. This 'new crisis of insecurity' is one of the reasons for the growth in animosity to private landlords. In 2018, the Conservative government consulted on proposals to introduce a system of three-year tenancies but did not introduce them. Their 2019 election manifesto promised to abolish 'no fault' evictions and in 2022 they published proposals to reform private renting (DLUHC, 2022a). The aim was to provide tenants with greater security, improve property conditions and allow landlords to regain possession on reasonable grounds more quickly. Most notably, 'no fault evictions' were to be abolished; and all existing and new tenants would move to periodic tenancies with annual rent reviews. These changes would represent a significant recalibration in tenancy law and create a more level playing field between landlords and tenants.

Rental affordability

As in many other advanced economies, there has been much public debate in England about rental affordability having become much worse than in the recent past. This in turn has prompted calls for the reintroduction of rent regulation in the private rental housing market. An important feature of this debate is that it is driven more by media stories and personal anecdotes than by robust data. In this section, we draw on the most recent English Housing Survey (2019/20) to examine affordability in the private rental market.

Table 5.3 shows the mean proportion of income that private tenants – and for comparison, social tenants – spent on rent in 2019/20. Unlike Australia and the United States, in England the government has not adopted a measure of rental affordability for policy purposes. However, the Office of National Statistics has used 30 per cent of income as a housing affordability benchmark. If one assumes that 30 per cent of gross income is the level beyond which expenditure on rent becomes unaffordable, then one could argue that, with a mean of 32 per cent of income spent on rent, tenants in England are on average living at the margins of rental affordability (the median was 26 per cent). When asked whether they were finding it easy or difficult to afford their rent, three-quarters of private tenants said it was easy and the other quarter that it was difficult (75 per cent versus 25 per cent).

However, there is considerable variation among private tenants in the share of their income that they spend on rent (see Table 5.3). In fact, there is a bi-modal distribution of rent burden among the different age groups of private renters: young people under 25 years and tenants aged 65 or older pay much more of their income in rent than do the age groups in between. Variation in average rent burden was even greater by socioeconomic group than by age. Among tenants in full-time paid work, the mean expenditure on rent in 2019/20 was 25 per cent of income (the median was 22 per cent) which is below the 30 per cent affordability threshold. But for other socioeconomic groups, the rent burden was much higher, and especially so for private tenants who were unemployed (54 per cent) and students in full-time education (65 per cent).

Not surprisingly, the share of income spent on rent falls as income rises. Taking the bottom two income quintiles together, about seven out of ten private tenants were paying more than 30 per cent of their income in rent in 2019/20. In the lowest income quintile, over half were spending their income on rent in 2019/20 (Table 5.3). These figures include housing benefit (HB) and suggests there is an underlying problem of benefit inadequacy. The generosity of HB for private tenants was cut back by the 2010 Conservative–Liberal Democrat coalition government (IFS, 2014). This significantly reduced the amount of benefit received and the number of tenants receiving HB. Meanwhile, working tax credits and out-of-work benefits – now merged along with HB into a single benefit called Universal Credit – were also cut back several times. Research on the impact of HB cuts found that over half of all private tenant recipients were running out of money most weeks (Kemp *et al*, 2014). The English Housing Survey shows one in seven (14 per cent) private tenants on HB were behind with their rent in 2019/20. The figure for non-recipients was 6 per cent. In addition to HB recipients, the other groups most likely to be behind with the rent were students and the unemployed (Table 5.4).

Expenditure on rent varies between and within regions. The rental affordability problem is more widespread in London than elsewhere in England. In London the mean spending by private tenants in 2019/20 was 42 per cent of income. This was much higher than in all other regions of England, which varied from 24 per cent in Yorkshire and Humberside to 34 per cent in the North-East. However, among *lower-income* private tenants, rental affordability is a widespread problem in England, but especially in London and the South of England. Taking the bottom two income deciles together, nine out of ten private tenants in London (93 per cent) and the South-East (91 per cent) were paying over 30 per cent of their income on rent in 2019/20. And three-quarters were doing so in the East of England (75 per cent) and in the South-West (76 per cent).

Thus, while there appears not to have been a universal private rental affordability crisis in 2019/20, there was one among low-income tenants, especially young adults, the elderly, unemployed people and HB recipients. This crisis was especially severe for low-income tenants in London and the South, where it also affected young professionals. Since then, the growing demand/supply mismatch in the new lettings market has increased rents in many localities and made rental affordability worse than in 2019/20. Moreover, the sharp post-pandemic increase in inflation, and the economic consequences of the Russian invasion of Ukraine, have created a nationwide cost-of-living crisis that will widen and deepen the rental affordability problems.

Landlords

Changing ownership

The ownership of private rental housing continues to be dominated by individuals and, therefore, it is still the 'cottage industry' that it was before the turn of the century. Recent estimates vary in the number of landlords in

Table 5.4: Rent arrears in the last 12 months

Row percentages	Behind	Up to date
Economic status		
Full-time work	6	94
Part-time work	12	88
Retired	7	93
Unemployed	23	77
Full-time education	15	86
other inactive	11	89
Household income quintile		
1 (lowest)	14	87
2	10	90
3	7	93
4	4	97
5 (highest)	4	96
Receiving housing benefit		
Yes	14	86
No	6	94
Age		
16–24	12	88
25–34	7	93
35–44	7	94
45–64	8	92
65–74	6	94
75 or over	~	93
Ethnic group		
Ethnic minority	10	90
White	7	93
Total	8	92

Note: ~ Insufficient data.

Source: Office of National Statistics: English Housing Survey 2019–2020.

England. Tax receipts in 2020 suggests 2.1 million. Other survey evidence suggests 2.5 million landlords (Rugg and Rhodes, 2018) or about 5 per cent of the adult population, with another 1.9 million having been landlords in the past. Nonetheless, the ownership of private rental housing began to change after the turn of the century and especially following the GFC. The proportion of dwellings owned by individuals rose from six in ten in the

Table 5.5: Proportion of private rental dwellings in England by landlord type

Landlord type	1993	2001	2003	2006	2010	2018	2021
Individuals	61	65	67	74	71	83	84
Companies	20	18	17	16	15	13	13
Other	19	17	16	10	14	4	3

Note: In Tables 5.5 and 5.6, data for the years 1993 to 2010 are based on representative samples of all dwellings in the PRS; those for 2018 and 2021 are based on a survey of landlords who (as required by law) had placed tenant deposits in a government approved scheme, weighted by the numbers of tenancies each landlord owned.
Sources: Crook and Kemp (2011; 2014); MHCLG (2019) and DLUHC (2022b).

1990s (just after deregulation) to eight in ten by 2022 (Table 5.5). Meanwhile, the proportion of dwellings owned by companies continued to fall, from 20 per cent in 2010 to 13 per cent in 2021 (Crook and Kemp, 2011, 2014; MHCLG, 2019; DLUHC, 2022b).

Several factors made rental housing more attractive to investors than it was before the turn of the century: rapid growth of house prices provided substantial capital gains, less attractive alternative investments, historically low interest rates and the availability of specialist BTL mortgages. Although macroprudential regulations introduced after the GFC placed restrictions on BTL landlord loan-to-value and interest-cover ratios, this was offset by the decline in interest rates to historically low levels and appeared not to have diminished the attractiveness of BTL investing. However, tax increases on residential landlords (discussed later in this chapter) introduced from 2016/17 do seem to have negatively affected investment in BTL property.

Landlord portfolio sizes have changed since the early 1990s in England (Crook and Kemp, 2011; 2014). The percentage of dwellings owned by landlords with less than five dwellings rose from 43 per cent to 61 per cent between 1993 and 2010 but then fell by 2021, suggesting a small growth in average portfolio size. In 2010, landlords owning just one property constituted 80 per cent of all landlords and owned 40 per cent of the total private rental stock, but by 2021 these respective proportions had fallen to 43 per cent and 20 per cent, again suggesting recent growth in average portfolio size (Table 5.6). There are few large private landlords, with some long established (for example, Grainger) and others more recently established (for example, Sigma Capital) but nothing like the scale of large landlords in North America or parts of mainland Europe.

The main source for the growth in the number of private rental homes in England continued to be transfers from the owner-occupied stock. However, some of the latter were originally local authority homes bought at substantial discounts from the market value by council tenants under the Right to Buy introduced in 1980 (Jones and Murie, 2006; Sprigings and

Table 5.6: Proportion of private rental dwellings in England by size of landlord portfolios

Dwellings	1993	2001	2003	2006	2010	2018	2021
1	26	30	33	35	40	21	20
2–4	17	23	22	23	21	31	32
5–9	12	13	11	14	8	18	18
10–99	26	21	23	21	19	27	27
100 or more	19	13	12	7	11	3	3

Sources: Crook and Kemp (2011; 2014); Office of National Statistics; MHCLG (2019) and DLUHC (2022b).

Smith, 2012). Murie (2022) estimated that 40 per cent of ex-Right to Buy homes in the UK have been sold to private landlords. Some new private rental homes have resulted from the conversion of former offices and shops into residential accommodation; a change of use that is no longer subject to planning control (Clifford *et al*, 2018). Only 10 per cent of properties in 2010 had been specifically constructed for private renting or were acquired newly built. Data from the 2021 survey of private landlords in England indicates that only 2 per cent of properties had been constructed for letting privately (DLUHC, 2022b). One in five private rental homes in 2020/ 21 had been built since 1990, although not necessarily originally for the sector (DLUHC, 2021). New supply has also come from the construction of apartment blocks in city centre regeneration projects with landlords purchasing flats 'off plan' and in niche markets, especially student housing. Unite and UPP Ltd – two of the largest providers of purpose-built student housing – have raised significant funds and achieved competitive returns (Knight Frank, 2017). Overseas companies have also invested in purpose-built student accommodation blocks and apartments in England. This includes private equity firms such as Blackstone and US real estate company Greystar.

Investment and management

An increased proportion of dwellings are now owned for investment purposes and landlords are now more dependent on rental lettings for their income. In 2010, two-thirds of rental properties had landlords who owned them for investment purposes (DCLG, 2011), rising to three-quarters by 2021; with an increase seeking rental income compared with capital growth (DLUHC, 2022b). While only 8 per cent of landlords in 2016 obtained half or more of their income from letting (Scanlon and Whitehead, 2016) over a quarter of the stock in 2018 was owned by landlords in that position (MHCLG, 2019).

Over half of the 2018 private rental stock was owned by landlords with a long-term view of their ownership, with three-quarters intending to re-let

Table 5.7: Whether landlords use a letting or managing agent by proportion of tenancies

Use agent?	%
Letting agent	34
Managing agent	5
Both letting and management services	9
Does not use an agent	52
Total	100

Source: Office of National Statistics: Survey of Private Landlords in England 2018.

vacancies and many willing to consider long-term tenancies provided they were able to regain possession more easily when tenants breached their lease (for arrears, anti-social behaviour, and so on). This evidence portrays a more mature and stable sector than in previous decades (Scanlon and Whitehead, 2016; Scanlon *et al*, 2021).

Although specialist student housing providers and new residential property companies have professional housing management, this is less true of many private individual landlords. Two in five used managing agents in 2010 but nearly half did so in 2021 (Table 5.7). Although there is a growing use of managing agents, they are not regulated, and many are not members of trade or professional bodies with codes of conduct. In 2010, two-thirds of private individual landlords had no relevant professional experience or qualifications, but this had risen to three-quarters by 2018. Landlord awareness of rental legislation and regulations had also increased compared with previous landlord surveys.

Because of the personal nature of management, individual landlords tend to manage market and business risks by investing in familiar places, usually close to where they live and work (Crook *et al*, 2012). Landlords manage their lettings in a very fragmented regulatory environment, with 36 pieces of legislation split between several government departments. Local authorities have enforcement powers, but these are mainly discretionary; and public spending cuts since 2010 have reduced their ability to take enforcement action. The system relies heavily on tenants enforcing their own rights, but there are limited redress arrangements, and the law requires neither licensing of most landlords nor proactive inspections of dwellings. Not surprisingly, an estimated 30 per cent of landlords fail to employ good practice (NAO, 2021).

Residential has outperformed commercial property (offices, shops, and so on) and other UK asset classes – such as equities and bonds – over the long term. In the long run, market rents tend to rise in line with average earnings and are much less prone than house prices to short-term fluctuations. Residential property also has lower volatility than, and low correlation with, other asset classes, thereby matching investor need for a mix of asset classes to diversify risk. Among BTL landlords, net income returns from rental housing have generally been between 3 per cent and 5 per cent (Scanlon and Whitehead, 2016) but total returns are much higher when capital gains are taken into account. Modelling of returns from geared BTL investment for all English regions found that they were significantly higher than from a FTSE 250 equity investment over the period from 1996 to 2018 (Jones and Mostafab, 2022). Studies of institutional investors confirm that residential property has outperformed commercial property and UK equities over the long term (German, 2016). For example, net yields for institutional investors in London and Manchester in 2019 were 4 per cent and 4.5 per cent while the yield on ten-year gilts was 0.7 per cent (Knight Frank, 2020).

Build-to-rent

These competitive net returns explain why there has been more interest in residential investment by institutional investors and other corporate landlords. This has been an ambition of governments of all political complexions since the deregulation of the sector in 1989. Their aims have been to attract large-scale, long-term investment in new high-quality dwellings, let to high professional standards on long-term tenancies, with an income-driven business approach creating emphasis on customer service and retaining tenants (DCLG, 2017). The hope was that letting portfolios would be large enough to achieve economies of scale and to manage market and business risks better than small-scale BTL landlords. BTR is also aimed at encouraging more tenure diversity on large developments and de-risking developments on large sites by completing the BTR element early in the build-out phase, thus reducing debt and equity funding (BPF, Savills and LSE, 2018).

Since rent deregulation in 1989, a range of government initiatives were introduced to stimulate investment by new corporate landlords in the PRS. They were not very successful initially because tax and legal impediments made it difficult to set up corporate landlords. In 2007, Real Estate Investment Trusts (REITs) were introduced to remove tax impediments to institutional investors in the private rental sector. However, it was existing commercial property companies that converted to REITs rather than new or existing residential property companies (Crook and Kemp, 2011; 2014). By 2015, institutional investors accounted for only 2 per cent of the value of the private rental market and yet their asset portfolios included substantial amounts of commercial rental property such as shops and offices.

There were until recently several reasons why institutions were reluctant to invest in rental housing (Crook and Kemp, 1999, 2011; BPF, Savills and LSE, 2018). First, portfolios of the size and quality, with good management and with proven returns, matching corporate owners' needs did not exist.

Second, net income returns on rental housing prior to the GFC were uncompetitive for financial institutions. Third, management costs were relatively high, and the professional PRS management platforms that existed were in their infancy. Fourth, the corporate residential market in England was neither mature nor liquid, yet these are important investment requirements for companies trading on stock markets. Fifth, the continued existence of poor stock conditions and bad management at the lower end of the rental market posed a reputation risk for institutional investors. And sixth, despite REITs providing full tax transparency, they still had some tax disadvantages.

Over the past decade, successive governments have taken further steps to tackle these barriers to institutional investment. In 2012, the government-commissioned Montague Review (DCLG, 2012) concluded that land, development and management costs had to be reduced because net income returns were too low. Town planning was critical because land valuations assumed completed dwellings were sold to owner-occupiers; and planning obligations requiring affordable housing meant that including private rental homes within a scheme made it unviable. The Montague Review argued that separating those who did initial development and letting from long-term ownership would remove development risk for long-term owners; and that local authorities and other housing providers could play a crucial role in facilitating and undertaking the development stage.

The 2010–2015 coalition government set up a £1 billion 'build to rent' fund for new private rental developments and a £3.5 billion guarantee fund (plus £3 billion in reserve) to underpin developments funded by fixed income debt. It also changed land-use planning policy to help foster PRS developments: it required planning to include BTR as an explicit form of housing to be identified in local plans, to ensure viability was addressed in planning negotiations, and to foster the building of 'affordable private renting' let on 'family friendly' three-year tenancies as an alternative to other forms of affordable housing.

Private rental housing is now more attractive to private funders and developments are also attracting forward funding of the initial development phase as well as long-term finance. New corporate landlords and their funders include property companies and developers, banks, building societies, pension and life assurance funds, investment fund managers, and housing associations. They also include sovereign wealth funds, venture capital as well as overseas investors. Many of the latter have long invested in residential property in other countries especially multi-family investors and developers in the United States and Canada.

The British Property Federation's 'build to rent map' showed that, by the third quarter of 2021, over 200,000 new BTR homes had been completed, were under construction or were being planned (BPF, 2021). Between 2012 and 2020, almost £22 billion had been invested in new BTR homes. Five per cent of all new homes built in the five years to March 2021 were specifically for private rental including 20 per cent of all new homes in London (House of Lords Built Environment Committee, 2022). The emergence of a BTR subsector is exemplified by the establishment of the first residential REIT when Sigma Capital, a property company building private rental family housing in the north of England, placed part of its portfolio in its new PRS REIT. The launch was oversubscribed (Sigma Capital Group, 2022). The surge in empty town centre shops has also provided BTR diversification opportunities for retailers. John Lewis, in partnership with financial institution Abrdn, plans to spend £500 million creating 10,000 new flats in its vacant shops (Lex, 2022).

Growth in the BTR subsector has also come from *not-for-profit* housing associations that have set up *for-profit* subsidiaries to develop new private rental housing. Most of this profit-oriented rental housing has not been targeted at the traditional housing association clientele of low-income and disadvantaged households, but rather at middle-income renters. However, an important rationale for this new investment in private rental homes has been to generate profits that can help subsidise their affordable rented homes, for which government grant funding for new construction has been substantially reduced. The evidence suggests that associations have constructed about a fifth of new BTR properties in England (Crook and Kemp, 2019).

Taxation

Private individual landlords are taxed at their marginal tax rates on their rental income net of running costs (management, maintenance, insurance, and so on). They cannot deduct any losses from their other taxable income ('negative gearing') although rental losses can be carried forward. Private housing landlords are not eligible for depreciation allowances, as the tax system assumes housing is a perpetual asset. Landlords are liable for nominal capital gains tax and pay stamp duty land tax on purchasing dwellings.

Companies are taxed on the net rental income from lettings at their relevant corporation tax rates, which mainly depends on company size. They pay stamp duty land tax when purchasing property and tax on capital gains at corporate tax rates. Property companies set up as REITs are taxed differently. REITs were introduced to avoid the problem of 'double taxation' with companies paying tax on profits and shareholders also paying tax on distributed profits.

In 2015, the Conservative government argued that competition from BTL landlords increased house prices and crowded out first-time home buyers and introduced three changes designed to make BTL investment less attractive. First, tax relief on private individual landlords' interest payments was restricted to the standard rate of tax (currently 20 per cent). Second, stamp duty land tax payable by private individual and corporate residential landlords was made subject to a 3 per cent surcharge. And, third, private individual and corporate residential landlords became subject to an 8 per cent capital gains tax surcharge. These three changes have resulted in the taxation of private individual landlords being even more disadvantaged than it already was compared with those in most other advanced economies (Scanlon *et al*, 2021).

Scanlon *et al* (2021) found that only 30 per cent of BTL landlords thought their plans would not be affected by these tax increases. Although some were putting plans on hold or stopping acquisitions, capital gains due to rising house prices and real rent increases could offset these tax changes. However, the 2021 survey of private landlords in England found that 29 per cent of properties had landlords who expected to reduce their portfolio, with many citing as reasons the tax changes and the government's proposed abolition of 'no fault evictions' (DLUHC, 2022b). In 2022, Rightmove and other major property portals reported that the supply of homes coming onto the lettings market had fallen substantially compared with the previous year; and that this had increased competition for properties and hence pushed up rents.

The COVID-19 pandemic

The onset of the COVID-19 pandemic exacerbated the challenges for tenants presented by insecure private rental tenancies. This was particularly the case for tenants with precarious jobs working in sectors – such as hospitality, public transport and retail – that were hard-hit by lockdowns (Resolution Foundation, 2020). In June/July 2020, 35 per cent of private tenants reported that their household monthly income had fallen by at least £100 due to COVID-19, a proportion that did not change subsequently (MHCLG, 2020; 2021a). Because people in health, delivery and other essential services continued to work during the lockdowns, they were more exposed than others to the virus. Hence, the safety of their living conditions was critical to their health and that of people living with them, especially in shared accommodation and residences with insufficient space to self-isolate if infected (Tunstall, 2021). The ability of adults, students and schoolchildren to work or study at home effectively was dependent on the size and amenities (including broadband connections) of their dwellings.

Government support

During the pandemic, the government provided unprecedented levels of financial support to the economy, including loans to businesses and funding to enable employers to furlough staff with the government paying up to 80 per cent of wages, subject to a cap. Workers with the virus that had to self-isolate received some limited income support. The government allowed property lettings and sales to continue, supported mortgage repayment holidays and created a temporary stamp duty holiday for house sales below £500,000 in price. It also extended some homeownership initiatives that were due to come to an end. Meanwhile, the Bank of England maintained its low interest rate and quantitative easing policies.

Temporary additional income support and increased rent allowances were introduced for tenants. Evictions were banned for a temporary period, except for the most serious cases. Landlords were allowed to continue health and safety inspections and urgent repairs; and were obliged to mitigate virus transmission in common areas and shared facilities (Jarman, 2020; MHCLG, 2021b). Many of these schemes were extended, often several times, because lockdowns were extended or reinstigated. Poverty lobbyists claimed not enough had been done, while landlords' associations claimed restrictions had damaged their businesses. Others were critical of the last-minute and often un-evidenced changes to government support (Jarman, 2020; JRF, 2020; HCLG, 2021).

Demand, rents and arrears

Rents fell in inner cities and rose in suburban and smaller towns and cities in the year to October 2020 (Hammond, 2021), reflecting rising demand for larger accommodation and gardens in response to the need for more working and safe space during lockdown. Significant outmigration of EU citizens during the pandemic (Gordon, 2021; Sumption, 2021) – especially those working in hospitality (O'Connor and Portes, 2021) and tourism – contributed to falling demand and rising supply in central locations.

In July 2020, a quarter of tenants reported that they were finding it more difficult to keep up with rent payments since COVID-19 restrictions had been put in place (MHCLG, 2020; 2021a). By the same date, the number of tenants in arrears had doubled (JRF, 2020; Pennington and Kleynhans, 2020; Resolution Foundation, 2021). Only 29 per cent of landlords in 2021 reported they had no rent arrears because of COVID-19. Seventy per cent of private tenants had no savings to fall back on and hence paid their rent and dealt with arrears by cutting back on other essentials and borrowing money to pay off arrears (DLUHC, 2022b). In response to lobbying by landlord associations and other critics, the government created a modest and temporary relief fund to help tenants pay off COVID-19 rent arrears.

Between July and September 2020, landlord possession claims, orders and warrants all fell by about 90 per cent compared to the same period in 2019 (Jarman, 2020). A parliamentary committee questioned why the government had stalled on its 2019 earlier commitment to improve tenants' security of tenure (HCLG, 2021). Landlord and tenant groups predicted that when the ban on evictions is lifted, there would be a wave of evictions among renters unable to pay rent during the pandemic, although others thought there would be a gradual rise and that some tenants would pursue other options including returning to the parental home (Whitehead and Holman, 2020). Landlord possession claims, orders and warrants have been rising since early 2021, but by the third quarter of 2022 remained below pre-COVID-19 levels.

Investment

Landlord associations estimated that around 23 per cent of landlords had lost rental income, 'with 9% of those landlords losing more than 20% of their rental income … and that almost a third of landlords planned to sell one or more properties over the next year' (HCLG, 2021: 30). And yet, landlord willingness to invest appeared not to have substantially fallen (Jarman, 2020). In November 2020, landlords made 15 per cent of agreed property purchases in Britain, more than at any time since December 2016 (Partridge, 2020). Investment in new-build private rental homes also continued unabated. Steps to support the housing market (for example, stamp duty holidays) helped landlords buy properties.

Preliminary assessment

A full assessment of the impact of COVID-19 is premature, but two points can be made at this point. First, the steps taken by the government to protect private tenants were necessary because of the deregulated nature of the tenure. They were 'emergency' measures, largely short-term and with frequent changes to the detail. Once some kind of 'new normal' is achieved, tenants in arrears will be at risk of homelessness. Second, the help given to homeowners via mortgage holidays, stamp duty holidays and the continuation of other support for home purchase, suggests that the government once again prioritised owner-occupation over private renting.

Conclusion

Since the turn of the century, the PRS in England has experienced considerable change. The number of privately renting households more than doubled and the proportions of them that were middle-aged or households with young children increased, while the share that was young adults decreased. The lengths of time that households were living in their current address and in the sector both increased. As a result, it is now less true than it was in the 1980s and 1990s (Boviard *et al*, 1985) that private rental housing is largely a sector providing transitional housing for young people prior to moving into homeownership after a few years or (if they are on low incomes) into social housing. It still performs that 'waiting room' role, of course, but it now houses a broader range of households and for longer than before.

The demand for private rental housing grew mainly because access to homeownership became more difficult, for reasons that we discussed in this chapter; and because the supply of local authority housing continued to shrink. Despite the substantial changes on the demand side, tenancy legislation has until very recently barely changed to reflect them. The great majority of private tenants have either one-year or six-month leases and very little security of tenure and pay market rents. Except for BTR firms, most landlords remain reluctant to offer longer-term tenancies. However, the growth of private renting – especially among middle-income households, who are more likely than young adults to vote – has given the sector a political salience and media attention that it has not had for decades (Kemp, 2015).

Low-income tenants face severe rental affordability problems, especially in London and the South where even young professionals now spend high shares of their income on rent. Rental affordability difficulties have been made worse by the post-pandemic surge in inflation and the economic consequences of the Russian invasion of Ukraine in February 2022. Faced with growing public concern about insecurity of tenure and rental affordability, in 2022 the Conservative government announced plans to tackle insecurity but not affordability, while the main opposition parties put forward plans to tackle both issues.

Meanwhile, the supply of private rental housing increased largely because the returns on alternative investments either fell or became more uncertain, giving individuals and corporate investors an incentive to enter the rental market or expand their portfolios. Although most of the additional private rental homes were formerly owner-occupied – including many ex-council dwellings sold under the Right to Buy – there has been growth in newly built homes, especially apartments, thereby helping to raise the quality of the rental stock. A BTR subsector has emerged over the last decade and is rapidly growing. And, as in some other advanced economies, the purpose-built private student housing subsector has also rapidly expanded.

These demand- and supply-side trajectories are the outcome of an array of economic, financial and sociodemographic trends, which we discussed in this chapter. Insofar as the growth of private renting is a consequence of official policy it is intervention in finance markets (such as quantitative easing) and in landlord taxation that have been pivotal rather than housing policy *per se*. Although some of the trajectories that we have discussed emerged from around the turn of the century, they either began or were given greater impetus by the GFC and the slow and relatively weak recovery from it in England. The COVID-19 pandemic profoundly impacted upon the rental market in the short term – and the repercussions of pandemic-related rent arrears will take a while to unfold – but appears unlikely to substantially alter the trajectories of change that we have discussed in this chapter.

Notes

[1] The chapter is about England rather than Britain (England, Wales and Scotland) or the UK (Britain and Northern Ireland) because housing policy is increasingly divergent between the constituent parts of the UK. Because of this diversity and chapter word-length constraints, it is difficult to do justice to Wales, Scotland and Northern Ireland while adequately covering the topics included in the book. In some cases, the chapter reports data that is available only at the Britain or UK level.

[2] Unless specified to the contrary, all data on households and dwellings in the text and tables are sourced from housing statistics available on the Department for Levelling-Up, Housing and Communities website at www.gov.uk and for which the authors wish to thank the Office of National Statistics.

References

Andrew, M. (2010) 'The changing route into owner occupation: the impact of student debt', *Housing Studies*, 25(1), 39–62.

Ball, M. (2006) *Buy-to-Let Ten Years On*, London, Association of Residential Letting Agents.

Boviard, E., Harloe, M. and Whitehead, C. (1985) 'Private rented housing: its current role', *Journal of Social Policy*, 14(1), 1–23.

BPF (British Property Federation) (2021) *Build to Rent Map of the UK*, London, BPF.

British Property Federation, Savills and London School of Economics (2018) *Unlocking the Benefits and Potential of Build to Rent?*, London, British Property Federation.

Clapham, D., Mackie, P., Orford, S., Buckley, K., Thomas, I., Atherton, I. and McNulty, U. (2012) *Housing Options and Solutions for Young People in 2020*, York, Joseph Rowntree Foundation.

Clifford, B.P., Ferm, J., Livingstone, N. and Canelas, P. (2018) *Assessing the Impacts of Extending Permitted Development Rights to Office-to-Residential Change of Use in England*, London, Royal Institution of Chartered Surveyors.

Crook, A.D.H., Ferrari, E.T. and Kemp, P.A. (2012) 'Knowing the area: the management of market and business risks by private landlords in Scotland', *Urban Studies*, 49(15), 3347–3363.

Crook, A.D.H. and Kemp, P.A. (1999) *Financial Institutions and Private Rented Housing*, York, Joseph Rowntree Foundation.

Crook, A.D.H and Kemp, P.A. (2011) *Transforming Private Landlords*, Oxford, Wiley Blackwell.

Crook, A.D.H. and Kemp, P.A. (eds) (2014) *Private Rental Housing: Comparative Perspectives*, Cheltenham, Edward Elgar.

Crook, A.D.H. and Kemp, P.A. (2019) 'In search of profit: housing association investment in private rental housing', *Housing Studies*, 39, 666–687.

DCLG (Department of Communities & Local Government) (2011) *Private Landlord Survey 2010*, London, DCLG.

DCLG (Department of Communities & Local Government) (2012) *Review of the Barriers to Institutional Investment in Private Rented Homes: Report of the 'Montague' Review*, London, DCLG.

DCLG (Department of Communities & Local Government) (2017) *Fixing Our Broken Housing Market*, Cm 9352, London, DCLG.

DLUHC (Department of Levelling Up, Housing & Communities) (2021) *English Housing Survey. Headline Report, 2020–21*, London, DLUHC.

DLUHC (Department of Levelling Up Homes & Communities) (2022a) *A FairerPrivate Rented Sector*, CP, 693, London, DLUHC.

DLUHC (Department of Levelling Up, Homes & Communities) (2022b) *English Private Landlord Survey 2021. Main Report*, London, DLUHC.

Doling, J. and Aundel, R. (2017) 'The end of mass homeownership? Changes in labour markets and housing temnure opportunities across Europe', *Journal of Housing and the Built Environment*, 32(4), 649–672.

German, J. (2016) *UK Residential Investment: Why Consider Investing in the UK Residential Market?* London, Invesco.

Gordon, I. (2021) *How Much has the UK's Overseas-born Population Actually Contracted Since the Onset of Covid19? A Research Note*, London, LSE.

Farnood, F. and Jones, C. (2023 'The changing image of the UK private landlords with the buy to let revolution', *Journal of Housing and the Built Environment*, 38(1), 241–259.

Hammond, G (2021) 'Flight to suburbs and beyond knocks inner-city rents', *The Financial Times*, 16–17 January, p 14.

HCLG (House of Commons Housing, Communities & Local Government Committee) (2021) *Protecting the Homeless and the Private Rented Sector: MHCLG's Response to Covid-19*, Sixth Report of Session 2019–21, HC 1329, London, House of Commons.

House of Lords Built Environment Committee (2022) *Meeting Housing Demand*, First Report of Session 2021–22, HL Paper 132, London, House of Lords.

IFS (Institute for Fiscal Studies) (2014) *Econometric Analysis of the Impacts of Local Housing Allowance Reforms of Existing Claimants*, London, Department for Work & Pensions.

Jarman, R. (2020) *What Next for the Private Rented Sector?*, London, Housing Quality Network.

Jones, C. and Murie, A. (2006) *The Right to Buy*, Oxford, Blackwell.

Jones, C. and Mostafab, A. (2022) 'The revival of private residential landlordism in Britain through the prism of changing returns', *Journal of Property Research*, 39(1), 56–76.

JRF (Joseph Rowntree Foundation) (2020) *Briefing: Struggling Renters Need a Lifeline this Winter*, York, JRF.

Kemp, P.A. (2015) 'Private renting after the global financial crisis', *Housing Studies*, 30(4), 601–620.

Kemp, P.A. and Kofner, S. (2010) 'Contrasting varieties of private renting: England and Germany', *International Journal of Housing Policy*, 10(4), 379–398.

Kemp, P.A., Cole, I., Beatty, C. and Foden, M. (2014) *The Impact of the Changes to the Local Housing Allowance in the Private Rented Sector: The Response of Tenants*, Research Report 872, London, Department for Work and Pensions.

Knight Frank (2017) *UK Student Housing Rental Update*, London, Knight Frank.

Knight Frank (2020) *Residential Yield Guide*, London, Knight Frank.

Lex (2022) 'John Lewis/Abrdn: aisle see you downstairs', *Financial Times*, 3–4 December, p 24.

MHCLG (Ministry of Housing, Communities & Local Government) (2019) *English Private Landlord Survey 2018: Main Report*, London, MHCLG.

MHCLG (Ministry of Housing, Communities & Local Government) (2020) *Household Resilience Study: Wave 1*, London, MHCLG.

MHCLG (Ministry of Housing, Communities & Local Government) (2021a) *English Housing Survey 2019–20*, London, MHCLG.

MHCLG (Ministry of Housing, Communities & Local Government) (2021b) *English Housing Survey: Household Resilience Study: Wave 2 November–December 2020*, London, MHCLG.

Murie, A. (2022) 'Right to buy: the long view of a key aspect of UK housing policy', in M. Stephens, J. Perry, P. Williams, P. and G. Young (eds) *UK Housing Review 2022*, London, Chartered Institute of Housing, pp 45–54.

NAO (National Audit Office) (2021) *Regulation of Private Renting, Report by the Comptroller and Auditor General, House of Commons Report Session 2021–22*, HC 863, London, NAO.

O'Connor, M. and Portes, J. (2021) *Estimating the UK Population During the Pandemic*, London, Economic Statistics Centre of Excellence.

Partridge, J. (2020) 'Buy-to-let sales booming as landlords make most of stamp duty discount', *The Guardian*, 14 December, p 34.

Pawson, H. and Mullins, D. (2010) *After Council Housing: Britain's New Social Landlords*, Basingstoke, Palgrave Macmillan.

Pennington, J. and Kleynhans, S. (2020) *Renters at Risk Getting Through the Coronavirus Crisis*, London, Shelter.

Resolution Foundation (2020) *Private Renters are at the Heart of Growing Housing Pressures*, London, Resolution Foundation.

Resolution Foundation (2021) *Getting Ahead or Falling Behind: Tackling the UK's Building Arrears Crisis*, London, Resolution Foundation.

Rex, J. and Moore, R. (1967) *Race, Community and Conflict: A Study of Sparkbrook*, Oxford, Oxford University Press.

Roberts, S. and Satsangi, M. (2021) 'The "bad landlord": origins and significance in contemporary housing policy and practice', *Housing, Theory and Society*, 38(4), 496–511.

Rugg, J. and Rhodes, D. (2018) *The Evolving Private Rented Sector: Its Contribution and Potential*, York, Centre for Housing Policy.

Scanlon, K. and Whitehead, C. (2016) *The Profile of UK Private Landlords*, London, Council of Mortgage Lenders.

Scanlon, K., Whitehead, C. and Blanc, F. (2021) *Private Landlords and Tax Changes*, London, LSE.

Sigma Capital Group (2022) *The PRS REIT PLC*, Edinburgh, Sigma Group.

Sprigings, N. and Smith, D.H. (2012) 'Unintended consequences: local housing allowance meets the right to buy', *People, Place and Policy Online*, 6(2), 58–75.

Stephens, M., Perry, J., Williams, P. and Young, G. (eds) *UK Housing Review 2022*, London, Chartered Institute of Housing.

Sumption, M. (2021) *Where Did all the Migrants Go? Migration Data During the Pandemic*, Oxford, Oxford University Migration Observatory.

Tunstall, B. (2021) 'How safe home?', *Town & Country Planning*, 90(4), 72–73.

Whitehead, C. and Holman, N. (2020) *Where Now for the Private Rented Sector?* London, LSE.

6

Private renting in the Netherlands: set to grow?

Marietta E.A. Haffner

Introduction

When private renting reached an all-time low of about 10 per cent of the housing stock in 2009, the Netherlands became one of the countries in Europe with the smallest private rental sector (PRS) (Haffner, 2014; 2018; Haffner *et al*, 2018). Private renting had decreased from a share of 60 per cent of the stock since the Second World War. This decline could not be called a surprise after decades of subsidising homeownership and social renting, while rents were controlled.

More recently, a turnaround took place with an increase of private rental stock. The most recent data series available in Figure 6.1 shows that in the period 2012–2021, the total occupied dwelling stock increased with a little over 640,000 units to more than 7.6 million units, spread over the three main owners. The increases of the different tenures effected a largely stable tenure distribution in the period 2012–2021: homeowners' market share remained at 58 per cent, while housing corporations – the social landlords – lost two percentage points of their share, ending up with a little over 29 per cent of occupied stock. Other landlords than social landlords (private landlords) gained three percentage points of market share (almost 240,000 dwellings), amounting to almost 13 per cent of occupied stock in 2021, slightly under one million occupied dwellings. Historically, this private rental stock has been in the hands of non-organisation or so-called individual or person landlords (individuals and couples) and organisations (institutional investors and other organisations) (Priemus, 1998; Haffner, 2014). The latter landlords were more likely to own the newer and higher-rent dwellings, while the former were more likely to target the lower end of the market. Whether rental dwellings are managed by estate agents depends on the choice of the investor/landlord (Haffner, 2014).

This chapter analyses the extent to which this turnaround from decline to rise shows structural dimensions and explores whether private renting is likely to continue to grow. This topic seems justified based on knowledge about such a trend in other countries. In many European countries so-called

Figure 6.1: Occupied dwelling stock by owner, the Netherlands, 2012*–2021

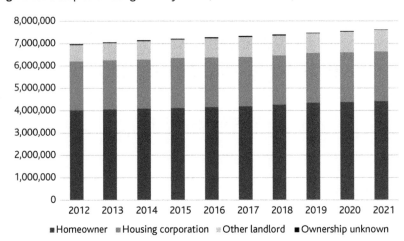

Note: * First year available in this series.

Source: CBS (2022a).

'market' renting has achieved a larger market share at the end of the past decade than at the beginning (Haffner and Elsinga, 2018; Haffner, 2020). The discussion in the literature about the urban affordability crisis (Wetzstein, 2017; Haffner and Hulse, 2021) shows the wider relevance.

To analyse and characterise the development in the PRS, this chapter first sets the scene in the next section with a short historic overview of the policy developments that have affected the PRS since the 1980s. This section also reflects on their impacts on the housing market that had been created post-Second World War, which caused private renting to lose ground: supporting a strong social rental sector and controlling rents, regardless of ownership of the dwelling, the latter to be considered a peculiarity in comparison to other countries (Haffner, 2014; 2018). After the brief review of these relevant policy changes since the 1980s that are suggested to have laid the groundwork for the turnaround in PRS market share around 2010, the state of the art in the PRS around 2010 is presented, as well as further developments around 2010 that may have contributed to the sector's increase in market share. Then the timeline is further followed analysing more recent developments, such as the more difficult access to homeownership and policies in response to the housing shortage and the COVID-19 pandemic and their expected impacts on the PRS.

Limiting rent control and the role of social landlords

Rent control, which was introduced after the Second World War in the rental sector, regardless of dwelling ownership, ceased to apply to newly built dwellings after 1989 and for existing dwellings with higher rents (subject to a required level of quality) in 1994. Therefore, rather than linking rent de-control to type of landlord, as is often the case in other countries, the rental market was divided into two segments: dwellings with regulated or controlled rents and those with deregulated, de-controlled or liberalised rents. The so-called liberalisation rent level has become the threshold rent level that separates the rent-controlled and rent-de-controlled renting from each other, irrespective of dwelling ownership. In 2021 this rent threshold amounted to €752.33 per month (Rijksoverheid, nda). The central government (still) determines the maximum increase of rent levels and liberalisation threshold once a year, while de-controlled rents are to be negotiated between landlord and tenant, also only once a year. Rental contracts with an indefinite term remained the standard.

A second move towards the market was effectuated in the 1990s when the financial requirements of the European Union (EU) about government budgets and debts heralded the cutting of the financial ties between subsidy recipients – social and private organisation landlords – and the subsidy provider – central government (Priemus, 1995; Haffner et al, 2009; Haffner, 2014). From then on, social landlords with the unchanged legal status of non-profit private organisation started operating as social entrepreneurs in competition with private landlords.

The role of social landlords was further limited by introducing an income limit for the allocation of social rental dwellings in 2011 (Elsinga et al, 2008; Haffner, 2018). This process that started with negotiations with the EU was finalised with the revised Housing Act of 2015 and had as its aim to create a level playing field between social and other landlords and to prevent subsidies (called state aid in EU terminology) leaking away because of market inefficiencies resulting from the non-level playing field. The 2015 Housing Act also required social landlords to largely abstain from commercial activities, like building and selling owner-occupied dwellings and building and letting rental dwellings in the liberalised segment.

A further change opened the door for the comeback of the PRS, when the 2010 coalition government of Conservatives and Christian Democrats, under the leadership of a Conservative Minister-President and its successors as of 2012 continued the mission of cutting back the autonomy and financial freedom of social landlords, also because of image issues (fraud, for example), while aiming to create more scope for action for private investors (Haffner, 2014). Next to the new framework of the 2015 Housing Act that curtailed the role of social landlords, in 2013 a new tax was introduced. The so-called landlord levy (Ministerie van Financiën, 2012; Priemus, 2014; Belastingdienst, 2021a) for the stock with a regulated rent owned by social and private landlords made the business of letting cheaper stock less attractive than before and relatively less attractive than letting stock with a de-controlled rent. To pay for the tax, extra rent increases for sitting tenants were needed and introduced for the low-rent stock. From 2013, the rent increases were also determined by the income level of the tenant (De Groot *et al*, 2016; Haffner, 2018). Another expected impact for this new regulation was that social tenants with a higher income would be stimulated to move to a middle-priced private rental dwelling or another dwelling to make room for another needy household in the rent-controlled stock. This was deemed necessary, as household income had become relevant at the moment of dwelling allocation, but not after the allocation moment, when living in a social rental dwelling.

The income dimension was not the only change in rent control, which was made more market conforming. The location of the dwelling was thus given a stronger impact on controlled rent levels from 2011 on. Furthermore, the 2016 Law on Tenant Mobility introduced stricter rent control for social than for private landlords in terms of limiting the increase of rents of their total stock (not only of individual dwellings), when taking rent pooling into consideration (Winter, 2016; Bharatsingh, 2017). Creating an exception for small private rental dwellings in Amsterdam and Utrecht by allowing their rents to be set higher than regulated based on dwelling quality standards was another move towards the market (Van der Molen, 2020).

Last, but not least, a regulation was put in place that allowed for more flexibility in type of rental contract than the indefinite one. The 2016 Law on Tenant Mobility allowed for more types of temporary rental contracts than those that had been introduced based on the Vacancy Law as a solution for owner-occupied dwellings that could not be sold in the aftermath of the GFC (Haffner, 2014; Winter, 2016; Bharatsingh, 2017; Huisman, 2020; Rijksoverheid, ndb). In comparison to the previous situation where all rental contracts were indefinite, these new types of contracts were time-expiring or temporary contracts; for example, letting based on five-year contracts (shared housing) or two-year contracts (independent housing). As a result, tenants had to cope with less tenancy security, while letting might be stimulated by more contract flexibility.

Market shares of (de-)controlled rental dwellings and the tenants

The previously described policy changes limited access to social renting for newcomers, potentially pushed out higher-income sitting tenants from social renting or pushed dwellings with sufficient quality into rent-de-control, once the sitting tenant moved out (Haffner, 2014; 2018). An example of the latter was a three-year rent freeze of the liberalisation rent level as of 2016, which effectively lowered the liberalisation rent level in comparison to the regulated rent increases (NUL20, 2014). In short, the changes mostly worked in favour of creating supply of private renting (Figures 6.1 and 6.2) and potential

Figure 6.2: Number of occupied rental dwellings (000s) by owner and rent (de-)control, the Netherlands, 2012*–2021

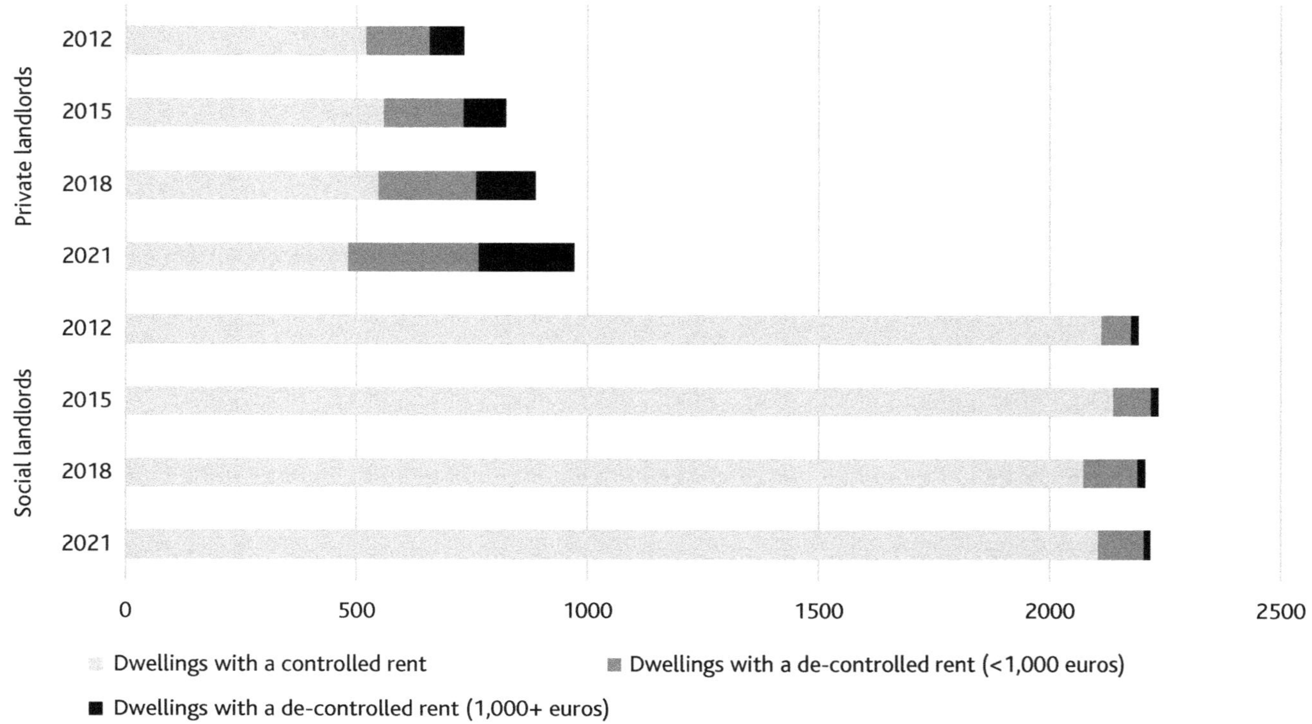

Dwellings with a controlled rent

Dwellings with a de-controlled rent (<1,000 euros)

Dwellings with a de-controlled rent (1,000+ euros)

Note: * First year available in this series.

Source: CBS (2022a).

supply of dwellings in the segment of liberalised private rents. By 2021 the share of dwellings with a de-controlled rent in the hands of private landlords had doubled to about half of their stock in comparison to 2012 when the share was almost 29 per cent of their stock. These de-controlled dwellings could have come from three sources according to CBS (2022a): former owner-occupied or rent-controlled rental dwellings or new construction.

Tenants were distributed across the (de-)controlled stock by income as follows. Most tenants lived in a social rental dwelling (41 per cent), while 28 per cent lived in private renting and 31 per cent in a rental dwelling with a liberalised rent in 2018 (Ministerie van Binnenlandse Zaken en Koninkrijksrelaties, 2019). The higher the income, the more likely a tenant lived in a rental dwelling with a liberalised rent: 76 per cent of high-income tenants, 49 per cent of middle-income tenants and 14 per cent of low-income tenants. Renting from a private landlord in the controlled segment accounted for one in three tenants with a low income, more than one in four tenants with a middle income, and almost one in six tenants with a high income. That lower-income tenants have come to increasingly live in the controlled rental segment, either housing corporation or private landlord, was a policy-induced trend by allocating more strictly according to income. While the housing corporation tenants were more likely to be retired or living on income support (61 per cent), those in private renting were increasingly likely to be employed or self-employed (62 per cent). Last, but not least, dwellings with a regulated rent have increasingly come to house singles, amounting to 58 per cent of housing corporation dwellings and 67 per cent of private rental dwellings.

Causes of the increase in private renting

As the previous sections show, policies have incrementally favoured investments in private renting by having made access to social renting more difficult, as well as the rent control for sitting tenants more focused on the policy target group for social renting. In addition, access to homeownership had become more difficult because of larger house price rises than income rises before the GFC (Haffner, 2014). In response to the GFC that caused three recessions in 2009, 2012 and 2013 (Haffner et al, 2017), the loan-to-value ratio and the loan-to-income ratio were restricted (stepwise) to reduce the risks of negative equity in the future. The effect of these measures was softened by a decreasing interest rate but reinforced the more difficult access to the sector (Boelhouwer and Schiffer, 2016; Haffner and Heylen, 2016). Such measures also reinforced the downward trend of nominal house prices due to the GFC (-16 per cent, 2008–2013; CBS, 2021a) and construction volume (Groenemeijer, 2021).

For private renting, the decreasing house prices in the period 2008–2013 made investment more attractive for professionals than before compared to alternative returns, particularly for the institutional investors who were interested in robust revenues. As is well-known, alternative returns consisted of low interest rates that the European Central Bank effected in its monetary response to the GFC (buying of government debts).

A final reason for new interest in private renting can most likely be associated with the statistical housing shortage that increased rapidly during the GFC. It was calculated to have grown by between 56,000 and 87,000 dwellings per year in the period of 2010–2015, while in the four years up to 2010 it also increased (Groenemeijer, 2021). The background to this calculated housing shortage was the increasing population, which increasingly had become immigration-led, while not so long ago (2006) the expectation was that population growth would be over by 2035 (Groenemeijer, 2021). Meanwhile, new supply decreased as a response to the GFC and the introduction of the landlord levy, among others.

Housing shortages push up house prices and de-controlled rents and thereby lower the risks of investment, as (direct and) indirect returns would become more likely. When the housing market started recovering after the shock from the GFC, house prices rose on average by 7.4 per cent in the period of 2013–2019, while inflation averaged 1.3 per cent and gross domestic product growth 3.8 per cent, indicating that the affordability of homeownership had decreased (Olsen and Tijm, 2021). At the same time, the housing shortage caused the growth in waiting lists for social renting (Kromhout and Wittkämper, 2019). The housing shortage was expected to increase further, exacerbating affordability problems, particularly in the cities, which in the literature has been recognised as a global phenomenon (Wetzstein, 2017; Haffner and Hulse, 2021). The statistical housing shortage has been forecasted to peak at 419,000 dwellings in 2025 (5.1 per cent of stock; Groenemeijer *et al*, 2020).

Non-institutional private rental investment on the increase

A new phenomenon on the rise were relatively small private investors (Michielsen *et al*, 2019, based on Aalbers *et al*, 2018). In 2018, private individual and couple investors (82 per cent) were the majority and company investors (12 per cent) the minority in this group of investors. Normal tax treatment is that the former are taxed in personal income tax either for 'normal' income from savings or other wealth (normal personal wealth management), while the latter are taxed either in personal income tax for business income or in corporate income tax (Haffner, 2014; Haffner *et al*, 2014; Bloem, 2021). The larger the rent revenues, the more likely a landlord will be paying corporate income tax with a maximum tax rate of 25 per cent, which is lower than the marginal tax rate for personal income tax (Belastingdienst, 2021a).

Up to 2012, private person investors when transacting sold more dwellings into homeownership than they bought, because of the 'value gap' in house prices between the owner-occupied housing and rental housing, particularly in cities (Conijn *et al*, 2019). Rent control caused house prices for rental dwellings with a sitting tenant with a permanent rental contract to be lower than prices for vacant housing.

As of 2013, when the economy recovered from the GFC, private individual investors with at least two dwellings in their portfolio started buying more dwellings than selling, particularly in cities (Van der Harst and de Vries, 2019). In 2009, private individual investors bought housing in 3.9 per cent of all housing transactions; this increased to 7.1 per cent in 2017. Most of these transactions were the responsibility of private investors with 3–5 dwellings in their portfolio. They were mostly selling their bigger dwellings but acquiring smaller apartments. While in 2013 they bought 1,332 more dwellings than they sold, the difference increased to more than 8,000 dwellings in 2017. In financial terms, private investors spent €3.8 billion on their acquisitions and €3.1 billion on their sales in 2017. The difference was positive, particularly for those with 6–9 dwellings in their portfolio.

Buying dwellings to let has become potentially an attractive business for many as alternative returns may be lower and/or less stable. Furthermore, the investment value of rental dwellings has gone up because rents have risen (Conijn *et al*, 2019). Since access to homeownership has become increasingly more difficult from 2010 onwards, the investor is able to pay a higher price for the dwelling than the first-time buyer. Consequently, the first-time buyer has most likely been increasingly crowded out of (popular) cities.

By 2019, about 280,000 private individual landlords with 475,000 units owned a little over 45 per cent of private rental stock – about 6 per cent of the dwelling stock (CBS, 2019, provisional numbers for 2018). Eight out of ten landlords owned one rental dwelling, 4 per cent owned five or more rental dwellings of which 250 landlords owned more than 50 rental dwellings. The likelihood of owning two or more dwellings was bigger when the landlord was of pension age (26 per cent) or self-employed (31 per cent) than when the landlord was employed (11 per cent), while most private individual landlords were employed (37 per cent), self-employed (27 per cent) or retired (20 per cent).

A quarter of the rental dwellings owned by private individual landlords were in the four biggest cities (Amsterdam, Rotterdam, Utrecht and The Hague). The share of private renting was relatively large in the university cities of Groningen (15 per cent) and Amsterdam (12 per cent), which is also the capital city, but also in The Hague (13 per cent), which houses the central government and parliament. In touristic municipalities such as Vaals (15 per cent) and Valkenburg aan de Geul (11 per cent) the share of the person/individual landlords was also relatively high. Such dwellings in student or touristic municipalities will have been more likely to be let to tourists by Airbnb or other platforms than elsewhere.

Institutional private rental investment on the increase

The 16 institutional investors in residential property are united in the Vereniging van Institutionele Beleggers in Vastgoed, Nederland (Association of Institutional Property Investors, Netherlands; IVBN). Institutional investors invest because of the funds that they manage for other purposes, such as pensions or insurances. The former revenues are exempted from corporate income tax, while the latter are not (Haffner, 2014; Haffner *et al*, 2014; Belastingdienst, 2021b).

IVBN-investors owned about 140,000 units (IVBN, 2020). This number amounted to more than 13 per cent of the private rental stock (Figure 6.2). Based on the IVBN 2019 renting survey, 75 per cent of their stock was part of the middle-priced rental segment with rents starting at the liberalisation rent level up to about €1,000 rent per month, 12 per cent of the lower-priced and 13 per cent of the higher-priced rental segment. As a reaction to the increasing housing shortage, IVBN members built 7,500 rental dwellings per year (IVBN, 2020). IVBN announced that members aim to build almost 31,000 units in the period 2020–2023.

The shortage of suitable mid-priced rental dwellings for middle-income households can be seen as structural and is hardly surprising considering the stronger focus of social landlords on their target group of lower-income households. The mid-priced rental segment with a rent starting at the liberalisation rent level had been largely missing, as it was not considered competitive for suppliers due to the subsidisation of social renting and homeownership (Haffner, 2014; 2018).

Investment in rental housing could also imply the acquisition of existing stock (most likely with sitting tenants) and not only new construction. According to Conijn *et al* (2019: 6), institutional investors either build new dwellings or buy portfolios from other institutional investors, rather than single dwellings. New rental construction is what developers have increasingly been aiming for according to Capital Value (2021). Whereas their order portfolio would have focused on homeownership a couple of years ago, middle-priced renting and homeownership development amounted to 28 per cent each.

In total, transaction volumes increased to €22.9 billion in 2020, an increase of more than one-fifth in comparison to 2019. This rise is explained with the stable investment context in comparison to other real estate in the year that the COVID-19 pandemic hit. International investors contributed €3.7 billion in 2020, embodying 32 per cent of transaction volume. The 85 transactions that took place amounted to an increase of 33 transactions compared to 2019. According to Capital Value (2021: 2–3), international investors find the Netherlands an attractive location for residential investment, not only because of the housing shortage (63 per cent), but also because of the stable economy and politics (81 per cent), as well as the relative attractive return (50 per cent). As their experience with the Netherlands increased, the international investors became increasingly interested in new construction. In 2020, 22 per cent of their investment realised 3,600 dwellings.

Tenants and their housing costs

Even though most rents are controlled, tenants on average paid a larger share of income on rent plus energy costs in 2018, as Table 6.1 shows, than owner-occupiers for which the cost-to-income ratio amounted to 23.4 per cent in 2021 (not in the table). With a housing cost-to-income ratio of 41.8 per cent, tenants renting from a private owner paid a higher share of their income on average for housing costs in 2021 than those renting from a social landlord with a ratio of 33.8 per cent. The increase of the ratio for private tenants by one percentage point between 2012 and 2021 implies that the total of housing costs including energy costs on average has risen more than disposable incomes, while for social tenants (renting from housing corporations) the average ratio in 2021 was more than one percentage point lower than for 2012. For social tenants the housing allowances will have been decisive (CPB, 2016; ABF, 2020; CBS, 2020), as well as the lower average energy costs per month (Table 6.1). As the latter declined on average for private tenants as well, private rents have increased relatively more on average. One explanation based on housing scarcity for middle-priced rental dwellings is offered by De Groot and Spiegelaar (2019) who observed that most of the rents of new tenants in the middle-priced private rental dwellings were close to the €1,000 per month that was considered 'segment maximum'. The extent of affordability (problems) will depend on household composition and income.

To understand the distribution of the average ratio for private tenants, Table 6.1 also shows these averages by household type. The household types with the highest ratios were the multi-person households with unrelated household members (51.1 per cent), single-person households (47.2 per cent) and to a lesser extent the one-parent families (39.2 per cent).

Housing shortage and private renting 're-regulation' policies

Hochstenbach and Ronald (2020: 1634) conceptualised the turnaround of private renting based on their case study of Amsterdam as one caused by 'regulated marketization'. They (2020: 1637) describe the 'state–initiated revival of private renting' first as less strict rent control making the return on private renting investment more attractive to investors (marketisation).

Table 6.1: Housing costs per month, including additional costs (euro) and housing cost-to-income ratio (%) by landlord and by renting from private owner by household type, the Netherlands, 2012, 2018, 2021 (cross-sectional data)

	Year	Net rent*	Additional housing costs**	Total housing costs	Housing cost-to-income ratio (%)
Renting from:					
Private owner	2012	560	183	743	40.8
	2018	657	181	837	42.4
	2021	782	162	944	41.8
Housing corporation	2012	376	173	549	34.9
	2018	430	170	600	36.0
	2021	468	153	622	33.8
Total	2012	416	175	591	36.2
	2018	496	173	669	37.8
	2021	568	156	723	36.3
Renting from private owner by household type					
Single person	2021	695	144	840	47.2
Multi-person (related household members)	2021	900	186	1,087	34.3
Lone-parent family	2021	713	191	904	39.2
Couple, total	2021	930	185	1,114	31.9
Couple, no children	2021	909	177	1,085	32.5
Couple, with child(ren)	2021	987	206	1,194	30.5
Multi-person (unrelated household members)	2021	1,093	200	1,293	51.1

Notes: *Housing allowances deducted, where relevant. **Including energy costs and municipal levies relevant to each household.

Source: CBS (2022b).

Second, stimulating new construction was municipality-led and regulated by attempting to take market interests into account while balancing this with their public role. Affordable middle-priced rental housing for key workers and other middle-income households was put on many municipal wish lists. This did not come as a surprise given the increase of the housing shortage, the small size of the middle-priced rental housing segment, the increase in middle-income groups who can no longer access either social renting or homeownership (Hoekstra and Boelhouwer, 2014), and the increase of the rents in relation to income between 2012 and 2018 (CBS, 2022b).

The number of municipalities that have developed policies to stimulate the provision of middle-priced private rental housing has increased from 40 per cent to 53 per cent within two years (Van der Molen, 2018). The expectation was that the municipalities would stimulate the realisation of 61,000 middle-priced rental dwellings for the demand estimated between 76,000 and 100,000 dwellings. The challenge was thereby to regulate price increases and/or speculation in the longer run after the construction of these dwellings. Linking such requirements to the land lease, if the land is owned by the municipality, may be one option. If a municipality owns the land, it has more options to implement so-called active land policy than if it does not own the land (VNG, 2018).

Even though the central government had pursued the objective of facilitating investment in private renting, the problems in the housing market caused by the shortage in housing also caused the central government to reconsider. For example, the 2014 Accommodation Act, which was adapted on 22 December 2020, offers municipalities a toolbox to handle the problems of touristic rentals in neighbourhoods where scarcity problems or livability problems exist. Municipalities may introduce regulation allowing for new limiting options: registration, permit or maximum number of nights (Ollongren, 2020). Such legislation will also be in line with the re-regulation dimension of 'regulated marketization' (Hochstenbach and Ronald, 2020), as will be the national regulation that the minister of housing proposed in 2019 to give market value of properties less weight in the determination of the quality of rental dwellings with a controlled rent (Van der Molen, 2020). The aim was to prevent the transfer of a larger number of rental dwellings with a controlled rent into the stock with a de-controlled rent, given the affordability problems.

Policy responses to the COVID-19 pandemic

When the COVID-19 pandemic hit in 2020, house prices continued rising (CBS, 2021a), even though economic indicators (gross national product, unemployment) were not developing favourably. Population growth in cities fell because of decreased numbers of immigration (CBS, 2021b). Pararius (2020), the largest independent website for housing offers as the website stated, reported first signs of decreasing liberalised rents in some cities. NUL20 (2021) reported in March of 2021 that in 2020 liberalised rents in Amsterdam, the biggest city, declined by almost 10 per cent on average.

Given the limited housing market impacts of the pandemic and given that the Netherlands has general safety net facilities in place – income support and housing allowances – no big policy initiatives were developed in first instance. To assure tenants, in 2020 central government agreed with the umbrella organisations of landlords that evictions were to be minimised, while government was going to send an emergency law to the parliament about extending during the pandemic the temporary contracts that were introduced after the GFC (Rijksoverheid, 2020).

By early 2021, the pandemic had not had a big impact on the housing market, while for financial hardship either temporary or more permanent solutions were in place. However, in the heat of the election campaign for the national elections in March of 2021, the Conservatives agreed that affordability problems had to be solved. Verberk *et al* (2019) showed that after three Conservative-led governments, the annual rent increases had resulted in 800,000 tenants who were estimated to have difficulty paying for basic consumption, implying an income problem rather than a housing problem (see also Woonbond, 2021).

However, to solve the affordability problems – except to go for more new construction to be organised by the new government – the response has been to introduce more rent control (Rijksoverheid, 2021a; 2021b). In February of 2021 the central government agreed on the parliament's proposal of a rent freeze for the annual 2021 rent revision date of 1 July for dwellings with a regulated rent (see also Ollongren, 2021). The large social and private landlords were to be compensated by lowering their landlord levy, in order to not endanger the aims of tackling the housing shortage. For small private landlords, the government intended to explore how they were to be compensated for their loss in revenues. Next to several other measures directed to social landlords, the since 1994 liberalised rents were controlled again as of 1 May 2021 for three years: the increase was maximised to 3.3 per cent, regardless of the rent increase agreed on in the individual rental contracts (Rijksoverheid, nda; 2021a; 2021b).

The latest rent control measures that central government implemented by 1 May 2022 was the 2019 proposal about rental housing quality with the aim to restrict the transfer from rental dwellings with a controlled rent into renting with a liberalised rent (Rijksoverheid, ndc). Central government also launched the proposal to re-regulate de-controlled rents for new tenancies to include the middle-priced rental dwelling (up to €1,000) (NUL20, 2022). The latter measure would reintroduce rent control for more than 25 per cent of stock in the hands of private landlords (Figure 6.2).

Next to the rent control measures, the central government also put in place a new design of the transfer tax to strengthen the position of the first-time buyer in comparison to the private person investor. The transfer tax for acquisition has been increased for the latter – any buyer not going to live in the acquired dwelling – to 8 per cent of house value. It exempts first-time buyers who are younger than 35 years of age, while other buyers who will occupy the dwelling themselves rather than let pay 2 per cent (Belastingdienst, 2021c). As of 1 April 2021, the eligible acquisition price was limited to €400,000. Plegt and de Vries (2021) showed the effect of this measure based on cadastral transactions. Private investors bought 30 per cent of their acquisitions of the last two years in the last quarter of 2020, right before the legislation changed on 1 January.

In summary, given not only the government objectives to counter the housing affordability problems, but also the rising rates of inflation (for energy) and the urgency of making progress on climate and sustainability goals, it remains to be seen whether the market share of private renting will be able to further grow as it did in the past decade.

Conclusion

After decades of decline, the past ten years witnessed a government-led revival of private renting. Central government has facilitated the growth of private renting, particularly the stock with a de-controlled rent by introducing national regulation, which made social renting and homeownership less accessible. Furthermore, rent control was no longer applicable to the private rental stock with a middle or higher rent (the de-controlled rent). At the same time, market developments since the GFC caused rental housing with a de-controlled rent to become attractive to global funds looking for returns. The share of dwellings with a de-controlled rent increased.

Meanwhile, local governments increasingly had to make efforts to realise and/or regulate middle-priced private renting for middle-income groups, including keyworkers in the middle of the urban affordability crisis. As the housing shortage has become top priority, in combination with affordability for renters, central government reinstated rent control in the private rental market stock with a de-controlled rent in 2021 and again in 2022 for three years. The central government also increased the transfer tax to discourage private non-institutional investors from buying dwellings and subsequently letting them to tenants rather than moving in themselves. This was done because private investors were able to outbid potential first-time buyers, thereby making house prices less affordable.

Given the turnaround in regulation of central government and the attempts by local governments to regulate middle- and low-priced rental housing, the most recent measures of central government could also be understood in terms of re-regulation of private renting in sight of perceived housing market problems. In combination with wider societal challenges in the fields of energy, climate and sustainability, the question arises whether the revival of private renting in the past ten years will be rather short-lived.

References
Aalbers, M., Bosma, J., Fernancdez, R. and Hochstenbach, C. (2018) *Buy-to-let: Gewikt en gewogen* (Buy-to-let: assessed), Leuven and Amsterdam, KU Leuven and UvA.

ABF (2020) *Waarom het gebruik van huurtoeslag steeg terwijl het economisch beter ging* (Why the use of housing allowances increased while the economic climate had been improving), https://www.abfresearch.nl/nieuws/waarom-het-gebruik-van-huurtoeslag-steeg-terwijl-het-economisch-beter-ging

Bharatsingh, S. (2017) *Mogelijkheden tot het tijdelijk (ver)huren van een woning verruimd. Wat verandert de Wet Doorstroming Huurmarkt 2015?* (Possibilities for temporarily renting a home have been increased. What will the 2015 rental market mobility act change?), https://www.elhannouche.nl/wat-verandert-de-wet-doorstroming-huurmarkt-2015/

Belastingdienst (2021a) *Verhuurderheffing* (Landlord levy), https://www.belastingdienst.nl/wps/wcm/connect/bldcontentnl/belastingdienst/zakelijk/overige_belastingen/verhuurderheffing/

Belastingdienst (2021b) *Tarieven voor de vennootschapsbelasting* (Tax rates of corporatakstax), https://www.belastingdienst.nl/wps/wcm/connect/bldcontentnl/belastingdienst/zakelijk/winst/vennootschapsbelasting/tarieven_vennootschapsbelasting

Belastingdienst (2021c) *Overdrachtsbelasting* (Transfer tax), https://www.belastingdienst.nl/wps/wcm/connect/bldcontentnl/belastingdienst/prive/woning/overdrachtsbelasting/

Bloem, E. (2021) *Huurinkomsten belasting. Basiskennis investeren in vastgoed* (Rent revenue taxation. Basic knowledge of real estate investment), https://vastgoedmentor.com/huurinkomsten-belasting/

Boelhouwer, P. and Schiffer, K. (2016) *Naar een hervorming van de woningmarkt: Niets doen is geen optie!* (Towards reform of the housing market: Doing nothing is not an option!), Delft, Technische Universiteit Delft.

Capital Value (2021) *De (woning)beleggingsmarkt in beeld 2021. Onderzoeksrapport. Samenvatting* (The (housing)investment market 2021 reviewed. Research report. Summary), Utrecht, Capital Value.

CBS (2019) *Bijna half miljoen woningen in particuliere verhuur* (Almost half a million private rental dwellings), https://www.cbs.nl/nl-nl/nieuws/2019/14/bijna-half-miljoen-woningen-in-particuliere-verhuur

CBS (2020) *Overheid; sociale uitkeringen* (Government; social benefits), https://opendata.cbs.nl/statline/#/CBS/nl/dataset/84121NED/table?ts=1616874711696

CBS (2021a) *Bestaande koopwoningen; verkoopprijzen, prijsindex 2015=100; mutaties gebruiksfunctie, regio* (Existing owner-occupied dwellings; prices, price index 2015=100), https://opendata.cbs.nl/#/CBS/nl/dataset/83906NED/table

CBS (2021b) *Bevolkingsgroei grotere steden stokt door lage immigratie* (Population growth in larger cities is stagnating because of low immigration) https://www.cbs.nl/nl-nl/nieuws/2021/01/bevolkingsgroei-grotere-steden-stokt-door-lage-immigratie

CBS (2022a) *Steeds minder gereguleerde huurwoningen beschikbaar* (Increasingly fewer rental dwellings with a regulated rent available), https://www.cbs.nl/nl-nl/nieuws/2022/42/steeds-minder-gereguleerde-huurwoningen-beschikbaar

CBS (2022b) *Housing Costs of Households: Household and Dwelling Characteristics*, https://opendata.cbs.nl/statline/#/CBS/en/dataset/84487 ENG/table?ts=1615661714862%20

Conijn, J., Meertens, V. and Schilder, F. (2019) *Buy-to-let verdringt starter van de koopwoningmarkt* (Buy-to-let is barring starters from owner-occupation), Amsterdam, ASRE.

CPB (2016) *De prijs voor betaalbaarheid: Opties voor meer doelmatigheid en effectiviteit in de huurtoeslag en het beleid voor de sociale huur* (The price of affordability: Options for more efficiency and effectiveness in housing benefit and social rental policy), Den Haag, Rijksoverheid.

De Groot, C. and Spiegelaar, L. (2019) *Too Soon to Celebrate Growth of Midmarket Rental in the Netherlands*, Utrecht, RaboBank/RaboResearch.

De Groot, C., Daalhuizen, F., Schilder, F. and Tennekes, J. (2016) *Betaalbaarheid van het wonen in de huursector: Verkenning van beleidsopties* (Affordability of housing in the rental sector: Exploration of policy options), Den Haag, PBL.

Elsinga, M., Haffner, M. and van der Heijden, H. (2008) 'Threats to the Dutch unitary rental market', *European Journal of Housing Policy*, 8(1), 21–37.

Groenemeijer, L. (2021) *Terugblik ontstaan woningtekort* (Reviewing the emergence of a housing shortage), Delft, ABF Research.

Groenemeijer, L., Gopal, K., Omtzigt, D. and van Leeuwen, G. (2020) *Vooruitzichten bevolking, huishoudens en woningmark: Prognose en Scenario's 2020–2035* (Prospects for population, households and housing market: Forecast and Scenarios 2020–2035), Delft, ABF Research.

Haffner, M.E.A. (2014) 'The Netherlands', in T. Crook and P.A. Kemp (eds) *Private Rental Housing: Comparative Perspectives*, Cheltenham, Edward Elgar, pp 48–70.

Haffner, M. (2018) 'The role of private renting in France and the Netherlands', in C.U. Schmid (ed.) *Tenancy Law and Housing Policy in Europe*, Cheltenham, Edward Elgar, pp 19–38.

Haffner, M. (2020) 'De Nederlandse particuliere huursector in Europees perspectief' (The Dutch private rental sector from a European perspective), *Real Estate Research Quarterly*, 19(2), 37–46.

Haffner, M. and Heylen, K. (2016) *De verdeling van de woonsubsidies naar inkomen en stedelijkheidsgraad: Vlaanderen en Nederland vergeleken* (The distribution of housing subsidies by income and degree of urbanization: Flanders and the Netherlands compared), Leuven, Steunpunt Wonen.

Haffner, M.E.A. and Elsinga, M.G. (2018) *Towards Inclusive Service Delivery through Social Investment in the Case of Housing* (Deliverable 6.3), Delft, Delft University of Technology.

Haffner, M.E.A. and Hulse, K. (2021) 'A fresh look at contemporary perspectives on urban housing affordability', *International Journal of Urban Sciences*, 25(1), 59–79.

Haffner, M., Hoekstra, J., Oxley, M. and van der Heijden, H. (2009) *Bridging the Gap between Market and Social Rented Housing in Six European Countries*, Amsterdam, IOS Press BV, https://repository.tudelft.nl/islandora/object/uuid%3Ad35c0ed4-7874-4413-8b90-25352ec8c980

Haffner, M., van der Veen, M. and Bounjouh, H. (2014) *National Report for the Netherlands*, Delft University of Technology, TENLAW, Tenancy Law and Housing Policy in Multi-level Europe (grant agreement no. 290694).

Haffner, M.E.A., Elsinga, M.G. and Mariën, A.A.A. (2017) *Social Disinvestment and Vulnerable Groups in Europe in the Aftermath of the Financial Crisis: The Case of Households that have Difficulties with Making Ends Meet in the Netherlands*, Delft, TU Delft/Leuven, HIVA-KU Leuven.

Haffner, M., Hegedüs, J. and Knorr-Siedow, T. (2018) 'The private rental sector in western Europe', in J. Hegedüs, M. Lux and V. Horváth (eds) *Private Rental Housing in Transition Counties: An Alternative to Owner Occupation?* London: Macmillan, pp 3–40.

Hochstenbach, C. and Ronald, R. (2020) 'The unlikely revival of private renting in Amsterdam: re-regulating a regulated housing market', *Environment and Planning A: Economy and Space*, 52(8), 1622–1642.

Hoekstra, J. and Boelhouwer, P. (2014) 'Falling between two stools? Middle-income groups in the Dutch housing market', *International Journal of Housing Policy*, 14(3), 301–313.

Huisman, C. (2020) *Insecure Tenure: The Precarisation of Rental Housing in the Netherlands*, Groningen, Rijksuniversiteit Groningen.

IVBN (2020) *Tweede Kamerverkiezingen 17 maart 2021: Sámen werken aan een gezonde woningmarkt voor iedereen* (Working together for a healthy housing market for everyone), Den Haag, IVBN.

Kromhout, S.C. and Wittkämper, L.M. (2019) *Stand van de woonruimteverdeling: wachttijden en verdeling in de praktijk* (State of the art of housing allocation: waiting times and allocation in practice), Amsterdam, RIGO.

Michielsen, J., de Vries, P. and Tatch, J. (2019) 'A comparative study on the Dutch and English buy-to-let market', in L. Bertalot, J. Johnson, D. Westig and S.G. Pérez (eds) *Hypostat: A Review of Europe's Mortgage and Housing Market*, Brussels, EMF, pp 15–21.

Ministerie van Binnenlandse Zaken en Koninkrijksrelaties (2019) *Ruimte voor wonen: De resultaten van het WoonOnderzoek Nederland 2018* (Space for living: The results of the analysis with the database WoonOnderzoekNederland 2018), Den Haag, Ministerie van Binnenlandse Zaken en Koninkrijksrelaties.

Ministerie van Financiën (2012) *Belastingplan 2013* (Taks plan 2013), Den Haag, Ministerie van Financiën.

NUL20 (2014) 'Liberalisatiegrens pas bevroren vanaf 2016' (Liberalisation rent level only frozen from 2016 on), *NUL20*, https://www.nul20.nl/lib eralisatiegrens-pas-bevroren-vanaf-2016

NUL20 (2021) 'Vrije sectorhuur Amsterdam: − 9.6%' (De-controlled rent Amsterdam − 9.6%), *NUL20*, https://www.nul20.nl/vrije-sectorhuur-amsterdam-96

NUL20 (2022) 'Regulering middenhuren gaat tot 1000 euro per maand' (Regulation of rents of middle-priced rental housing up to 1000 euro per month) *NUL20*, https://www.nul20.nl/regulering-middenhu ren-gaat-tot-1000-euro-maand

Ollongren, K.H. (2020) 'Besluit van 22 december 2020, houdende vaststelling van het tijdstip van inwerkingtreding van de wet van 7 oktober 2020 tot wijziging van de Huisvestingswet 2014 en de Gemeentewet in verband met de aanpak van ongewenste neveneffecten van toeristische verhuur van woonruimte en woonoverlast (Wet toeristische verhuur van woonruimte) (Stb. 2020, 460)' (Decision of 22 December 2020, tourist rental housing act), *Staatsblad*, 566, 29 December, https://zoek.officielebek endmakingen.nl/stb-2020-566.html

Ollongren, K.H. (2021) *Uitvoering motie Beckerman* (Execution of Second Chamber resolution of chamber member Beckerman), Brief aan de Tweede Kamer, Kenmerk 2021-0000087305, 17 February, Den Haag, Ministerie van Binnenlandse Zaken en Koninkrijksrelaties.

Olsen, J. and Tijm, J. (2021) *Stedelijk bouwen, agglomeratie-effecten en woningprijzen* (Urban building, agglomeration effects and house prices), Den Haag, CPB.

Pararius (2020) *Dalende huurprijzen in grote en middelgrote steden* (Falling rents in large and medium-sized cities), https://www.pararius.nl/nieuws/dale nde-huurprijzen-in-grote-en-middelgrote-steden

Plegt, M. and de Vries, P. (2021) 'Vierde kwartaal 2020 topperiode voor particuliere investeerders' (Fourth quarter 2020 peak period for private investors), *ESB* online, 21 April, https://login.tudelft.nl/sso/ module.php/core/loginuserpass.php?AuthState=_3b1457de84129e7 da12c6cafb5e01d53a56f8d3766%3Ahttps%3A%2F%2Flogin.tudelft. nl%2Fsso%2Fsaml2%2Fidp%2FSSOService.php%3Fspentityid%3Dht tps%253A%252F%252Fengine.surfconext.nl%252Fauthentication%252 Fsp%252Fmetadata%26cookieTime%3D1686133652

Priemus, H. (1995) 'How to abolish social housing: the Dutch case', *International Journal of Urban and Regional Research*, 19(1), 145–155.

Priemus, H. (1998) 'Commercial rented housing: two sectors in the Netherlands', *Netherlands Journal of Housing and the Built Environment*, 13(3), 255–278.

Priemus, H. (2014) 'Is the landlord levy a threat to the rented housing sector? The case of the Netherlands', *International Journal of Housing Policy*, 14(1), 98–106.

Rijksoverheid (nda) *Welke regels gelden er voor een huurverhoging* (What rules apply to a rent increase?), https://www.rijksoverheid.nl/onderwerpen/woning-huren/vraag-en-antwoord/welke-regels-gelden-er-voor-een-huurverhoging

Rijksoverheid (ndb) *Welke mogelijkheden heb ik om mijn woning tijdelijk te verhuren?* (What options do I have for temporarily renting my home?), https://www.rijksoverheid.nl/onderwerpen/woning-verhuren/vraag-en-antwoord/welke-mogelijkheden-heb-ik-om-mijn-woning-tijdelijk-te-verhuren

Rijksoverheid (ndc) *Kan ik huurverlaging krijgen als de WOZ-waarde minder meetelt bij de puntentelling van mijn huurwoning?* (Can I get a rent reduction if the WOZ value counts less in the quality points of my rental home?), https://www.rijksoverheid.nl/onderwerpen/woning-huren/vraag-en-antwoord/kan-ik-huurverlaging-krijgen-als-de-woz-waarde-minder-meetelt-bij-de-puntentelling-van-mijn-huurwoning

Rijksoverheid (2020) *Geen huisuitzettingen en verlenging tijdelijke huurcontracten* (No evictions and renewal of temporary leases), https://www.rijksoverheid.nl/actueel/nieuws/2020/03/26/geen-huisuitzettingen-en-verlenging-tijdelijke-huurcontracten.

Rijksoverheid (2021a) *Huren in gereguleerde sector in 2021 niet verhoogd* (Rents in regulated sector not increased in 2021), https://www.rijksoverheid.nl/onderwerpen/woning-huren/nieuws/2021/02/17/huren-in-gereguleerde-sector-in-2021-niet-verhoogd

Rijksoverheid (2021b) *Eerste Kamer stemt in met drie wetten die wonen betaalbaar houden voor huurders* (The Senate approves three laws that keep housing affordable for tenants), https://www.rijksoverheid.nl/actueel/nieuws/2021/03/23/eerste-kamer-stemt-in-met-drie-wetten-die-wonen-betaalbaar-houden-voor-huurders

Van der Molen, F. (2018) 'Dweilen met de kraan open?' (Mopping with the faucet open?), *NUL20*, 94, 18–20.

Van der Molen, F. (2020) 'Liberaliseren woningen wordt lastiger' (Liberalising of dwelling rents will be more difficult), *NUL20*, 104, 24–25.

Van der Harst, F. and de Vries, P. (2019) *In beeld: de groeiende rol van particuliere verhuurders op de Nederlandse woningmarkt* (Overview: the growing role of private landlords in the Dutch housing market), n.l., Kadaster.

Verberk, M., Warnaar, M. and Bos, J. (2019) *Hoe gaan mensen om met hoge woonlasten? Een onderzoek naar het effect van hoge woonlasten op de overige uitgaven* (How do people deal with high housing costs? A study into the effects of high housing costs on other expenditures), Den Haag, Nibud.

VNG (2018) *Grondbeleid voor Raadsleden. Wat U als raadslid moet weten over grondeleid* (Land policy for Councilors. What you as a Councilor need to know about land policy), Den Haag, Vereniging van Nederlandse Gemeenten.

Wetzstein, S. (2017) 'The global urban housing affordability crisis', *Urban Studies*, 54(4), 3159–3177.

Winter, A.C. (2016) *De nieuwe Wet Doorstroming huurvnmarkt: wat verandert er per 1 juli 2016 voor u?* (The new rental market transition act: what will change for you as of 1 July 2016?), Blog, https://boutadvocaten.nl/blog/nieuwe-wet-doorstroming-huurmarkt-verandert-er-per-1-juli-2016/

Woonbond (2021) *Kamer stemt over beloftes huurbevriezing in kieswijzer* (Second Chamber votes on rent freeze promises in electoral guide), https://www.woonbond.nl/nieuws/kamer-stemt-over-beloftes-huurbevriezing-kieswijzer

7

Suppressive regulation and lower political esteem: private renting in Germany at the beginning of decline

Stefan Kofner

Introduction

In contrast to most other advanced economies, where private renting is more or less a residual sector focused on the poor and those unable to buy their home, the German private rental sector is still a cornerstone of housing provision and serves a broad range of households. As in many other countries, though, individual private landlords dominate in the German private rental sector (PRS). There is no doubt that the PRS is a key pillar of the German housing system. In summary, this system is characterised by:

1. strong tenancy security for decades, interrupted only by deregulation legislation in the 1960s;
2. a system of only temporary subsidies for social housing at moderate profits, which has led to a permanent shrinking of the social housing stock;
3. building up of a large rental housing stock via extensive and continuous housing subsidies and generous tax treatment in the past (1949–2005);
4. Stop-go housing subsidies since 2006 while maintaining relative tenure neutrality.

In the German case, the author prefers to define the PRS according to ownership. A rental dwelling thus belongs to the PRS if it is owned by a private person, a group of private persons or by a private company. For pragmatic reasons, this definition includes social housing owned by private landlords because only the owner groups, but not the status of the apartments in their respective housing portfolio, is statistically recorded. But this does not affect more than 2 per cent of the sector's housing stock.

Structure of supply and demand in the private rental housing market

The German housing market is characterised by specific structures that distinguish it very clearly from other housing markets. The essential aspect here is the role of renting and particularly private renting. It is quantitatively and qualitatively quite different from the private rental market in other early industrialised Western countries, where homeownership is more widespread.

Supply side: a very large cottage industry

The most striking characteristic of the German private rental sector from a comparative perspective is its size: almost 80 per cent per cent of the rental market and more than 45 per cent of the total housing market.

As in many other countries, individual private landlords rather than property companies and financial institutions, dominate in the German PRS (see Table 7.1). In urban areas professional landlords tend to dominate in the private rental market; but in rural areas, smaller towns and suburbs, small-scale operators are often more common. In Germany, private individuals account for 63 per cent of all rented dwellings and 79 per cent of privately rented dwellings. As elsewhere, they are a very heterogeneous group of actors in the housing market, with diverse aims and backgrounds. Self-employed people and civil servants are significantly over-represented among individual landlords (16 per cent self-employed and 11 per cent civil servants compared with 5 per cent and 3 per cent respectively in the total population). The proportion of pensioners among private owners is just as high as in the population as a whole (42 per cent). The vast majority are amateur landlords with less than 15 dwellings who self-manage their portfolios. Forty-five per cent of their apartments were purchased and 24

Table 7.1: Number (millions) and percentage (%) of dwellings by type of owner

Year	Owner-occupied	Individual private rental	Private company	Total private rental	Public	Coop-erative	Non-profit	Total
2011	17.3 (43%)	15.0 (37%)	3.2 (8%)	18.2 (45%)	2.6 (6%)	2.1 (5%)	0.3 (1%)	40.5 (100%)
2014	17.0 (42%)	14.3 (35%)	4.2 (10%)	18.5 (45%)	2.7 (7%)	2.1 (5%)	0.3 (1%)	40.6 (100%)
2018	17.7 (43%)	15.0 (36%)	3.9 (9%)	18.9 (45%)	2.5 (6%)	2.1 (5%)	0.2 (1%)	41.4 (100%)

Sources: Zensus 2011 Sonderauswertung; Mikrozensus Zusatzerhebung zur Wohnsituation 2014; 2018; GdW-Jahresstatistik 2014, 2018.

per cent inherited. Another 25 per cent was newly built and 12 per cent were acquired by gift or transfer. Unlike in the liberal market economies, individual private landlords have a very long-term investment horizon and a marked preference for security of investment (BBSR, 2015).

Institutional landlords own a minority of the rental stock in Germany. Corporate landlords account for 17 per cent of all rented dwellings and 21 per cent of the private rental housing stock. This includes private housing companies, insurance companies, pension funds and property funds. Since the late 1990s a few large-scale financial investor property companies, many of which are owned by global private equity companies, have entered the German PRS. They have built up large housing portfolios by taking over housing companies from public sector organisations and manufacturing firms. The legacy of these investors, who liquidated their investments at a profit after the financial crisis subsided, are a handful of very large, listed housing companies such as Vonovia, Deutsche Wohnen and LEG (TRAWOS, 2012; BBSR, 2017).

Other institutional investment in PRS dwellings occurs only rarely. Open-ended property funds tend to ignore residential buildings (Scope Analysis, 2019). Close-ended property funds concentrate on certain niches of the residential market, such as historic monuments and student dwellings. Insurance and pension funds usually have a very low share of real estate in their portfolios. On average, it is far below the legal maximum share of 25 per cent: the effective real estate share is only 3.7 per cent among German primary insurers (GDV, 2020). Recently, however, the housing portfolios of the two Southern German Landesbanken (Bayern, Baden-Württemberg) were sold to consortiums of German institutional investors. The background to this were stipulations imposed by the European Commission in connection with the bailout of these banks. German Real Estate Investment Trusts are not allowed to invest in existing residential buildings (Kofner, 2007).

Nowadays, public opinion relating to takeovers of public housing companies is very hostile. There are even efforts and initiatives aiming at re-municipalising the privatised apartments (Jensen, 2020) or even expropriating the new owners. After a successful referendum the Berlin Senate must enact a law according to which all profit-oriented companies with at least 3,000 dwellings are to be socialised. The amount of compensation was to be set 'well below the market value' at 30–40 per cent of this value (Beck *et al*, 2020: 5–6).

While the performance record of the German capital market in terms of allocating equity funds to residential investment is still modest, the German PRS has become a sought-after safe-haven investment for international and domestic capital in the wake of the global financial crisis. However, these investments are no longer large portfolio transactions, but rather individual purchases.

In Germany, there is no distinct mortgage market segment for buy-to-let mortgages. Private apartment buildings or condominiums for rent are financed by the same lenders as owner-occupied homes, that is, commercial banks, building societies ('Bausparkassen'), cooperative banks and public-sector banks such as development banks and locally operating savings banks. Savings banks, cooperative banks and building societies together provide more than 70 per cent of the financing for private housing construction. Compared to homeownership financing, neither the interest rates, nor the loan-to-value requirements are systematically higher for buy-to-let mortgages. The loan conditions for rented multi-family buildings depend on the characteristics of the individual property and the amount of the loan. So-called 'Tableau conditions' with fixed interest rates – depending on certain objective characteristics of the borrower and the collateral, such as, for example, in private home finance – are not available. However, the conditions for the financing of multi-family houses closely depend on the conditions for owner-occupied housing. Lenders obviously believe that both types of mortgages have a comparable default risk.

In general, the supply-side structure of the German housing market seems well-balanced. In large parts of the country, there is an effective and only slightly distorted choice between tenures and landlord groups (that is, public landlords, private landlords and cooperatives). There is also effective competition between tenures and landlord groups (Kofner, 2014b).

However, the dominant role of private landlords could be endangered in the long run. The new federal government, which has been in office since December 2021, not only plans to further tighten the rent price laws (see section on 'Local reference rent: loss of market orientation') but also wants to restrict tax incentives to non-profit housing companies and to significantly increase the share of social housing in new construction.

Compared with the nearly 19 million privately rented apartments, the social housing sector (defined as publicly subsidised, not publicly owned, apartments) still appears very small. The number of social dwellings is currently only one million and is still shrinking. Back in 1987 the total number of social dwellings was four million. Thus, the sector is just a shadow of its former self. The declining importance of social housing is due to the reduction of federal subsidies and to the temporary character of the subsidies. But here a trend reversal is about to begin: the new federal government wants to increase the number of social housing units completed annually to 100,000 (Koalitionsvertrag, 2021), which would be approximately a threefold increase.

The German social housing sector has contributed to the growth of the private rental sector in the past, either by the expiry of the social status of the dwellings after the subsidy had been paid back, or by the sale of whole housing companies to the private sector (Voigtländer,

2006). Moreover, the social housing sector causes only limited distortion of competition. It is well integrated in most respects with the private sector.

Demand side: private renting as the most widespread tenure

In Germany, there are more tenant than owner households. Tenant households are the predominant group with a share of 56 per cent. About 45 per cent of all households are tenants of private landlords. Among poorer households, the share of tenants is particularly high: 67 per cent of households with a net income between €1,500 and €2,000 are tenants; and the share of tenants is much higher among households with incomes below €1,500. Although the share of tenants decreases with increasing household income, there are many tenants among higher earners, in contrast to many other advanced economies. Among those with household incomes above €4,500, the share of tenants is 29 per cent; and among households with incomes between €3,200 and €4,500, 42 per cent are tenants (Statistische Ämter des Bundes und der Länder, 2019).

There is also a dependence between household size and the share of tenants. While 72 per cent of one-person households – the largest group of households – are tenants, the share of homeowners is above 50 per cent in all other groups and rises with household size. Also, the smaller the household, and the lower household income, the higher is the probability that it is a tenant household. The homeownership rates by age groups reflect the fact that first-time buyers/builders are relatively old compared to other advanced economies. In 2015, the homeownership rate among households aged under 35 years was only 13 per cent; and among those aged from 35 to 44 years, tenants dominated with a share of 61 per cent. Moreover, the homeownership rate in both age groups has declined significantly since 2010 (Voigtländer and Hude, 2017). Thus, most young- and middle-aged households in Germany are tenants.

Emergence of today's housing market structures

It is an important question how these distinct German housing market structures emerged. On the eve of the First World War, a share of the PRS of about 90 per cent of the total housing stock was typical in industrialised countries (Department of Environment, 1977; Howenstine, 1981). Since then, long-term decline in the share of households living in private rental housing has taken place in most advanced economies. However, the decline was much less pronounced in Germany. In the first half of the 20th century, small private landlords were by far the largest landlord group in Germany. Even the boom in social housing construction after the Second World War did not put the dominance of the private landlord into question. In 1961, the share of small private landlords was 42.7 per cent of the total housing stock and 64.5 per cent of the rental housing stock. There is evidence that the market share of private landlords was even higher in 1950 (Statistisches Bundesamt, 2000).

According to the German experience after the Second World War, the essential prerequisite for a well-developed rental sector is a combination of tax incentives for rental housing and protective regulation, that is, eviction protection and third generation rent control according to the classification of Arnott (1995; 2003). In Germany, renting offers a long-term perspective, and this has counteracted a more pronounced relative contraction of the sector (Kofner, 2014a).

The tax treatment of housing investment in Germany after the Second World War was particularly attractive for small private landlords; and that was a decisive factor for their large market share. Generous depreciation allowances, deductibility of maintenance and repair costs and negative gearing, combined with tax-free capital gain, ensured that rental housing was mostly well maintained and prevented some of the richer households from buying their home. This helped to prevent the emergence of prejudice against renting as a tenure in Germany.

The other side of the coin of the large German rental sector is a low homeownership rate by international comparison. There is much less cultural fixation on homeownership (Huber and Schmidt, 2019) in Germany than in many Anglophone countries and private renting is not seen as an inferior tenure. However, culture can be shaped by housing policy and housing market conditions, at least in the long run.

The German PRS has always provided for a wide range of housing quality and hence German households do not need to become homeowners to access the standard of housing that they require. Open-ended tenancies and very strong tenancy security for decades (Kofner, 2014b) has ensured that private renting can provide long-term or even lifetime accommodation for households in Germany. Rent regulation ensures that tenants are not exposed to sharp, short-term increases in rents, even in tight housing markets. Hence, rental housing is regarded as a stable and reliable tenure – almost as secure as owner-occupied housing – even if the security associated with it has been compromised somewhat in recent years by rising rents and housing shortages in some places.

All these factors have helped to maintain demand for private renting relative to homeownership among many moderate and well-off households (Kemp and Kofner, 2010). Only in the 1970s, and between the late 1980s and the turn of the century, has the rate of homeownership moved upward, and even then, only a little. Not surprisingly, the German homeownership rate is subject to significant regional differentiation. The share of tenants is particularly high in large parts of Eastern Germany, in northern North Rhine-Westphalia, and in certain urban areas such as Berlin (where it is 83 per cent).

Widening gap between housing demand and supply since 2005

The market situation on the German housing market has changed significantly since around 2010. Housing completions have increasingly lagged behind net immigration, which has again risen significantly. This has led to increasing market tension in the housing markets, albeit with large spatial differences.

Demand side: ever-growing demographic pressure

When Angela Merkel became chancellor in 2005, German housing markets were not under demographic pressure: the balance of cross-border migration was at a low level, as was fertility. The population had remained virtually unchanged for ten years at just over 82 million people and remained at that level while the population aged. This population development continued until the end of the decade when a fundamental trend reversal occurred. Only household numbers have grown by about half a per cent per year between 2005 and 2010 because of the continuing trend towards ever smaller average household sizes.

The surplus of births over deaths has been negative in Germany since the 1970s, and this has not changed to date. In contrast, immigration has exerted growing demographic pressure on housing markets since 2010, not only globally but especially in the spatial hotspots of housing need. The establishment of full free movement of workers for the Central and Eastern European EU-8 accession countries from May 2011 (and later for Bulgaria, Romania and Croatia); and the government's decision in 2015 not to close Germany's borders in the face of the large influx of refugees, have contributed to this situation.

Between 2010 and 2020, a net cumulative of 4.8 million people immigrated to Germany. This corresponds to an additional housing demand of more than two million dwellings and a housing completion output of around seven years. Subsequently, the total population started to grow significantly again and the annual growth rate of the number of private households also increased significantly.

Supply side: long-run shortfall in housing completions

German housing markets were by no means relaxed across the board when Angela Merkel took office in 2005. There was no momentum in house prices at that time, but the vacancy rate, as measured by the Techem–empirica vacancy index, was only 2.5 per cent in Western Germany and significantly lower in Baden-Württemberg, Bavaria and Hamburg.

However, the powerful and long-term demographic and housing policy narrative of the time was still 'shrinkage and stock orientation'. Housing policy challenges like social housing, housing for the elderly or climate protection were to be met primarily not via new construction, but rather by means of adaptation and modernisation of the existing housing stock. It was assumed that it would be possible to do without a broad-based support for new construction; and hence the two most important housing policy subsidies for owner-occupied and rental housing were abolished on 1 January 2006, which left the housing market to its own devices for the next 12 years.

Not least because of these drastic changes in housing policy, housing completions reached ever new lows. In 2006, 250,000 dwellings were built, followed by a continuous decline to a low of only 160,000 dwellings in 2009 and 2010. It was not until 2012 that the 200,000 level for housing completions was exceeded again. And it was not until 2020 that completions reached 300,000, a total last surpassed in 2001 (Statistisches Bundesamt, 2021). Despite the tightening of demand, housing completions per 1,000 inhabitants were not above the EU average in 2018, at 3.7 units. The Scandinavian countries, as well as France and Poland, had much higher completion rates (Wunsch, 2019). For many years, according to the available housing need forecasts (Pestel-Institut, 2019) not even the purely demographically derived housing demand was met, not to mention the at least equally high additional demand for replacement due to the ageing of the housing stock. Moreover, only 28 per cent of currently completed dwellings (2020) are rental apartments, including only a relatively small number of social housing and other affordable dwellings.

Growing market tension

In view of the population and household figures, which have been rising significantly again since 2010, and the insufficient number of newly completed dwellings, the consequences were not long in coming: rents as well as land and house prices have increased strongly since 2010. Meanwhile, the vacancy rate began to fall further from an already low level. However, housing policy remained largely inactive even in the face of an ever more urgent need for action.

The trends in key housing market tension indicators – vacancies, rents, house prices – can be described as follows. The apartment vacancy rate in Germany peaked in 2006 at 4.1 per cent. Since then, the vacancy rate has fallen continuously and was only 2.8 per cent in 2019 and remained at this level in 2020 (empirica, 2021). This corresponds to around 600,000 vacant multi-storey apartments across Germany. The vacancy rate in growth regions continues to fall, most recently to 1.9 per cent (2019), while it continues to rise significantly in shrinking regions and is now 8.6 per cent. East Germany has significantly higher vacancy rates than West Germany and the lowest reserves of vacant apartments are reported in Southern Germany.

There is a spatial correlation between vacancies and rents because rent increases are easier to implement where housing is scarce. According to the micro census supplementary survey, the average 'net cold rent' (that is, excluding all extra costs) per square metre was €6.90 in 2018. Compared to the year 2010, this represents an increase of €1.47 (equivalent to 27 per cent). In the seven largest metropolitan cities, rents were well above the overall average at €8.90, while in the rural districts they were considerably lower.

Quoted rents increased by 38.6 per cent in the period 2008–2018 from €6.07 to €8.41 (Bundesregierung, 2019). However, only the rents in the group of the 15 district-free cities with more than 500,000 inhabitants have shown above-average increases in the last ten years (BMI, 2021: 24). In Eastern Germany, according to the data of the real estate brokerage portal immowelt, quoted rents are relatively low in general, but with the major exception of the cities of Berlin (€11.40, 104 per cent growth between 2009 and 2019, first-time rent €13.50) and Potsdam and their respective surrounding areas. Otherwise, there are only a few growth poles in the east with above-average rent levels. In Western Germany, Bavaria and Baden-Württemberg have particularly high rent levels, especially in the metropolitan areas around major cities such as Stuttgart and Munich. Other high-price regions are the Rhine and Rhine-Main region and Hamburg.

The average rent burden ratio of private households, as measured by supplementary micro census surveys, has risen by 4 percentage points since 2010 to 27 per cent in 2018 (reference value is gross cold rent, that is, without extra costs for heating). The individual burden depends on place of residence, income and household size. While the seven largest metropolises clearly exceed the average rent burden with 29.5 per cent, the burden ratio in Germany's rural districts is only around 25 per cent (Statistisches Bundesamt, 2019).

Households with a net income of less than €1,700 also have a far above average burden. In the period 1993–2013, the housing cost burden increased significantly solely for the lowest fifth of the income distribution (Dustmann *et al*, 2018). The rent burden also depends very clearly on age with the over-60s being particularly burdened. Households receiving housing allowances (Wohngeld) had a rent burden of 39.0 per cent before, and 27.3 per cent after, receipt of housing allowances in 2019 (Wohngeld- und Mietenbericht, 2020). For single-person households, the comparative figures are 46.4 per cent and 34.2 per cent, respectively.

All in all, high and significantly rising rents and rent burdens are largely a metropolitan phenomenon in Germany, except for a larger area in the south and south-west. Accordingly, the commercial success of private landlords also depends to a large extent on the location of their properties. Only in certain regions have shortages driven rents up significantly.

The development of rents, but also other factors such as ever lower mortgage interest rates, have not left the development of property prices in Germany untouched. Regardless of which house price index is used, they all show the same picture: the turn of the millennium was initially followed by a decade of relatively stable house prices, and it was not until 2011 that a relatively steep upward trajectory began. While prices for owner-occupied housing rose by around 80 per cent between 2010 and 2021, prices for multi-family houses increased even more sharply, by more than 100 per cent (as measured by the VDP capital value index provided by VDP Verband Deutscher Pfandbriefbanken).

This sharp increase in property prices has a very pronounced distribution effect in Germany because of the much lower property ownership rate as compared with other European countries. There are simply far fewer property owners who could benefit from rising house prices. Moreover, real estate wealth is extremely concentrated in Germany. Baldenius, Kohl and Schularick have estimated the inflation-adjusted increase in wealth due to the rise in house prices in the period 2011–2018 at €2.8 or €1.3 trillion, depending on whether one uses the price data from Bulwiengesa or from the Organisation for Economic Co-operation and Development. The distribution of the real capital gains over that period was also lop-sided: of the €2.8 trillion, €1.5 trillion went to the top 10 per cent and another €1.2 trillion to the 50th to 90th percentile (Baldenius *et al*, 2020).

As property prices have risen much faster than residential rents, the net cold rent multipliers (ratio of the price of a real estate investment to its annual rental income before extra costs and expenses) have generally risen sharply recently, especially at the focal points of housing need. Multipliers above 20 are now common in major cities (Munich 2019: 43, Berlin: 31, Frankfurt and Hamburg: 28, Cologne: 24). This means that the returns from the purchase of apartment buildings are now very modest, while landlords who have been invested for a long time benefited from substantial capital gains. The danger of regional real estate bubbles is growing.

Stifling regulatory momentum

The worsening housing shortages in more and more cities have forced politicians to act. Housing subsidies, however, were extended only after a long delay and only for a limited period. The answer to the problem was tighter regulation first and foremost – against a background of an already highly regulated system. Rent regulation has tended to set stricter boundaries on the yields of landlords in recent years than in previous housing cycles. Also, for the first time it included new lettings, with the result that rents do not follow closely market scarcity anymore.

The basis of the German system of rent price formation remains the local reference rent (LRR) – in principle, an average of the rents competing landlords demand for apartments of comparable quality. The LRR is an artificial concept, however, not to be confused with a market rent. There are other factors determining rent levels apart from the LRR. The costs for the modernisation of a dwelling have direct consequences for the maximum permissible rent, but those rent increases are unconnected with the LRR system. What is more, the LRR is the most common, but not the only admissible contractual framework for the determination of future rent increases. There are two more – the index-linked rent and the stepped rent – but they are not so common and must be agreed separately.

In 2013, a hitherto unbroken tide of legislative measures started with the aim of limiting the growth in rents. This fundamentally changed the entire character of the German system of rent price formation. One cannot seriously call it a market-oriented system any longer. Rather, it functions according to its own rules.

Local reference rent: loss of market orientation

The cornerstone of German rental price law is the LRR. The LRR determines the permissible rents in existing leases and – since 2015 – also those for new leases. Thus, the scope of this rent control mechanism has been significantly expanded. The LRR corresponds to the average rent collected in the community for housing of similar quality but is not a purely empirical concept. The quality comparison is limited to certain normative criteria: type of dwelling, location, size, property condition and equipment provided in the apartment. The calculation of the LRR includes rents from new leases as well as rents increased in existing contracts but excludes rents from ongoing rental contracts if not raised (Kofner, 2014b). The LRR is an artificial construct that only partially and imperfectly reflects the empirical conditions, and its market orientation has suffered decisively from recent legislative interventions:

- Since 2013 *lower rent caps* in ongoing contracts are applicable in the hot spots of housing need and the new coalition government plans to reduce them even further.
- Since 2015, a close *linkage of the newly agreed rents to the LRR* (Mietpreisbremse, Rent Brake) was established.
- Since 2020, rents agreed upon or changed *in the last six years* were included in the LRR (only four years before).

Moreover, the adjustment of the rental indices (Mietspiegel) reflecting the LRR to market developments is often delayed. In the past, there were huge local differences in the practical application of the rules for the determination of the LRR. Recently, however, legislation has triggered a clear trend towards standardisation in this field. For municipalities with more than 50,000 inhabitants, a rent index is now obligatory, and a federal legal ordinance has led to the standardisation of the methodology of local rent indices.

The scope of permissible rent increases in ongoing contracts is not only limited by the LRR, but also by an additional rent cap which limits the scope for rent increases over three years to a maximum of 20 per cent even if the relevant LRR would permit a higher rent increase. Rent increases that were legitimately made due to modernisation activities or increased operating costs remain unconsidered whatsoever. The state governments can nominate municipalities with severe housing shortages where the maximum rate is only 15 per cent (11 per cent according to the plans of the new federal government). The rent caps are primarily a problem for the housing industry, when rent controls for social rental apartments expire.

The Rent Brake, which was originally set to expire in 2020, has been extended to 2025 and shall be further extended to 2029 according to the 2021 coalition agreement. Also, it has been made more stringent in terms of claims for recovery in the event of violations. As a result of the introduction of the Rent Brake, the price formation mechanism of the LRR has been severely distorted and the self-referentiality and artificiality of the system has increased substantially.

Rent Brake: severe restraint on returns from private letting

Under the Rent Brake (Mietpreisbremse) which came into force on 1 June 2015, newly agreed rents were also made subject to a substantial limitation for the first time, although certain exceptions apply. Thus, the boundaries of market division have been extended. The brake limits rents for newly signed leases at 10 per cent above the respective LRR in areas with 'tight housing markets' to be determined by the state governments according to certain housing market related and demographic criteria stipulated in the federal civil code.

Ongoing leases are not affected by the new regulation. Rents must not be reduced in ongoing rental agreements, even if they are more than 10 per cent above the LRR. In addition, in case of a lease renewal, the rent level already achieved in the previous lease can be maintained. To avoid a counter-productive impact on investment incentives, additional exemptions from the Rent Brake apply for new rental dwellings and for the first lease agreement after a comprehensive modernisation.

In general, the LRR system is a possible answer to certain forms of market failure in the housing markets. These are the relationship-specific investments of tenants (Knappe and Funk, 1993; Kofner, 1996; SVR, 2013) and the low elasticities of supply and demand in the housing market. A reasonable solution would be such that both rents in existing contracts and newly agreed rents are sufficiently limited to ensure fair burden-sharing between insiders and outsiders. Nevertheless, the medium-term market orientation of the system and its ability to balance supply and demand should be preserved. However, it is doubtful if these requirements are met by the German Rent Brake.

First, the Rent Brake severely disrupts the LRR system. In case of rising market tension, it slows down the growth of re-letting rents – the only dynamic element in the process of adjustment of the LRR – and this results in a lower growth path of the LRR, *ceteris paribus* (Kofner, 2015). With the Rent Brake, the LRR has largely *lost its medium-term market orientation*. This leads to dysfunctional markets that cannot find their way back to equilibrium by themselves. The Rent Brake also affects the *spatial allocation function of rents*: It boosts rather than limits demand at the focal points of housing needs. This is likely to be at the expense of tenant groups with market access problems and also promotes the emergence of black markets (Kholodilin and Ulbricht, 2014).

From the perspective of tenants, the new rules substantially violate the principle of 'equal rent for equal housing quality'. What the individual tenant must pay now also depends very much on the date when the rental contract was agreed, the contractual pre-history of the respective apartment, and its year of construction. These arbitrary differentiations are not linked with objective criteria such as the economic and social situation of the tenants or the quality of the building. From the point of view of private landlords, the Rent Brake means a severe reduction in their rental income. They can no longer achieve significant mark-ups on rent when re-letting. Apart from that, the LRR as a reference for rent increases in current contracts is also developing less dynamically. This makes evasive reactions such as sale, complex modernisation or conversion into condominiums more likely. Finally, we should not forget that regional housing deficits can only be reduced by additional housing completions (SVR, 2013) or a fall in the number of households, and not by regulatory intervention in the formation of market prices.

'Mietendeckel Berlin': regulation taken to extremes

In Berlin, the left-wing Senate attempted to introduce even more drastic price regulations than the federal Rent Brake. Berlin's housing market has undergone significant change. The vacancy rate has fallen steadily and now stands at just 0.8 per cent. Also, rents more than doubled between 2008 and 2018. Against this background, in February 2020 the Senate enacted a somewhat primitive system of maximum rents called Mietendeckel (Rent

Price Cap), affecting both existing and newly agreed rents. However, in April 2021 the Federal Constitutional Court determined that the Berlin state government did not have legislative competence in this field of legislation in the first place, with the result that Berlin's Mietendeckel expired after being in force for over a year (Decision of the Federal Constitutional Court of 25 March 2021). The main provisions of the Mietendeckel were:

- Freezing of rents from the cut-off date of 18 June 2019. From 2022, it was planned to annually increase the stop rents in line with the rate of inflation, but by no more than 1.3 per cent.
- Limitation of newly agreed rents by a system of maximum rents based on the Berlin rent index of 2013. There were differentiations according to year of construction and equipment, but not according to residential location. Modernisation costs could only be apportioned to the extent of €1 per square metre and month (as compared to €3 and €2, respectively, according to the federal civil code BGB (*Bürgerliches Gesetzbuch*/the German civil code).
- Reduction of 'excessive' rents in ongoing contracts to the relevant level according to the Rent Table plus 20 per cent, with surcharges and discounts depending on the residential location (range of €1.02 per square metre).

The impact of the Mietendeckel on Berlin's housing market was differentiated (Kofner, 2021; Dolls *et al*, 2020). As new housing was not affected by the rent cap, it did not result in a slump in new housing permits and completions. The Mietendeckel dampened the development of rents somewhat, although rents for apartments built in 2014 or later increased rapidly because they were exempt from the new state regulations.

Even though older apartments could be rented more cheaply, apartment seekers hardly had a chance to find one anymore. According to Immobilienscout24, the number of rental apartments built before 2014 advertised on their portal fell by 60 per cent within one year. Apartments were converted into condominiums or landlords left them vacant. In addition, Berlin's Mietendeckel resulted in spending cuts on modernisation and refurbishment.

All in all, the Mietendeckel did not fulfil expectations. It produced arbitrary distributional effects and significantly exacerbated the housing shortage. From the point of view of private landlords, it was symbolic of a complete departure from a balancing regulatory approach that also considers the economic interests of landlords.

Reallocation of modernisation costs imminent

The treatment of modernisation costs in terms of related rent increases is regulated outside the LRR system (Gesell and Siegmund, 2019). Landlords can impose incurred modernisation costs on their tenants in yearly portions. The capacity to raise rents in line with modernisation costs is an important element of the incentive system to maintain and improve residential buildings and keep the housing stock in good condition. This is also true for the climate change and the age-appropriate adaptation of the stock.

However, the modernisation allocation may decrease housing affordability for certain tenant groups and accelerate gentrification processes in some places (Schiebe, 2015). This is especially true in tight regional housing markets and that was the reason for the legislator to reduce the apportionment, even though without regional differentiation. With effect from the beginning of 2019, the annually apportionable share of the modernisation costs was reduced from 11 per cent to 8 per cent. Furthermore, limits were introduced on the maximum amount of the apportionment: the monthly rent may not increase by more than €3 per square metre of living space within six years. If the monthly rent before the rent increase is less than €7 per square metre, it may not be increased by more than €2.

In the current capital market, residential modernisation is still a profitable business, especially if the landlord can collect the full 8 per cent modernisation apportionment. The caps, however, severely reduce the investable amount of capital to only €450 or €300 per square metre, respectively. If landlords invest more, they get no return for it in the rent. Thus, the caps will result in a slower rate of modernisation in the housing stock. The trade-offs of the modernisation apportionment have become all too obvious: The more modernisation incentive, the higher the rent increases and vice versa. This trade-off can only be mitigated if the landlord makes use of public subsidies for the modernisation, which reduce the modernisation-related rent increase accordingly.

Remarkably enough, the new Berlin coalition wants to try to solve the financing of climate change protection in the residential building sector within the tenant–landlord relationship. They want to examine 'a rapid changeover to the partial warm rent' (Koalitionsvertrag, 2021; 91) and, if possible, abolish the modernisation apportionment for energy efficiency improvements. The basic idea of this partial warm rent is: on top of the net cold rent, tenants also pay for 'basic heating costs' for their apartment and will be also responsible for the user-dependent share of heating costs, which result from their own heating behaviour. However, these different types of costs are unlikely to be clearly distinguishable from each other. Another problem with this approach is that the tenants would have to pay the largest part of the climate change cost, as they would have little benefit from the fuel costs saved by the landlord's investments. Landlords, not the tenants, should enjoy these benefits so that they have an incentive to invest in them.

On top of that, the new coalition plans to deal with the increased costs due to the progressively rising CO_2 price outside of this partial warm rent system, either by splitting them in half between tenants and landlords or in the form of a 'graduated model according to building energy classes'.

Conversion of rental apartments into condominiums even more difficult

Conversion to condominium ownership is a kind of safety valve for landlords when rent law excessively restricts their ability to charge competitive rents on their properties. Hence, it is not surprising that measures have been introduced to restrict conversions to condominiums.

In the case of conversion to condominium ownership, additional protection against eviction applies in the form of a three-year lock-in period. The prerequisite is that the condominium ownership was established after the letting of the apartment and then sold. State governments may extend the lock-in period up to ten years by statutory order.

Apart from this, conversion can be made subject to approval by means of preservation statutes. Furthermore, since June 2021, a general approval requirement for conversions is also in effect for housing markets with excess demand. Exceptions apply, among other things, to buildings with no more than five flats, in cases of inheritance, or if the apartments are largely sold to the tenants.

Taxation and subsidisation of rental housing facing fundamental realignment

Since 2006, neither rental housing nor homeownership had been noticeably promoted by the government. The abolition of the declining balance depreciation scheme for newly built rental housing and of the homeownership grant (*Eigenheimzulage*) enacted back then were a government initiative to improve the budget situation, but without taking into account housing market-related considerations and enforced against heavy resistance of the affected lobby groups (Woebken-Ekert, 2005). It was only in 2018 that efforts were once again made to boost housing construction via subsidies.

Resumption of broad-scale housing subsidisation with tried-and-tested instruments (2018–2021)

For a long period, the federal government responded to the demographically induced upsurge in housing demand observed since around 2010 by introducing rent price legislation, but not by subsidy policy. In the owner-occupied sector, mortgage interest is not deductible because for tax purposes the home is regarded as a consumption good. Hence, no taxation of imputed rent and no deductions of any sort are applied. There is also no taxation of capital gains.

The federal government announced its 'housing offensive' in its 2018 coalition agreement, which, in addition to more rent control legislation, a quantitative completion target and additional funds for social housing construction, also included two large, but time-limited subsidies again, one for homeownership and the other for new rental housing construction (Koalitionsvertrag, 2018).

Just under €10 billion was made available for the *Baukindergeld* subsidy of €12,000 per existing child of the builder or buyer of a new or an existing house for owner-occupancy (Merkblatt Baukindergeld der KfW, 2021). The grant was introduced retrospectively from 1 January 2018 and was available until the end of March 2021. This did not make a significant contribution to combating the urban housing shortage, nor – because of its short duration – to the growth of homeownership in Germany.

The not exactly new instrument for promoting rental housing construction was special depreciation allowances. It complemented the existing German tax system for private landlords, whose main features are:

- Capital gains taxation privilege encouraging long-term investment in rental property: capital gains from the private sale of residential buildings held for more than ten years are usually tax-free.
- Depreciation allowances (linear) at 2 per cent – or 2.5 per cent for older buildings – broadly in line with economic depreciation.
- Higher depreciation scheme as an incentive to invest in buildings under historic monument protection and buildings located in statutory redevelopment or preservation areas (according to German income tax law 9 per cent per year in the first eight years after purchase).
- Mortgage interest tax relief.
- Immediate deduction of repair expenses from rent income.
- Negative gearing: landlords may offset losses from rental property against their other sources of taxable income.

Between 2018 and 2021 this tax regime, which could be considered tenure neutral, was again supplemented by special depreciation allowances for the creation of new housing. These were primarily aimed at small private investors, as the law contained a cap of €200,000 on the *de minimis* subsidies attributable to an investor over a three-year period. Up to 5 per cent of the acquisition or production costs (excluding land, subject to cost limits) could be claimed annually during the first four years in addition to the regular linear depreciation at 2 per cent per year. Thus, within the first four years, a total of up to 28 per cent of the costs could be considered as depreciation for tax purposes.

The fiscal incidence of such special depreciation allowances is problematic, as the instrument also encounters high demand markets in many places where housing supply is not very elastic, also due to the lack of building land and spare capacity in the construction industry. Under such market conditions, extra depreciation allowances may also lead to rising land prices because of the presumably lower elasticity of land supply.

Compared with other countries, the German housing subsidy system has always assured tenure neutrality by and large. The subsidy floodgates were sometimes closed and sometimes opened again, but always in parallel for both tenures. Whether this will continue in the future is not entirely clear.

A new start in housing subsidies since 2022

Since the two most important housing subsidies expired in 2021, the new federal coalition government has great scope for redesigning the funding landscape. Indeed, it wants to break new ground with housing subsidy instruments. According to the 2021 coalition agreement, the promotion of homeownership is to be more accurately targeted with allowances for land transfer tax and a sharper focus of the subsidies on threshold and lower-income households with a particular emphasis on their loan financing.

A fundamental change of course is intended in rental housing subsidisation. The focus is to be on social housing construction and public interest housing (*Wohnungsgemeinnützigkeit*) which was abolished in 1990. Limited-profit housing is to be reintroduced in a new form in Germany. Housing subsidies are to be concentrated on this new kind of housing organisations, which shall use them to create affordable housing with a permanent social commitment.

With this fundamental reorientation, privately financed housing construction will become less important in the German housing system. To the extent that these plans work out, private landlords will face more competition from cheap, subsidised housing. However, they can try to build social housing themselves. This will probably be necessary because the capacities of municipal and cooperative housing companies are limited. However, small amateur landlords are often likely to be overwhelmed by the complex bureaucracy involved in social housing.

The COVID-19 pandemic

For two years, the COVID-19 pandemic kept Germany on tenterhooks. However, the impact on the rental housing market has been limited so far.

A moratorium on rent payments and consumer loans was in place in Germany for the months of April to June 2020. If tenants had not paid their rent during this period due to COVID-19, this had no consequences for the landlord's right to terminate the lease. However, corresponding rent debts had to be paid back by 30 June 2022 at the latest. The instalments for mortgage loans must also be paid again, whereby the total repayment period is shifted back by three months.

Whether and how the COVID-19 crisis will affect the private rental sector is difficult to answer at present. It is not yet clear to what extent population settlement and migration patterns will be affected by the pandemic in the long run. What can be observed is that a great deal is currently being invested in modernising and equipping owner-occupied properties. There has been no reversal of the trend in rents and property prices. At best, there are signs of a slowdown in rent increases in the country's metropolises.

Conclusion

Private renting is still the most important housing tenure for households in Germany. However, the operating environment of the private rental sector has been subject to profound changes in recent years. Triggered by housing shortages in more and more cities and regions, the regulatory screws have been tightened noticeably, albeit with regional differentiation. The rents for new leases are now subject to significant restrictions. The city state of Berlin even tried to introduce a primitive form of administered rents but was stopped from doing so by the Constitutional Court. Nevertheless, with these important changes, the market orientation of the German LRR system has been largely lost and, according to the 2021 coalition agreement, the situation will not change in this legislative period.

It is striking that the tone of the public discourse on housing has changed for the worse in recent years. There are also increasing calls for the expropriation of larger private housing companies. In Berlin, a referendum on the matter was successful. There is no longer a consensus on the regulatory framework of the rental housing market. The positions have hardened and the relationship between the interest groups on both sides has developed for the worse.

Confidence in the ability of free housing markets to solve supply problems has clearly declined. For private landlords, this means that on the one hand they have opportunities for windfall gains and rising rents, but on the other hand they are increasingly deprived of these opportunities by regulatory intervention in a political climate that is becoming more and more hostile to them.

The decisive event for the further development was the federal election in September 2021. It marks a crossroads: the new government wants to proceed with more intervention, much more social housing and a new kind of housing organisation serving the public interest as central players on the supply side, which the Green Party, among others, has long advocated. This last aspect will require a lot of groundwork and will only take effect after a long delay.

The ideas of the new coalition government on how to share the burden of climate change protection in the building sector are still unclear. A balance must be found here between technical requirements and subsidies. There is a tendency towards fundamental and complex solutions that may come too late to address the pressing problems in time.

The signs do not necessarily point to an increase in the importance of the PRS. From a long-term perspective we have learned in the 16 Merkel years that more preventive action is needed in view of the slow speed of adjustment of housing markets. Housing policy must provide for the necessary incentives and resources for new residential construction (land, building capacity) in a timely and regionally targeted manner.

References

Arnott, R. (1995) 'Time for revisionism on rent control?', *Journal of Economic Perspectives*, 9(1), 99–120.

Arnott, R. (2003) 'Tenancy rent control', *Swedish Economic Policy Review*, 10(1), 89–121.

Baldenius, T., Kohl, S. and Schularick, M. (2020) 'Die neue Wohnungsfrage: Gewinner und Verlierer des deutschen Immobilienbooms' (The new housing question: winners and losers of the German real estate boom), *Leviathan*, 48(2), 195–236.

Beck, I., Brendl, C. and Kinefss, G. (2020) *Vergesellschaftung von Wohnungskonzernen in Deutschland? Eine (kritische) Betrachtung an der Schnittstelle von Grund- und Menschenrechten* (Nationalisation of housing corporations in Germany? A (critical) consideration at the interface of fundamental and human rights), Freiburger Informationspapiere zum Völkerrecht und Öffentlichen Recht, Issue 4/2020.

BBSR (Bundesinstitut für Bau-, Stadt- und Raumforschung) (Federal Institute for Research on Building, Urban Affairs and Spatial Development) (2015) *Privateigentümer von Mietwohnungen in Mehrfamilienhäusern* (Private Owners of Multi-Family Rental Housing, BBSR Online Publication, February, https://www.bbsr.bund.de/BBSR/DE/veroeffentlichungen/bbsr-online/2015/ON022015.html

BBSR (Bundesinstitut für Bau-, Stadt- und Raumforschung) (2017) *Börsennotierte Wohnungsunternehmen als neue Akteure auf dem Wohnungsmarkt – Börsengänge und ihre Auswirkungen* (Listed housing companies as new players on the housing market – IPOs and their impact), BBSR Online Publication 01/2017, https://www.bbsr.bund.de/BBSR/DE/veroeffentlichungen/bbsr-online/2017/bbsr-online-01-2017.html

BMI (Bundesministerium des Innern, für Bau und Heimat) (2021) *Faktenblätter zum deutschen Wohnungsmarkt 2021* (Factsheets on the German Housing Market 2021, as of February 2021).

Bundesregierung (2019) Antwort der Bundesregierung auf die Kleine Anfrage der Fraktion DIE LINKE (Answer of the Federal Government to the Small Parliamentary Enquiry of the parliamentary group DIE LINKE), Parliamentary printed matter 19/12786, 18 August.

CBRE-empirica-Leerstandsindex 2021, empirica (2021) *Marktaktive Leerstandsquote auf dem deutschen Wohnungsmarkt im Jahr 2020 nach Bundesländern* (Market active vacancy rate in the German housing market in 2020 by federal state), Statista GmbH, https://de.statista.com/statistik/daten/studie/258755/umfrage/marktaktive-leerstandsquote-von-wohnungen-nach-bundeslaendern/

Department of Environment (1977) *Housing Policy: Technical Volume*, London, HMSO.

Dolls, M., Fuest, C., Krolage, C., Neumeier, F. and Stöhlker, D. (2020) 'Ökonomische Effekte des Berliner Mietendeckels' (Economic effects of the Berlin rent ceiling), *ifo Schnelldienst*, 73(3).

Dustmann, C., Fitzenberger, B. and Zimmermann, M. (2018) *Housing Expenditures and Income Inequality*, ZEW Discussion Paper No. 18–048, Mannheim.

GDV (Gesamtverband der Deutschen Versicherungswirtschaft) (Statistical Pocketbook of the Insurance Industry) (2020) *Statistisches Taschenbuch der Versicherungswirtschaft 2020* (Statistical Pocketbook of the Insurance Industry 2020), Berlin: German Insurance Association.

Gesell, B. and Siegmund, A. (2019) 'Mietrecht in Zeiten des Wohnungsmangels: Modernisierungsmieterhöhung und Abwehrrechte des Mieters' (Tenancy law in times of housing shortage: modernisation rent increase and tenant's rights of defence), *NZM – Neue Zeitschrift für Miet- und Wohnungsrecht*, 489–506.

Gesetz zur Mietenbegrenzung im Wohnungswesen in Berlin (MietenWoG Bln) (2020) February Fundstelle, GVBl. 2020 (50), Gliederungs-Nr: 233–14. Law.

Howenstine, J. (1981) 'Private rental housing abroad: dwindling supply stirs concern', *Monthly Labor Review*, 104(9), 38–42.

Huber, S.J. and Schmidt, T. (2019) 'Cross-country differences in homeownership: a cultural phenomenon?', Deutsche Bundesbank Discussion Paper, No. 40/2019.

ImmoScout24 (2020) 'Mietendeckel-Analyse von ImmoScout24: Kaum Entlastung auf dem Berliner Wohnungsmarkt & Im Gegenteil: Das Wohnungsangebot sinkt kontinuierlich und der Nachfragedruck nimmt zu' (Rent cap analysis by ImmoScout24: Hardly any relief on the Berlin housing market and on the contrary: The supply of housing is continuously decreasing and the pressure of demand is increasing), 19 October 2020, Press release, https://www.presseportal.de/pm/31321/4737434

Jensen, I. (2020) 'Wohnraum als soziale Infrastruktur: Ansätze zur (Re-) Kommunalisierung von Wohnraum betrachtet am Beispiel Berlin' (Housing as social infrastructure: approaches to the (Re-)Municipalisation of housing taking the example of Berlin), in B. Schönig and L. Vollmer (eds) *Wohnungsfragen ohne Ende?! Ressourcen für eine soziale Wohnraumversorgung* (Housing issues without end?! Resources for social housing provision), Bielefeld, transcript, pp 147–162.

Kemp, P.A. and Kofner, S. (2010) 'Contrasting varieties of private renting: England and Germany', *International Journal of Housing Policy*, 10(4), 379–398.

Kholodilin, K.A. and Ulbricht, D. (2014) 'Mietpreisbremse: Wohnungsmarktregulierung bringt mehr Schaden als Nutzen' (Rent price cap: housing market regulation does more harm than good), *DIW Wochenbericht*, 81(15), 319–327.

Knappe, E. and Funk, L. (1993) 'Marktlösung oder Staatseingriffe?' ('Market solution or state intervention?), in *Landeszentrale für politische Bildung Baden-Württemberg: Wohnungsbaupolitik* (State Agency for Civic Education Baden-Württemberg: housing policy), Stuttgart, Kohlhammer, pp 53–74.

Koalitionsvertrag zwischen CDU, CSU und SPD, 19. Legis-laturperiode (Coalition agreement between CDU, CSU and SPD, 19th legislative period) (2018) Ein neuer Aufbruch für Europa, eine neue Dynamik für Deutschland, ein neuer Zusammenhalt für unser Land (A new departure for Europe, a new dynamic for Germany, a new cohesion for our country), Berlin, 12 March, coalition treaty, https://www.bundesregierung.de/breg-de/themen/koalitionsvertrag-zwischen-cdu-csu-und-spd-195906

Koalitionsvertrag zwischen SPD, Bündnis 90/Die Grünen und FDP, 20. Legislaturperiode (Coalition agreement between SPD, Bündnis 90/ Die Grünen and FDP, 20th legislative period) (2021) Mehr Fortschritt wagen: Bündnis für Freiheit, Gerechtigkeit und Nachhaltigkeit (Daring more progress: alliance for freedom, justice and sustainability), Berlin, 24 November, coalition treaty, https://www.bundesregierung.de/breg-de/service/gesetzesvorhaben/koalitionsvertrag-2021-1990800

Kofner, S. (1996) 'Vergleichsmietensystem und Kündigungsrecht: Reform der Regulierungen des Wohnungsmarktes?' (Local reference rent system and termination law: reforming housing market regulations?), *Zeitschrift für Wirtschaftspolitik* (Journal of Economic Policy), 3(45), 397–424.

Kofner, S. (2007) 'Wohnimmobilien als Investitionsobjekte der deutschen REITs' (Residential real estate as investment object of German REITs), *Wohnungswirtschaft und Mietrecht*, 60, 183–185.

Kofner, S. (2014a) 'The German housing system: fundamentally resilient?', *Journal of Housing and the Built Environment*, 29(2), 255–275.

Kofner, S. (2014b) *The Private Rental Sector in Germany*, OECD Consultancy Report, CreateSpace Independent Publishing Platform, https://amzn.to/3nvJ3Oq

Kofner, S. (2015) 'The new German rent price cap and its impact on rent price formation and investment incentives', paper presented at the ENHR Conference Lissabon, 12 June.

Kofner, S. (2021) 'Ein Jahr Berliner Mietendeckel: Die Illusion bleibt' (One Year of the Berlin Rent Cap: The Illusion Remains), *Junge Freiheit*, 21 February.

Merkblatt Baukindergeld der KfW (2021) *KfW Bank*, 22 January, https://www.kfw.de/inlandsfoerderung/Privatpersonen/Neubau/F%C3%B6rderprodukte/Baukindergeld-(424)/

Pestel-Institut (2019) 'Wohnungsbedarf, Wohnungsbauziel der Bundesregierung, Wohnungsneubaunachfrage und Wirtschaftlichkeit des Wohnungsneubaus' (Housing demand, housing construction target of the Federal Government, demand for new housing and economic viability of new housing construction), Study, various associations of the German construction and real estate industry, https://www.baustoffindustrie.de/fileadmin/user_upload/bbs/Dateien/Downloadarchiv/Wohnungsbau/Pestel-Kurzstudie__Wohnungsbedarf__Wohnungsbauziel_der_Bundesregierung__Wohnungsneubaunachfrage_und_Wirtschaftlichkeit_des_Wohnungsneubaus__.pdf

Sachverständigenrat für die Begutachtung der gesamtwirtschaftlichen Entwicklung (SVR) (German Council of Economic Experts) (2013) 'Gegen eine rückwärtsgewandte Wirtschaftspolitik' (Against a backward-looking economic policy), Annual Report, 13 November 2013.

Schiebe, C. (2015) 'The displacement of tenants by energy-related modernization in Berlin', Berlin, Humboldt-Universität zu Berlin.

Scope Analysis (2019) *Offene Immobilienfonds: Marktstudie und Ratings 2019* (Open-ended real estate funds: market study and ratings 2019), Frankfurt, Scope Analysis GmbH Berlin.

Statistische Ämter des Bundes und der Länder (Statistical Offices of the Federal and State governments) (2019) *Wohnen in Deutschland: Zusatzprogramm des Mikrozensus 2018* (Housing in Germany: Supplementary programme of the Microcensus 2018), https://www.destatis.de/DE/Themen/Gesellschaft-Umwelt/Wohnen/_inhalt.html;jsessionid=F3C47234F85D6D232233A329A881A803.live722#sprg229134

Statistisches Bundesamt (Federal Statistical Office) (2000) *50 Jahre Wohnen in Deutschland* (50 years of housing in Germany), Stuttgart, Metzler-Poeschel.

Statistisches Bundesamt (2019) Wohnen 2018: Mieten und Mietbelastung in Metropolen besonders hoch' (Housing 2018: Rents and rent burden particularly high in metropolitan areas), Press Release No. N 001, 1 October 2019.

Statistisches Bundesamt (2021) 'Bauen und Wohnen: Baufertigstellungen von Wohn- und Nichtwohngebäuden u.a. nach Bauherren' (Building and housing: Construction completions of residential and non-residential buildings, among others, by builder), Lange Reihen z.T. ab 1980, *Federal Statistical Bureau*, data series.

TRAWOS (Institut für Transformation, Wohnen und Soziale Raumentwicklung) (Institute for Transformation, Housing and Social Spatial Development) (2012) *Aktuelle Geschäftsmodelle von Finanzinvestoren im Themenfeld Wohnungswirtschaftlicher Wandel und neue Finanzinvestoren* (Current business models of financial investors in the thematic field of housing industry change and new financial investors), Report, Enquête Commission on Housing Industry Change and New Financial Investors on the Housing Markets in NRW, Görlitz, Hochschule Zittau/Görlitz.

Voigtländer, M. (2006) 'Mietwohnungsmarkt und Wohneigentum: Zwei Seiten einer Medaille' (Rental Housing Market and Home Ownership: Two Sides of the Same Coin), Gutachten für den Verband deutscher Pfandbriefbanken (Expert report for the Association of German Pfandbrief Banks).

Voigtländer, M. and Hude, M. (2017) 'Trends in der Wohneigentumsbildung' (Trends in home ownership), Expert Report for the Schwäbisch Hall Foundation bauen-leben-wohnen.

Woebken-Ekert (2005) 'Bausparen: Die letzte Bastion' (Savings and Loans: The Last Bastion), *Die Zeit*, 25 August.

Wohngeld- und Mietenbericht (Housing allowances and Rent Report) (2020) Bundesministerium des Innern, für Bau und Heimat 2021 (Federal Ministry of the Interior, for Building and Home Affairs 2021), Government report, https://www.bmi.bund.de/SharedDocs/downloads/DE/veroeffe ntlichungen/2021/06/bericht-bauwirtschaft.pdf;jsessionid=F6BCC3468 6058F37515AEB3BB4729CC9.1_cid295?__blob=publicationFile&v=1

Wunsch, S. (2019) *Europavergleich: Deutschland nur Mittelmaß beim Wohnungsbau* (European comparison: Germany only mediocre in housing construction), GEWOS Institute for Urban, Regional and Housing Research, https:// gewos.de/2019/02/07/europavergleich-deutschland-nur-mittelmass-beim-wohnungsbau/

Zensus (2011) Bevölkerungs- und Wohnungszählung 2011 (Population and Housing Census 2011), Statistisches Bundesamt, Wiesbaden, https://www.zensus2011.de/SharedDocs/Downloads/DE/Publikationen/Aufsaetze_Archiv/2016_12_NRW_Zensus_Vielfalt.pdf?__blob=publicationFile&v=2

8

Private renting in Denmark: foreign investors in the crosshairs

Kath Scanlon

Introduction

Internationally, Denmark is admired by housing experts for its pioneering approach to co-housing, for the tenant democracy of its social housing estates, and for the clean lines of its modern residential architecture. Its private rented sector (PRS) is discussed mainly, if at all, in terms of the complexity of the rent-control system. Arguably, though, the PRS is now the most interesting of Danish housing tenures, as in recent years the sector has become a political battleground. Politicians have adopted measures to try to deter certain overseas investors whose activities, they say, have pushed up private rents in cities. Similar debates are taking place in other countries and the Danish experience may offer some lessons, though similar forces can have very different effects in different places. As always with housing, context is all.

The basics: tenures, dwellings, landlords and tenants

Tenure split and dwelling types

Denmark's PRS declined steadily in size over the last half of the 20th century. The proportion of privately rented dwellings more than halved in 50 years, from 39.8 per cent in 1960 to 14 per cent in 2010 (Table 8.1). As late as 2014, a leading authority wrote that: 'Like most other countries in Europe, the Danish PRS has been in decline for many years (and) … it must be expected that the sector will be further diminished in the years to come' (Skifter Andersen, 2014: 99, 124). In the last ten years, however, this decline has reversed and the PRS began to grow in country as a whole and in the capital. In Copenhagen the sector now accounts for 23 per cent of occupied dwellings, up from 19 per cent in 2010.

Dwellings

Most Danish PRS housing is purpose-built and tenure-specific and tends to be older than the dwelling stock as a whole. About a third of PRS

Table 8.1: Inhabited dwellings by tenure, Denmark and Copenhagen, 2010 and 2020

	Denmark		Copenhagen	
	2010	**2020**	**2010**	**2020**
Private rent	14%	19%	19%	23%
Owner-occupation (including co-ops)	58%	56%	51%	50%
Social rent	22%	22%	21%	20%
Other/unknown	3%	2%	7%	6%

Source: Author's calculations based on Statistics Denmark housing table builder (nd).

Figure 8.1: Dwellings by year of construction: private rental sector and overall dwelling stock, 2020

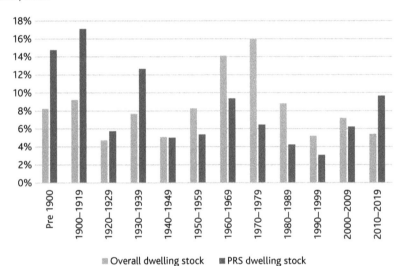

Source: Author's calculations based on Statistics Denmark housing table builder (nd).

homes were built before 1920 (Figure 8.1) compared with one in six of all homes.

Under Danish law, different regulations apply to various physical types of buildings, so it is meaningful to subdivide the PRS into dwelling types. Danish experts consider the true PRS to consist of dwellings in rental-only buildings with three or more units; that is, multi-family blocks. These make up about two-thirds of the overall PRS stock and more than three-quarters of the homes owned by company landlords (Table 8.2). Multi-unit properties have historically been affected by both rent-control regulations and restrictions on division of ownership, which de facto means that it is not possible to change the tenure of many private rental dwellings.

Table 8.2: Dwelling types: private rental sector as a whole and dwellings owned by companies, 2020

	% of all PRS stock	% owned by company landlords
Detached house/farmhouse	21	8
Semi-detached or terraced house	11	12
Dwellings in blocks of flats	66	77
Student accommodation	1	2
Other	1	1

Source: Author's calculations based on Statistics Denmark housing table builder (nd).

New construction of private rental dwellings ceased in the 1970s but started again in the 1980s, mostly funded by institutional investors. This resumption was partly to do with developments in the *social* rented sector, which is of generally high quality and preferred to the PRS. Rules for construction of new social housing imposed a maximum cost per square metre, which meant it was impossible to build high-quality new social homes in the best locations, especially in the Copenhagen area (Christoffersen, 2010; Liliegreen, 2020). This left a gap in the market for high-quality rental units. New PRS construction continued to increase in the first two decades of the millennium (Figure 8.1). These newer homes are more likely to be in the hands of company owners, who own 51 per cent of PRS dwellings overall, but 78 per cent of those built since 1990 and 64 per cent of PRS dwellings in Copenhagen.

In Denmark, the tenure of buildings is generally fixed and can only be altered with difficulty – according to Christoffersen (2010: 29), 'when a house is originally established in a given tenure, there are important restrictions and barriers regarding later change of tenure'. Multi-family rental buildings cannot generally be sold as individual units to owner-occupiers. This has been a matter of political contention, and there have been periods when restructuring ownership to allow sale of individual flats was permitted as part of urban regeneration programmes or to encourage owner-occupation or the formation of cooperatives (functionally also a type of owner-occupation). The current position is that some rental buildings – listed buildings or those built since 1999 – can be broken up and sold as owner-occupied flats. In addition, any rental building with more than six units can be sold at market price to tenants if they create a cooperative, although the tenants only have right of first refusal and cannot force a sale (that is, there is no 'right to buy'). In the late 1990s these buildings could be bought cheaply and came with significant tax breaks and resulted in many conversions to cooperatives (Ball, 2001). It is generally prohibited to demolish private rented housing.

After 2007 there was an influx to the sector of newly constructed flats that were originally destined for owner-occupation; when the post-global financial crisis (GFC) decline in the housing market made them impossible to sell they were changed to private rental. Similarly, new high-density developments built for sale during the COVID-19 pandemic have instead been turned into rental schemes, at least initially.

In recent years there has been an upsurge in construction of private student housing in Copenhagen and other major university cities, driven by the shortage of small affordable rental units in the wider market. One such project, built using shipping containers on reclaimed land in Copenhagen harbour, was initially ten times oversubscribed even though rents were relatively expensive (Liliegreen, 2020).

Landlords

In tandem with the increase in sector size, there has been a notable shift in the composition of landlords. In 2010 most privately rented homes were owned by private individuals or couples, but by 2020 the majority were in company ownership, as corporate owners both bought existing bocks and built new ones. Companies now own almost two-thirds of PRS dwellings in the capital, and 51 per cent in the country as a whole (Table 8.3). There are no Real Estate Investment Trusts in Denmark.

Residential buildings are the largest single category of commercial real estate investment in Copenhagen, according to market analysts. From 2003 to 2007 there was an annual tax-incentive programme for institutional investors in the PRS, as well as a subsidy to private developers to build dedicated student accommodation. In 2016, the residential sector accounted for 41 per cent of investment transactions, versus 28 per cent for offices, 13 per cent for retail and 18 per cent other (Sadolin and Albæk, 2017).

Even though institutional investors have been significant in the Danish market for decades, corporate landlordism – and specifically the involvement of overseas investors – has become a contentious political issue in the last few years (see Box 8.1). Danish pension funds are major investors in residential buildings, owning about 10–15 per cent of PRS properties (Copenhagen Economics, 2019), and individuals with defined-contribution pensions can choose what proportion of their own funds to allocate to real estate.

Table 8.3: Private rental sector landlord types, Denmark and Copenhagen, 2010 and 2020

	Denmark		Copenhagen	
	2010	2020	2010	2020
Private individuals	60%	49%	52%	36%
Companies	40%	51%	48%	64%

Source: Author's calculations based on Statistics Denmark housing table builder (nd).

Box 8.1: The Blackstone intervention (*Blackstone indgrebet*)

Since 1996, landlords have been able to move a property from cost-based rents to the higher *lejedes værdi* rents by carrying out a 'thorough renovation' that includes improvements in energy efficiency. The likely effects of the provision have long been recognised: Skifter Andersen said in 2014 that 'this loophole, in the course of time, will diminish the effect of strong rent control. In particular, professional landlords in the cities will use this possibility to systematically transfer dwellings to a higher quality level and obtain higher rents' (2014: 99). Such renovations have led to rent increases of as much as 100 per cent in Copenhagen (Liliegreen, 2020).

When the current national government in Denmark took office in 2019, the coalition agreement included a promise to take action to stop short-term speculation by investors in the rental market, especially in Copenhagen. The policy has been spearheaded by housing minister Kaare Dybvad Bek of the Social Democratic Party, who said, 'We should put our foot down and say clearly that we in Denmark decide how our capital city should develop. That is not a decision we leave to foreign investment funds' (quoted in Kastberg, 2020). Kaare Dybvad said he was inspired in part by the film *Push*, about the campaign against Blackstone by former UN Special Rapporteur for Housing Leilani Farha, which premiered in the Danish capital.

The new legislation is known colloquially as the 'Blackstone intervention', and is targeted at the US-based investment firm whose activities in Denmark have been blamed for rent increases in big cities. Blackstone first entered the Danish market in 2014 and now owns about 2,300 homes, mostly in Copenhagen, through its subsidiary Kereby. Farha is one high-profile critic: she wrote that in Denmark Blackstone buys buildings housing poor and low-income tenants, 'undertakes repairs or refurbishment, and then increases the rents—often exorbitantly—driving existing tenants out, and replacing them with higher income tenants' (Deva and Farha, 2019: 5).

After parliamentary debate in early 2020, new laws came into effect in July 2020 that significantly tighten the requirements for rent-increasing renovations. Under the new laws:

• the energy-efficiency requirements are higher;
• improvements must be certified by municipal authorities;
• landlords are forbidden from offering tenants a payment to move out to enable renovation (formerly a common practice);
• courts or the rent board must give more weight to the rents of comparable flats when deciding how much rent is allowable after renovations;
• landlords who buy rental properties with cost-based rents cannot raise rents to *det lejedes værdi* for the first five years after the transaction, and then only for new tenants.

Taken together, the measures make it harder and more expensive for landlords (all landlords, not just big investors) to raise rents. The goal, Kaare Dybvad has said, is to enable key workers such as bus drivers and kindergarten teachers to live near their work in costly cities like Copenhagen.

Unsurprisingly, the Danish tenants' organisation says the new measures are a victory for tenants, while the Danish Property Federation has called them a disaster. Recent analysis by Cushman and Wakefield, reported in the Danish financial newspaper *Børsen*, says 'international investors have disappeared completely' from the Danish property market since the laws were passed, and that investors including Danish pension funds are now looking to Sweden and Norway (Thomasen, 2021).

The volume of institutional investment has grown significantly in the last decade. In 2017, foreign investors accounted for 76 per cent of residential real estate transactions by value, up from 21 per cent in 2012 (Skifter Andersen, 2019, citing Cushman and Wakefield data). Although Blackstone is the best-known overseas firm, it is not the largest investor: the Swedish company Heimstaden has invested far more in Danish residential property. While the political spotlight has been on overseas investors, there are several major Danish property companies, including NREP (Nordic Real Estate Partners) and the unlisted DADES (Det Almindelige Danske Ejendomsselskab [The ordinary Danish real estate company]), which own residential buildings as well as commercial and retail properties.

Since 2002, to attract investment into the private rental market, the profits of pension funds and insurance companies from investments in the PRS have been taxed at 15.3 per cent rather than the normal corporate rate of 30 per cent. Parents of university students are also tax-favoured landlords, according to the Organisation for Economic co-operation and Development (OECD), which said 'current regulation allows parents to set below-market rents and receive tax allowances for the deficit' (OECD, 2019: 30). At the instigation of Radikale Venstre, one of the major political parties, legislation has recently been introduced to eliminate the tax allowances (Liliegreen, 2020). The OECD also criticised the fact that children living in flats owned by their parents are allowed to claim housing benefit for low-income tenants.

Tenants

The PRS is generally not a tenure of choice. There is a strong cultural preference for owner-occupation in Denmark; indeed, the ratio of mortgage debt to gross domestic product is among the highest in the world. Those who cannot afford owner-occupation would generally prefer to live in the

Figure 8.2: Age distribution of residents of private rental sector and owner-occupied homes, 2020

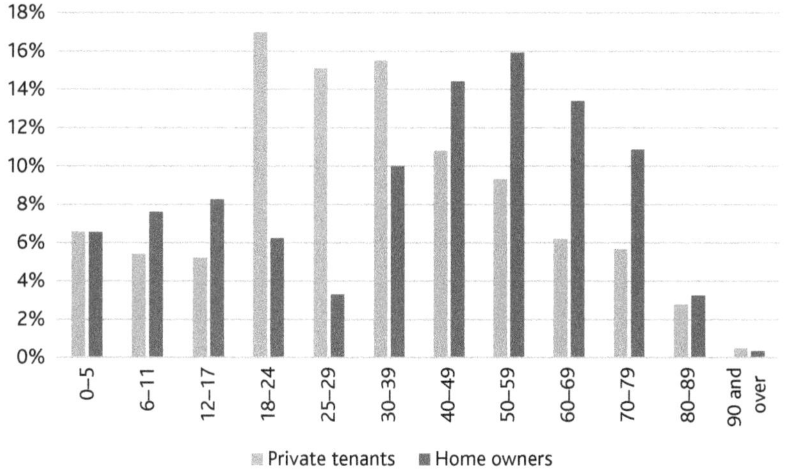

Private tenants ■ Home owners

Source: Author's calculations based on Statistics Denmark housing table builder (nd).

social rented sector, which is mostly in good condition, non-stigmatised and accommodates a wide range of households.

Households in private renting are more likely to be young: about half of those living in privately rented homes are between the ages of 18 and 39, while from age 40 onwards more individuals live in owner-occupied homes (Figure 8.2). Since 2010, this pattern has become more marked: the proportion of younger private tenants has risen, and that of older households has fallen. Private tenants are more often single and in receipt of housing benefit. Except for a small minority of wealthy tenants, they generally have lower incomes than owner-occupiers and residents of cooperatives. The typical private renting household had an income 30 per cent below the Danish average in 2000. And in 2010, private tenants' average disposable income was DKK 165,000, compared with DKK 280,000 for private landlords (The Danish Economic Council, 2001; Kristensen, 2012). Tenants are also more likely to be out of work and less likely to own their own businesses. Ethnic minorities are much more likely to live in social housing than in private rental, in part because municipalities until recently had a legal obligation to provide permanent accommodation for all refugees (Liliegreen, 2020).

The young tend to live for relatively short periods in private rental (as little as 1.2 years for young couples under the age of 30) while those over 60 live on average for 19 years in the tenure (Skifter Andersen, 2010: table 11.4). Students are over-represented in the sector, especially in the bigger cities with universities.

Especially in the capital, the rental market is tight, and a public viewing for an available unit can attract up to 50 potential tenants. It is not uncommon for landlords to ask for three months' rent in advance plus a deposit of equal size, which is difficult on ordinary incomes. There are local–authority schemes to lend money for deposits, but if the landlord is a private individual, they often refuse for fear of contributing to 'speculation'.

Tenure security and rent control

In general, rules about tenancies, rents and dwellings in the private rented sector apply across the whole country. Within this national framework, local authorities can apply policies that reflect local circumstances.

The private tenancy

In Denmark, the bundle of rights acquired by the private tenant includes rights only afforded to owners in, for example, the Anglo-Saxon countries. Private tenants generally have the right to occupy a dwelling indefinitely and landlords may evict only for certain reasons specified in law. The acceptable reasons are few and include rent arrears, serious misconduct or requiring the dwelling for the landlord's own use, though not for the use of an adult child or another relative (Norberg and Juul-Sandberg, 2018). Tenants can also be evicted if the building is to be demolished or renovated (in which case the landlord must find the tenant a new home), if the dwelling belongs to an employer where the tenant no longer works, or if the tenant has engaged in serious misbehaviour.

Landlords are permitted to use time-limited contracts only in certain circumstances, such as temporary relocation abroad or plans to sell the dwelling (Norberg and Juul-Sandberg, 2018). Tenants can sublet their homes for up to two years in case of need, such as illness or temporary transfer for work reasons. They can also sublet up to half of their dwelling to unrelated persons, without a time limit and with no requirement for permission from the landlord.

When a rented property is sold the sitting tenant remains in place, with their existing rental contract in force. Spouses can assume a tenancy if a tenant dies, as can cohabitants if they were living in the dwelling for at least two years. In the case of divorce or separation, the parties can decide which should take over the tenancy.

Landlords are responsible for maintaining and decorating the homes, and for choosing the decorative details, although if the parties agree, this responsibility can be transferred to the tenant.

Development of Danish rent control

Indefinite tenure usually goes together with rent control, as otherwise the landlord could force the tenant to leave simply by raising the rent to an unaffordable level. The Danish rent-control system dates to the early part of the 20th century, and most of the Danish private rental stock is still subject to some form of rent control.

The first regulation of rents in Denmark was a rent freeze in 1916, imposed in response to big rent increases in the first year of the First World War. Rent committees were set up by municipalities to ensure that the freeze was adhered to, and tenants' rights protected. After 1918, the freeze was gradually relaxed and was removed in 1931. Rent regulation was then imposed 'temporarily' in March 1939, 'for fear of strong rent rises during the coming world war, and of shortages of material for new construction' (Lunde, 2010: 263). This was of a piece with the creation of redistributive welfare state structures through the 1930s. The state in effect compelled landlords to subsidise rents, and the result was virtually to shut down private investment in rental dwellings, ending the prolific construction of new rental buildings in the 1930s. In addition to the rent freeze, there were other temporary measures including bans on evictions and demolitions, a ban on owning more than one house, and forced auctions of empty homes.

In the period after 1945, the stock of Danish housing grew due to massive state subsidies for new construction of social housing, and the post-war housing shortages disappeared. Rent control, however, remained and became a tool for redistribution. Rather than eliminate the rent regulations (which were still categorised as 'temporary') politicians added to them. The oft-amended law governing rent control during the post-war period was the rent control Act (*Lejeloven*), under which rents are determined by 'the value of the rented dwelling'. This was not a synonym for market rents, but in practice meant rents were based on the rents of similar units in terms of location, type, size, quality and standard (OECD, 2006). There were various changes to the system in the 1950s, including permitting smaller communes to do away with regulation, but no change in principle.

In 1966, however, there was political agreement about the desirability in principle of removing rent regulation and allowing rents to move with the market. It was felt that a one-off change would be too drastic, so a scheme was devised that was intended to gradually bring rents in both private and social rented housing up to market levels by 1974. But the scheme, which was based on fixed annual percentage increases in rent, did not anticipate the high inflation of the early 1970s and was not adjusted to take it into account. In 1974, rents in the private rented sector were at roughly the same level in real terms as they had been in 1967 (OECD, 1999; Christoffersen, 2010).

The 1966 agreement also for the first time allowed for the division of ownership in former rental buildings, to permit creation of owner-occupied apartments. There were minimum requirements regarding the physical condition and facilities, and new multi-unit buildings could be owner-occupied from the beginning. This led to the exodus of the best quality parts of the private rented sector from the tenure. After 1975 this type of change increased greatly, as tenant cooperatives were given the right of first refusal on sale of rental buildings. The calculation of sales prices was regulated in such a way as to deny the original owners any possibility of capital gains. This avenue of tenure change was closed in 1979 for most properties.

In 1975 a supplementary rent-control act (*Boligreguleringsloven*) was passed; this act introduced a system of cost-based rents. Municipalities could choose whether to apply the earlier *Lejeloven* or the new regime. The new system implied an increase in rents in 1976 of about 30 per cent in real terms (OECD, 1999).

The lack of maintenance in the PRS that resulted from rent control was addressed by a series of urban renewal programmes in the 1970s, and again from 1985 to 2000. These did not explicitly target the private rental dwellings, but as these were in worst repair they benefited most. As part of the renewal strategy, many older, smaller apartments were combined to form bigger units, contributing to the current shortage of small, cheap flats for low-income households and students (Liliegreen, 2020).

In 1991 rent control was lifted, for new buildings only, on negotiation of a new lease. Subsequent rent rises are limited to the cost of living. In 2004, landlords were allowed to charge market rents for new rooftop penthouse apartments built on top of otherwise rent-controlled buildings.

Current rent regulation

There are two main systems for controlling rents on new tenancies. These regulate both initial asking rents for new tenancies, and within-tenancy rent increases, in dwellings built before 1991. The one that affects most properties is the running-cost system or *omkostningsbestemt husleje* (OMK), which applies in Copenhagen and surrounding areas, and in most major cities. The permitted rent under the OMK system is intended to cover the landlord's running costs plus an owner's yield based on loan costs or the assessed value of the property, and a fixed amount for exterior maintenance; the calculation method is set out in the legislation. Rents can be raised if the running costs exceed the existing rent, or if the landlord has made improvements. In all, just under one-half of PRS dwellings are regulated under this system, including 88 per cent of buildings with between 11 and 20 units. Individual local governments (communes) can decide whether to apply the running-cost system in their areas, and 79 of Denmark's communes do so.

In the other 19 municipalities – mainly smaller towns – a second rent-control system applies for properties built for 1992. This system permits somewhat higher rents (though still below the notional market clearing level) and is known as *det lejedes værdi* (DLV), which translates as value of the tenancy or the value of the rented dwelling. This system is based on comparisons with rents for similar properties. In 2019 it was estimated that there were 121,000 OMK homes in the country, and 50,000 DLV (Copenhagen Economics, 2019).

Landlords can bring their units out of the purview of OMV or running-cost regulation by carrying out a 'thorough renovation'; this is known as a 'paragraph 5 clause 2' renovation. After this, rents can be set according to the DLV system. Renovations and rent increases are on a unit-by-unit basis, so there are buildings where some units are renovated and have near-market rents, while others are unrenovated and have OMV-regulated rents.

Calculation of rents is complex. The rent control systems that apply to new leases have already been described, but Liliegreen (2020) observes that in fact there are four different systems in operation, as the various changes in regulation sometimes applied only to housing constructed subsequently, while existing housing remained subject to the previous regulatory regime.

There is a system of rent tribunals that deals with disputes between landlords and tenants. Experts agree, however, that the layering of rent-control systems and the complexity of calculations leads to a lack of transparency, and that it is often impossible in practice for lay people to determine how much rent they should be paying (Edlund, 2003; Norberg and Juul-Sandberg, 2018).

Arguments for policy change

Experts both internal and external have been proposing reform of Danish rent regulation for decades. The Danish Economic Council said in 1970 that there was no longer a shortage of housing in Denmark and advocated the elimination of rent regulation, but to no avail. In 1987 the Ølgaard Commission was appointed to look at housing policy and published its report the following year. It focused mainly on social housing and said that lifting rent control on the private sector would be a political gesture without real effect as long as the subsidies given to other tenures were unchanged (Christoffersen, 2010: 123). In 1994 a rent law commission (Lejelovskommissionen) was set up to look specifically at rent regulation. Its 1997 report (Lejelovskommissionnen, 1997) recommended only marginal changes and did not address the issue of differing subsidies to different tenures.

In a widely cited 2001 report on the country's housing market, the Danish Economic Council made the case for relaxation leading to eventual elimination of rent regulation. The OECD has been a consistent critic of this element of Danish housing policy, devoting chapters to housing in its 1999 and 2006 economic surveys of Denmark. Its 2016 and 2019 economic surveys also recommended easing rent regulation and reducing housing subsidies. An OECD expert advocated establishment of a commission to investigate the scope for a bigger PRS and said rents could be made more flexible by reducing the investment threshold for rent-increasing improvements and allowing more scope for comparisons of flats when determining similar rents (Smidova, 2016). The first suggestion was not acted upon; as for the second and third, the Blackstone intervention (see Box 8.1) moved policy in the opposite direction.

The criticisms are based on the effect of the regulations on the utilisation and maintenance of the stock. Rents paid do not necessarily relate to the unit's desirability in terms of location, size and general attractiveness, leading to overconsumption of housing, lock-in effects, and an insider/outsider split, where desirable homes are acquired based on insider knowledge.

In terms of maintenance, until the late 1990s the formulae used for the various rent-control regimes applied a standard amount for maintenance which did not reflect differences in buildings' physical condition or location, and landlords were limited in their ability to pass these costs on to tenants. This led to underinvestment, and the OECD in 1999 identified 'a back-log of maintenance work of about DKr 12 billion (1989 prices) for the pre-1950 stock' (OECD, 1999: 115).

The maintenance charges were increased in the late 1990s, which improved maintenance somewhat. Of greater importance though were the effects of a widespread urban renewal programme in the early 1990s. Most of the housing improved was private rental housing. 'Most of the urban renewal projects (were) carried out with the landlord as contractor, for whom the urban renewal project typically replaces and finances maintenance investment that the landlord otherwise would have had to undertake at a later stage to keep up the value of his housing capital' (OECD, 1999: 117). The OECD points out that:

> One of the main lessons to be drawn from the experiences of Denmark and many other European countries is that rent controls, most often without proper regard for incentives to maintenance, have serious long-term effects on the quality of the relevant housing stock, in the end necessitating heavy government outlays to offset the deterioration of the capital stock. (OECD, 1999: 116)

In the past few years, what is variously called the financialisation or commodification of housing has entered the national political debate (see Box 8.1). The main concern of politicians and housing advocates is the effect on lower- and middle-income tenants of rapid rises in urban private rents. These increases are blamed on the speculative activities of capital-rich overseas investors. While the OECD and many economists have long argued that the housing system would perform better if the PRS were regulated less, the opponents of financialisation see tighter regulation as the way forward.

Taxes and subsidies

Private landlords' yields are taxed more than the returns of owners of other types of residential property (Lunde, 2021). Landlords (private individuals or companies) pay income tax on their rental income and can offset interest charges and operating costs; by contrast, owner-occupiers are not taxed on imputed rental income. Losses on rental property can be offset against other types of income ('negative gearing'). Rental income for individual landlords is taxed at the same rate as other types of income, at rates that range from 47 per cent to 60 per cent, while corporations or companies pay a corporate tax rate of 56.5 per cent, except for certain tax-favoured institutional investors. Since 2002, the profits of pension funds and insurance companies from investments in private rented property have been taxed at a very favourable 15.3 per cent.

Private landlords, like other property owners, are subject to municipal land-value tax; the average rate in 2020 was 2.75 per cent of assessed value. These values are very much out of date (Lunde and Whitehead, 2021), and the need for updating the land-tax system has long been a favourite topic of mainstream Danish economists. Reforms have recently been introduced although they are not due to take effect until 2024 because of difficulties updating the tax-collection IT systems.

Landlords can deduct 4 per cent per annum of the purchase price of the building only (that is, not including the land value). All private landlords must pay capital gains tax – though the payment can be delayed if the proceeds are used to buy another property – while owner-occupiers are exempt.

The tax system is not tenure neutral: other housing tenures in Denmark receive higher levels of subsidy and tax relief. Owner-occupiers benefit from mortgage tax relief, while the construction of social housing and new cooperatives is subsidised by the state. Neither social housing providers nor cooperatives are subject to income tax, although conversely, they must bear the full burden of mortgage interest.

Housing benefit

Private tenants are eligible for housing benefit, which is divided in two types: *boligsikring* is for economically active persons, and *boligydelse* is for pensioners; about 75 per cent of expenditure is on the latter. The amount of benefit payable is related to housing expenditure and household income. To encourage beneficiaries to economise, housing benefit does not cover the full rent. Housing benefit is administered by local authorities, who must cover 25 per cent of the costs for employed people and 50 per cent for pensioners. This creates an incentive for municipalities to steer people towards lower-cost PRS accommodation.

In 1999, some 10 per cent of tenants in the PRS received regular housing benefit and 15 per cent received housing benefit for pensioners. These figures were much lower than for social housing tenants: 16 per cent and 25 per cent respectively (*Det Økonomiske Råd* / The Danish Economic Council, 2001: table III.7).

Prices for rental buildings: the financial crisis and beyond

In the run-up to the GFC, the biggest price increases were seen in large blocks of flats, whose values rose about 200 per cent from the year 2000 to the market peak in 2007–2008. The price falls occasioned by the GFC led to several failures of company landlords: the government-appointed expert commission that investigated the effects of the financial crisis found that the residential-property industry had been more affected than other industries, experiencing 339 bankruptcies in 2010 versus 39 in 2006 (Ministry of Industry, Business and Financial Affairs, 2013: 143).

Before the property market collapsed in 2008, prices for rental buildings had risen so much that interest payments could be up to ten times rental incomes. After 2008, prices regained a relationship to rents and values fell steeply. After the crisis it came to light that in the period leading up to the bust, a small number of speculators pushed up the prices of residential buildings by colluding to sell properties to each other at artificially inflated prices (Sandøe and Svaneborg, 2013), and the State Prosecutor for Economic Crime charged some of the biggest offenders.

Official statistics show that in 2020, real prices in Denmark for residential buildings with four or more units were slightly lower than they had been in 2011. In Copenhagen they were about 18 per cent above 2011 levels, having dropped significantly from a peak in 2017 (Figure 8.3). The figures are, however, based on a small number of transactions (708 across the country in the most recent year, of which 56 were in Copenhagen), and the marked fluctuations may reflect composition effects.

Affordability

Rents are highest in the major cities of Copenhagen, Aarhus, Aalborg and Odense, and in new buildings (Figure 8.4). This is not only because post-1991 buildings are exempt from rent control, but also because the city government of Copenhagen since 2005 required that the average size of dwellings in new residential blocks should be at least 95 square metres (Liliegreen, 2020). This regulation, intended to foster construction of good-quality homes, also had the effect of blocking development of smaller, cheaper units, and the rule was relaxed somewhat from 2015. Per square

Figure 8.3: Prices of residential rental blocks, Denmark and Copenhagen, 2011–2020

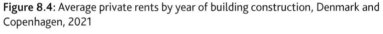

Note: Nominal price per building with 4+ units, DKK 000. Four-quarter moving average. Index 2011 = 100.

Source: Author's calculations based on Statistics Denmark housing table builder (nd).

Figure 8.4: Average private rents by year of building construction, Denmark and Copenhagen, 2021

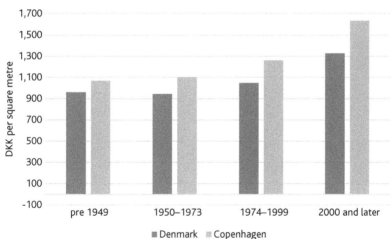

Note: DKK per square metre.

Source: Author's calculations based on data from Bolig- og Planstyrelse's Boligstat.dk (2020).

metre, rents for purpose-built flats are about 25 per cent higher than for other dwelling types.

National statistics consumer-spending figures show that average real rents across the private and social sectors have risen over last decades (Figure 8.5). Rents fell sharply after the GFC, then resumed their upward trend.

Figure 8.5: Average real rents for rented flats, 1994–2019 (DKK per annum)

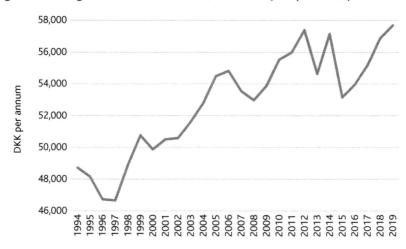

Note: Includes both private and social rented units.

Source: Author's calculations based on Statistics Denmark housing table builder.

Disruptors: digital platforms, Airbnb, COVID

Some rental transactions begin online, but not all vacant properties are offered on the open market: the high demand, especially in big cities, means landlords can often easily find tenants without advertising and prefer to rent to people they already know (Skifter Andersen, 2014). In many countries the digital marketplace for housing is concentrated in a few online portals, but Denmark has several including specialists in student rentals, single rooms in shared houses and housing for expatriates. Some of these portals gather information on prospective tenants and allow landlords to exclude, for example, certain household types.[1] The competition holds prices down and on some of the main portals landlords can list properties for free.

While Airbnb and similar platforms operate in Denmark, the phenomenon of short-term rentals has been less of a political issue than in many European capitals, possibly because Danish weather and Danish prices limit the tourist influx. The biggest impact has been to remove from the market rooms that were previously rented out to university students. From May 2018, properties can be let on a short-term basis for a maximum of 70 days per year (OECD, 2019). The property sector has also seen fintech innovations: for example, The Many, a crowdfunding platform for PRS properties.

The COVID-19 pandemic had less effect in Denmark than in many countries: the strong welfare-state structure largely replaced the incomes of those who lost employment, and tenure security has protected tenants from eviction. It was not felt necessary to introduce COVID-19-specific regulations such as a ban on evictions.

One of the biggest online portals reported in January 2021 that they had seen strong growth in the number of rental units on the market since the start of the pandemic, which they attributed to a fall in tourist arrivals and Airbnb use (BoligPortal, 2021). Demand for rented flats was holding up and indeed growing, as erstwhile potential buyers decided to rent instead because of economic insecurity. As in many other advanced economies, there was a shift in demand towards dwellings with outside space and bigger floor areas.

Conclusion

Private renting in Denmark is highly regulated, even in comparison with other continental European systems. This regulation suppresses net yields, and investment returns from rental property traditionally came largely from capital gains (Skifter Andersen, 2014).

Denmark's PRS is distinctive also for the major role of local institutional investors. This has long been a feature of the Danish system, in contrast to many other countries where the involvement of such investors has been more recent. Corporate investment was positively incentivised by tax breaks, as such owners were seen to offer stable long-term funding and professional management, analogous in some ways to the housing associations that operate Denmark's social rented housing.

In recent years, though, overseas investors have increasingly bought up rental property and applied the strict profit maximisation approach favoured in some American business schools. One consequence of rent control is that there is excess demand for private renting, especially in big cities. Private landlords who are able to raise rents can boost profits and usually manage to find tenants, and the legislation has long allowed for rent increases on improvement of the housing. But although wholesale renovations and associated rent increases were legal, this was not an approach that most local landlords adopted. The entry of new investors who did not operate according to tacit Danish rules caused a political backlash.

What is happening in Denmark is part of a wider European debate. In late 2020 the European Parliament's Committee on Employment and Social Affairs adopted a report critical of financialisation in the housing market, which said that 'recent scale-up of foreign and corporate investments in residential urban property has transformed patterns of ownership, raise(d) concerns on the social fabric of a city and on who can be held accountable for citizen's rights to adequate and affordable housing' (Joint Research Centre, 2019, quoted in van Sparrentak, 2020). Thinking perhaps of Denmark's initiative, the author calls on EU member states and cities to 'redefine their relationship with private investors, international financial institutions and financial markets to reclaim housing as a human right' (van Sparrentak, 2020: 27).

With the Blackstone intervention, Denmark initiated the first skirmish in what may become a wider political war against international investors. The actions of these market actors are perceived to be at the root of housing affordability problems. But while Blackstone and other corporates have indeed raised rents in the properties they own (and improved the physical fabric), they are not solely or even mainly to blame for lack of affordability in the PRS: this problem has much deeper roots. Over the next few years, we will find out whether Denmark's pioneering initiative leads, as its proponents hope, to restructuring of ownership in the Danish PRS and clear improvements for tenants' stability and affordability, or whether it brings with it significant unintended consequences.

Note

[1] https://www.boligportal.dk/en/rent-out

References

Andersen, M.L. (2019) 'Boligreguleringslovens S5, stk.2' (Housing Regulation Act, Paragraph 5, subsection 2), *Magasinet: Boligøkonomisk Videncenter* (The Magazine of the Knowledge Center for Housing Economics), 32, December.

Ball, M. (2001) *RICS Review of European Housing Markets 2001*, London, RICS.

BoligPortal (2021) 'Corona og fremtidens boligmarked' (Coronavirus and the future housing market), https://www.boligportal.dk/blog/viden/cor ona-og-fremtidens-boligmarked/

Boligstat.dk (2020) Rent statistics, *Social- og Boligstyrelsen* (Social and Housing Agency), https://boligstat.dk/SASStoredProcess/guest?_program=/Bolig stat/Hovedmenu

Christoffersen, H. (2010) *Den private ejendomsudlejnings betydning for samfundet* (The Private Rental Sector's Role in Society), Copenhagen, Ejendomsforening Danmark.

Copenhagen Economics (2019) *Regulering af private udlejnings ejedomme: Konsekvenser af et indgreb i boligreguleringslovens § 5 stk. 2* (Regulation of Private Rented Buildings: Consequences of a change in housing regulation 5.2), report commissioned by EjendomDanmark.

Danish Economic Council (2001) *Dansk Økonomi forår 2001 Kapitel III: Boligmarkedet – Skævt og ineffektivt* (Spring Report 2001: The Housing Market – Unequal and Inefficient), http://www.dors.dk/sw1163.asp

Deva, S. and Farha, L. (2019) Letter to Stephen Schwarzman, Blackstone CEO, https://www.ohchr.org/Documents/Issues/Housing/Financializat ion/OL_OTH_17_2019.pdf

Edlund, H. (2003) *European University Institute Tenancy Law Project: Final Report Denmark*, http://www.eui.eu/Documents/DepartmentsCentres/Law/ResearchTeaching/ResearchThemes/EuropeanPrivateLaw/TenancyLawProject/TenancyLawDenmark.pdf

Joint Research Centre (2019) *The Future of Cities: Opportunities, Challenges and the Way Forward*, Luxembourg, Publications Office of the European Union, https://ec.europa.eu/jrc/en/publication/eur-scientific-and-technical-research-reports/future-cities

Kastberg, L. (2020) 'Nu er Blackstone-indgrebet en realitet: Træder i kraft 1. juli' (Now the Blackstone intervention is a reality: It comes into force 1 July), *Berlinske*, 4 June, https://www.berlingske.dk/dine-penge/nu-er-blackstone-indgrebet-en-realitet-traeder-i-kraft-1-juli

Kristensen, J.B. (2012) *Konsekvenser af huslejeregulering på det private udlejningsboligmarked: en Mikroøkonomisk undersøgelse for 2000'erne* (Consequences of rent regulation in the private rented housing market: a microeconomic analysis for the 2000s), DREAM, https://www.bvc.dk/media/1437/konsekvenser-af-husleje-regulering-paa-det-private-udlejnings-marked.pdf

Lejelovskommissionen (The Danish Governmental Commission on Rent Legislation) (1997) *Lejeforhold: Lejelovskommissionens betæankning* (Rent relations: The rent law commission's report), Copenhagen, Housing Ministry.

Liliegreen, C. (2020) 'Housing construction in the market periphery – Denmark', in M. Tunström (ed) *Building Affordable Homes: Challenges and Solutions in the Nordic Region*, NORDREGIO, https://norden.diva-portal.org/smash/get/diva2:1420468/FULLTEXT01.pdf

LLO (Lejernes Landsorganisation) (2020) *Vi Lejere*, https://llo.dk/om-llo/vi-lejere

Lunde, J. (2010) 'Private lejeboliger: Den misrøgtede boligform må gentænkes' (Private rental housing: the neglected tenure must be re-thought), in H. Christoffersen *Den private ejendomsudlejnings betydning for samfundet* (The Private Rental Sector's Role in Society), Copenhagen, Ejendomsforening Danmark, pp 245–286.

Lunde, J. (2021) 'Hjælp til skatteminister Bødskov' (Help for tax minister Bødskov), *Jyllandsposten*, 9 April.

Lunde, J. and Whitehead, C. (2021) *How Taxation Varies Between Owner-Occupation, Private Renting and Other Housing Tenures in European Countries: An Overview*, UK Collaborative Centre for Housing Evidence, https://housingevidence.ac.uk/wp-content/uploads/2021/02/European-Housing-Taxation-report-1.pdf

Rangvid, J., Grosen, A., Østrup, F., Møgelvang-Hansen, P., Jensen, H.F., Thomsen, J., *et al* (2013) 'Den finansielle krise i Danmark - årsager, konsekvenser og læring' (The financial crisis in Denmark: reasons, consequences and learning), *The Rangvid Report*, Copenhagen, Ministry of Industry, Business and Financial Affairs.

Norberg, P. and Juul-Sandberg, J. (2018) 'Rent control and other aspects of tenancy law in Sweden, Denmark and Finland: how can a balance be struck between protection of tenants' rights and landlords' ownership rights in welfare states?', in C. Schmid (ed) *Tenancy Law and Housing Policy in Europe: Towards Regulatory Equilibrium*, Cheltenham, Edward Elgar, pp 260–293.

OECD (1999) 'Chapter IV: policies for the housing market', in *OECD Economic Surveys: Denmark*, http://www.oecd-ilibrary.org/docserver/download/fulltext/1099131e.pdf?expires=1297269379&id=0000&accname=ocid71015720&checksum=A59628CDD25C5B9B6D9B78DED9EB0A8D

OECD (2006) 'Chapter 4: housing: less subsidy and more flexibility', in *OECD Economic Surveys: Denmark*, http://www.oecd-ilibrary.org/economics/oecd-economic-surveys-denmark-2006/housing_eco_surveys-dnk-2006-6-en

OECD (2019) *OECD Economic Surveys: Denmark 2019*, Paris, OECD Publishing, https://doi.org/10.1787/eco_surveys-dnk-2019-en

Sadolin and Albæk (S&A) (2017) Copenhagen Property Market report.

Sandøe, N. and Svaneborg, T.G. (2013) *Andre Folks Penge – Historien om den danske finanskrise* (Other people's money: History of the Danish financial crisis), Copenhagen, Jylands-Postens Forlag.

Skifter Andersen, A.H. (2010) 'Den private udlejningssektor nu og i fremtiden' (The private rented sector now and in future), in *Den private ejendomsudlejnings betydning for samfundet* (*The private rental sector's role in society*), Copenhagen, Ejendomsforeningen Danmark, pp 175–210.

Skifter Andersen, H. (2014) 'Denmark', in T. Crook and P.A. Kemp (eds) *Private Rental Housing: Comparative Perspectives*, Cheltenham, Edward Elgar, pp 99–124.

Smidova, Z. (2016) 'Betting the house in Denmark', OECD Economics Department Working Paper No. 1337.

Statistics Denmark housing table builder (nd) https://www.statistikbanken.dk/statbank5a/default.asp?w=1920

Thomasen, E. (2021) 'Blackstone indgreb stopper udenlandske investorer' (Blackstone intervention stops foreign investors), *Børsen*, 2 February, https://borsen.dk/nyheder/ejendomme/blackstoneindgreb-stopper-udenlandske-investorer

Van Sparrentak, K. (2020) *Report on Access to Decent and Affordable Housing for All (2019/2187(INI))*, European Parliament Committee on Employment and Social Affairs, https://www.europarl.europa.eu/doceo/document/A-9-2020-0247_EN.pdf

9

Norway: booming housing market and increasing small-scale landlordism

Mary Ann Stamsø

Introduction

The key features of the Norwegian housing system are a large homeowner sector, with sustained real house price increases; a private rental sector (PRS) dominated by small-scale investors; and a residual social rental sector. Even though Norway has a generous welfare benefit system, the housing sector is relatively market-oriented and housing policy is modest in terms of benefits and social housing. Low interest rates, increasing incomes, favourable taxation and a rental sector with poor housing conditions that appears not to provide an attractive alternative, have maintained a high demand for homeownership. However, increasing affordability problems have caused a cautious political commitment for affordable housing and a rental sector with long-term contracts and rents below market rent, as an alternative to the market-based housing sector.

This chapter begins by presenting the main features of Norwegian housing policy in the context of the country's welfare regime and political economy more generally. It explores the dynamics and change within the PRS in relation to other tenures and the development of the housing market. Housing finance, subsidies, regulation and tax policy are also discussed. Further sections analyse developments in relation to the composition of the rental market, the secondary property market, housing conditions and rent levels. The chapter then takes a deeper look into characteristics of the tenants in the rental market in relation to the homeowner market. The chapter ends with an analysis of effect of the COVID-19 pandemic on the housing market and the PRS.

Housing policy in context

Type of government and welfare state regime

The Norwegian economy, often referred to as welfare capitalism, has a mix of free market activity and government intervention, and a closely integrated welfare system. Norway is part of the Nordic welfare state, also

Table 9.1: Public social expenditures in Norway, as a percentage of gross domestic product (Organisation for Economic Co-operation and Development average in brackets)

Public social expenditures in total	25.3 (20.6)
Old age	8.9 (7.4)
Health	6.5 (5.6)
Housing	0.1 (0.3)
Gini coefficient	0.26 (0.32)

Note: Year 2017/19 or latest available.
Source: OECD (2021a).

classified as the social democratic welfare model by Esping-Andersen (1990). Key characteristics of this model are comprehensive, public-financed and universalistic benefits; corporatist coordination with three-party cooperation between the state, and the main employer and employee organisations; and egalitarian outcomes. Income from petroleum activity, with heavy state ownership, puts Norway in an exceptional position compared to other countries. The oil fund, labelled the Government Pensions Fund Global, serves to shield the economy from ups and downs in oil revenue, as a financial reserve, and as a long-term savings plan so that both current and futures generations get to benefit from the oil wealth. The importance of this fund is shown by relatively limited impact on the housing market from the global financial crisis and the COVID-19 pandemic, as discussed later in the chapter.

As Table 9.1 shows, there is a high level of public social expenditures, and a relatively low level of income inequality, in Norway. High gross domestic product (GDP), and in particular per capita GDP, results in much higher figures for total public social spending in most sectors than the Organisation for Economic Co-operation and Development (OECD) average. However, public spending on housing is low, including expenditures in cash and kind, on social housing and individual transfers, and not tax subsidies. By comparison, public spending on housing as a percentage of GDP in other Nordic welfare states ranked between 0.4 per cent and 0.8 per cent.

Responsibility for housing policy

In Norway, the state and the municipalities share the responsibility for housing. In some areas of housing policy, various forms of cooperation between these government levels exist. Social work in connection with housing, such as helping homeless people or others in particular need, is carried out by municipalities in agreement with the state and with state funding. The state is mainly responsible for the funding of means-tested instruments while the municipalities are mainly responsible for administration. For households in need the State Housing Bank offers loan and grants to first-time homeowners, grants for adapting dwellings for disabled and elderly people, a national housing allowance programme and housing for disabled and elderly for residential care. The municipalities allocate these instruments. In addition, some municipalities in high price areas have their own housing allowance. The municipalities have the responsibility for social housing. However, the State Housing Bank offers grants to municipalities, companies and foundation for construction and improvement of social housing and for student dwellings.

Housing provision and policy

In Norway, one of the key political housing goals since the Second World War has been homeownership and remains so today. Rental housing is regarded as a transitional stage in people's housing career and is mostly a phenomenon among low-income groups and a temporary solution for younger households. Homeownership accounts for 77 per cent of households (82 per cent of individuals). The rental sector is consequently modest in size, accounting for 23 per cent of households including 4 per cent who live in social rented housing.

An egalitarian housing policy after the Second World War, carried out within the owner-occupied sector, laid the foundation of today's tenure structure. The expansion of homeownership was implemented through regulation of house prices in cooperative housing and individual owner-occupied housing; strict regulation of interest rates and the availability of credit; allocation of large-scale universal subsidies through grants and loans for all homeowners; and a favourable taxation system. In addition, rents in most blocks of flats in big cities were regulated in the period 1940–1982, and condominium conversion was forbidden in the period 1976–1982. Social housing was reduced, and Norway built up a cooperative housing sector in urban areas representing an alternative to social renting for middle- and low-income groups. The co-op sector was strongly regulated by prices and access through membership and seniority and received reasonable loans from the state. Through these instruments, mainly distributed by the State Housing Bank, Norway built up a housing sector of good quality (Stamsø, 2009). In addition, egalitarian traditions in Norwegian society, characterised as small-scale industry and agriculture and no legacy of aristocracy, influenced the structure of housing and housing policy that supported homeownership (Annaniassen, 2006). A high rate of homeownership also relates to a low degree of urbanisation, and in big cities the transformation of private rentals owned by large-scale landlords to condominiums in the 1980s (Wessel, 2002).

A critical political view of the PRS after the Second World War also formed the political choices that were made towards the sector (Annaniassen, 2006).

After deregulation of the housing and financial sectors in the mid-1980s, a more liberalised bank system was introduced. The co-op sector transformed from functioning as social housing, to being almost like the homeownership sector by implementing market prices, and the loss of the significance of membership and seniority as access criteria. Co-op housing is today regarded as homeownership, as only small differences exist, the most important being restrictions on letting, and exemption for co-ops of the 2.5 per cent stamp duty. As this transformation of the co-op sector did not lead to an increase in social housing (municipal owned housing) in the following years, a relatively high share of housing on market terms exists in Norway. The housing market then went through a boom from 1985 to 1988, followed by a bust, economic downturn, and a banking crisis until 1992. A gradual transition of universal to means-tested housing instruments followed. In big cities, private rent regulation was removed in 1982 for new tenancies and gradually phased out for existing tenancies in pre-world war blocks of flats in the period 2000–2010. Since then, private rents have been mainly set at market levels.

Large-scale private landlords were generally replaced by small-scale private individual landlords. This change reflected the absence of subsidies for large-scale landlords and the fact that many small-scale landlords were not taxed on their rental income. Private individuals who could afford it regarded owning an extra dwelling as a good investment. Meanwhile, long-term tenancies were gradually replaced by short-term ones, as renting came to be seen as a temporary housing situation; and for their part, landlords preferred short-term tenancies as it gave them the flexibility to withdraw from the rental market (Stamsø, 2009).

Today, about 3 per cent of the housing stock consists of social housing owned by the municipalities (public housing) and about 1 per cent through subletting, implying that in total social rentals account for 4 per cent (Grebstad, 2020; Statistics Norway, 2021c). However, a large proportion of social housing are care homes and just over half are let to socially or financially disadvantaged households (Holmøy, 2018). Social housing rents are determined by the municipalities, resulting in market rents in the most metropolitan areas and rents based on costs in other areas (Barlindhaug et al, 2018).

Table 9.2 shows the development in the tenure pattern in Norway from 1920 to 2020, at national level and in the capital Oslo. At the national level, the homeownership rate increased up to the turn of the century and then stabilised. Renting declined up to 1990, and particularly so during the 1980s, and stabilised from the turn of the century. In Oslo, a similar development has taken place in homeownership, but cooperatives have declined since 1990 and renting has increased.

Table 9.2: Tenancy in Norway and Oslo from 1920 to 2020 by household (%)

	1920	1950	1970	1980	1990	2001	2011	2020
Norway								
Owner-occupied +	53		53	50	59	63	63	63
Cooperatives			13	17	19	14	14	14
Rented	47		34	33	22	23	23	24
Oslo								
Owner-occupied	5	12	12		28	36	36	36
Cooperatives		24	39		48	35	34	32
Rented	95	64	43		24	29	30	32

Note: + Owning alone or condominiums.
Source: Statistics Norway (2021a; 2021b; 2021c).

Housing market

In Norway, house prices have experienced a long-term boom, interrupted only by minor declines. In real terms, house prices increased by 469 per cent between 1992 and 2020 (Statistics Norway, 2021d). Nominal house prices increased by 206 per cent from January 2003 to June 2021 (Figure 9.1). The strong and long-term increase in house prices in Norway are caused by increase in income, an historical low interest rate, urbanisation, housing construction not keeping up with the demand, favourable tax policy, and not least an expectation of rising house prices. Norway has the fifth highest house prices among the OECD countries (OECD, 2021b).

In 2007, the financial crisis caused a temporary – and in an international context – comparatively small fall in house prices. This was because the Norwegian economy could benefit from the sovereign oil fund and the public budget surplus to pursue counter-cyclical policies. As in other countries, the banks suffered from large losses due to investing in US subprime or other unsecured loans. This was because of tightening of the banks' lending practices and new rules of capital adequacy introduced in 1991, after the bank crisis, to ensure that the banks had at all times a sound capital adequacy and thereby a good solvency. Another temporary house price decrease occurred in 2014 due to a marked fall in oil prices; and again in 2017 because of tightening of the mortgage regulations and an increase in supply of dwellings.

Table 9.3 shows there has been a significant increase in house prices compared to disposable incomes in the past ten years and especially so in Oslo. Household debt as a percentage of disposable incomes increased over the same period. In 2019, Norway ranked second highest among OECD countries on household debt as a percentage of disposable income and highest

Figure 9.1: Nominal and seasonally adjusted house price index, existing dwellings, 2003–2021

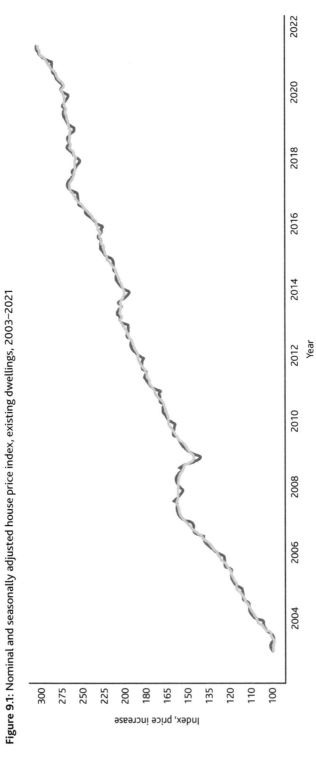

Source: Real Estate Norway FINN and Eiendomsverdi AS (2021).

Table 9.3: House prices, median salary and household debt

	2021	Change last 10 years
Average national house price, June 2021 (sqm in parentheses)	4,392,883 (48,192) NOK	+68%
Average Oslo house price, December 2021 (sqm in parentheses)	6,369,474 (85,657) NOK	+102%
Median yearly salary (2020)	529,800 NOK	+25%
Households debt as % of disposal income (2020)	239%	+20%

Note: By 31 December 2020 the exchange rate of 100 NOK was 11.7198 USD, 9.5508 EUR and 8.5865 GBP.

Source: Real Estate Norway, FINN and Eiendomsverdi AS (2021), Statistics Norway (2021e), OECD (2021c).

as a percentage of GDP (IMF, 2020; OECD, 2021c). Rising household debt is a tricky issue: it can be ameliorated by the existence of an extensive welfare safety net, but it also increases wealth inequality which runs counter to the aims and ideals of the Nordic welfare model (Tranøy et al, 2020). Debt is particularly increasing among younger people, as more and more have debt ratios up to 400–500 per cent of gross income (The Financial Supervisory Authority of Norway, 2020). Highly leveraged homeowners are particularly vulnerable to rising interest rates or economic recession. The high household debt rate also represents a risk to society as it amplifies downturns when there is a strong decline in demand across the economy. As most mortgages in Norway have floating interest rates, this could trigger a downturn in the event of high interest rate increases in a short time. According to the OECD and International Monetary Fund, the high debt and the Norwegian property market remain the principal domestic vulnerability concerns (OECD, 2019; IMF, 2020).

Norway is also experiencing an increasingly uneven housing wealth distribution, both geographically and between generations. In Norway, this process operates across at least three generations, and grandparents' homeowner status as well as their degree of urbanisation appears to have a substantial effect on young adults' tenure status and house value (Galster and Wessel, 2019). Killengreen Revold et al (2018) show that most young home buyers finance the purchase with a mortgage, and that half of home buyers aged 20–29 years receive financial assistance from their parents when buying a dwelling. Eggum and Røed Larsen (2021) found that the Gini-index of house values has increased from 0.26 on January 2007 to 0.29 in January 2019, an increase of 10 per cent, and that capital gains accumulated in the housing market in the same period varied substantial according to urbanisation and date of birth.

Challenges in housing policy

Major challenges in the homeowner country Norway are, first, that long-term house price inflation is widely seen in positive ways as benefiting the 'insiders' in the housing market; and, second, that the possibility for homeowners of making capital gains has gained decisive importance. This has made it difficult to bring about changes in housing policy. Within the rental sector, the high proportion of small-scale private landlords contributes to lower market stability and predictability. However, for low- and middle-income households paying market rents, the government is under pressure to make changes to enable them to cope with increasing affordability problems and the instability of the rental market. Some politicians, researchers and citizens now argue for the importance of a 'third housing sector' in Norway (Oslo municipality, 2019a; Prosser, 2020).

A third housing sector is broadly defined as an alternative to (1) the market-oriented private rental sector and (2) to social housing aimed at the most vulnerable. It includes both ownership and renting on more reasonable terms than the market provides. Important elements are non-commercial terms where profits return to the dwellings with the goal of offering affordable housing; and co-ownership housing in non-profit-driven organisations. Although affordable housing and non-profit housing for people with middle or lower incomes are common in many countries, it has been difficult to achieve in Norway.

Some minor projects have taken place in recent years to secure affordable ownership in the construction of new dwellings. The 'From rent to owning' model offers housing to tenants without equity, giving them an agreement to rent for some years and then the opportunity to buy the dwelling at the price that applied at the time of the initial rental agreement. In some cases, the rents are below market rent, as where there exists an agreement between the developer, the municipality, and the State Housing Bank (NBBL, 2021). This model is also used by some municipalities, who buy dwellings and offer renting-to-owning agreements to tenants in particular need. These schemes often include rents below market level, start-up loans and housing allowances (Veiviseren.no, 2021). Shared ownership, started by OBOS (*Oslo Bolig- og Sparelag*/Oslo Housing and Saving cooperation), the leading co-op in Norway, is another model. The tenant buys the dwelling in corporate ownership with OBOS, owning 50 per cent or more of the equity, with the opportunity to increase their share up to complete ownership, with OBOS owning the remaining part. The tenant pays market rent for the part that OBOS owns (in addition to their share of the common costs) as does OBOS. When selling the dwelling, OBOS have a right of first refusal, except if the sale is to a close family member such as a spouse, cohabitant or child. (OBOS, 2021a). 'Bostart' is another project from OBOS offering new dwellings below market price, where OBOS have the right to buy the dwelling back at the initial price paid by the buyer adjusted for the increase in value in the meantime (OBOS, 2021b). All these projects are within the homeowner sector and not affordable to most low-income groups that are not entitled to social housing or means-tested housing instruments, or to middle-income groups in urban areas.

Projects within the rental sector are currently relatively marginal. One is agreements between municipalities and private companies for the construction and purchase of rental housing, which gives the municipality an option to allocate up to 40 per cent of these dwellings during a period of 20 years to disadvantaged groups, and the companies can get a basic loan from The State Housing Bank. If the companies get grants and a basic loan from the State Housing Bank, the project periods are at least 30 years. Rents are set at average rent level and contracts for five years or more (Veiviseren. no, 2021). One challenge is that currently the Planning and Building Act does not provide municipalities with the right to impose certain disposition conditions on private developers or to offer housing at below market prices; only to buy a certain share of the dwellings in new construction projects. The government has taken some modest steps towards rental housing. One is to consider changing the provision of the Rent Act on minimum time in leases during 2021. Another is to provide the Housing Bank with a framework to provide more loans for private rental housing (National Strategy for Social Housing Policy, 2021–2024). The current city council in Oslo municipality have some more significant plans for affordable dwellings, within the concept of a third housing sector, but these are pilot projects within both renting and owning (Oslo municipality, 2019b; 2019c).

Finance, taxation and regulation

Subsidies

Housing allowances from the State Housing Bank are the most evident subsidy in housing the poorest and the homeless. The amount of allowance received varies according to income and housing expenditures up to an approved ceiling that varies with location and household size.

As Table 9.4 indicates, the share of recipients renting has increased, particularly within the PRS, and their income compared to the average salary has declined. The housing allowance has not increased in line with increases in either house prices or rents. While the total number of recipients has decreased, among young people it has increased: in 2010, 34 per cent of recipients were under 35 years of age, but by 2020 it had risen to 40 per cent (The State Housing Bank, 2021). A municipal housing allowance also exists in many municipalities, as a supplement to the national housing allowance. In 2020, 7,689 households received municipal housing allowances in Oslo

Table 9.4: Distribution of housing allowance from the State Housing Bank, 2010 and 2020

	Total amount	Number of recipients	Amount % of housing expenditure	Housing expenditure > ceiling	Income % of median salary	Renters % (PRS in parentheses)
2010	3.4 bn NOK	146,790	37%	51%	33%	82% (48%)
2020	3.8 bn NOK	124,250	37%	60%	27%	89% (61%)

Source: The State Housing Bank (2021), Statistics Norway (2021e).

(Statistics Norway, 2021f). Public spending on housing allowances as a percentage of GDP is low in an international context: only 0.08 per cent in 2019 compared with the OECD average of 0.26 per cent (OECD, 2021b).

The State Housing Bank also offers start-up loans, distributed by the municipalities, intended for those who do not have the equity required by banks to provide home loans, which in 2020 amounted to 13.7 billion NOK, distributed to 8,078 households at an average 87 per cent of the housing value (The State Housing Bank, 2021). Municipalities also offer grants for first-time home buyers as a supplement to start-up loans to disadvantaged groups. Social assistance is not a housing instrument, but it is significant within housing in cases where housing policy instruments are deemed to be insufficient. According to the Social Service Act (2009) social services are obliged to provide financial support for housing, to find temporary accommodation and to help provide permanent housing.

Tax breaks and tax relief on homeownership constitutes the most comprehensive public support within the housing sector. Norway also stands out internationally in granting unlimited deductibility of debt interest. The Ministry of Finance has estimated that the tax expenses (subsidies) of housing and secondary homes total 11.5 billion NOK. Meanwhile, the discount in wealth tax due to low tax value was estimated at 29.9 billion NOK in 2020 (Ministry of Finance, 2021a). In 2019 property tax amounted to 1.3 per cent of GDP and 3.2 per cent of tax revenues, which is well below the OECD average (OECD, 2021d). This favourable taxation system has been regularly criticised by various government-mandated reports, as well as by the International Monetary Fund and OECD, for being a prominent weak spot in economic policy, as it contributes to greater inequality, inefficient resource allocation, high house prices, high debt and risk to the society (for example, NOU, 2014: 13; OECD, 2019; The Norway towards 2025 Committee, 2021). However, significant change is a political hard nut to crack. It seems like a typical insider–outsider problem favouring the majority – the homeowners – at the expense of the outsiders – the renters and would-be first-time home buyers. Rich homeowners benefit the most through the favouritism in wealth tax and the interest deductibility.

Taxation

Individuals pay net wealth tax at a rate of 0.85 per cent on their taxable net wealth, in excess of a basic allowance of NOK 1.5 million in 2020. Spouses are granted one basic allowance each. The taxable value of assets is in principle equal to their market value. However, residential properties and other immovable properties are valued well below market value: for primary homes, it is 25 per cent of market value, 30 per cent for second homes, and 90 per cent for secondary properties.

Each municipality decides whether to levy property tax, within the limitations laid down in the Property Tax Act. In 2020, 319 of 356 municipalities levied this tax. The property tax rate, if any, can be levied at between 0.2 per cent and 0.4 per cent of the valuation basis, to be determined by valuation every tenth year. The municipalities may also choose to use the net wealth tax bases in the valuation of residential property. Furthermore, the municipalities may choose to apply a discount in their valuation of properties and a minimum allowance to reduce the valuation basis of residential properties. Since 2017, the municipalities may opt for exempting holiday homes from property tax. Because of all these exemptions, the property tax is low and amounted on average to 3,901 NOK on a detached house of 120 square metres in 2020. In total, property tax on housing and secondary homes amounted to 7.2 billion NOK in 2020, which is low in an international context as a percentage of GDP (Statistics Norway, 2021g; OECD, 2021). Stamp duty is levied on the buyer of a property, at a rate of 2.5 per cent of the market price, but co-op housing is exempted. Stamp duty tax was valued at 10.5 billion NOK in 2020 (Ministry of Finance, 2021a).

There is a taxation on capital gains from the sale of primary homes and secondary homes at a rate of 22 per cent. However, seldom levied on individuals, since it is not applicable if the owner has owned the house for at least one year, the secondary home for at least five years, lived in the home at least one of the two years, or used the secondary home at least five of the last eight years. Interest rates on debt, including mortgage, are deductible at a rate of 22 per cent, in unlimited amounts. Tax on imputed rent was abolished in 2005, and inheritance tax from 2014.

In the case of private renting, where the owner lives in the same house, the income from rent on such units is entirely tax-free if the value of the rented part does not exceed 50 per cent of the rentable value for the whole house. Tax exemption also apply for rental income below 20,000 NOK per year. Other private individual landlords pay tax on net income at a rate of 22 per cent, for income above 20,000 NOK in 2020. Large-scale landlords have significantly higher taxes, since they are subjected to tax rules applying to business, where letting out five or more dwellings is deemed to be a business and both the company and dividends are taxed.

Increases in tax have mainly taken place on secondary properties (not second homes) and on short-term lettings such as Airbnb. The tax value of secondary property has increased steadily over the last ten years, rising from 40 per cent of market value in 2010 to 90 per cent in 2020. On 1 January 2018, government introduced a tax on short-term rentals in one's own home, including Airbnb. When renting out parts of the apartment or the entire apartment the owner lives in, for less than 30 days at a time, the owner is taxed on rental income exceeding 10,000 NOK during the year, in 2020. The 30-day rule applies to each rental. Eighty-five per cent of the rental income is taxable, at a rate of 22 per cent. Companies that provide short-term rentals, such as Airbnb, were from 1 January 2020 required to report to the tax authorities. They must give information on every landlord, the amount of income and renting period in all rental conditions. This is to prevent a black economy and to give similar conditions among the providers within and outside the sharing economy (Capita, 2019). Compared to other rental dwellings, taxation of short-term rents implies a stricter taxation. The mortgage interest tax deduction was steadily decreased from 28 per cent in 2013 to 22 per cent in 2019. By contrast, in 2020 the maximum rate of property tax for homeowners was reduced from 0.7 per cent to 0.5 per cent, and from 2021 to 0.4 per cent (Ministry of Finance, 2021a).

Regulation

In Norway, tenants and landlords are protected by the Norwegian Landlord and Tenant Act (2000). Tenants' rights in the private rental market primary concern protection against notice of termination and against unreasonable rental fees. Unless otherwise decided, the duration of tenancy contracts is time unlimited. The Act allows for fixed-term tenancies of three years, and for special reasons, for shorter time. Unlimited contracts give the tenant much stronger rights than time-limited contracts. The landlord cannot terminate the tenancy contract without just cause. A just cause could be that the landlord wants to use the dwelling for her/himself, the building is to be demolished or rebuilt, or if the tenant has failed to fulfil the obligations of the contract. Tenants can terminate the contract at any time. There are separate rules if the owner lives in the same house.

The rent in new tenancy agreements cannot exceed the current market rent. The Act allows for adjusting rents in ongoing tenancies after three years, and then every third year, to the average rent on similar dwellings in the same area. This provision covers time-unlimited contracts and time-limited contracts longer than three years. The Act also allows for adjusting rents in accordance with the consumer price index, one year after the last rent adjustment. According to the Act, deposits for private rental dwellings are to be limited to a maximum of four months' rent.

Rents vary by the quality and the location of the dwellings. However, in the rental market other conditions also matter, such as the length of tenancy and type of landlord. In 2018, 75 per cent of the tenants were paying market rent (Statistics Norway, 2018). Rent levels increase steadily by the number of rooms in the dwelling and average rents in Oslo and Bærum are much higher than in other cities in Norway.

Rental contracts that have lasted some years have lower rents than newer contracts because they are more seldomly adjusted by the landlord and hence long-standing tenants benefit from a discount from the market level. Rents in Norway have increased less in recent years, and vary less by location, by comparison with house prices. In an international context, rent increases are at the average among OECD countries in the period from 2005 to 2019 (OECD, 2021b).

Rents in social housing are based on average rents in similar dwellings in the same area, which means approximately market rents. This principle is followed in most urban areas, where most social rental homes are located (Barlindhaug *et al*, 2018). There is no restriction on converting the tenure status of dwellings in Norway today.

Since 2015, the government set a temporary framework for all residential mortgage lending, which has been changed three times. Currently, the rules require a maximum debt rate of five times gross income, a maximum 85 per cent loan-to-value ratio, and down payment for loans with a loan-to-value ratio of more than 60 per cent. In Oslo, the maximum loan-to-value ratio is set to 60 per cent for secondary properties to halt the growth in buy-to-let lettings. The regulations are subject to a 'flexibility quota', which during normal times allow banks to deviate from the requirements for 10 per cent of their mortgage lending (8 per cent in Oslo) (Ministry of Finance, 2021b).

Composition of the rental market

In 2018 the ownership of rental housing was as follows: employers 2 per cent, private large-scale corporates 10 per cent, organisations and private foundations (including student associations) 8 per cent, private individuals (including relatives/friends) 69 per cent, municipalities 8 per cent, and others 3 per cent. Further, 41 per cent of the tenants lived in the same building as the owner (Statistics Norway, 2018).

Table 9.5 shows rental ownership in the five largest cities in 2006 and 2018. There has been a significant increase in private individual landlords, and for some cities private large-scale corporates. The first category, relatives/ friends/employer/other, mainly operates with rents below market level because of the relationship between the tenant and the landlord. The latter landlord segment decreased substantially in all five cities, which implies a shift towards more profit-oriented rental landlordism.

Table 9.5: Ownership of rental housing in Oslo and other large cities, 2006 and 2020 (% of rental sector)

	Oslo	Bergen	Stavanger	Trondheim	Tromsø
2006					
Relatives/friends/employer/other	19	21	19	17	28
Private individual	35	41	52	40	45
Private large-scale corporate	32	25	7	22	12
Municipalities	10	11	20	14	9
Student dwellings	4	2	2	7	6
2020					
Relatives/friends/employers/other	7	10	8	10	13
Private individual	40	52	64	52	68
Private large-scale corporate	44	30	17	32	10
Municipalities	6	5	8	4	7
Student dwellings	4	3	3	3	2

Source: Statistics Norway (2021h).

Short-term lettings

Norway, as in many other countries, have seen the emergence of short-term and online rental accommodation. The most evident is Airbnb, which quickly spread from the early starting point in 2008. Airbnb continued to grow year by year until 2020. The development has taken place particularly in areas with comprehensive and increased tourism, both in large cities and the surrounding areas and in rural areas. By the number of reserved rooms Airbnb increased by 45 per cent in 2018 from the previous year – while hotels increased by only 2 per cent – and increased by nearly 30 per cent in 2019. Total income from Airbnb increased by 30 per cent from 2018 to 2019 and amounted to three billion NOK in 2019. The median host rental income was 44,068 NOK (Capita, 2018, 2019).

Concerns about the short-term rental market expressed by the hotel industry and local populations have led to several measures by the authorities (NOU, 2017:4). New legislation within the residential real estate law was asserted from 1 January 2020 to limit short-term lettings (rental on a daily or weekly basis during a 30-day period) for homeowners. In condominiums, owners are only allowed short term lettings for a maximum of 90 days a year. Homeowner associations are allowed to shorten that limit to 60 days or increase it to 120 days. In housing cooperatives, the new legislation allows for short-term lettings for the first time, and for a maximum of 30 days a year. In addition, the law prohibits private individuals and private companies from buying more than two residential units in the same homeowner's association. In 2018 and 2020, new tax rules on short-term leases were introduced (as discussed earlier).

Digital platforms have become important for tenants looking for rental homes, for landlords seeking tenants, and for agents and rental brokers managing rental properties on behalf of landlords. They seek to ensure safe rental conditions and a correct rental price for both landlords and tenants throughout the rental period, at the cost of the landlord. For the landlords they arrange all the practicalities with advertisements, views, lease and deposit, a credit and reference check of the tenants and ensure that the condition of the accommodation is thoroughly documented when moving in and moving out. In addition to Airbnb, there are online platforms for both landlords and people or companies seeking separate apartments for short-term letting according to temporary employment, apartments that are options between long-term apartment rentals and short-term hotel stays. There are also investment companies offering guidelines for property investments for both small-scale and large-scale landlords.

Secondary properties

Owning an additional dwelling beyond one's home (except second homes) has several motives and purposes, such as an investment, wealth accumulation, to increase current income by letting out, to commuter housing, second homes in the city, intergenerational support, or keeping a low valued vacated home in the countryside. Table 9.6 reveals that owning two or more dwellings is relatively common in Norway, accounting for about one in ten households in 2019, and the share increased by about 50 per cent between 1988 and 2010, followed by a minor increase since then.

Since these properties do not include second homes, it is probably high by an international context. Ownership of second homes is also high in Norway, as 24 per cent of households owned a secondary home in 2018 (Statistics Norway, 2021i; 2021j).

Measured by the housing stock, there were 399,855 such secondary properties registered in Norway, in the third quarter of 2020, which constitutes about 15 per cent of the housing stock (Ambita and Norges Eiendomsmeglerforbund, 2020). The EU-SILC 2018 showed that 10.5 per cent of households owned one additional dwelling, 1.4 per cent owned two and 0.6 per cent owned three or more additional dwellings either in Norway or abroad (Statistics Norway, 2018). The ownership of secondary properties is geographically widespread, but in most rural areas a higher percentage of households owned additional dwellings (Statistics Norway, 2021k). Properties owned abroad are mostly located in Sweden, followed by the US and then the UK.

Table 9.6: Households owning two or more dwellings, Norway, 1988–2019

	1988	2010	2019
Per cent of households	6.2	9.7	10.1
Market value primary home (NOK)		2,404,000	3,751,300
Market value secondary property (NOK)		1,773,200	2,906,200

Note: The numbers only include dwellings not in the same house as the owner, other than the main dwelling of the owner.

Source: Statistics Norway (1988; 2021i).

Transparency International Norway examined the ownership of a selection of properties owned by legal persons and foreign individuals, in the two most attractive downtown areas in Oslo, characterised by high urban, business and housing development, with a view to money laundering in the real estate market. They found a significant element of ownership in tax havens, a certain proportion of natural and legal persons registered in countries with a moderate to high level of corruption, and in some properties, there was a complicated ownership structure that allows access and identification of real licensees difficult (Transparency International Norway, 2021).

Rental housing quality

Data on the rental sector unfortunately does not distinguish between PRS and social rented housing. Table 9.7 measures housing size by the number of rooms and by square metres for renters and homeowners. In general, renters live in smaller dwellings than homeowners do, and co-ops fall in between. Even if there are marginal differences between homeowners and co-op residents today, there are still differences in the size of the dwellings, mainly because co-ops are in urban areas with smaller dwellings, often in blocks of flats, and these dwellings function as social housing. Renters mainly occupy one-room dwellings and those less than 40 square metres. The average numbers of rooms are somewhat higher than average for OECD countries (OECD, 2021b).

In 2020, 4 per cent of homeowners, 7 per cent of co-op owners and 14 per cent of renters were overcrowded. The official Norwegian measure of overcrowding measures households living in dwellings where the number of rooms is fewer than the number of persons, or one person living in one room (kitchen, bath, hallway and small rooms below six square metres do not count) and the dwelling is smaller than 25 square metres. In Oslo, the numbers were respectively 7 per cent, 11 per cent and 23 per cent (Statistics Norway, 2021c). In an international context, overcrowding is not high in Norway (OECD, 2021b).

Table 9.7: Number of rooms and square metres, percentage of households, owners and renters, 2007 and 2018

	Owner-occupied		Cooperatives		Renters	
	2007	2018	2007	2018	2007	2018
1 room	1	1	2	2	14	21
2 rooms	5	6	25	23	37	40
3 rooms	15	17	37	41	27	22
4 rooms	26	24	26	23	10	10
5 rooms	24	22	9	8	7	4
6 rooms	15	16	1	2	3	2
7 rooms+	15	15	1	1	3	1
< 40 sq. m.	0	1	2	4	13	23
40–59 sq. m.	3	4	16	16	23	24
60–79 sq. m.	8	9	39	37	26	27
80–99 sq. m.	13	12	25	20	15	12
100–129 sq. m.	25	21	13	17	12	9
130–159 sq. m.	19	16	3	5	5	3
160+ sq. m.	32	37	1	1	6	3

Source: Statistics Norway (2021k).

Rents and contracts

As for house prices, rents vary by the quality and the location of the dwellings. In addition, in the rental market other conditions also matter, such as the length of tenancy and type of landlord. In 2018, 75 per cent of the tenants paid market rent (Statistics Norway, 2018). Table 9.8 show that the level of rents increases steadily by the number of rooms in the dwellings. We can also see that average rents in the most urban areas, Oslo and Bærum, are about double those in the least urban areas for one-room dwellings, and between twice and three times for four-room and five-room dwellings.

Contracts that have lasted some years have lower rents than newer contracts, and the difference from the newest tenancies increase by the length of tenancies, so that long-term tenancies are more seldom adjusted and so get a form of discount. Between the year 2006 and 2020, rents on new tenancies (entered current year), in other words market rents, increased by 140 per cent and older tenancies (contract entered more than six years ago) by 144 per cent. Compared to house prices, rents have increased less and vary less according to location. In an international context the increase in rents are at the average among OECD countries, in the period 2005 to 2019 (OECD, 2021b).

Table 9.8: Variation of monthly rent by urbanisation and dwelling size, NOK, 2021

	1-room	2-room	3-room	4-room	5-room+
Oslo and Bærum	8,750	12,080	14,810	18,410	22,270
Akershus	..	9,510	11,250	12,120	12,760
Bergen	6,610	9,150	11,310	13,710	18,930
Trondheim	6,990	9,560	11,560	14,150	20,020
Stavanger	..	8,740	10,780	12,390	..
20,000 and more inhabitants	6,380	7,960	9,540	10,790	13,100
2,000–19,999 inhabitants	4,970	6,960	7,960	9,080	9,710
200–1,999 inhabitants	..	5,890	7,100	7,320	7,930

Notes: By 31 December 2020 the exchange rate of 100 NOK was 11.7198 USD, 9.5508 EUR and 8.5865 GBP. Akershus is the neighbouring county of Oslo. The municipality Bærum is excluded from Akershus and added to Oslo. Bergen, Trondheim and Stavanger are, except Oslo, in that order, the largest cities in Norway.

Source: Statistics Norway (2021h).

In Norway short-term contracts dominate the rental market, partly because rental dominates among younger households as a temporary housing situation, and because renting is viewed as a temporary solution. In 2018, among those with time-limited contracts, 86 per cent had contracts for three years or less (Statistics Norway, 2018). Some tenants rent for a longer time or forever, mostly disadvantaged people or people in particular need.

Newer statistics on differences in rents according to type of landlord are not available. However, figures from 2013 showed that rents were highest for private companies, second highest for private individuals not in any relation to the tenant, third highest for private individuals related to the tenant through friendship or kinship, fourth highest for employers or others, and lowest for municipalities (social housing) or student dwellings (Ogbamichael et al, 2013).

Tenants in the rental sector

Table 9.9 shows that within the short time span from 2015 to 2020, the share of renters increased for low-income and vulnerable groups receiving housing allowances or social assistance. The opposite development took place for homeowners, while for the co-op sector there was little change. The table also shows increasing rents and decreasing homeownership (including co-ops) for the youngest age groups. This is a result of increasing house prices. The decline in homeownership has been a long-term trend among economically disadvantaged groups – people with low levels of education,

Table 9.9: Housing tenure by household economy and age, 2015 and 2020

	Owner-occupiers		Cooperatives		Renters	
	2015	2020	2015	2020	2015	2020
Income quartile						
Lowest	36	34	13	13	51	53
Second	61	61	17	17	21	22
Third	73	73	15	15	11	12
Highest	82	82	11	11	7	7
Benefit receipt						
Housing allowance	22	20	13	10	66	70
Social assistance	29	25	8	7	63	68
Social security, age < 67	45	45	17	16	38	39
Social security, age ≥ 67	64	66	18	17	18	17
Age group						
20–29	51	49	13	12	37	39
30–39	64	63	14	14	22	23
40–49	75	74	11	10	14	16
50–66	78	78	12	11	10	10
67–79	76	77	14	13	10	10

Source: Statistics Norway (2021c).

low income, recipients of social assistance and dwelling support – and among young adults aged 20 to 34, since the global financial crisis and as a result of the tightening of the mortgage terms (Killengreen Revold *et al*, 2018).

Affordability

As seen from Table 9.10, total yearly expenditures have increased by a marginal amount for homeowners and more for co-op residents. This is probably because co-ops mostly are in central areas where housing prices are highest, and where the numbers of younger people entering the housing market are higher. Homeowners are mostly located in rural areas, even if they are also located in urban and rural areas. Total expenditures have increased most for renters, probably because more renters live in urban areas, and that interest rates decreased from 2012 to 2018, which lowered total expenditures for homeowners and cooperatives, even if the house price increase could outweigh the interest rates effect for the latest entering the market. This partly explains the development in the percentage of households having housing expenditures more than 25 per cent of disposable income. However, the

Table 9.10: Housing expenditures and affordability by tenure, 2012 and 2018

	Owner-occupier		Cooperatives		Renters	
	2012	2018	2012	2018	2012	2018
Total yearly housing expenditure (NOK)	69,159	71,273	86,516	98,745	61,178	76,823
High housing expenditure (%)	13	11	35	34	49	59
Very high housing expenditure (%)	3	3	6	4	12	12

Note: At 31 December 2012, the exchange rate of 100 NOK was 55.912 USD, 7.756 EUR and 9.0399 GBP. At 31 Decmeber 2018, 100 NOK was 8.6911 USD, 9.9448 EUR and 11.0672 GBP.

Source: Statistics Norway (2021k).

increase of 10 per cent for renters also relates to more low-income groups among renters.

Housing cost burdens are relatively high in Norway in an international context. Within the rental sector the average housing cost burden (rent as share of disposable income) was 30.3 per cent in 2018, ranking second highest among OECD countries (OECD, 2021b).

The COVID-19 pandemic

On 26 February 2020, Norway received its first proven case of COVID-19. The government and the authorities implemented measures to limit the spread of the virus at an early stage. On 12 March the government introduced the first lockdown measures to contain the spread of the disease, including closing kindergartens, educational institutions, small and large businesses, restaurants, sports and cultural events, along with the introduction of travel restrictions, working from home and social distancing. The measures were eased before the summer, but were later reintroduced to varying degrees, and more stringently in March 2021 due to a major new outbreak of infections. In terms of health effects, Norway has performed better than most countries, measured by the extent of infections and the number of people seriously ill and dead by the end of August 2021. (Statistics Norway, 2021l).

To stabilise the economy, and to curb the economic downturn, the authorities also introduced comprehensive policy measures. Among these were a change in the redundancy regulations in that the state took a larger share of the burden; extension of unemployment benefits; various support schemes, such as tax relief, loans, guarantees and capital; compensation for reduced earnings for companies and businesses; and various measures for cultural, sports and other organisations. To maintain financial stability, the counter-cyclical capital buffer requirement for banks was reduced from 2.5 per cent to 1 per cent (Statistics Norway, 2021l).

The COVID-19 pandemic had a deep negative impact on the economy, compounded by the tightening of global financial conditions and decline in oil prices in the first months of 2020. Mainland GDP was 4.7 per cent lower than expected in 2020. The unemployment rate reached more than 10 per cent right after the first lockdown and 5 per cent in the fourth quarter of 2020 (excluding layoffs under three months). Increased public transfers shielded households and businesses, so that much of the decline in incomes and revenues fell on the state. However, with the gradual reopening of society with lower spread of infection, vaccines and relief of infection control, GDP for mainland Norway increased by 1.4 per cent from the first to the second quarter of 2021, and employment also rose. By June 2021, GDP for mainland Norway was back at about the same level as February 2020 (Statistics Norway, 2021l). Financial reserves from petroleum revenue gave Norway significant benefits in economic counter-cycle policy; and the use of oil money under COVID-19 was higher than during the global financial crisis. In addition to the various measures, the existing comprehensive welfare benefit schemes slowed down the negative economic effect of COVID-19 as they acted as automatic stabilisers and dampened the effects of the crisis on the economy. Further, financial support for sickness rights may have contributed to people staying home when they became ill, thus making the fight against the virus easier than it would otherwise have been. However, some households were hit extra hard, such as people with temporary or otherwise insecure employment.

The most significant measure affecting housing has been that the Norwegian State Bank brought the main policy rate of interest down to zero, the lowest ever. This reduced borrowing costs for corporate organisations and households but at the expense of rising house prices. Mortgage lending regulations were also relaxed by temporarily allowing banks to deviate from the flexibility quota, up to 20 per cent of new loans during the second and third quarters of 2020 for the whole country. Spending by the State Housing Bank on housing allowances expanded by 500 million NOK and on loans by five billion NOK (Ministry of Local Government and Modernisation, 2020).

As seen from Figure 9.1, house prices continued to increase during the pandemic period. Real house prices increased by 7.5 per cent at national level, and 10.5 per cent in Oslo, in 2020, continuing in the first months of 2021 and then the increase slowed. The PRS experienced the opposite development. Sharply after the pandemic outbreak, empty dwellings increased, because of students staying with their parents, reduced mobility in the labour market, and lower economic immigration. This created a heated public debate and criticism of the fact that landlords qualified for the government support schemes for business, since it could lead them to speculating in leaving the dwellings empty to receive more support rather than lowering the rent. To qualify for a compensation scheme, the company had to have employees and a loss of turnover of at least 30 per cent, which entitled them to a refund of up to 85 per cent of the company's unavoidable fixed costs. The support scheme thus included only large-scale landlords, to receive partial compensation for operating costs related to rent, insurance and other fixed costs. Some landlords reduced the rents. The rental survey showed that, at the national level, rents for one-room dwellings reduced by 7 per cent in 2020 compared with the previous year but increased for the rest. Another consequence of the pandemic was that new housing construction starts fell by 5 per cent and by 3 per cent for dwellings, in 2020; and completions by 4 per cent and 6 per cent respectively (Statistics Norway, 2021m). Demand for short-term rentals such as Airbnb likewise fell due a combination of COVID-19 and travel restrictions.

There will probably be several longer-term implications of the pandemic on housing. One is increasing housing prices and rents for some years due to the reduction in construction. Another is that the virus outbreak forced changes in work processes with more home working and more use of digital tools and digital technology. The scope of home working will then probably be higher than before the pandemic and reduce the benefits of living close to the workplace. This could change the settlement structure by lowering demand in the centre of big cities, and increases demand around the big cities, areas with good commuting opportunities, in smaller cities and in rural areas. The need for an extra room for a home office could contribute to the demand for larger dwellings, and thereby reduce demand in the most urban areas. Consequently, the growth in house prices and rents and the supply of dwellings may slow down in big cities and increase around big cities and in rural areas. Maybe this also will affect tenancies, as homeownership is easier to achieve outside the urban areas. For Norway's case, it could maintain a high rate of ownership, higher than otherwise, and then lower PRS than otherwise.

However, the rising international inflation caused by low interest rates in the COVID-19 period, was drastically worsened in 2022 by the energy crisis from the war in Ukraine and economic instability. The Norwegian State Bank started to increase the main policy rate at the end of 2021 followed by further increases in 2022 due to increasing inflation. A following economic downturn or even recession may then also apply to Norway. Then unemployment, economic hardship and higher interest rates will probably result in affordability problems and declining house prices, which may increase the PRS. These effects may also increase the pressure of affordable housing on policy makers, described as 'the third housing sector' initially in the chapter.

Conclusion

Path dependencies embedded in a historically shaped provision system play key roles in housing outcomes in Norway today, most notably a very high level of homeownership, limited involvement of property companies in the PRS and a residual social housing sector. Favourable taxation, historically low interest rates, and a rental sector not considered a good alternative, have maintained a high demand for homeownership along with high and rising house prices, and very high household debt. However, homeownership among the youngest and among low-income groups has fallen, with a consequent increase in the PRS. Small-scale private landlords dominate the rental market and have increased in later years. The rental sector is characterised by lower quality housing, short-term contracts, market-based rents and an increasing affordability problem for tenants. Although there are some differences in rents based on the type of landlord. Norway has a cautious political commitment to affordable housing and a rental sector with long-term contracts and below market rents, as an alternative to the market-based housing sector. Overall, in an international context Norway coped reasonably well in response to COVID-19. The pandemic had a deep and negative impact on the economy. However, low interest rates, increased public transfers and a comprehensive welfare safety net shielded households and businesses to a large degree, and house prices increased.

References

Ambita and Norges Eiendomsmeglerforbund (2020) 'Førstegangskjøpere og sekundærboliger' [First Time Homeowners and Secondary Properties], Report 2020 Q3, https://www.nef.no/wp-content/uploads/2020/12/Forstegangskjopere-og-sekundaerboliger_2020-Q3.pdf

Annaniassen, E. (2006) 'Norge – det socialdemokratiska ägerlandet' [Norway – the social democratic homeowner country] in B. Bengtsson (ed) *Varför så olika? Nordisk bostadspolitikk I jämförande historiskt ljus* [Why so Different? Nordic Housing Policy in a Comparative Historical Perspective], pp 159-218, Malmö, Égalité.

Barlindhaug, R., Holm, A., Lied, C., Ruud, M.E., Sommervoll, D.E. and Søholt, S. (2018) 'Storbyenes praksis for å hjelpe vanskeligstilte på utleieboligmarkedet' [The cities' practice of helping disadvantaged on the rental housing market], NIBR Report 2018:12.

Capita (2018) *Romdøgn for Airbnb og Hotell i Norge – 2018* [Numbers of Rooms per Day and Night for Airbnb and Hotels in Norway], https://www.nhoreiseliv.no/contentassets/c55367fac9c84a08bc9b370aebd9698a/capia_airbnb_hotell_norge2018.pdf

Capita (2019) *Skatt og inntekt Airbnb Norge* [Taxes and income Airbnb Norway], https://www.nhoreiseliv.no/contentassets/d4439e132c894c52a3af7200a25189a0/airbnb_skatt_est.2019.pdf

Eggum, T. and Røed Larsen, T.E. (2021) 'Is the housing market an inequality generator?', Housing Lab Working Paper Series, 2021/2.

Esping-Andersen, G. (1990) *The Three Worlds of Welfare Capitalism*, Cambridge, Polity Press.

The Financial Supervisory Authority of Norway (2020) *Boliglånsundersøkelsen 2020* [The Mortgage Survey 2020], https://www.finanstilsynet.no/conten tassets/283fc01171fb41a3bb618d2ee664ebc4/boliglansundersokelsen_2 020.pdf

Galster, G. and Wessel, T. (2019) 'Reproduction of social inequality through housing: a three-generational study from Norway', *Social Science Research*, 78(2), 119–136.

Grebstad, U. (2020) *Mer bruk av midlertidige boliger* [More Use of Temporary Housing], Statistics Norway, Municipal Housing, https://www.ssb.no/ bygg-bolig-og-eiendom/artikler-og-publikasjoner/kommunale-boli ger-arkiv

Holmøy, A. (2018) *Bruk av kommunale boliger* [Use of Municipal Housing], Reports 2018/15, Statistics Norway, https://ssb.brage.unit.no/ssb-xmlui/ bitstream/handle/11250/2499054/RAPP2018-15_web.pdf?isAllowed= y&sequence=1

IMF (International Monetary Fund) (2020) *Norway Financial System Stability Assessment*, IMF Country Report No. 20/259, https://www.imf.org/en/ Publications/CR/Issues/2020/08/07/Norway-Financial-System-Stabil ity-Assessment-Press-Release-and-Statement-by-the-Executive-49670

Killengreen Revold, M. (2019) *Færre unge kjøper bolig* [Fewer Young People Buy Housing], Statistics Norway, Reports 2019/23.

Killengreen Revold, M., Sandvik, L. and With, M.L. (2018) *Bolig og boforhold – for befolkningen og utsatte grupper* [Housing and Housing Condition – for the Population and Vulnerable Groups], Statistics Norway, Reports 2018/13.

Ministry of Finance (2021a) *Prop. 1 LS (2020–2021) for Budsjettåret 2021 Skatter, avgifter og toll 2021* [Prop. 1 LS (2020–2021) for the Budget Year 2021: Taxes, Fees and Customs 2021], https://www.regjeringen.no/no/ dokumenter/prop.-1-l-20202021/id2768694/?ch=26

Ministry of Finance (2021b) *Boliglånsforskriften 1. januar 2020–31. desember 2020* [The Mortgage Regulations 1 January 2020–31. December 2020], https://www.regjeringen.no/no/tema/okonomi-og-budsjett/fina nsmarkedene/boliglansforskriften-1.-januar-202031.-desember-2020/ id2679449/

Ministry of Local Government and Modernisation (2020) *Alle trenger et trygt hjem. Nasjonal strategi for den sosiale boligpolitikken (2021–2024)* [Everyone Needs a Safe Home. National Strategy for Social Housing Policy (2021– 2024)], https://www.regjeringen.no/contentassets/c2d6de6c12d548449 5d4ddeb7d103ad5/oppdatert-versjon-alle-trenger-en-nytt-hjem.pdf

NBBL (2021) *Boligbyggelagenes løsninger* [Housing Association's Housing Solutions], https://www.nbbl.no/om-oss/interessepolitikk/leie-til-eie/

National Strategy for Social Housing Policy (2021–2024) https://www.regj eringen.no/no/dokumenter/nasjonal-strategi-for-den-sosiale-boligpolitik ken-2021-2024/id2788470/

The Norway towards 2025 Committee (2021) 'Noen utfordringer for en balansert og bærekraftig økonomisk utvikling etter pandemien: Innspill til Perspektivmeldingen 2021 fra utvalget Norge mot 2025' ['Some challenges for a balanced and sustainable economic development after the pandemic: Input to the Perspective Report 2021 from the Norway towards 2025 committee'], https://www.norgemot2025.no/files/2021/ 02/Norge-mot-2025-rapport-feb-2021.pdf

NOU (Norwegian Official report) (2014:13) *Capital Taxation in an International Economy*, https://www.regjeringen.no/en/dokumenter/nou-2014-13/id2342691/?ch=13

NOU (Official Norwegian Reports) (2017:4) *Sharing Economy – Opportunities and Challenges*, https://www.regjeringen.no/en/dokumenter/nou-2017-4/id2537495/

OBOS (2021a) *OBOS deleie* [OBOS Shared Ownership], https://nye.obos. no/ny-bolig/artikler/generelle/deleie/

OBOS (2021b) *OBOS Bostart* [OBOS Residence start], https://nye.obos. no/ny-bolig/artikler/generelle/obos-bostart/

OECD (2019) *Economic Surveys Norway*, https://www.oecd.org/economy/ surveys/Norway-2019-OECD-Economic%20Survey_Overview.pdf

OECD (2021a) *Social Expenditure Database*, https://www.oecd.org/social/ expenditure.htm

OECD (2021b) *OECD Affordable Housing Database*, http://www.oecd.org/ housing/data/affordable-housing-database/

OECD (2021c) *Household Debt*, https://data.oecd.org/hha/household-debt.htm

OECD (2021d) *Tax on Property (Indicator)*, https://data.oecd.org/tax/tax-on-property.htm

Ogbamichael, T, Holmøy, A. and Nygaard, R. (2013) 'Utvidlelse av leiemarkedsundersøkelsen' [Extension of the rental market survey], https:// www.ssb.no/priser-og-prisindekser/artikler-og-publikasjoner/_attachm ent/108690?_ts=13e1c8515a0

Oslo municipality (2019a) 'Kunnskapsgrunnlag for en kommunal boligpolitikk' [Knowledge basis for a municipal housing policy], https:// www.oslo.kommune.no/getfile.php/13325532-1558347273/Tjenes ter%20og%20tilbud/Politikk%20og%20administrasjon/Byutvikling/ Kunnskapsgrunnlag%20for%20en%20kommunal%20boligpolitikk.pdf

Oslo municipality (2019b) 'Nye veier til egen bolig' [New roads to own home], City council case 145/19, https://tjenester.oslo.kommune.no/ekst ern/einnsyn-fillager/filtjeneste/fil?virksomhet=976819853&filnavn=vedl egg%2F2019_05%2F1308121_1_1.pdf

Oslo municipality (2019c) 'Sak 47 Nye veier til egen bolig – Byrådssak 145 av 23.05.2019' [Case 47 New roads to own home – City Council case 145 of 23.05.2019], City council decision, https://www.oslo.kommune.no/dok/Bystyret/2020_02/1346909_1_1.PDF

Prosser, S. (2020) 'Den tredje boligsektor: Hva det kan bli, og hvorfor vi trenger det' [The third housing sector: what it can be, and why we need it], *Tidsskrift for boligforskning*, 3(2), 180–192.

Real Estate Norway, FINN and Eiendomsverdi AS (2021) *Housing Price Statistics*, https://eiendomnorge.no/boligprisstatistikk/

Stamsø, M.A. (2009) 'Housing and the welfare state in Norway', *Scandinavian Political Studies*, 31(4), 1–26.

The State Housing Bank (2021) 'Statistikkbanken' [Statistic Bank], https://statistikk.husbanken.no/

Statistics Norway (1988) *Survey of Housing Conditions*, https://www.ssb.no/historisk-statistikk/emner/personlig-okonomi-og-boforhold

Statistics Norway (2018) *EU-SILC 2018*, https://doi.org/10.18712/NSD-NSD2671-V6

Statistics Norway (2021a) *Population and Housing Census*, https://www.ssb.no/a/histstat/publikasjoner/

Statistics Norway (2021b) *Population and Housing Census*, https://www.ssb.no/statbank/list/fobbolig

Statistics Norway (2021c) *Housing Conditions, Register-Based*, https://www.ssb.no/statbank/list/boforhold

Statistics Norway (2021d) *Price Index for Existing Dwellings*, https://www.ssb.no/priser-og-prisindekser/statistikker/bpi

Statistics Norway (2021e) *Earnings*, https://www.ssb.no/en/arbeid-og-lonn/statistikker/lonnansatt/aar

Statistics Norway (2021f) *Table 12013: Basic Data – Other Municipal Assistance for Dwellings (M) 2015 – 2020*, https://www.ssb.no/en/statbank/table/12013/

Statistics Norway (2021g) *Property Tax*, https://www.ssb.no/en/offentlig-sektor/statistikker/eiendomsskatt

Statistic Norway (2021h) *Rental Market Survey*, https://www.ssb.no/en/statbank/list/lmu

Statistic Norway (2021i) *Table 10315: Formuesrekneskap for hushald. Sum, tal hushald og gjennomsnitt for hushald med beløp 2010 – 2019* [10315: Property Accounts for Households. Total, Number of Households and Average for Households with Amounts 2010 – 2019], https://www.ssb.no/statbank/table/10315/

Statistics Norway (2021j) *Survey of Consumer Expenditures*, https://www.ssb.no/en/statbank/list/fbu

Statistics Norway (2021k) *Housing Conditions, Survey on Living Conditions*, https://www.ssb.no/en/bygg-bolig-og-eiendom/statistikker/bo

Statistics Norway (2021l) *Norge under Korona/COVID-19 Statistikk om koronakrisen* [Norway under Korona/COVID-19 Statistics on the Corona Crisis], https://www.ssb.no/korona/statistikk-om-koronakrisen#blokk-5

Statistics Norway (2021m) *Byggeareal* [Building Area], https://www.ssb.no/bygg-bolig-og-eiendom/statistikker/byggeareal/aar

Tranøy, B.S, Stamsø M.A., and Hjertaker I. (2020) 'Equality as a driver of inequality? Universalistic welfare, generalised creditworthiness and financialised housing markets', *West European Politics*, 43(2), 390–411.

Transparency International Norway (2021) *Hvem eier Oslo? Hvitvaskingsrisiko i eiendomsmarkedet Oslo* [Who Owns Oslo? Money Laundering Risk in the Real Estate Market Oslo], http://transparency.no/2021/01/27/hvem-eier-oslo-hvitvaskingsrisiko-i-eiendomsmarkedet/

Veiviseren.no (2021) *For bolig og tjenesteområde* [For Housing and Service Area], https://www.veiviseren.no/stotte-i-arbeidsprosess/leie-og-kjop-av-bolig/leie-til-eie-for-vanskeligstilte

Wessel, T. (2002) 'Fra leie til eie – konvertering av leiegårder i norske byer' [From rent to ownership – conversion of tenancies in Norwegian cities], *Tidsskrift for samfunnsforskning*, 3, 299–331.

10

Private rented markets in Spain and housing affordability

Montserrat Pareja-Eastaway and Teresa Sánchez-Martínez

Introduction

The Spanish housing system historically has been characterised by an imbalance in tenure in favour of homeownership and a social housing stock that is either residual or completely neglected. Since the mid–20th century, housing policies have not been impartial regarding this situation. In fact, housing provision in Spain has focused greatly on the homeownership sector, reducing social housing stock over time, and granting the private rented sector (PRS) the benefit of several regulations that have failed to change its downward course.

Analysis of the PRS in Spain cannot be decontextualised from the characteristics of the Spanish housing system at large. The Spanish PRS has often performed the role of social housing during booms in the housing market, as low–income households could not afford to enter any other form of tenure (Pareja-Eastaway, 2010; Pareja-Eastaway and Sánchez Martínez, 2016; López-Rodríguez and Matea *l*, 2019). Thus, rather than fulfilling the well-known theoretical functions of the PRS throughout the typical housing career (that is, first housing access or increasing socioeconomic mobility), in Spain, the PRS has partially solved the issue of housing access for disadvantaged groups. However, the rise in demand without a proper response from the supply side has contributed to a generalised increase in rents, which has also been aggravated in recent years by the popularity of temporary subletting for tourist purposes.

The narrow PRS is one factor that has partially prevented Spain from engaging in resilient reactions to the economic and financial crisis of 2008 and the recent COVID-19 pandemic, both of which have created an unstable framework for employment and economic growth and have had a negative impact on housing affordability. Since access to homeownership has been removed from the equation during these crises – due to the tightening of credit conditions for obtaining a mortgage and the sector's bad reputation stemming from the increase in evictions carried out, among other issues – the growing pressure to find affordable housing is central to the Spanish housing debate (Pareja-Eastaway and Sánchez Martínez, 2016; López-Rodríguez and Matea, 2019). The historical trajectory of the Spanish housing system has currently left the authorities with fewer alternatives than in the past to grant adequate housing access, placing the PRS squarely in the spotlight of housing policy design.

The 21st century finds the Spanish PRS in a critical situation: on the one hand, it likely represents the most interesting alternative for alleviating the lack of affordable housing available in the country (Módenes Cabrerizo, 2019). On the other, tenants living in rented accommodation are experiencing excessive housing burden costs: in fact, Spain currently registers the highest housing burden cost in the European Union. In addition, the quality of dwellings in the sector is generally poor and although some efforts are currently underway to support the retrofitting of private rented dwellings, there is still a long way to go. While demand is guaranteed, the supply side of the market is struggling to fill the gap of years of neglect and lack of interest on the part of landlords, due to the low profitability of private rented dwellings.

The policy debate around the PRS is currently very active in Spain (Pareja-Eastaway and Sánchez Martínez, 2017; García-Montalvo, 2019; 2020). The country recently approved a new Housing Plan, Royal Decree (7/2019) which centres on 'urgent measures for housing and the rented market' that are mainly focused on easing the pressure of rising rents and facilitating affordable housing in the sector. The relative degree of freedom that Autonomous Communities (ACs) and local governments have under this umbrella is presently generating a controversial debate. On the one hand, measures such as rent control or the expropriation of housing for reasons of social interest are being considered (Argelich Comelles, 2017). On the other, there are political and economic discrepancies regarding the efficiency of these instruments designed to improve the functioning of the private rental market, as well as questions about their constitutionality, in some cases (Pareja-Eastaway and Sánchez Martínez, 2009; Nasarre-Aznar and Molina-Roig, 2017; López-Rodríguez and Matea, 2020; Ponce, 2020; Algaba Ros, 2021).

In this chapter we discuss the PRS in Spain and its consistently diminishing participation in the Spanish housing system, despite several regulatory attempts to redirect this trend. This downward progression has been accompanied by the worsening of living conditions in rented dwellings, which has only been made worse by the effects of both the global financial crisis (GFC) of 2008 and the COVID-19 pandemic. Scholars and policy makers alike currently agree on the need for a dramatic change in this pathway, given that the problem of affordability cannot be solved without considering the private rented sector as a key segment of development. Here, we argue that a structural change in the PRS's trajectory can be achieved by considering the multifaceted aspects of the sector in the context of the wider territory. The diversity of functions and attributes of the Spanish PRS is expanding; therefore, national strategies and policies should be considered as a framework that then allows for further tailored interventions to be made at lower levels of government, especially at the local level. After all, a solution in one area will not necessarily work in another. In this regard, there is an intermediate step related to the knowledge available in the sector that must be solved: currently, statistics about formalised rent contracts are missing. This information is only available in terms of the supply prices disclosed by private companies, such as Fotocasa and Idealista. Since there is a large deficit of information, it is hard to believe that institutional decisions are supported by effective diagnoses of the current situation, especially considering the lack of homogeneity and the fragmentation of the data that is available (Rodríguez Alonso and Espinoza Pino, 2018).

We begin with an overview of the continuously falling trajectory of the PRS's participation in Spanish housing tenure, which has ended with only a slight rebound after 2008. Next, a discussion of the characteristics of supply and demand in the Spanish PRS will follow, considering the increasing vulnerability of tenants, the rise of temporary subletting and the large fragmentation of the supply of available rented housing. We pay particular attention to the sector's changing regulations and its overall lack of effectiveness in providing adequate affordable housing. We also include an in-depth analysis of the short-term and likely long-term effects of the COVID-19 pandemic on the Spanish PRS, as well as policies that aim to address it. Finally, we will discuss the relationship between the PRS and the problem of affordability in the country and will suggest possible courses of action.

A turning point in the downward trajectory? The private rental sector's recent evolution in Spain

For decades, the rented sector in Spain has not offered a real alternative to homeownership in terms of housing tenure. The explanation for this phenomenon can be found in the non-neutral nature of housing policies in Spain – which have essentially encouraged the acquisition (rather than the rental) of housing since the mid-20th century – coupled with the favourable conditions of the financial market in terms of mortgage lending. In addition, the rented sector in Spain has long been the scene of diverse and wide-ranging regulatory measures. While rent control legislation has opted to freeze rents and to extend contracts indefinitely, it has also depleted the market's capacity to generate new rented housing supply until 1985, when a drastic liberalisation measure was adopted that still did not represent a clear recovery for the sector. In fact, the rent regulations adopted that year eliminated the possible incentives for maintaining a healthy rented sector. As a result, Spain is internationally known as a country where a certain 'culture' or 'ideology' of homeownership predominates (Ronald, 2008).

The diminishing participation of the rented stock in the housing market has gone hand in hand with the decrease of (publicly rented) social housing in the country (Pareja-Eastaway and San Martin, 2002). The continuous decrease in social housing stock has left the private rented sector as the sole alternative to homeownership. In contrast, homeownership has slightly reduced its participation in the country's housing stock, decreasing from 79.5 per cent in 2004 to 75.9 per cent in 2019. When compared to other European countries, Spain is no longer among those with the highest rates of participation in the homeownership sector. Romania (95.8 per cent), Hungary (91.7 per cent), Poland (84.2 per cent) and Norway (80.3 per cent) each reflect higher percentages than Spain, while Italy (72.4 per cent), The Netherlands (68.9 per cent) and Sweden (63.6 per cent) show percentages that are below Spain. The relative decrease in the housing stock devoted to homeownership has been counterbalanced by a relative increase in the rented sector: in 2008, the PRS represented 11 per cent of the housing stock, while in 2019 its participation reached 15.4 per cent.

The financial and economic crisis of 2008 was a turning point from which the private rental market grew in Spain. However, the same was not true for social housing or housing with rents under the market price. On the contrary, the social housing sector has experienced a continuous decline, one that has been further accentuated since the real estate boom during the 2000s. These trends indicate that the private rental market will need to offset the downward trend in rental housing by offering dwellings with rents below the market rate (Pareja-Eastaway and Sánchez-Martínez, 2016; see Figure 10.1).

The lack of a strong rented sector presents considerable secondary problems in Spain, such as the enormous level of indebtedness of homeowners that should be living in another form of tenure, as well as the persistence of a hidden demand for social housing.

According to the European Survey of Income and Living Conditions, 24.1 per cent of the Spanish population currently lives in rented housing, a figure that is lower than the rest of the countries of the European Union, which sees an average of 30.2 per cent of the population living in rented housing (EU-SILC, Eurostat, 2019). The distribution between private and public rents in Spain is as follows: 15.4 per cent of the population lives in rented housing at market price and 8.7 per cent in rented housing at a lower price than the market price (which includes rent subsidised by the public sector: 2.7 per cent, and rent-free housing: 6 per cent).

However, although the weight of rented housing is comparatively low in Spain compared to European levels, in the last 15 years there has been

Figure 10.1: Evolution of privately rented housing and housing rented below the market price in Spain, 2004–2019*

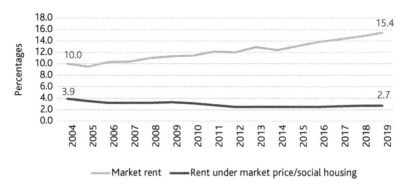

Market rent ——Rent under market price/social housing

Note: * Excluding rent-free housing.

Source: INE (National Statistics Institute) databases 2019: Living Conditions Survey (ECV).

a growing increase in the percentage of private rented housing: from 10 per cent in 2004 to 15.4 per cent in 2019 – an increase of more than 50 per cent on average, with differing intensities in the country's 17 ACs (see Figure 10.2a). It is also important to highlight the significant differences in the size of the private rented market between the regions with the greatest weight in the rented market – such as the Balearic Islands (31.7 per cent), Catalonia (23.1 per cent), Madrid (19.7 per cent) and the Canary Islands (17 per cent) – and the regions with the lowest weight, such as Extremadura and Galicia (each 8.1 per cent) (Figure 10.2b). The demand for rented housing has increased in Spain's most populous cities, where the greatest concentration of economic activity and migratory flows are found (European Commission, 2019; Hornbeck and Moretti, 2019).

The recent changes arising in the Spanish private rented market are similar to those occurring in other European countries. The growth of large cities and the pressures exerted by the varied components of demand are forcing local, regional and national governments to instate a diverse range of measures to address the lack of affordable housing. The current situation in Spain is a direct consequence of the 2008 GFC, which changed the foundations of the housing system. The increase in unemployment, the rise in temporary housing contracts and the decrease of household income are key consequences of the crisis and some of the main reasons for changes in the housing system. Despite the beginnings of economic recovery that commenced in 2013, difficulties in housing access are determined by the continued inability of low-income groups to find permanent occupation, as the labour market is still highly unstable and precarious and particularly affects young households (Anghel *et al*, 2018; Lozano and Rentería, 2018). Since 2008, the reluctance of financial entities to grant new mortgage loans

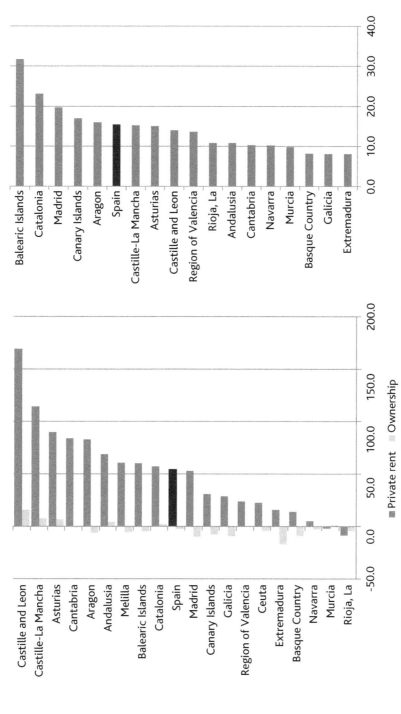

Figure 10.2: (a) Variation of households living in homeownership and private rented dwellings, 2004–2019; (b) private rented housing stock in Spain in 2019

Source: Own elaboration based on Institute of Statistics Spain (INE) Survey of living conditions (several years).

Figure 10.3: Rent growth in Autonomous Communities, 2015–2020 (%)

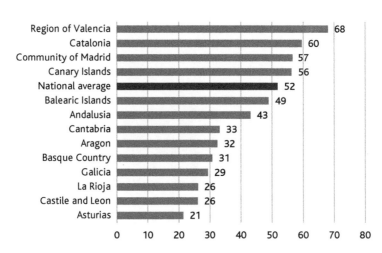

Source: Statista, 2020, residential rental market in Spain (based on Fotocasa.es).

to Spanish households, as well as these households' relative inability to pay part of the costs of acquisition with their savings, should also be considered determinants of the increase in demand for private rented housing. Likewise, the elimination of tax deductions for home purchases as of January 2013 also represents a change in the biases inherent in housing policy, which for more than 40 years actively focused on promoting access to homeownership.

As in many other European countries, pressures from the demand side and the relative lack of adaptation to changing housing needs – evidenced by the dwindling supply of rented dwellings – have led to a considerable increase in rents in the last five years. On average, Spanish rents increased around 51 per cent per square metre between 2015 and 2020. The intensity of this generalised rise in rents differs according to the AC, with a spectrum ranging from a maximum increase of 68.02 per cent in the Region of Valencia to a minimum increase of 21.39 per cent in Asturias (see Figure 10.3).

As we will see later in the chapter, the pressure exerted by the increase in private rent demand has pushed up rents, given the scarce supply in this market. This fact, together with the stagnation of household incomes, has caused many tenants to face high housing costs that bear an excessive burden on their family budgets and therefore increase their financial vulnerability.

Young, overburdened by debt and temporarily employed: the tenant profile in Spain

According to the latest Housing and Rent Barometer prepared by the Centre for Sociological Research (CIS, 2018), which surveys the reasons to live in a particular type of housing tenure in Spain, 42.3 per cent of Spanish renting households claimed that the main reason they opted for the rented market was their inability to buy a home due to a lack of income, followed by 14.9 per cent of respondents who did not want to take on a mortgage and an additional 14.9 per cent of respondents who stated that a rented home allows them greater socioeconomic mobility.

The rented market has often been considered a first step in an individual's housing career for most segments of the Spanish population. In fact, it is precisely the group comprised of young households has shown the highest increase in the number of rented housing tenants in Spain. The notable proportion of rented housing currently occupied by households aged 16–29 years old must be emphasised: 52.1 per cent, while the 30–44-year-old age bracket represents a further 32 per cent of the rented housing market in Spain. This indicates a marked increase from the end of the 1990s, when these young households occupied 18 per cent and 11.8 per cent of the rental market, respectively (Figure 10.4a).

Although there is a growing trend in rising rents for all types of households across the rented market, this increase is higher for households whose primary earner is unemployed (27.8 per cent in 2018) or employed under a temporary contract (37.3 per cent in 2018). The combination of low income and the risk of job loss makes it difficult for a significant percentage of households to access a home mortgage, though they also struggle to pay their rents at existing market prices (Figure 10.4b).

The implications of the lack of social housing in Spain are extremely important when it comes to providing affordable housing to vulnerable households, a group that has increased considerably due to the dramatic impact of both the GFC and the COVID-19 pandemic. In the aftermath of the financial crisis, many home buyers were unemployed and faced eviction due to their inability to pay their mortgages. Given the shortage of social housing, evicted families ended up living in privately rented accommodation, moving in with family or friends, benefiting from the so-called 'Mediterranean mattress', which refers to the relevance of a network of family and friends (Allen *et al*, 2004), subletting rooms in shared flats or even squatting in empty dwellings. Unsurprisingly, the distribution of tenants in Spain by salary (in euros, 2020) shows that the majority belong to lower income segments (see Figure 10.5).

Another collective that has steadily increased its presence in the PRS is the multifaceted group of immigrants living in Spain. In 2010, 46.3 per cent of immigrants from the European Union lived in the PRS, while 71.2 per cent of immigrants arriving from the rest of the world also lived in rented accommodation. In comparison, only 8.9 per cent of Spanish households lived in rented housing at the same time. Independent of country of origin, all households have increased their participation in the PRS in 2020, though

Figure 10.4: Tenant profile by age and employment: (a) age; (b) employment situation of economically active households

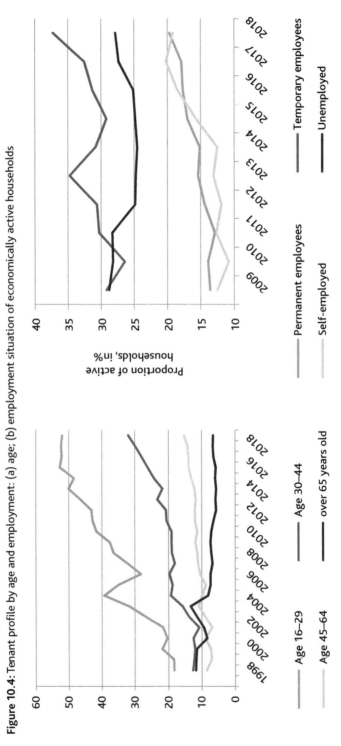

Source: Own elaboration using INE (National Statistics Institute) databases: Household Panel (HP) and Living Conditions Survey (ECV) (several years).

Figure 10.5: Distribution of tenants in Spain by annual salary in euros, 2020

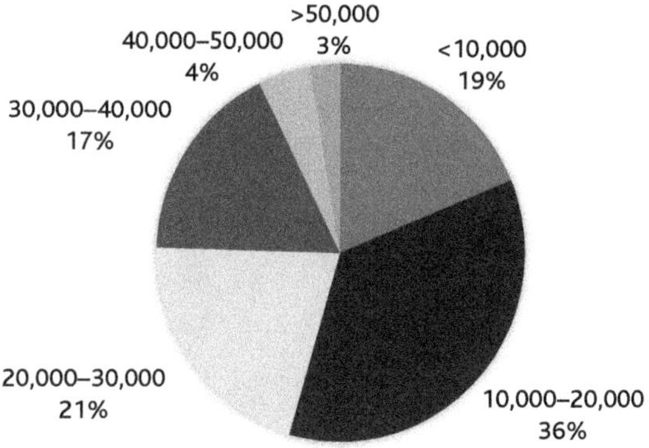

Source: Statista, 2020, Residential rental market in Spain (based on Alquiler Seguro).

with varying intensities: while the percentage of Spanish households living in the private rented market has more than doubled since 2010 (15.4 per cent), immigrant households from the EU and from the rest of the world have increased to 60.5 per cent and 79.3 per cent, respectively. Low-income immigrants have traditionally targeted the private rented market as a first step in their housing career in their new host country, while demand from middle- and high-income immigrants has mainly been directed toward homeownership, particularly the purchase of second homes in heavily touristic areas. Two important considerations should be made regarding the future of homeownership and the private rented market after 2020: on the one hand, the impact Brexit may have on British homeowners in Spain and, on the other, the possible lifestyle changes surrounding leisure consumption and life in post-pandemic Spanish society. Both aspects may have considerable impact on the demand for second homes, which might also affect the private rented market in certain areas of Spain.

Since 2008 rents have experienced a notable growth in many main metropolitan areas, rising far above both home sales prices and standard wages. Households have also witnessed a steep rise in their housing expenditures compared to their net incomes. In fact, Spain has one of the highest proportions in Europe of households whose spending on housing costs constitutes an overburden when viewed in relation to their net incomes (Figure 10.6). According to Eurostat's criteria, a household is in a situation of cost overburden when it spends more than 40 per cent of its income on housing. Such situations are far more common for tenants in the rented market, who generally exhibit a higher degree of vulnerability than homeowners in terms of tenure stability and financial situations, regardless of whether homeowners have outstanding mortgage payments. Thus, the degree of precariousness Spanish tenants experience is currently

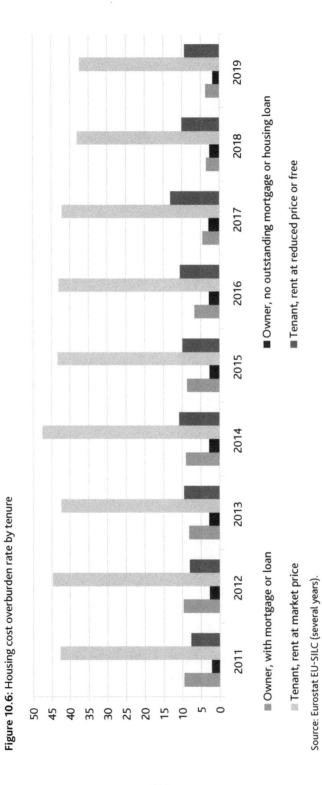

Figure 10.6: Housing cost overburden rate by tenure

■ Owner, with mortgage or loan
■ Owner, no outstanding mortgage or housing loan
■ Tenant, rent at market price
■ Tenant, rent at reduced price or free

Source: Eurostat EU-SILC (several years).

converging with a housing model that is heading towards insecurity (Módenes Cabrerizo, 2019).

Increased vulnerability of tenants in Spain

Clearly, in the aftermath of the GFC there has been a general increase in the financial vulnerability of both homeowners and tenants. An important indicator of the functioning of the housing market is the housing cost overburden rate, which measures the number of households for which the percentage of spending on housing services represents more than 40 per cent of their disposable income. As shown in Figure 10.7, many Spanish households that live in dwellings paying the market rent also bear the burden of a rise in housing expenses that, in many cases, is nearly double the European average. In 2019, 37 per cent of households in Spain spent more than 40 per cent of their net disposable income on their rent in the private market, compared to an average of 26 per cent in the other EU28 countries. Likewise, while 14 per cent of Spanish households faced housing expenses that represented more than 75 per cent of their net disposable income, this same percentage dropped to just 7 per cent in the EU28.

Turning to the number of evictions carried out in the rental sector, it is very difficult to identify the number of households that have been displaced from their homes on a national scale, due to the lack of statistical data. Until 2012, official statistics did not distinguish between types of tenure when calculating evictions. However, considering the available data, Figure 10.8 shows how evictions increased considerably after the outbreak of the 2008 crisis. In 2012, the rented sector comprised most evictions, accounting for 78 per cent of the total, though evictions due to mortgage defaults were substantial in the years thereafter and were recorded at nearly the same rate as in the rented sector. Mortgage evictions are one of the most important and tragic social manifestations of the real estate crisis of 2008. The increase in crime derived from high unemployment, the growing precariousness of work and the reduction of wages have increased the number of foreclosures recorded from just over 10,000 at the beginning of the century to around 70,000 per year since 2012 (Méndez Gutiérrez del Valle and Plaza Tabasco, 2016; Rodríguez Alonso and Espinoza Pino, 20182018).

In recent years, evictions in the rented sector have become far more relevant, reaching 72 per cent of all evictions recorded in 2020. Data for 2020 shows a steep drop in evictions overall, with just 30,000 households experiencing eviction. This rate is like that of 2008, before the GFC. However, it should be considered that exceptional measures (such as moratoriums on eviction) were implemented due to the COVID-19 pandemic, a topic we will discuss elsewhere in this chapter.

Figure 10.7: Percentage of households experiencing housing overburden (percentage of housing cost over disposable income) in Spain and EU28, 2010–2019

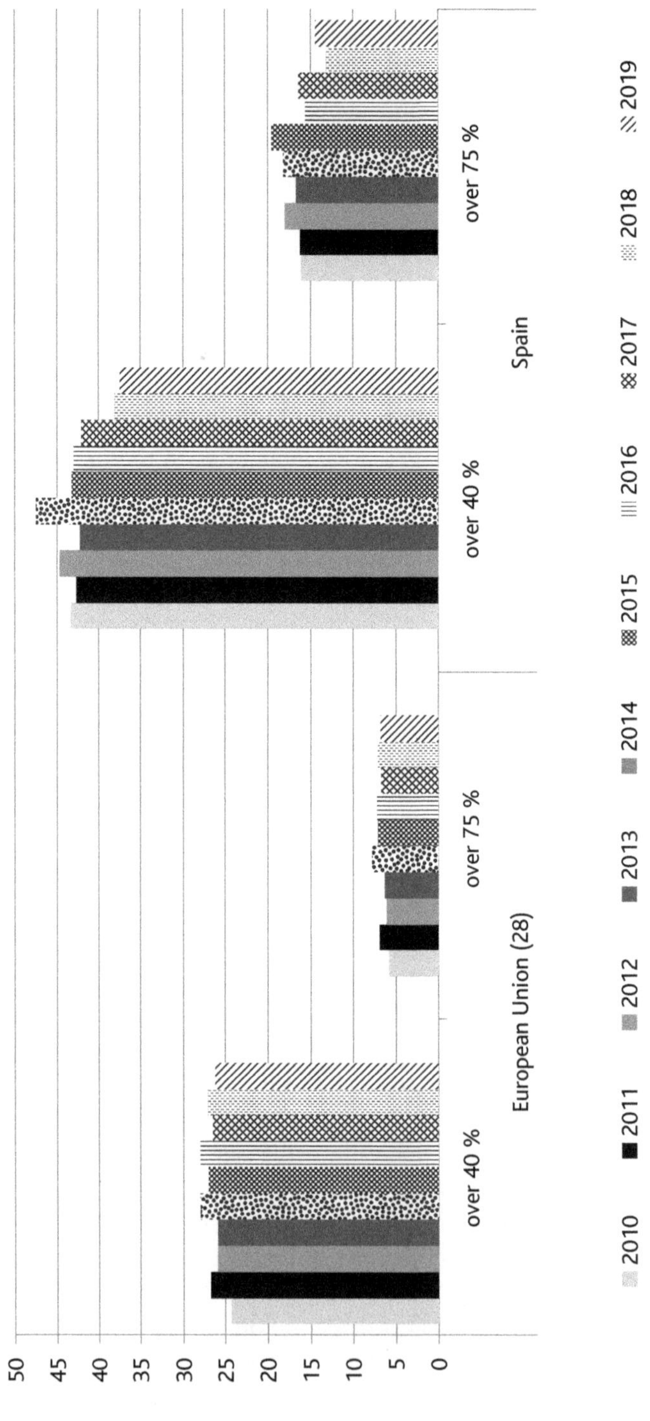

Source: Eurostat EU-SILC (several years).

Figure 10.8: Foreclosures and evictions in Spain, 2008–2020 (*)

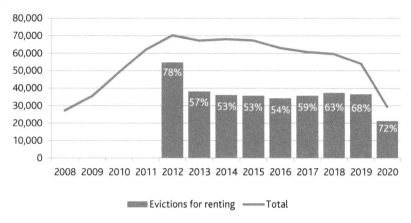

Note (*): Total includes foreclosures and evictions in all tenures.
Source: Consejo General del Poder Judicial (CGPJ) (2020).

A fragmented supply with emerging new players

Rental supply in Spain has traditionally been fragmented, as many landlords are individuals and there has been limited participation by large companies or public bodies acting as managers of rented housing stock. Several factors explain this situation, including: the lack of incentives for increasing (or even maintaining) the supply of private rented housing; the pressure exerted by strong regulations in the sector until 1985; the attractiveness of a booming homeownership sector; the low profitability of private rented housing when compared to other possible investments and the lack of professional property managers of rented housing.

The GFC considerably changed this situation: many financial entities became the legal owners of a large stock of housing which was mainly accumulated due to mortgage defaults and the subsequent evictions of homeowners. In fact, Sareb, a private company with a public mission to alleviate banks of their toxic assets, was created in 2012 as part of the joint plan set out in the same year by the Spanish state and the European Commission to recapitalise the financial entities most affected by the crisis. In 2012 and 2013, Sareb purchased around 200,000 troubled assets for a reduced price established by the Bank of Spain (€50.8 million), which included developer loans and properties. In turn, Sareb provided liquidity to these banks by paying them with bonds guaranteed by the Public Treasury, which the banks could then exchange for cash in the Central European Bank. Apart from finishing uncompleted construction projects before selling and effectively selling the assets in their portfolio, since 2012 Sareb has reserved 'a pool of 15,000 properties for social purposes in collaboration with the Public

Table 10.1: Profiles of landlords in Spain

	2014	2018
	%	%
Private individual	78.9	81.5
Company dedicated to rental of housing	12.0	9.3
Public administration	4.3	6.9
Employers of one household member	1.0	0.2
Non-profit organisation/other answer	1.9	1.4
Don't know/didn't answer	2.0	0.8

Source: Centre for Sociological Research (CIS) (2018).

Administration, to alleviate the problem of affordable housing in Spain' (Sareb, 2023) (Sareb website, accessed on 21 April 2021). According to their statistics, they have assigned around 3,000 properties to varied ACs and town councils.

This fragmented ownership and lack of professionalism in property management has characterised the private rented supply for decades. According to the Housing and Rent Barometer (CIS, 2018), between 2014 and 2018, individual owners of rented properties increased by 2.6 per cent, representing more than two-thirds of the private rented supply in 2018 (Table 10.1).

During the housing boom prior to 2008, large investors did not consider the Spanish rented market attractive enough for investment, as expectations on returns from buying or building and later selling in the homeownership market were much higher (see Figure 10.9).

Returns on investments in rented housing have traditionally been stable, hovering around 5 per cent, while returns on investments in the homeownership market have been highly volatile. This marked difference is due to individual expectations or speculations on the future evolution of housing prices and rents. However, the observed increase in rents and rental profitability in recent years has increased the attractiveness of rented housing as an investment instrument, seen mainly from 2013 to 2019. This has aroused the interest of investors, with the market undergoing a profound transformation due to the development of SOCIMIs (Real Estate Investment Trusts, or REITs) (García-Vaquero et al, 2020). However, although it is still an embryonic market and these entities still hold a reduced portion of the total housing stock (which is largely concentrated in the metropolitan areas of Madrid and Barcelona), they have increased their presence in the housing market notably. For example, in the city of Barcelona, legal entities represented around 25 per cent of the residential rental homes in 2018 (Observatori Metropolità de l'Habitatge de Barcelona, 2018).

Figure 10.9: Profitability in the housing sector (*)

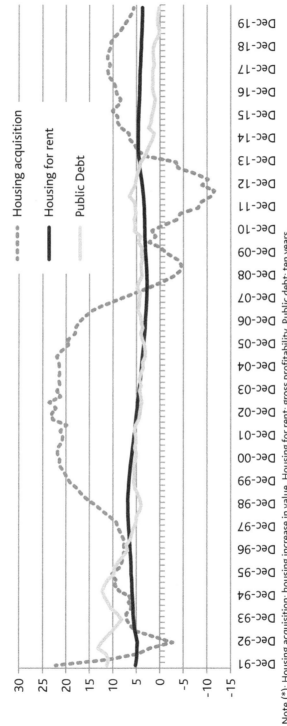

Note (*): Housing acquisition: housing increase in value. Housing for rent: gross profitability. Public debt: ten years.

Source: Bank of Spain (several years).

Temporary subletting: an urban dilemma

In recent years, many Spanish cities have employed strategies to increase tourism, with the sector constituting an important source of economic specialisation and income. In cities like Barcelona, the strong presence of temporary subletting platforms (such as Airbnb and Booking.com) has led to changes in many neighbourhoods, narrowing the spectrum of affordable housing by converting homes into lucrative short-term tourist accommodations and contributing to the displacement of residents (Cócola Gant, 2016).

The rapid expansion of city tourism and short-term rentals has recently attracted great interest, both in public opinion and among policy makers. This is due to the rising tensions that it is causing regarding prices in a reduced market such as that of rented housing in Spain; these tensions are especially pronounced in large tourist cities. Short-term rental platforms could aggravate the problem of housing affordability in large cities such as Barcelona, Madrid, Malaga, Mallorca, Seville and Valencia, among others, where tourism is popular and the difference in profitability between long-term rental to residents or short stays for tourists is high (Garcia-López *et al*, 2020). As Figure 10.10 shows, despite the COVID-19 effect, in 2020 it was more profitable to rent housing to tourists than to long-term residents in all districts of Madrid except in Arganzuela, Ciudad Lineal and Puente de Vallecas. In Barcelona, without exception, profitability was higher for tourist rentals in all districts.

Professional managers in the rented sector: reacting to the attractiveness of the sector

As we have already mentioned, the private rented sector is dominated by individual landowners. For many years, the management of the rented sector lacked professional guidance: there were no specialists in dealing with private properties, as there were no clear incentives to do so. In recent years, two aspects have changed this situation: on the one hand, the onset of short periods of temporary subletting into tourists as a profitable adventure in many Spanish cities and rural areas has opened a new window of opportunity for professional managers, most of whom are devoted to amassing portfolios of individual owners without receiving any returns on their properties. These professional managers deal with all the required transactions (usually including maintenance and repairs to the property, as well as collecting rent payments) and, depending on the area, they may supervise a considerable portfolio of properties. Up until the COVID-19 pandemic, there was a great degree of opportunism within this sector, as returns were extremely high. It is likely that the managers who survive the initial shock of the pandemic will constitute an efficient group of professionals in the sector.

Figure 10.10: Profitability of residential versus tourist renting, Madrid and Barcelona, 2020 (€ per month)

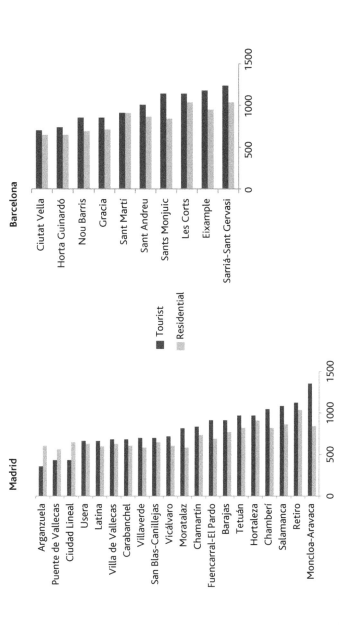

Notes: For residential rentals, figures represent earnings after the deduction of taxes and monthly expenses for rent management services, per month. For tourist rentals, figures represent earnings from a property rented 24 nights per month, after the deduction of bills, taxes and other expenses for rent management services.

Source: Statista (2020) residential rental market in Spain (based on Alquiler Seguro).

Figure 10.11: Profitability of investment in rented housing, 2010–2020 (%)

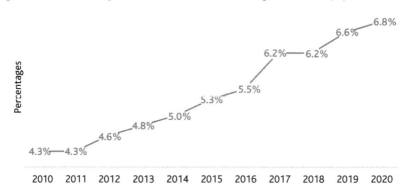

Note: Profitability calculated the annual rental income as a percentage of the value of the property.
Source: Statista (2020) residential rental housing in Spain (based on Fotocasa [2020]).

On the other hand, in the aftermath of the GFC, foreign investors have identified the Spanish private rented sector as being particularly profitable; thus, large investments in REITs, have taken place. From 2013 to 2019, the number of registered SOCIMIs increased from 2 to 90 while the value of their controlled assets rose from €0.1 million in 2013 to €46 million by the end of 2019 (García-Vaquero and Roibas, 2020) (Figure 10.11). However, by 2019, 82 per cent of the assets held by SOCIMIs were not residential: hotels, offices, commercial offices, shopping centres and logistic centres were the main alternatives.

It is worth stressing the fact that, in some cases, investors have bought (publicly rented) social housing directly from the ACs[1] responsible for their management. Despite alleviating the budgetary difficulties of the public sector, this situation has also exacerbated the already limited stock of public housing and has indirectly harmed the private rented market, as its role in providing social housing has become increasingly more relevant. Thus, the unstructured and disorganised management scheme of social housing in Spain (Lambea Llop, 2016) runs parallel to the similar management style of the private rented sector. A wide range of entities manage the social housing sector, including for-profit and non-profit private entities, foundations, housing cooperatives, associations, religious organisations and confederations (Alberdi, 2014). The private rented market currently benefits from entities who are already familiar with the management of social housing stock, as they are used to dealing with the private stock bought by public authorities for affordable purposes. The case of Barcelona is of particular interest in this regard, as the Local Housing Agency has acquired several units in the private market that are intended to be managed by the non-profit sector under certain requirements related to the entity's expertise, the targeted collective of users, the maximum rent charged and the duration of their tenancies. The ownership of the dwellings will remain public, but their use will be transferred to the different non-profit entities.

The rented sector and the National Housing Plan (2018–2021)

In 2018, a New Housing Plan was approved for the period 2018–2021. Its main objective is to rebalance tenure in the Spanish housing system, paying special attention to the expansion of the rented sector.

On the demand side, direct subsidies were the most relevant measure aiming to help low-income families, the young and the elderly, and vulnerable families in the position of being evicted. Diverse requirements were considered in terms of households' eligibility, though the amount of the subsidy obtained is based mainly on maximum income and the degree of disability of the tenant, as well as the cost of rent paid for the home. These subsidies vary between 40 per cent and 50 per cent of the current rent. On the supply side, the main beneficiaries of this new law are foundations, social enterprises and associations, self-constructed cooperatives, and non-for-profit organisations, among others. Subsidies are granted per dwelling and vary depending on the income of the tenants up to a maximum of 50 per cent of the investment made in the building of the dwellings for rent.

The ACs are tasked with implementing these measures, depending on their priorities and budgets.

The regulation of the rented sector in Spain: a heated debate

The regulation or deregulation of the private rented market is currently included in many local agendas in Europe again. Over the last ten years, the introduction of new forms of regulating the market has been discussed and, in some cases, even approved. During Spain's dictatorship (1936–1975) and beyond, until 1985, the country had already experienced a long period of frozen rents and indefinite contracts, accompanied by strong governmental support for homeownership. The consequences of many decades of robust intervention in the rented market left the sector in a poor situation: the quality of rented dwellings was below average compared to owner-occupied housing, due to the lack of incentives for landlords to invest in maintenance and repairs. Furthermore, the number of dwellings in the rented market had steadily decreased to figures that were among the lowest in Europe. In 1985, together with other measures intended to improve the competitiveness and efficiency of the country, the rented sector became completely liberalised. However, the consequences of the sector's deregulation did not change its pathway towards a narrow PRS with diverse situations in terms of rents, security of tenure and returns.

Two attempts have been made to increase regulations in the sector, which were mainly focused on establishing the minimum number of years for rental contracts and the automatic updating of rents. In the recent past, the rented sector has become the object of a new housing plan focused on stimulating the supply side of the market. The Royal Decree (7/2019) of 'urgent measures for housing and the rented market' aims to ameliorate the negative effects of higher rents and prices on tenure security and affordability. The minimum duration of contracts has increased from three to five years, with an additional extension allowed for a maximum of three years. If both parties agree, the contract can be renewed as much as they wish. The maximum increase of rents will be determined yearly by the increase of the annual Consumer Price Index. An agreement should be formalised between both parties with respect to the exchange of improvements in or to the accommodation for an increase in the rent. Furthermore, the tenant's housing security will be defined accordingly in the terms of the contract, which will stipulate the owner's possible reasons for terminating the contract. Finally, a variety of situations in the household (including the presence of vulnerable or disabled people living in the property) will extend the contract's validity, even after the death of the original contract holder.

Two aspects of the current law are worth stressing: first, concerning evictions, the law requires a mandatory report on the potential vulnerability of the household. If the tenancy of vulnerable persons is detected, the eviction procedure will be postponed for a month (or three if the owner is a company) in order to seek a suitable solution for the tenants. Second, despite the increase of temporary subletting in the country, the law does not currently consider this situation in any capacity. However, an existing rule determines that if three-fifths of the votes of owners/landlords of the community are against the possibility of temporary subletting in the building, this may forbid the establishment of a touristic apartment within the community.

Furthermore, a major innovation found in the current regulation is the establishment of a National Index of Reference to monitor the rented market. ACs will use this index to enact their responsibility for housing policies in their individual jurisdictions. As a result of this index and its use in the varied contexts of Spain's ACs, in June 2020 the Ministry introduced a new official statistic on the rented market. The National System of Reference of Rent Prices proposes a price index for the wider Spanish territory based on 11.2 million rent contracts signed between 2015 and 2018. The detailed information that this new tool provides will (theoretically) allow for the identification of areas with extreme pressure on rent prices and, thus, will intervene to soften this tension. Up until now, the measurement of rented prices has been left in the hands of real estate agencies which, rather than using the transaction price, were measuring the supply price and therefore creating a certain bias, while not including the possible negotiations of buyers and sellers. Simultaneously, other subnational agencies like the Observatori Metropolità de l'Habitatge (Metropolitan Housing Observatory) in Catalonia, are producing their own price indexes (based on two real estate agencies, Habitaclia and Fotocasa).

The political and academic debates regarding the application of rent controls in certain locations run parallel to what is happening in other European areas where the pressure on rents is very high. In particular, the municipality of Barcelona, one of the main promoters of this measure, is pushing to adopt a selective measure that will limit the maximum threshold of rents.

The rented sector and the effects of COVID-19

Housing plays a doubly significant role in the situation caused by the COVID-19 pandemic. On the one hand, home-based lockdowns have formed a key part of the measures taken to combat the pandemic by reducing community transmission of the disease, so having stable accommodation is an indispensable condition of living in the COVID-19 era. On the other hand, the stagnation of labour income which had already begun to affect many households because of the 2008 crisis is now joined by further income loss or stagnation due to the COVID-19 crisis. Many households have once again seen their income reduced, while others have had to temporarily abandon their labour activity and be put on furloughs; still others, unfortunately, have become unemployed. When we add to this list the increase in rental prices that have already been taking place in recent years, the relevance of spending on housing in relation to total income has risen considerably, leading to an unsustainable financial situation for many households (Observatori Metropolità de l'Habitatge de Barcelona, 2020).

This situation has led the Spanish government to establish extraordinary measures in the rented sector which affect both tenants and landlords. These primarily aim to protect the most vulnerable tenants by ensuring greater housing stability during periods of lockdown and by mitigating their financial difficulties. These measures have been extended and modified over the recent months, since the start of the pandemic in March 2020 (Box 10.1). These measures have had a direct impact on the number of evictions carried out during 2020. In 2019, the total number of evictions in the rented sector was 14,193, while in 2020, just 6,915 evictions occurred. In ACs such as Madrid and Catalonia, this constitutes a reduction of nearly 50 per cent. In Barcelona, for example, 22.5 per cent of households living in the rented sector have negotiated a rent postponement or reduction, with a success rate of 55.2 per cent (Observatori Metropolità de l'Habitatge de Barcelona, 2020).

The economic and health uncertainties caused by the COVID-19 pandemic have inspired changes in the trends of the rental market in Spain.

Box 10.1: Measures to mitigate the economic and social impact of COVID-19 in the private rental market

1. **Evictions**
   - Exceptional suspension of rental evictions for vulnerable homes with no alternative due to the COVID-19 crisis.
   - Maximum term of six months (from 2 April to 2 October 2020).
2. **Extension of lease contracts**
   - The automatic renewal of rental contracts that expire in the three months following the entry into law of this rule is implemented. This extension will be six months and the terms and conditions of the current contract will be maintained.
3. **Moratorium on rent payment**

For large holders of housing, both public and private, including the Social Housing Fund or financial entities. It is understood that this term refers to those entities who own more than ten properties.

The tenant can choose between:

- a 50 per cent reduction in rent for the duration of the State of Alarm decreed by the government and the following monthly payments if that period is insufficient in relation to the situation of vulnerability caused by COVID-19; or
- a moratorium on the payment of rent will be extended while the State of Alarm lasts or while the situation of vulnerability persists. Once this situation is overcome, the tenant will return the unpaid installment or installments over a period not exceeding three years, without any type of penalty or interest being applied.
- A maximum term of four months is applicable in both cases.

For small and medium landlords. In these circumstances, the tenant may request a postponement in the payment of his rent if he or she is in a vulnerable situation. The landlord will have seven days to accept it, propose an alternative or reject it.

If there is no agreement, the tenant will have access to a program of temporary financing aid at zero cost with the state's guarantee.

4. **Official Credit Institute (ICO) credit line for COVID-19 lease**
   - The tenant may request a loan, paid directly to the landlord, for up to six monthly payments of the rental income, to be returned within a maximum period of ten years. This loan will be granted by one of the major credit institutions and will have the endorsement of the state, through the Official Credit Institute, which will sign the corresponding agreement with the Ministry of Transport, Mobility and Urban Agenda.

- Repayment period of up to six years, exceptionally extendable for another four and without, in any case, accruing any type of expenses and interests for the applicant.

5. **Aid programme to help minimise the economic and social impact of COVID-19 on rents of habitual residence** (until 31 December 2021)
   - Concession of rental aid, through direct award, to tenants of a habitual residence who prove that they are in a situation of economic and social vulnerability because of COVID-19, which will be determined by the ACs and the cities of Ceuta and Melilla.
   - Amount of the aid: maximum of €900/month and 100 per cent of the rental income, up to a period of six months, being able to include as the first monthly payment that which corresponds with the month of April 2020.

6. **An essential requirement to qualify for these measures is to prove that you are in a situation of economic vulnerability:**
   - In a situation of unemployment, within a furlough situation, reduced working hours due to the care of elders or minors. In the case of a business owner or other similar circumstances, suffering a substantial loss of income or rental income, plus expenses and supplies when basic income is greater than or equal to 35 per cent of net income, or when income is less than three times the Public Indicator of Multiple Effect Income (IPREM).

Namely, the most dynamic Spanish cities have ended the year with historic drops in rental housing stock and in falling prices, as we may observe in Figures 10.12a and 10.12b.

Conclusion

The Spanish real estate market is characterised by an imbalanced tenure system, which features the predominance of homeownership, a reduced private rented market, and a completely neglected and residual social housing stock. This situation is inherited from the policies that have been carried out since the middle of the last century, which were primarily focused on facilitating housing access through homeownership.

The lack of rental housing has become a problem of vital importance in Spain, especially since the 2008 GFC and the COVID-19 pandemic. In the absence of social housing, the demand for privately rented units is under great pressure, causing prices to skyrocket. This situation, in which the PRS performs the function of social housing, fundamentally affects young people, immigrants and the country's most vulnerable households, who have seen their working conditions worsen, leading to precarious, unstable employment contracts with low wages. The lack of housing available for rent has produced severely negative implications in Spain, fundamentally when it comes to providing affordable housing to these vulnerable households. Many Spanish households living in rented accommodation bear an overburden in housing

Figure 10.12: Price and number of units in the rented market, variation January–December 2020, Madrid and Barcelona

a) **Rent prices**

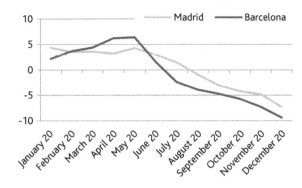

b) **Number of units**

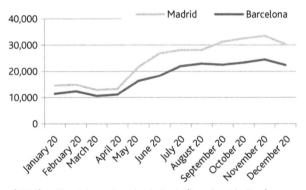

Source: Statista (2020) residential rental market in Spain (based on Idealista).

spending that, in many cases, doubles the European average. This has caused a significant increase in the number of evictions due to non-payment of rent.

Apart from the rented sector's inability to meet the demand for housing from vulnerable households, another booming demand complicates the picture: that of short-term tourist rentals. The rapid expansion of urban tourism and short-term rentals is raising prices even further in a market as tight as the PRS in Spain. The enormous difference in profitability between rentals meant for long-term residential use and short stays for tourists has aggravated the problem of housing affordability in large cities such as Barcelona, Madrid, Malaga, Mallorca, Seville and Valencia.

The rental supply in Spain is mostly fragmented into dwellings owned by small individual landowners. However, emerging new actors are identified: both public and private, for-profit and non-profit companies that are still few in number but are capable of offering the necessary volume of rental housing that the market needs, and at an affordable price that is also appropriate for social housing. The professionalisation of the sector is key to ensuring a stable framework for the relationship between supply and demand, as well as enforcing compliance with public requirements regarding the minimum percentage of affordable housing in any new development.

Current rent regulation in Spain is situated in what is termed 'third generation' rent control: the regulation of rent during, but not between, tenancies (also termed tenancy rent control), which is intended to mitigate the negative effects of increased rent prices on security of tenure and affordability. These regulations provide for a minimum duration of rental contracts, which has been increased from three to five years and allow for an additional extension of up to three years. The regulations also determine the possible reasons for which the owner may terminate the contract, to offer greater security to tenants in vulnerable situations.

An intense debate is now taking place in Spain regarding the application of rent controls or other forms of regulation, given the extreme increase in rental prices in certain areas. This debate is firmly in line with similar debates in neighbouring countries. However, the positions taken are widely divided, both from an academic and an institutional point of view. Municipalities such as Barcelona advocate for the implementation of rent controls in the city, especially in those areas considered to be under pressure due to high rents. This would be an exceptional measure since contracts are currently limited to a maximum period of five years. To carry out this type of sweeping legal change, it is critical to have official statistics with detailed and updated information on rent prices in varied areas of the city or the country. Unfortunately, the lack of adequate statistical data has been a dominant issue in Spain for many years, particularly in the region of Catalonia. This situation is currently being corrected with the June 2020 publication of the new National Rental Price Reference Index, a pricing system for rental housing that allows landlords and tenants to calculate the average values of monthly rent per square metre, with wide disaggregation throughout the territory. With this new statistic, it may be possible to implement a cap on rent increases in tense areas, especially if a low supply of rental housing persists. This index is expected to be updated frequently.

On a broader scale, the most widely agreed alternative to rent control (on the part of both politicians and academics) is the commitment to measures aimed at increasing the supply of rented housing stock. The Royal Decree (7/ 2019) of 'urgent measures for housing and the rented market' is aligned with this purpose. It establishes several measures to combat the shortage of private rent supply, such as the establishment of agreements between tenants and private homeowners to discount repairs made by tenants from their monthly rent prices. Certain possibilities are neglected, however, such as introducing tax incentives to landowners who wish to carry out renovations to their dwellings involving additions to the structure. Furthermore, the agreement made between the national government and Sareb to allocate part of the toxic assets derived from the GFC is a lost opportunity to constitute a larger stock of both social and affordable housing in Spain, as very few houses have finally been used for this purpose. Many sectors demand more initiatives in this regard. An increased stock of accessible, publicly regulated housing for rent could be built progressively, in collaboration with the private sector, provided all the actors involved take on a firm commitment to not selling the dwellings to their tenants in the future, as has happened in the past.

Despite the timid reactions of national authorities, the present moment constitutes a perfect opportunity to rebuild a political strategy based upon the right to housing and the right to the city. The creation of a significant stock of rented housing will take some time, so the creation of a framework that allows a selective cap on rents should not be ruled out.

Note

[1] For instance, the regional government of Madrid sold around 5,000 social rental dwellings to investment funds, including Goldman Sachs and Blackstone.

References

Alberdi, B. (2014) 'Social housing in Spain', in K. Scanlon, C. Whitehead and M. Fernández Arrigoitia (eds) *Social Housing in Europe*, Oxford, Wiley-Blackwell, pp 223–237.

Algaba Ros, S. (2021) 'El control de la renta en el arrendamiento de vivienda' (Rent control in housing rental), *InDret,* 1, 46–86, https://doi.org/10.31009/InDret.2021.i1.02

Allen J., Barlow, J., Leal, J., Maloutas, T. and Padovani, L. (2004) *Housing and Welfare in Southern Europe*, London, Blackwell Publishing, https://doi.org/10.1002/9780470757536.fmatter

Anghel, B., Basso, H., Bover, O., Casado, J.M., Hospido, L., Izquierdo, M. *et al* (2018) 'La desigualdad de la renta, el consumo y la riqueza en España' (Inequality of income, consumption and wealth in Spain), *Documentos Ocasionales*, 1806, Banco de España.

Argelich Comelles, C. (2017) 'The temporary expropriation of dwellings and other housing measures for vulnerable people in the Act 4/2016 of Catalonia', *Revista Jurídica del Notariado*, 102–103, April–September.

CIS (Centre for Sociological Research) (2018) *Housing and Rental Barometer.* Studio n°3212, Ministry of the Presidency of Spain, http://www.cis.es/cis/export/sites/default/-Archivos/Marginales/3200_3219/3212/es3212mar.html

Cócola Gant, A. (2016) 'Holiday rentals: the new gentrification battlefront' *Sociological Research Online*, 21(3), 112–120, https://doi.org/10.5153/sro.4071

Consejo General del Poder Judicial (CGPJ) (2020) *Datos sobre el efecto de la crisis en los órganos judiciales por Tribunal Superior de Justicia* (Data on the effect of the crisis on judicial bodies by the Superior Court of Justice), https://www.poderjudicial.es/cgpj/es/Temas/Estadistica-Judicial/Estudios-e-Informes/Efecto-de-la-Crisis-en-los-organos-judiciales/

European Commission (2019) 'Housing affordability and sustainability in the EU', analytical report, https://ec.europa.eu/docsroom/documents/38481/attachments/1/translations/en/renditions/native

Eurostat (2019) 'Distribution of population by tenure status, type of household and income group', EU-SILC survey [ilc_lvho02].

Fotocasa (2020) The house for rent in Spain in the year 2020, https://s36360.pcdn.co/wp-content/uploads/2021/01/La-vivienda-en-alquiler-en-2020.pdf

Garcia-López, M.A., Jofre-Monseny, J., Martínez-Mazza, R. and Segú M. (2020) 'Do short-term rental platforms affect housing markets? Evidence from Airbnb in Barcelona', *Journal of Urban Economics*, 119, 103278, https://doi.org/10.1016/j.jue.2020.103278

García-Montalvo, J. (2019) 'Retos del mercado del alquiler en España' (Challenges of the rental market in Spain), *Cuadernos de Información Económica*, 269, 1–11.

García-Montalvo, J. (2020) 'Controla alquileres que algo queda…o no' (Control rents that something remains... or not), *Expansión*, 28 February.

García-Vaquero, V. and Roibás, I. (2020) Evolución reciente de las SOCIMI en España (Recent evolution of SOCIMIs in Spain), Artículos Analíticos, Boletín Económico, 2/2020, Banco de España.

Hornbeck, R. and Moretti, E. (2019) *Estimating Who Benefits From Productivity Growth: Direct and Indirect Effects of City Manufacturing TFP Growth on Wages, Rents, and Inequality*, Working Paper, University of Chicago Booth School of Business.

Idealista database (2020) 'Evolution of the rental market in Spain', https://www.idealista.com/sala-de-prensa/informes-precio-vivienda/alquiler/

INE (2019) Living Conditions Survey (ECV). Households by tenure status of housing, https://www.ine.es/dynt3/inebase/es/index.htm?padre=1927&capsel=1925

Lambea Llop N. (2016) 'Social housing management models in Spain', *Revista Catalana de Dret Públic*, 52, 115–128, http://revistes.eapc.gencat.cat/index.php/rcdp/article/view/10.2436-20.8030.01.69/n52-lambea-en.pdf

López-Rodríguez, D. and Matea, M.L. (2019) 'Evolución reciente del mercado del alquiler de vivienda en España' (Recent evolution of the housing rental market in Spain), *Artículos Analíticos*, Boletín Económico, 3/2019, Banco de España.

López-Rodríguez, D. and Matea, M.L. (2020) 'La intervención pública en el mercado del alquiler de vivienda: una revisión de la experiencia internacional' (Public intervention in the housing rental market: a review of the international experience), *Artículos Analíticos*, Boletín Económico, 2002/2020, Banco de España.

Lozano, M. and Rentería, E. (2018) 'El imparable aumento de los años en precariedad laboral de los adultos jóvenes en España (The unstoppable increase in years of job insecurity for young adults in Spain), 1987–2017', *Perspectivs Demogràfiques*, 12, 1–4.

Méndez Gutiérrez del Valle, R. and Plaza Tabasco, J. (2016) 'Crisis inmobiliaria y desahucios hipotecarios en España: una perspectiva geográfica' (Real estate crisis and mortgage evictions in Spain: a geographical perspective), *Boletín de la Asociación de Geógrafos Españoles*, 71, 99–127.

Módenes Cabrerizo, J.A. (2019) 'The unsustainable rise of residential insecurity in Spain', *Perspectives Demogràfiques*, 13, 1–4, DOI: 10.46710/ ced.pd.eng.13

Nasarre-Aznar, S. and Molina-Roig, E. (2017) 'A legal perspective of the current challenges of the Spanish residential rental market', *International Journal of Law in the Built Environment*, 9(2), 108–122, https://doi.org/ 10.1108/IJLBE-03-2017-0013

Observatori Metropolità de l'Habitatge de Barcelona (2018) *Presentació de l'Informe L'habitatge a la metròpoli de Barcelona*, https://www.ohb.cat/wp-content/uploads/2019/07/20190703-Presentaci%C3%B3-informe.pdf

Observatori Metropolità de l'Habitatge de Barcelona (2020) *Medidas dirigidas al alquiler para paliar los efectos del Covid-19 en España, Alemania y Francia* (Measures Targeted at Renting to Mitigate the Effects of Covid-19 in Spain, Germany and France), https://www.ohb.cat/wp-content/uploads/2020/ 07/LAB-regulacion-internacional-alquiler-Covid-19-.pdf

Pareja-Eastaway, M. (2010) 'El régimen de tenencia de la vivienda en España' (The housing tenure regime in Spain), in J. Leal Maldonado (ed) *La política de vivienda en España* (Housing policy in Spain), Madrid, pp 101–128.

Pareja-Eastaway, M. and San Martin, I. (2002) 'The tenure imbalance in Spain: the need for social housing policy', *Urban Studies*, 39(2), 283–295.

Pareja-Eastaway, M. and Sánchez Martínez, M.T. (2009) 'European rental markets: regulation or liberalization? The Spanish case', in P. Arestis, P. Mooslechner and K. Wagner (eds) *Housing Market Challenges in Europe and the United States – Any Solutions Available*, Hampshire, Palgrave Macmillan, pp 131–157.

Pareja-Eastaway, M. and Sánchez Martínez, M.T. (2016) 'Social housing in Spain: what role does the private rented market play?', *Journal of Housing and the Built Environment*, 32, 377–395.

Pareja-Eastaway, M. and Sánchez Martínez, M.T. (2017) 'More social housing? A critical analysis on social housing provision in Spain', *Critical Housing Analysis*, 4(1), 124–131.

Ponce, J. (2020) '¿Es constitucional la ley catalana que limita el precio de los alquileres? (I y II)' (Is the Catalan law that limits rental prices constitutional?), Hay Derecho, *Expansión*, https://hayderecho.expansion.com/2020/10/04/es-constitucional-la-ley-catalana-que-limita-el-precio-de-los-alquileres-i/ y https://hayderecho.expansion.com/2020/11/19/es-constitucional-la-ley-catalana-que-limita-el-precio-de-los-alquileres-ii/

Rodríguez Alonso, R. and Espinoza Pino, M. (2018) 'De la especulación al derecho a la vivienda: Más allá de las contradicciones del modelo inmobiliario español' (From speculation to the right to housing: Beyond the contradictions of the Spanish real estate model), *Traficantes de sueños*, https://www.academia.edu/35595699/De_la_especulaci%C3%B3n_al_derecho_a_la_vivienda_M%C3%A1s_all%C3%A1_de_las_contradicciones_del_modelo_inmobiliario_espa%C3%B1ol

Ronald, R. (2008) *The Ideology of Home Ownership: Homeowner Societies and the Role of Housing*, Basingstoke, Palgrave Macmillan. DOI: 10.1057/9780230582286

Sareb (2023) 'Since 2012: nine years of meticulous work with our portfolio. What we have achieved so far', https://www.sareb.es/nuestro-trabajo/logros/

Statista (2020) 'Housing rent prices in Spain between June 2015 and June 2020, by autonomous community (in euros per square meter)' in *Residential rental market in Spain*, https://www.statista.com/topics/7506/residential-rental-market-in-spain/#topicOverview

11

The short-run impact of COVID-19 on the private rented sector

Tony Crook

Introduction

COVID-19 is a new SARS (severe acute respiratory syndrome) coronavirus disease. It spread rapidly from its origins in Wuhan, China; and despite many countries having tackled previous pandemics, many were wholly unprepared. Globalisation and technical convergence have resulted in new forms of non-calculable uncertainty where cities were the worst hit by COVID-19 because their densities and interactions facilitated the transmission of the virus and within cities the most deprived neighbourhoods were the worst hit of all (Bryson *et al*, 2021). To cope with the threat, economies were shut down with major supply shocks followed by major demand shocks worldwide, wiping off huge proportions of global gross domestic product (GDP) in a matter of months and destabilising money markets. Fiscal and monetary policy came together as economies and money markets were put on life support by governments, sustaining businesses, jobs and incomes, and by central banks supporting liquidity through massive purchases of, mainly government, bonds (Tooze, 2021).

Housing was both part of the way the virus was transmitted and one of the consequences of the shutdowns and market adjustments that resulted from attempts to contain the spread of the virus. This chapter explores the short-run impact of COVID-19 on the private rented sector (PRS) of the housing market in the countries discussed in earlier chapters of this volume. It considers the evidence in three contexts: first, to assess if the nature of these countries varieties of capitalism and welfare regimes are related to governments' COVID-19 interventions in the PRS; second, to examine subnational as well as national responses; and third to assess if policy interventions can be framed by ideas about path dependency and historical institutionalism.

First, this chapter examines each country's responses to COVID-19 in the light of an earlier comparison of the PRS in developed countries (Crook and Kemp, 2014). That showed how policies on regulation of rents and security of tenure and the extent of investment by corporate and institutional landlords were related to their types of economy and welfare regimes, using typologies developed by Hall and Soskice (2001) on varieties of capitalism and by Esping-Andersen (1990) on types of welfare regime. The 2014 book showed that the PRS in liberal market economies and welfare regimes tended to have deregulated sectors and limited investment by corporate landlords whereas other types of economy and welfare regimes were more likely to have greater regulation and more ownership by corporate landlords.

These classifications have been contested, not the least that welfare regimes do not always 'read across' from welfare to housing because (among other things) the globalisation of financial markets and the growing reliance by households on asset-based welfare weakens the link between welfare regimes and welfare outcomes, as households seek to manage risks. Nonetheless, recent studies indicate that welfare regimes do still 'map onto' housing. For example, a recent study focused on Europe, showed that these relationships have endured, although in some liberal welfare regimes and market economies aspects of rent regulation have been introduced but targeted at particular cities or regions where rents have risen significantly (Kettunen and Ruonavaara, 2020). Another recent analysis has also shown that these relationships have been sustained over time while also responding to changing circumstances (for example, see Dewilde, 2017). Hence, Blackwell and Kohl (2019) argue that one should look at trajectories over time, not simply cross-sectional studies, in examining the validity of typologies in explaining outcomes.

Second, research on cross-country differences (for example, Stephens, 2011, 2020) has moved away from focusing only on ideas about convergence and on nation states to examine the roles of both supra and subnational bodies. More emphasis is now placed on integrating higher level structures and forces with the institutional details than can better help explain differences and similarities. One such study of PRS policy has examined the extent to which policy is centralised or is the responsibility of subnational governments, fostering the possibility of diverse responses within nation states to COVID-19 (Kholodilin, 2021). As Béland *et al* (2021) have also noted, divergences in policy legacies, political institutions in federal structures and political partisanship led to significant differences in how notionally similar liberal market economies and welfare regimes responded to COVID-19. Understanding these subnational divergences is critical because COVID-19 has had asymmetric impacts on regions and housing markets (Coyle, 2020). Some households with the ability to move relocated and consumed more and safer space while substandard housing in some disadvantaged communities whose residents were less able to move undermined their residents' resilience to virus transmission (Brown *et al*, 2020; Davenport *et al*, 2020; Nanda *et al*, 2020; Sokol and Pataccini, 2020; McCann and Ortega-Argilés, 2021; Maclennan *et al*, 2021).

Third, the concept of path dependency helps explain how existing institutional arrangements shape the ways in which how governments respond to major events, such as COVID-19, that require action but which do not undermine the existence of those institutions (Pierson, 2004). Hence, at least in the short term, it is likely that the constraints or existing legacies imposed by types of economy and welfare systems have determined how governments have responded. On the other hand, given the serious, sudden and widespread impact of COVID-19, governments had to take urgent steps to combat its impact on health and economic life, steps described as 'emergency Keynesianism' (Ban, 2020; Bremer and McDaniel, 2020) during which normal fiscal disciplines were suspended, with 13.5 per cent of global GDP spent on emergency funding worldwide (*The Economist*, 2021a).

These responses were often more agile than those made in response to earlier crises (for example, the global financial crisis) and many were different from what might have been predicted under wholly path-dependent scenarios. Nonetheless, it is likely that these emergency responses had to draw upon existing mechanisms (hence path dependency) but also to be adapted to the crisis as existing measures were expanded or extended and new measures drawn up (Moreira and Hick, 2021). Commentators had reservations about how these emergency responses undermined democratic accountability by limiting prior debates when such measures were enacted (Omerod and Davoudi, 2021). Historical institutionalists (Krasner, 1984) argued that critical junctures in the form of exogenous events can result in transformative change. Hence it is possible that COVID-19 has been a critical juncture and that the short-term adaptations to the crisis will lead to more permanent changes in welfare policy, including those designed to better address existing regional and housing inequalities that the pandemic showed up in sharper relief (*The Economist*, 2021a; McCann and Ortega-Argilés, 2021). Meanwhile, the COVID-19 shutdowns enabled many households to save more because spending options were reduced for the duration. Once the lockdowns were removed, some of this excess saving found its way into the housing market and, supported by very low borrowing costs, increased house prices. Consequently, the housing market price effects of COVID-19 may have exacerbated existing housing inequalities (Strauss and Smith, 2021).

To explore the impact of COVID-19 on the private rental market, this chapter has four further sections. First, a discussion of the wide range of factors related to the pandemic that potentially impacted on the PRS. Second, a 'drawing together' in a summary of the detailed evidence on the approaches adopted in each country based on the previous chapters in this book. Third, an assessment of whether the nature of each country's type of economy and welfare regime was central to the way they tackled the impact. The final section draws some necessarily provisional conclusions about the short-run impact of the COVID-19 pandemic of the PRS and reflects on how far the crisis is likely to provoke new thinking about the PRS given how critical junctures can bring new ways of thinking into the frame. Hence, this analysis inevitably focuses on the short term.

The potential short-term impact of COVID-19 on demand and supply in the private rented sector

Given what we know about the PRS (discussed in earlier chapters) this section considers some *a priori* arguments about the likely impact of COVID-19 before the next section discusses the evidence of what happened in each country studied in this volume.

Demand for private renting

On the demand side, tenants' incomes, and ability to pay rent, will potentially have been reduced if economies have 'shut down', depending on whether this imposition has been country-wide or restricted to only parts of each country. How this has affected PRS tenants will depend on their jobs, the approach governments have taken to allowing economic activity to continue during the pandemic and how essential services have been kept open (Kholodilin, 2021). Those working in health, transport and delivery services, and food retailing will have kept working and been paid. Construction activity is also likely to have continued. In other sectors, the extent of 'shutdown' is likely to have varied, with many in service industries including financial and professional services (and some education sectors) being able to operate remotely from their offices with many staff working online from home and again being paid. But other sectors may have been shut down to varying degrees including non-essential retail and hospitality. The impact of employees in these latter sectors depends on the extent to which government have stepped in to pay some or all of the wages of these staff, that is, through new so-called 'furlough' schemes or through extending existing employment protection programmes. It will also depend on the extent of government support for businesses enabling them to keep going without making staff redundant.

How these government economic decisions and employment support mechanisms affected PRS tenants depends on the occupational and other social and economic attributes of tenants and their specific housing circumstances (see, for example, Benfer *et al*, 2021; Byrne, 2021). As previous chapters have shown, PRS tenants tend to work more than the average in sectors that have been 'closed', especially in hospitality and non-essential retail services, but also in low-paid service sectors which have stayed 'open', including delivery services. In addition, the PRS houses many students living away from home and students are a key part of the 'demand side' of the PRS. Where higher education has moved largely online students have been faced with a choice of staying at home or moving to their university town. Their decisions will affect overall supply of the PRS where such student homes and flats become void.

As well as the pandemic affecting livelihoods and rent-paying abilities, the nature of PRS accommodation has also affected tenants' ability to do their jobs and to do so without any heightened risk of infection (Brown et al, 2020). Households with school-aged children doing online learning and adults working from home will have needed adequate space and good internet connections to be able to work effectively. Any such PRS households without adequate space will therefore, all other things being equal, have had an incentive to seek out new accommodation giving them the space they need and at the same time seek new homes in less crowded neighbourhoods with access to open space, including private gardens.

However, not all PRS households will have been able to relocate to larger (and safer) homes. Those living in shared accommodation including bedsits and other forms of multiple occupation with shared communal and/ or circulation space will have had an increased risk of infection (Kenway and Holden, 2020), especially when they are sharing with those still going out to work and at greater risk of contracting the virus from co-workers or others. Although many countries have required those who are infected or in contact with someone else who has been infected to isolate, their risk to others depends first on whether they can afford to lose income by isolating and second whether their homes allow them to keep safe from others. The increase in higher densities and apartments in city centres may have contributed to the spread of the virus (Sturzaker, 2021). In many ways, the existing precariousness of PRS tenants' dependency on low-paid jobs and insecure accommodation has reinforced their exposure to the virus (Byrne, 2021). As Nathan (2021) has observed in a case study of the spread of the pandemic in UK cities, including London, urban housing, labour market conditions and deprivation are key explanatory factors to the density of cases and the way the virus spreads.

In the short run, for other and less vulnerable households, more home-working will have reduced long-distance commuting and may lead to higher levels of satisfaction with working at home depending on the location, size and type of accommodation. Already on the evidence to date, there has been a significant increase in demand for (and prices of) suburban homes with the opposite trend in the case of city centre homes (Grant, 2020; Cox, 2021a; The Economist, 2021b; Gallent and Madeddu, 2021). In the longer run, this change in home/work living patterns may reverse the recent trend to city centre living involving small PRS flats in high-density neighbourhoods as part of regeneration policies because these may now be a negative factor in nurturing good health (Hubbard, 2020; Jones and Grigsby-Toussaint, 2020; Maddedu and Clifford, 2021; Bryson et al, 2021; Dockerill et al,

2021). Some (see, for example, Batty, 2020) have argued the pandemic might spell the end of compact city policies. Not all commentators accept this (see Nathan [2021] for a summary of the arguments). Some argue that COVID-19 will not stop the trend towards larger and denser cities because 'the human tolerance of risk in pursuit and wealth and well-being is too high for that' (Webster, 2020). This latter view is shared by Glaeser and Cutler (2021), who argue that cities will continue to thrive, despite pandemics, given their importance to new business development and social interaction. This depends on steps being taken, among others, to improve community and public health and city governance in relation to education, affordable housing and criminal justice, and making them smarter and less regulatory in approach. Others have argued that city planning will need to return to its historical origins in dealing with the unhealthy nature of cities in the 19th century by enhancing cities' resilience and preparedness for future pandemics by minimising virus transmission (see, for example, Andres *et al*, 2022). Yet others wonder if remote working, which has characterised the pandemic, becomes a more permanent part of working life cities will lose their magnetic attractions and compact city policies will be replaced by more decentralised 'garden city' forms of urban living (Lennon, 2021).

To sum up so far, COVID-19 is likely to have had a significant impact on demand for the PRS but the impacts will be strongly related to the jobs and other lives of tenants living in the sector. Not all will have been able to pay their rent or to relocate to safer and healthier accommodation. The impact on the latter tenants will depend heavily on the nature of the pre-existing regulatory frameworks and government support both for those losing jobs or some element of their income and support for rent payment for all tenants. In countries with deregulated legal framework for the PRS, the combination of job and income losses presents an acute challenge for governments if a large proportion of tenants has significant rent arrears arising from the impact of the virus on their income. In pre-COVID-19 times, landlords would be able to proceed to secure evictions but in the pandemic governments have a choice as to whether to pause these until 'normal times' are resumed and to consider increasing levels of rent support to limit the scale of arrears. Landlords, too, have choices and may be willing to 'forgive' arrears especially if the tenants have never caused them concerns before. In countries with a greater degree of regulation and support for income and rent payments it is possible that these pre-existing regulatory frameworks and support systems will have been sufficient to cope with income losses and inability to pay rents. In countries where families are important components of their welfare system there is likely to have been more reliance on non-state agencies. In addition to addressing income stress among tenants, governments will also have had to ensure that PRS accommodation remains safe, especially in shared accommodation, in order at reduce transmission of the virus and to protect tenants, for example by ensuring common parts are well ventilated and regularly cleaned. In many countries these latter regulations are enforced at the local level and of course in some countries much of regulatory policy about rents and security of tenure is similarly the responsibility of subnational bodies. There are the beginnings of research exploring the way local bodies have responded to COVID-19 (for example, Hambleton, 2021) but also critical commentary in England of how central government dominance and central fiscal controls of local spending restricted local governments' ability to respond to the pandemic (Warner et al, 2021).

The supply of private renting

On the supply side, there are four possible impacts. First, and related to the effect on tenants' income, landlords may well find they lose rent and, depending on how governments decide to support tenants, be unable to evict them, at least until more normal conditions arrive. They will also be faced with deciding if they need to adjust rents downwards in order to continue to receive an income stream, perhaps granting existing tenants some 'rent holidays'. Notably, residential REIT (Real Estate Investment Trust) values fell in many countries (OECD, 2021).

Second, landlords will be affected by any general support for all businesses, although this may not be available for those landlords who operate as individuals and not as companies. Such support could include the opportunity to furlough any directly employed staff in circumstances where landlords need to curtail aspects of the business plus any other support including granting 'holidays' for loan repayment or relevant taxes (for example, by deferring payments). These business mitigations might be partially sufficient to cover rental losses.

Third, there may also be impacts from steps governments take to support the economy and housing markets in general but which benefit private landlords as a result. The latter might include any supply-side incentives designed for example to keep housing construction (see OECD, 2021) going, including any temporary waivers of taxes on purchasing land or newly completed units (and on housing transactions in general). It might also include measures to temporarily waive aspects of consents required to build new homes or convert existing property into homes. The latter may be related to measures governments take to deal with the scale of vacant office and retail premises where there is evidence that the move to working from home and online retailing may become a more permanent feature of economies and not just a short-term response to the pandemic. More generally, in so far as central banks have played key roles to support economies through low interest rates and other measures such as quantitative easing, these will have kept landlords' debt interest payments down while asset prices will have been supported. In combination, these should have made acquiring existing or newly built property attractive. But any decline in city rents may undermine some recent investments (Nanda *et al*, 2020).

Fourth, the collapse of tourism in many major cities because of travel and other restrictions will have resulted in a big drop in demand for short-term holiday lettings, including via the Airbnb platform (for example, Cox [2021b] for evidence for Barcelona, Lisbon, London and Venice). One consequence of this could be that some of these lettings return to the longer-term lettings market thereby increasing the supply, at least in the short term, with potential consequences for depressing rents of new lettings. This could be dramatic given the scale of Airbnb lettings in major cities and their concentration in a few locations (for example, Shrabina *et al*, 2023).

To sum up on the supply side, there will have been several forces moving in different directions. Landlords may have suffered rent losses and found their returns significantly depressed but will not necessarily have had easy options to sell up especially if regulations make it difficult to secure possession. The 'burden' of rent losses may be mitigated by the extent of any support from government both specifically in relation to rents and to businesses in general, although the latter is likely to have been more important to corporate than to individual landlords. Nonetheless, despite this support, the losses may lead some landlords to sell up, especially smaller landlords for whom losses may be difficult to sustain. On the other hand, government support for housing markets and construction plus macroeconomic policy may have created a favourable context for additional investment in both existing and newly built property.

The overall picture

Pulling the demand and supply-side factors together to assess from first principles the likely short-run impact of COVID-19 on the PRS is not easy but it is feasible to suggest that the most difficult settings will be in countries with liberal market economies and liberal welfare regimes where landlords may well have faced significant rent losses. That is, unless government stepped in to support demand (including landlord subsidies) while introducing temporary rent freezes and/or eviction freezes. In other countries the existing regulatory frameworks and support system for rents and those out of work may well have mitigated the impact of COVID-19 on tenants' ability to pay rents and sustain their tenancies. At the same time there may well have been changes to tenants' preferences with more demand for lower density and safer forms of accommodation, leading to higher rents in suburban settings. In other settings, especially in cities with high proportions of holiday lettings, demand may have fallen while supply has risen, resulting in higher levels of vacancies and falling rents. While some landlords may decide to leave the market, others, especially larger landlords whose incomes derive principally from the PRS, may well have looked to maintain or even increase their stock given a more favourable investment climate.

The chapter now examines these propositions by examining what has happened in each of the countries studied in this book (see also Byrne [2021], Kholodilin [2021] and OECD [2021] for evidence drawn from a wider range of countries which suggests that suspending evictions was the most widely practised intervention globally; and Colpher [2020] for a summary and analysis of governments' overall responses to COVID-19 in Europe and how they related to a number of theoretical frameworks on government decision-making under crisis).

Evidence of the short-run impact of COVID-19

This section brings together the evidence presented in the country chapters about the impact of COVID-19 and looks at four key themes:

1. the general approach of governments to supporting economies during the pandemic;
2. trends in demand and rents;
3. support for tenants and impact on arrears and evictions;
4. evidence on investment, including government support for landlords and evidence of landlords exiting the sector or making new investments.

The evidence in this section classifies the case study countries into three categories using the same taxonomy used in Crook and Kemp (2014) and briefly discussed previously. Australia, England, Ireland (not included in the 2014 study) and the United States have been classified as liberal market economies and welfare regimes; Denmark, Germany, the Netherlands and Norway as co-ordinated market economies and social-democratic or conservative welfare regimes; Spain was classified as a mixed market economy (with a Mediterranean welfare regime).

General approach of governments

The country chapters indicate that many countries took steps to combat the virus entering their countries (where they could) and pursued restrictions and lockdowns on economic and other activity to suppress social contact and prevent transmission of the virus.

Liberal market economies shut borders (but to varying degrees and extents) and had restrictions on activity including lockdowns of various lengths and in different ways in particular subnational jurisdictions. They also supported their economies with very significant public spending where the lockdowns prevented business operating including payments to support businesses that were shut down to help them retain employees (especially hospitality, tourism and non-essential retail where in most countries PRS tenants were over-represented among employees) and some temporary increases in unemployment assistance to staff who lost jobs. In Australia a Job Keeper subsidy was introduced to help business retain employees while unemployment assistance rates were doubled for a temporary period. In England, the government provided loans to firms and other organisations whose businesses were interrupted and enabled them to 'furlough' staff with the government paying up to 80 per cent of wages, subject to a cap. Workers having to isolate if they caught the virus received some limited income support. The Bank of England maintained its low interest rate and quantitative easing policy. In Ireland, a flat-rate payment of €350 per week was made available to workers who became unemployed as a result of the pandemic. A temporary wage subsidy scheme was also set up to subsidise the salaries of employees in firms affected by the pandemic. By May 2020, approximately 46 per cent of the labour force were on some form of income-related support and PRS tenants were more likely than other households to work in the economic sectors that were shut down. Likewise, in the United States those most likely to lose jobs were in travel, hospitality and retail, typically earning low wages whereas those in professional and other businesses were less likely to have lost work. To combat loss of earnings, the US Congress passed measures including payments to households earning below a specific amount, enhanced unemployed insurance benefits support for small businesses, and loan forbearance for homeowners and landlords with federally backed mortgages. These types of measures were expensive. For example, in Australia the Job Keeper provisions cost AUS$90 billion but appear to have been successful in keeping unemployment lower than would otherwise have been the case and potentially helped businesses bounce back once COVID-19 restrictions were eased. In the United States measures costing US$5 trillion were introduced in the year to March 2021.

Rather different approaches were typical in countries with other types of economies and welfare regimes. In Denmark, for example, as well as having lower levels of infection than many other countries COVID-19 also has had less effect on PRS households than in many other countries because a strong welfare state helped largely to replace the incomes of those who lost employment because of the virus. A similar picture prevailed in Germany where existing unemployment insurance covers about 60 per cent of former earnings (up to a maximum) and a similar subsidy for employees on reduced hours. Germany also has provision that help tenants with rent payments in terms of actual costs of tenancies provided they are reasonable (and if not reasonable will cover them until they find something that is judged reasonable). In the Netherlands, given the limited housing market impacts of the pandemic and the fact that the Netherlands had safety net facilities in place – income support and housing allowances – no big policy initiatives were developed, although some modifications were made to rent regulation measures. Norway undertook significant monetary measures including reducing banks' capital buffers, reducing the central bank's main interest rate to zero, and fiscal measures that provided more support for redundant employees based upon existing welfare measures. Financial support for businesses, including private landlords and cultural organisations, through tax reliefs, loans and guarantees, was also introduced. As a result, the costs of the significant recession and decline in GDP fell on the state and not on those whose lives were impacted by lockdowns and were funded by the significant reserves arising from oil revenues. Spain, with a more mixed market economy, had a rather different experience with the government taking significant measures to protect tenants losing jobs and landlords losing incomes with a range of measures to protect vulnerable tenants who had lost jobs or been furloughed with measures related to the scale of their landlords' portfolios.

Trends in demand and rents

Taking first the experience of countries with liberal market economies and welfare regimes, our country chapters reveal a very common pattern. In Australia, vacancies initially rose and rents fell, especially in rental markets near universities, but subsequently demand increased for lower density locations as people wanted accommodation and locations more suited to working from home. House prices and rents increased in these locations with both landlords and homeowners competing to buy property with adverse impacts on existing communities in these locations. England experienced a similar trend with vacancies rising in inner cities and city centres and rents falling (with the opposite in suburban locations) with this 'relocation effect' being compounded by the high vacancies in short-term tourist lets and by out-migration of EU citizens following Brexit and COVID-19. At the same time, since not all private tenants were able to move, overcrowding increased with potentially adverse impact on virus transmission. There was a similar pattern in Ireland with the number of lettings increasing as short-term holiday lettings came onto the mainstream market while rent inflation fell to its lowest level for nearly a decade, a reflection of the additional supply and the fall in tenants' incomes. In the United States, rents fell in many metropolitan areas as families sought to relocate to suburban locations to secure more space both within the home and outside.

In the other economies studied in this volume, the picture is broadly the same. In Denmark, reports suggested an increase in lettings partly because accommodation being used for holiday lets, including via the Airbnb booking platform, came onto the main lettings market. Demand did not decline as households postponed potential decisions to buy and not to rent, but demand shifted to lettings with more space inside and outside the dwelling. In Germany, there is evidence of investment in improvement to owner-occupied property and some fall in the rate of rent increases in the main cities. In the Netherlands, partly because of the demand effect of a fall in the numbers of in-migrants, liberalised rents started falling in 2020 in some cities and by 10 per cent in Amsterdam. In Norway, vacant dwellings rose partly because students stayed at home and not in their university town, partly because tourist lettings declined, and partly (it was alleged) because the support scheme for businesses incentivised qualifying large-scale landlords to leave dwellings empty. In Spain, the major cities experienced declining rental stock and falling rents.

Support for tenants and impact on arrears and evictions

In liberal market economies governments took significant (albeit mainly temporary) measures to protect tenants from the impact of lost income on their ability to pay rents. These included measures to suspend evictions because of rent arrears and direct help with rent. In Australia, there were initial measures to harmonise state and territory policy on eviction and rent increase moratoria, measures that were later extended. Some states increased rental assistance payments. Landlords were also encouraged to negotiate rent reductions or payment deferrals with tenants unable to pay, notwithstanding the asymmetric imbalances in power between landlords and tenants. Low-income and young tenants were those most likely to be in arrears and/or need support but so too were landlords who relied on rent payments to service loans on their lettings portfolios. The government's support for jobs appeared to be a more effective way of helping tenants in difficulties than the rent arrears and evictions measures. In England, temporary additional income support and increased rent allowance measures were introduced for tenants. Evictions were banned for a temporary six-month period, except for the most serious cases, while guidance about managing arrears, including through mediation, was introduced. Many of these schemes were extended, often several times, because lockdowns were extended and/or re-instigated. By July 2020 a quarter of tenants were finding it more difficult to keep up with rent payments since COVID-19 restrictions had been put in place and the numbers in arrears had doubled, raising concerns about the likely scale of evictions when restrictions cease, with lobbyists arguing for a government relief fund to pay tenants' arrears. In March 2020, Ireland introduced a temporary rent and evictions freeze later extended until July 2020 when they were replaced by more targeted measures designed to protect tenants at risk of rent increases or of eviction (because of arrears) or who were eligible for state income support (but requiring tenants to declare that they were eligible). The eviction and rent increase moratoria also applied to areas which had the highest health-related restrictions. The qualifying criteria for rent supplement payments in Ireland were also widened. Initial evidence on the impact of these measures suggests that the evictions freeze was successfully implemented and that rent arrears did not significantly increase. The evidence from the United States showed that in early 2021 nearly one in five of all renters were in arrears and a third had little confidence that they could pay their next month's rent. Millions of renters were thus at risk of losing their homes, but a range of eviction moratoria stalled most evictions. Although arrears continued to accumulate the recent measures passed by the US Congress provide emergency rental assistance, which were intended to cover these arrears and enable renters to continue to occupy their homes. In August 2021 these eviction measures were extended in counties where transmission rates are high and will enable more rental assistance to be targeted on private tenants there. Research evidence suggests that not only did this assistance help with paying rents (although tenants still experienced difficulties meeting other needs), but that it also resulted in short-term improved mental as well as financial health for those in receipt of the assistance, compared with those who were not (Airgood-Obrycki, 2022).

In countries with different market economies and welfare regimes the approaches and outcomes were different. In Denmark, existing arrangements related to security and rents meant that no additional measures were needed to protect PRS tenants from the impact of COVID-19 on their ability to pay rents and to protect them from eviction. In Germany, a similar picture prevailed and there has also been a temporary moratorium on rent payments that do not impact of landlords' right to seek possession, provided accumulated arrears are paid off by a fixed date in 2022. The Netherlands has measures about rents and security in place as well as income support and housing allowances and hence no major new initiatives were mounted to deal with the impact of COVID-19 on the PRS. However, in the light of evidence that PRS tenants were having difficulties paying rents, the national government agreed with landlords that evictions were to be minimised and it also made permanent the temporary tenancy contracts introduced after the global financial crisis. In addition to help tenants pay rents for existing dwellings with regulated rents a temporary rent freeze was introduced for a year in 2021 with compensation paid to landlords with large portfolios. In dwellings where rents had been liberalised or where income-based rents were charged, future increases have been limited by new indices set so that new construction is still viable. In Norway existing welfare schemes slowed down the negative economic effects of the virus as they acted as automatic stabilisers and dampened the effects of the crisis. For example, housing benefit costs expanded by 500 million NOK during the middle of 2020. Moreover, the central bank took its rate down to zero thus lowering loan costs with significant effects on households and the housing market.

Spain took many new steps to combat the impact of COVID-19 on the PRS. These primarily aimed to protect the most vulnerable tenants (those who lost their jobs, were furloughed or on short hours). These measures were extended and modified. They included the temporary suspension of evictions of vulnerable people; lease and term extensions for six months; a moratorium on rent payments to large landlords enabling rent to be deferred with negotiated deferment for smaller landlords; loans (and grants for the vulnerable) to help tenants pay their rent. There were also arrangements to help landlords who have lost rental income. As a result of these measures evictions fell substantially with evidence from the main cities showing a 50 per cent fall and also of a quarter of tenants negotiating rent reductions or payment deferment.

Evidence on investment and landlords' returns

In Australia, there was a shortage of rentals in the locations favoured by those seeking more space inside and outside their homes with households relocating from the major cities to the suburbs or elsewhere. Investor landlords returned to bidding for properties for sale, putting additional pressure on house prices and thereby increasing demand for private rental from households priced out of the owner-occupier market.

In England, landlord associations estimated that around a quarter of landlords had lost rental income and that almost a third of landlords planned to sell one or more properties over the next year. On the other hand, the 'appetite' to invest appeared not to have been dramatically 'dented' during the pandemic. In November 2020, landlords made 15 per cent of agreed property purchases in England, Wales and Scotland, more than at any time since December 2016. Investment in new-build private rental housing also continued unabated with the macroeconomic environment of low interest rates and increasing asset house prices fostering new deals including those financed by overseas investors. Steps to support the housing market (for example, stamp duty tax holidays) also helped landlords, albeit not deliberately targeted at them. In Ireland, landlords were able to claim help if non-payment of rent created financial hardship for them (in the sense of being unable to service debt on a property let out). In the United States, evidence suggested that owners of small portfolios were hit the hardest by rent arrears, whereas owners of larger portfolios appeared to experience only small increases in arrears.

In the Netherlands, the revised measures in relation to rent regulation were designed to protect landlords' returns and nurture new construction as well as to protect tenants. Norway introduced support on landlords' unavoidable fixed costs for those who employed staff and where their rent loss meant turnover fell 30 per cent or more. In Norway, the central bank cut its main interest rate to zero, which lowered costs for landlords while the fall in construction may well lead to higher house prices and rents.

Summary

The evidence in this section suggests that the experience of dealing with COVID-19 has broadly matched the *a priori* expectations of state and market responses discussed in the previous section. PRS tenants were more likely than households in other tenures to work in precarious jobs in many retail and hospitality sectors where work was low-paid and insecure. Many lost their jobs or were furloughed and governments addressed this by special initiatives or additional funding to existing welfare programmes. Governments also sought to protect housing either by introducing new approaches to limit rents and evictions, amendments to existing regulatory protection in the PRS (sometimes targeted to specific locations, subsectors of the PRS or specific, usually vulnerable, tenants) or by having in place adequate existing protections on rents and evictions to support tenants during the pandemic. Markets responded too: some tenants moved to homes and locations with more indoor and outdoor space, with rents falling in central city locations and rising in the suburbs. Although many landlords lost income there was also evidence that macroeconomic adjustments and specific tax and other protections of housing market and construction activity provided an economic environment for continuing investment in the PRS. But there were also important differences between countries and these are explored in the next section.

Have government policies to support the private rental sector during COVID-19 been related to types of market economy and welfare state?

Table 11.1 shows in summary form the extent of government interventions specific to the private rental sector based upon the evidence in the previous section and the country chapters in this volume. It is evident from the previous section that the liberal market economy countries generally initiated significant 'emergency' types of intervention in the labour markets to protect (to different extents) workers whose jobs disappeared or where workers were temporarily furloughed, not least the large numbers of private tenants working in hospitality and non-essential retail sectors. With some exceptions, countries with other types of economy tended to let their existing welfare mechanisms take the strain, although clearly this involved significant additional public expenditure. In contrast, in liberal market

Table 11.1: COVID-19 measures in the private rental sector by types of economy

Intervention	Liberal market economies and liberal welfare regimes	Co-ordinated market economies and social-democratic or conservative welfare regimes	Mixed market economies and Mediterranean welfare regimes
Rent freezes or deferrals	Yes, Australia (states) Yes, Ireland (targeted) No, England No, USA	No, Denmark Yes, Germany but temporary Yes, Netherlands but targeted No, Norway	Yes, Spain but targeted and related to landlord size
Eviction freezes	Yes, Australia (state specific) Yes, England Yes, Ireland Yes, USA	No, Denmark, No, Germany Yes, Netherlands but focused No, Norway	Yes, Spain for vulnerable
Financial support for tenants	Yes, Australia (some states) Yes, England (temporary) Yes, Ireland Yes, USA	No, Denmark No, Germany Yes, Netherlands targeted and temporary No, Norway	Yes, Spain for vulnerable
Support for landlords	Yes, Australia to incentivise rent freezes, and so on Yes, England via general business support Yes, Ireland if loss of rent, and so on Yes, USA via forbearance of federal-backed loans	Yes, Norway support for business landlords Yes, Netherlands (re: rent freeze) No, Germany No, Denmark	Yes, Spain related to landlord size

Source: Collated from information in country chapters in this volume.

economies, existing mechanisms tended not to suffice and hence COVID-19 specific initiatives to safeguard jobs and income were needed, again with significant additional public expenditure.

Looking at Table 11.1, a similar contrast between liberal market and other economies in terms of specific interventions to protect tenants (and landlords) in the PRS can be discerned. In liberal market economies governments (and states within countries where relevant) were more likely than in other countries to have introduced some form of rent and eviction freeze, together with some direct financial support for tenants and for landlords. This was not universally the case and there were exceptions, as Table 11.1 confirms. In contrast, in countries with other types of economy, governments (and devolved states) were much less likely to have introduced additional controls including rent and eviction freezes and support for tenants and landlords.

There were exceptions but these tended to be targeted and not universal (for example, as in the Netherlands, related to the type of rent regulation involved) and were also connected with a desire on governments' part to ensure these temporary freezes (or restrictions) did not impair investment in construction. Spain, the only example of a mixed market economy, intervened in all four ways but generally related to targeted support for vulnerable tenants and to protect the finances of specific types of landlords.

The evidence suggests a mix of reacting to a critical juncture in liberal market economies with new interventions but that path dependency enabled countries with other types of economy and welfare regime to cope with their (mainly) existing arrangements intact. In the former the deregulated nature of the PRS mean that without new interventions the loss of tenants' incomes would have led to massive arrears and evictions and losses for landlords: hence the rent and eviction freezes and support for both tenants and landlords. In other countries the existing welfare and PRS regulatory arrangements for rents and security meant that (in most cases) there was no need for a universal adoption of new approaches save those to address specific cases where either vulnerability or increased rents would impact badly on tenants (and hence landlords' incomes) and on new construction.

However, it seems doubtful (on current evidence) that this critical juncture in terms of emergency COVID-19 necessitated interventions in the PRS in liberal market countries will lead to more permanent changes. One example of an exception to this is England, where its government has announced that it will proceed with some permanent restrictions on automatic evictions at the end of fixed-term leases (DLUHC, 2022). This had been announced two years ago but not implemented: hence the decision to implement seems likely to have been provoked by the threat of mass evictions during COVID-19 and especially thereafter when the virus is less of a threat to health and jobs.

Conclusion

Because PRS tenants are more likely than other households to work in low-paid jobs, especially in hospitality and non-essential retail (including in the gig economy) they have been particularly exposed to the loss of income resulting from measures taken to control the virus. They have also been more exposed to the virus because of living in accommodation which is multi-occupied and in high-density neighbourhoods. Taken together this has impaired their ability to pay rent from earned income even when benefiting from temporary wage support measures. Despite these labour market interventions, governments in liberal market economies with limited regulation of rents and security in the PRS have found it also necessary to introduce temporary measures to protect tenants (and also support landlords' finances). In other countries with different types of economy and welfare regimes where there has been more regulation of the PRS (in terms of rents and security) a combination of general welfare support and the existing regulatory arrangements have not required the much more extensive PRS regulatory intervention seen in liberal market economies. But despite these differences all countries discussed in this volume have massively expanded public spending ('emergency Keynsianism') either through the automatic stabilisers built into welfare systems or through special measures in the labour market to protect incomes. In both cases the state has massively protected its PRS albeit in different ways

In addition to these differences there have also been marked similarities. In most countries studied in this volume there have been significant changes to housing preferences with those able to move and able to buy and rent new homes seeking to purchase (or rent) homes with more space both inside and outside the dwelling. At the same time, measures taken to support economies and the housing market have resulted in significant increases in house prices arising from low interest rates and specific measures to support housing construction and transactions with consequent impacts on the profitability and attractiveness of PRS investment. And in countries with federal systems of government the PRS-specific interventions had been led by the relevant state or territory government and in others the interventions have sometimes been related to the market conditions and the intensity of infections prevailing in particular locations.

It is a moot point as to whether a critical juncture has been reached and whether these trends are a temporary adaptation to the specific circumstances of COVID-19 (more people working from home; ensuring greater security for tenants losing jobs and income) or whether it will result in a more permanent shift not only in the location of PRS stock but also in changing approaches to the regulation of the sector. Thus in the context of the greater systemic risks facing advanced economies (Beck, 1992), which it is difficult for individuals to mitigate, future shocks to the housing market (whether financial or environmental) and specifically to the PRS may be better mitigated and withstood by new approaches to regulation drawing on the experience of dealing with the virus and not need the crisis management that has been necessary in responding to COVID-19.

References

Airgood-Obrycki, W. (2022) *The Short-Term Benefits of Emergency Rental Assistance*, Cambridge, MA, Harvard University, Joint Center for Housing Studies, https://www.jchs.harvard.edu/sites/default/files/research/files/harvard_jchs_short_term_era_benefits_airgood-obrycki_2022.pdf

Andres, L., Bryson, J.R., Mehanna, H. and Moawad, P. (2022) 'Learning from COVID-19 and planning post-pandemic cities to reduce pathogentransmission pathways', *Town Planning Review,* ahead of print, DOI: https://doi.org/10.3828/tpr.2022.5

Ban, C. (2020) *Emergency Keynesianism 2.0: The Political Economy of Fiscal Policy in Europe during the Corona Crisis*, Copenhagen, Copenhagen Business School, https://research.cbs.dk/en/publications/emergency-keynesianism-20-the-political-economy-of-fiscal-policy-

Batty, M. (2020) 'The coronavirus crisis: what will the post-pandemic city look like', *Environment & Planning B: Urban Analytics and City Science*, 47(4), 547–555.

Beck, U. (1992) *Risk Society: Towards a New Modernity*, London, SAGE.

Béland, D., Cantillon, B., Hick, R. and Moreira, A. (2021) 'Social policy in the face of a global pandemic: policy responses to the COVID-19 crisis', *Social Policy & Administration*, 55(2), 249–260.

Benfer, E.A., Vlahov, D., Long, M.Y., Walker-Wells, E., Pttemger, J.L., Gonsalves, G. and Keene, D.E. (2021) 'Eviction, health inequity, and the spread of COVID-19: housing policy as a primary pandemic mitigation strategy', *Journal of Urban Health*, 98, 1–12.

Blackwell, T. and Kohl, S. (2019) 'Historicizing housing typologies: beyond welfare state regimes and varieties of residential capitalism', *Housing Studies*, 34(2), 298–318.

Bremer, B. and McDaniel, S. (2020) 'The ideational foundations of social democratic austerity in the context of the great recession', *Socio-Economic Review*, 18(2), 439–463.

Brown, P., Newton, D., Armitage, R. and Monchuk, L. (2020) *Lockdown. Rundown. Breakdown: The COVID-19 Lockdown and the Impact of Poor-Quality Housing on Occupants in the North of England*, Newcastle, The Northern Housing Consortium, https://www.northern-consortium.org.uk/wp-content/uploads/2020/10/Lockdown.-Rundown.-Breakdown..pdfortium.

Bryson, J.R., Andrees, L., Ersoy, A. and Reardon, L. (eds) (2021) 'A year into the pandemic: shifts, improvisations and impacts for places, people and policy', in *Living with Pandemics: Places, People and Policy*, Cheltenham, Edward Elgar, pp 2–35.

Byrne, M. (2021) *The Impact of COVID-19 on the Private Rental Sector: Emerging International Evidence*, Dublin, University College Dublin, https://publicpolicy.ie/perspectives/the-impact-of-covid-19-on-the-private-rental-sector-emerging-international-evidence/

Colpher, B. (2020) 'Public policy responses to COVID-19 in Europe', *European Policy Analysis*, 6(2), 126–137.

Cox, H. (2021a) 'Melbourne maelstrom', *Financial Times*, 30 and 31 January, p 3.

Cox, H. (2021b) 'Too good to be true', *Financial Times*, 24 and 25 February, pp 1–2.

Coyle, D. (2020) *Beyond the Pandemic, What Should We Do?*, Cambridge, The University of Cambridge, https://www.cam.ac.uk/stories/BeyondThePandemic_productivity

Crook, A.D.H. and Kemp, P.A. (2014) 'Comparing countries', in A.D.H. Crook and P.A. Kemp (eds) *Private Rental Housing: Comparative Perspectives*, Cheltenham, Edward Elgar, pp 224–246.

Davenport, A., Farquharson, C., Rasul, I., Sibieta, L. and Stoye, G. (2020) *The Geography of the COVID-19 Crisis in England*, London, Institute for Fiscal Studies, https://www.ifs.org.uk/uploads/The-Geography-of-the-COVID-19-crisis-in-England -final.pdf

Dewilde, C. (2017) 'Do housing regimes matter? Assessing the concept of housing regimes through configurations of housing outcomes', *International Journal of Social Welfare*, 26, 384–404.

DLUHC (Department of Levelling Up Homes & Communities) (2022) *A Fairer Private Rented Sector*, London, DLUHC, CP, 693, https://assets.pub lishing.service.gov.uk/government/uploads/system/uploads/attachment_data/file/1083381/A_fairer_private_rented_sector_print.pdf

Dockerill, B., Hess, D.B., Lord, A., Sturzaker, J. and Sykes, O. (2021) 'Putting the COVID-19 pandemic into perspective: urban planning scholars react to a changed world', *Town Planning Review*, 92(1), 1–2.

The Economist (2021a) 'Shelter from the storm', *The Economist*, 6 March, pp 17–18.

The Economist (2021b) 'Global property: the race for space', *The Economist*, 10 April, pp 69–70.

Esping-Andersen, G. (1990) *The Three Worlds of Welfare Capitalism*, Cambridge, Polity Press.

Gallent, N. and Madeddu, M. (2021) 'Covid-19 and London's decentralising housing market – what are the planning implications?', *Planning Practice & Research*, 36(5), 567–577.

Glaeser, E. and Cutler, D. (2021) *Survival of the City: Living and Thriving in an Age of Isolation,* London, Basic Books.

Grant, J. (2020) 'Pandemic challenges to planning prescriptions: how Covid-19 is changing the way we think about planning', *Planning Theory & Practice*, 21(5), 659–667.

Greve, B., Blomquist, P., Hvinden, B. and van Gerven, M. (2020) 'Nordic welfare states – still standing or changed by the COVID-19 crisis?', *Social Policy & Administration*, 55, 295–311.

Hall, P.A. and Soskice, D. (2001) 'An introduction to varieties of capitalism', in P.A. Hall and D. Soskice (eds) *Varieties of Capitalism, the Institutional Foundations of Comparative Advantage*, Oxford, Oxford University Press.

Hambleton, R. (2021) *Cities and Communities Beyond COVID-19: How Local Leadership Can Change Our Future for the Better*, Bristol, Policy Press.

Hubbard, P. (2020) *How COVID-19 Might Change the Way We Live and Work for Good*, London, Kings College London, https://www.kcl.ac.uk/how-covid-19-might-change-the-way-we-live-and-work-for-good

Jones, A. and Grigsby-Toussaint, D.S. (2021) 'Housing stability and the residential context of the COVID-19 pandemic', *Cities & Health*, 5(S1), S159–S161.

Kenway, P and Holden, J. (2020) *Excess Deaths in the Time of Covid Reflect the British State's Indifference to How Society Really Works*, London, New Policy Institute, https://www.npi.org.uk/files/3415/8938/9004/Excess_deaths_in_the_time_of_Covid.pdf

Kettunen, H. and Ruonavaara, H. (2021) 'Rent regulation in 21st century Europe: comparative perspectives', *Housing Studies*, 36(9), 1446–1468.

Kholodilin, K.A. (2021) 'Housing policy during COVID-19 crisis: challenges and solutions', DIW focus, No. 2, Deutsches Institut für Wirtschaftsforschung (DIW), Berlin, https://www.econstor.eu/handle/10419/219095

Krasner, S.D. (1984) 'Approaches to the state: alternative conceptions and historical dynamics', *Comparative Politics*, 16(2), 223–246.

Lennon, M. (2023) 'Planning and the post-pandemic city', *Planning Theory & Practice*, 24(1), 140–143.

Maclennan, D., Miao, J.T. Christie, L. and Long, J. (2021) 'Raising productivity and housing the economy', in P. McCann and T. Vorley (eds) *Productivity and the Pandemic, Challenges and Insights from Covid-19*, Cheltenham, Edward Elgar, pp 191–204.

Maddedu, M. and Clifford, B. (2021) 'Housing quality, permitted development and the role of regulation after COVID-19', *Town Planning Review*, 92(1), 41–48.

McCann, P. and Ortega-Argilés, R. (2021) 'The Covid-19 shock: the UK national and regional implications in the light of international evidence', in P. McCann and T. Vorley (eds) *Productivity and the Pandemic, Challenges and Insights from Covid-19*, Cheltenham, Edward Elgar, pp 1–15.

Moreira, A. and Hick, R. (2021) 'COVID-19, the Great Recession and social policy: is this time different?', *Social Policy & Administration*, 55(2), 261–279.

Nanda, A., Thanos, S., Valtonen, E., Xu, Y. and Zandieh, R. (2020) 'Forced homeward: the COVID-19 implications for housing', *Town Planning Review*, 92(1), 25–31.

Nathan, M. (2021) 'The city and the virus', *Urban Studies*, online first, https://doi-org.sheffield.idm.oclc.org/10.1177/00420980211058383

OECD (2021) *Housing Amid Covid-19: Policy Responses and Challenges*, Paris, OECD, https://www.oecd.org/coronavirus/policy-responses/housing-amid-covid-19-policy-responses-and-challenges-cfdc08a8/#contactinfo-d7e3269

Omerod, E. and Davoudi, S. (2021) 'Governing the pandemic: democracy at the time of emergency', *Town Planning Review*, 92(3), 323–328.

Pierson, P. (2004) *Politics in Time*, Princeton, Princeton University Press.

Shrabina, Z., Arcaute, E. and Batty, M. (2021) 'Airbnb and its potential impact on the London housing market', *Urban Studies*, 59(1), 197–221.

Sokol, M. and Pataccini, L. (2020) 'Winners and losers in coronavirus times: financialisation, financial chains and emerging economic geographies of the covid-19 pandemic', *Tijdschrift voor Economische en Sociale Geografie*, 111(3), 401–415.

Stephens, M. (2011) 'Comparative housing research: a system embedded approach', *International Journal of Housing Policy*, 11(4), 337–356.

Stephens, M. (2020) 'How housing systems are changing and why: a critique of Kemeny's Theory of Housing Regimes', *Housing Theory & Society*, 37(5), 521–547.

Strauss, D. and Smith, C. (2021) 'Pandemic cements the housing gap', *The Economist*, 26 and 27 June, p 8.

Sturzaker, J. (2021) 'The people: where will they go?', *Town Planning Review*, 92(1), 11–17.

Tooze, A. (2021) *Shutdown: How Covid Shook the World's Economy*, London, Allen Lane, Penguin Press.

Warner, S., Richards, D., Coyle, D. and Smith, M.J. (2021) 'English devolution and the covid-19 pandemic: governing dilemmas in the shadow of the treasury', *The Political Quarterly*, 92(2), 321–330.

Webster, C. (2020) 'How high can we go? Urban density, infectious versus chronic disease, and the adaptive resilience of cities', *Town Planning Review*, 92(1), 123–130.

12

Change and continuity in private rental housing

Peter A. Kemp

This book has explored trends in private rental housing in the advanced economies over the past two decades. On the demand side, these trajectories include growth in private renting and more families, couples and higher-income households living in the private rented sector (PRS). On the supply side, developments include the increasing numbers of private individual landlords and the growing importance of various types of large-scale corporate landlords. Internet-based PropTech platforms have become increasingly important in the process of matching tenants and landlords. And the emergence and rapid growth of Airbnb, and other internet-based nightly accommodation hosts, has impacted upon housing supply, prices and rents in popular tourist localities. Taken together, these developments represent a significant, and to some extent, unexpected, change in the nature and role of private rental housing in the first two decades of the 21st century. It is not a wholesale transformation of the sector but rather, to a greater or less extent, a 'recalibration' of private renting and its contribution to housing provision in the advanced economies.

The contributions to this book highlight the pivotal impact that the global financial crisis (GFC) has had on recent trajectories of change in private renting. It was the largest economic shock to hit the advanced economies (AEs) since the Great Depression in the interwar years. The subprime mortgage crisis was an important catalyst behind the onset of the GFC and the accompanying fall in house prices in many AEs. It also prompted central banks to introduce macroprudential controls on mortgage lending to households and buy-to-let (BTL) landlords. In the aftermath of the GFC, interest rates declined to historically unprecedented low levels, as central banks cut their policy rates and introduced quantitative easing. One consequence of this new era of cheap money was to decrease bond yields and increase house prices (Mian and Sufi, 2014; Tooze, 2018).

Viewed from an historical institutionalist perspective, the GFC created a 'critical juncture' (Pierson, 2004) that helped to shift private renting and owner occupation onto altered trajectories – 'developmental paths' – involving variable degrees of re-growth of the former and decline of the latter across many of the AEs. However, that tenure transformation was also the outcome of much more slow-moving demographic and economic trends that were helping to reshape at the margins the role and nature of private renting in many AEs. In historical institutionalist terms, institutional change is not only the outcome of disruptive shocks like the GFC but can also result from incremental but ultimately cumulative transformative processes. Streeck and Thelen (2005) describe this as 'transformation without disruption'. The transformative changes in private rental trajectories explored in this book are the outcome of both the disruptive effects of the GFC and the more slow-moving but ultimately transformative demographic and socioeconomic trends.

Transformative change

Much of the scholarly debate on these changes in private rental housing has focused on the impact of the GFC (for example, Aalbors, 2016; Fuller, 2021). And, as Chapters 2 to 10 show, to a greater or lesser extent the GFC did have a transformative impact on private renting in all nine countries covered in this book. Nevertheless, many of the changes in private rental housing were underway *before* the GFC (Kemp, 2015). In England and Ireland, for example, the increase in private renting began just after the turn of the century. In New Zealand the re-growth of private renting began during the late 20th century. Moreover, in some AEs, the growth in private renting among young adults began before the GFC, but this new trend was offset by increasing owner-occupation rates among elderly households. In England, for example, the growth of private renting among young adults aged under 25 years began as early as the 1980s (Resolution Foundation, 2021). In Australia, homeownership has been falling among young adults aged 25 to 34 years, and households aged 35 to 44 years, since the 1980s. Between 1982 and 2007, the homeownership rate fell from 56 per cent to 39 per cent among the former and from 75 per cent to 64 per cent among the latter (Wood and Ong, 2015). Instead of buying their home, increasing numbers of young adults are renting it from a private landlord. In short, while the changes in the role and nature of private rental housing that have taken place or come to notice since the turn of the century are the outcome, not only of the path-disrupting economic shock of the GFC, but also of more slow-moving, gradual forces. In this section, we present an overview of the latter before moving onto the former.

Academic research in housing studies has emphasised the causal role of financialisation in the transformation of contemporary housing markets in the AEs and beyond (for example, Aalbors, 2016; van Loon and Aalbers, 2017; Fields, 2018; Martin *et al*, 2018). As Fuller (2021) among others has noted, there is no agreed definition of this term and some have contested its usefulness. Leaving that debate to one side, the financialisation of housing and the wider economy is not a new phenomenon, but rather one that has been ongoing since the late 20th century (Krippner, 2011). It was enabled by the deregulation and subsequent internationalisation of financial markets from the 1980s. It was further facilitated by the invention of the World Wide Web, which made possible the development of internet portals; the globalisation of information; and the instantaneous, electronic transmission of capital within and between countries. The sharp increase in the volume of residential mortgage-backed securities from the late 1990s in the United States – and their purchase by banks and investors in the United States, Europe and elsewhere – was one of the *precursors* to the GFC, not a *consequence* of it. Meanwhile, the acquisition of former social and company housing organisations in Germany by private equity firms began in the 1990s (Kofner, 2006; 2014; Wijburg and Aalbers, 2017). Wijburg *et al* (2018) referred to the opportunistic acquisitions of these former social rental portfolios as 'Financialisation 1.0'.

A further component of this pre-GFC phase of financialisation has been the sale of local authority homes in Ireland and in England – and elsewhere in Britain – to sitting tenants. In this way, as Byrne (Chapter 4, this volume) points out, local authority housing has acted as a subsidised pathway into homeownership for many low- and moderate- income council tenants. However, once the new owners have passed the minimum holding period, they can choose to move somewhere else and let their former council home to private renters or to sell it on the open market, either to owner-occupiers or to private landlords (Sprigings and Smith, 2012). Sales to private landlords are not negligible. Indeed, Murie (2022) has estimated that about 40 per cent of dwellings sold under the Right to Buy are now in the private rented sector. In other words, while the Right to Buy was promoted to increase the number of *owner-occupiers*, it has also indirectly provided housing landlords with access to a supply of relatively low-cost *dwellings* to let.

The flow of ex-council homes into the private rental market is part of a broader process of transfers from the owner-occupied sector into the PRS and vice versa. In Australia (Hulse, Chapter 2, this volume) and in England (Crook and Kemp, Chapter 5, this volume) most private landlords buy second-hand rather more than newly built properties. Indeed, in these two countries, there has long been a significant two-way flow of homes between owner-occupation and private renting. The same is very likely true in other countries where the PRS is dominated by small-scale BTL landlords and that have no restrictions on the sale of rental apartments to owner-occupiers. For most of the post-1945 period, the net flow of dwellings was from the owner-occupied to the PRS. But with the decline in homeownership, the net outflow reversed, with more dwellings moving from the owner-occupied sector to the PRS, rather than the other way around. Meanwhile, as Martin *et al* (2022) have shown in their Australian study, there is considerable turnover of *landlords* with the PRS, with many new investors entering, and subsequently exiting, the sector, often after a relatively short period.

A further important cause behind the partial re-growth and changes in private rental housing is the secular decline in interest rates, which began in the 1980s and 1990s (Kemp, 2015). Other things being equal, lower interest rates enable households and housing investors to take out a larger mortgage with which to buy a new dwelling or remortgage an existing one. Increasing purchasing power without a commensurate rise in housing supply, of course, will tend to push up house prices. Although other factors may have been at work, the secular decline in interest rates facilitated the marked increase in house prices that began in most AEs in the mid- to late-1990s. In turn, the increase in real house prices enabled owner-occupiers to accumulate wealth via tax-free capital gains, some of which was invested in rental housing by better-off households, thereby giving further upward momentum to house prices (Ronald and Kadi, 2018).

The fact that house prices increased by more than incomes over that period is arguably the most important reason why fewer young and moderate-income households have been able to buy their home, or have rented for longer, than their parents did (Whitehead and Williams, 2017). While low interest rates make mortgage repayments easier to afford, the sharp increase in house prices compared with disposable incomes means it takes longer to save up for the deposit on a home purchase than it did in the mid-1990s. It is not so much the cost of the mortgage repayments that has reduced the number of young adults buying their home; rather, it is the amount of down payment they need to make to get a mortgage (Whitehead and Williams, 2017).

In addition, a complex of gradual but profound sociodemographic trends has also increased the demand for private rental housing. Later marriage and later child-rearing – life events that often prompt moves from renting to owner-occupation – have increased the length of time for which younger households rent their home. To some extent, the rise of cohabitation has had a similar impact on entry into owner-occupation. Likewise, the growth in higher education participation rates since the 1990s has also pushed back the age of entry into owner-occupation among young adults. Moreover, in countries such as Australia, England and the United States, where university students pay substantial tuition fees, repayment of these loans has reduced their ability to save for a deposit and thereby lengthened the time after graduation that they rent their accommodation (Andrews, 2010).

Nevertheless, and as the chapters in this volume show, the GFC has had a far-reaching impact on private rental housing markets. In the first place, the GFC was the biggest economic shock to hit the AEs since the onset of the Great Depression in the interwar years. The credit crunch and disorganisation in global capital markets that occurred during the GFC created the need to reconsider the growing role of finance in the wider economy, including the risks to financial stability arising from the growth in novel and opaque financial instruments and in 'shadow banking' (Turner, 2016). The impact of the GFC varied across the AEs, with countries such as Ireland, Spain, the UK and the United States having been affected very much more than Australia and Norway. Moreover, among those worst affected, the recovery from the GFC was slow and more attenuated by comparison with the Great Depression and other major recessions since the Second World War.

The introduction of quantitative easing – the purchase of government and corporate bonds by central banks – to keep interest rates low and (it was hoped) thereby stimulate investment and consumption helped bring nominal interest rates down to historically low, and in some countries negative, levels. As many analysts have pointed out, this ultra-cheap money policy boosted the demand for assets – including residential property – from households and corporate investors (Turner, 2016). Quantitative easing lowered the return on government and corporate bonds, which in turn prompted a 'search for yield' among investors. And among other assets, this new search for higher-yielding outlets led pension funds, insurance companies, private equity firms, other corporate organisations and better-off households to invest in the private rental housing market or increase their exposure to it (Kemp, 2015). As a result, private rental housing has become a new international asset class (van Loon and Aalbers, 2017; Fields, 2018; Fuller, 2021). Wijburg et al (2018) referred to this development as 'Financialisation 2.0'.

A further important reason why the GFC had a profound impact on housing – including private rental markets – is that it was not an *exogeneous* shock of the kind discussed by 'punctuated equilibrium' theorists of institutional change (for example, North, 1990; Steinmo et al, 1992). Instead, it was an *endogenous shock*, with roots in the securitisation of the rapidly expanding US subprime mortgage market (and other forms of collateralised debt obligations) and the accompanying sale of the securitised mortgage bundles on the global financial market (Mian and Sufi, 2014). The GFC shook the very foundations of the RMBS (residential mortgage-backed securities) market and the growth of homeownership among subprime and other marginal borrowers based upon it. Central banks and policy makers had little choice but to introduce measures to ensure that bank lending to home buyers was more prudent and better regulated than it had been in the decade prior to the GFC. Hence, one outcome of the GFC was the introduction by central banks of macroprudential tools to increase the resilience of the mortgage market and improve economic stability. These macroprudential tools included limits on loan-to-value ratios and borrower affordability tests (Turner, 2016). Thus, the GFC proved to be the catalyst for mortgage market changes that have reduced the ability of households at the rent/buy margin to move from renting to purchasing their home.

One further outcome of the GFC was the rise of mortgage foreclosures and evictions of borrowers who were no longer able to keep up with their mortgage payments (Immergluck, 2015; Martin and Niedt, 2015). This increased both the demand for and the supply of rental homes. In their contributions to this volume, Byrne, Pareja-Eastaway and Sánchez-Martínez, and Schwartz highlight how the foreclosure crises in Ireland, Spain and the USA respectively led to a growth in private renting among households that had lost their home. As well as increasing the number of households needing to rent their homes after losing their owner-occupied one, the foreclosure crisis created a one-off increase in the supply of vacant homes for sale at property auctions, many of which were bought for rental rather than occupation, in some cases by private equity firms like Blackstone (Fields and Uffer, 2016; Christophers, 2022) and other large corporate landlords (Mills *et al*, 2019).

Change and continuity

In summary, the changes in private rental housing demand and supply that we have examined in this book were the product of both (1) slow-moving social, demographic and economic trends; and (2) the economic shock of the GFC. However, the extent and pattern of change in private renting has not been uniform across the AEs, but rather variegated in important ways. That is hardly surprising, of course, because the trends and developments that prompted change were not uniform across the AEs. Rather, they unfolded in different economic, housing, welfare state, legal and cultural contexts, and policy settings. Housing provision, in other words, is embedded within a broader political economy (Stephens, 2011; Aalbers, 2016; Gallent, 2019).

The growth in households renting privately was about ten percentage points in England and Ireland, but significantly smaller than that in Australia, Denmark, the Netherlands, Norway, Spain and the United States. Meanwhile, the size of the German private rental sector was relatively stable over the first two decades of the 21st century. The types of households renting from private landlords did not change much in Germany over that period. But in the other AEs, the types of households diversified to a greater or lesser extent, to include more working and better-off households, more couples, and more families with dependent children.

Large corporate landlords such as pension funds, insurance companies and private equity firms increased substantially in seven of the nine countries – and especially so in Denmark and Ireland – but much less so in Australia and Norway (Martin *et al*, 2018). Since the turn of the century, PropTech firms providing information and services to tenants, landlords and prospective investors have become ubiquitous in the rental (and owner-occupied) housing market (Rogers, 2017; Fields and Rogers, 2021; Fields, 2022). Scanlon notes that in Denmark, where there is a shortage of rental housing, many landlords prefer to let their accommodation to people who they know. In England, recent years have witnessed a marked increase in mergers and acquisitions among letting agent firms, and Hulse explains that a similar process is ongoing in Australia.

Despite the significant changes in private rental housing that have taken place in many AEs since the turn of the century, there is much that has not changed. Again, this is hardly surprising. Institutions are relatively enduring configurations and highly path dependent. Hence, as Streeck and Thelen (2005) argued, transformation tends to take place gradually over time, as new institutions become increasingly important and gradually displace previously dominant ones. Major economic shocks have the potential to generate quicker, more radical and system-wide change. But even so, the transformations resulting from them invariably take some years to take place, as actors shape and respond to the new institutional configurations and the opportunities that are thereby created. Hence, it may be some time before their effects become fully apparent.

Despite the increased involvement of large corporate landlords in most of the countries covered in this book, small-scale private individual landlords still dominate the rental market in Australia, England, Ireland, Germany, Norway and Spain. In Denmark, as Scanlon explains, large corporate landlords were responsible for most of the growth in private rental housing over the past decade and now account for the majority (60 per cent) of homes in the PRS. This remarkably quick rise to ascendancy was the outcome of new construction rather than buying existing portfolios from private landlords. In countries like England and Australia where small-scale landlords dominate the supply of rental homes, the limited availability of portfolios large enough to attract the interest of financial institutions wishing to enter the PRS has forced them to focus on new-build developments (Crook and Kemp, 2011).

Relatively short, fixed-term tenancies continue to be dominant in private rental housing markets in the liberal market economies. And yet the evidence indicates that in Australia (Morris *et al*, 2021) England and Ireland, the proportion of tenants who are long-term renters has increased and the share of tenants who are elderly has also risen. These types of households are more likely than young adults to prefer long-term tenancies. Short-term tenancies make it relatively easy for landlords to ask their tenants to leave at the end of the contract. Not surprisingly, therefore, insecurity of tenure has become a pressing policy issue in liberal market economies. In Chapter 4, Byrne shows that, while major reforms of landlord–tenant law in 2004 and 2016 aimed to significantly strengthen tenant protection in Ireland, in practice

Table 12.1: Variegated private renting

Trend / policy issue	AUS	DE	DK	ENG	IE	NL	NOR	ESP	USA
PRS growth?	✔		✔	✔	✔	✔	✔	✔	✔
Broader role?	✔			✔	✔	✔		✔	✔
Increase in large corporate landlords?		✔	✔	✔	✔	✔	✔	✔	✔
PropTech dominant?	✔	✔		✔	✔	✔	✔	✔	✔
Indefinite leases?		✔	✔			✔	✔		
Airbnb concerns?	✔	✔		✔	✔	✔	✔	✔	✔
Affordability concerns	✔	✔	✔	✔	✔	✔	✔	✔	✔
Rent regulation?		✔	✔		✔	✔	✔	✔	
Anti-landlord sentiment?		✔	✔	✔	✔				

Sources: Chapters 2 to 10, this volume.

they were undermined by structural factors that remained unchanged. As a result, insecurity continues to be a pressing concern there for low-income private tenants. In England, 'no-fault' evictions are to be made illegal and tenants' rights improved more generally.

Indefinite leases have long been the default rental contract in Germany, Denmark, the Netherlands and Norway (Table 12.1). As a result, tenants have much stronger security of tenancy and, in the great majority of cases, can remain in their rental home for the very long term. However, in Norway, while indefinite leases are the default, legislation enacted in 2000 allowed fixed-term tenancies of up to three years and they dominate the market. It is also now possible in the Netherlands to let rental homes on fixed-term contracts (Haffner, Chapter 6, this volume). As Scanlon notes in Chapter 8, and Stamsø explains in Chapter 9, the private rental sectors in Denmark and in Norway, respectively, are widely seen as providing a largely transitional role, housing young adult tenants for a short period prior to buying their home; and the average duration of private renting is very short.

Rental affordability

In all nine countries, the affordability of rental housing is a public concern. This reflects the fact that rents have risen significantly in these countries, as the Organisation for Economic Co-operation and Development data for the period from 2005 to 2020 show. The crisis in rental affordability is by no means confined to the nine case study countries. Indeed, Wetzstein (2017) has argued it is a global one. Housing affordability, of course, is not simply about rents but also about incomes. If rents rise in line with incomes, affordability is not getting worse but staying roughly the same. In general, research on housing affordability is based on household surveys. Using the EU's 'housing cost overburden rate' to compute affordability, for example, Hick *et al* (2022) examined trends in affordability in European countries between 2010 and 2018. In this measure, households are deemed to be facing affordability problems if they spend more than 40 per cent of their disposable income on housing. They found that the cost overburden rate increased in some European countries between 2010 and 2018, but in others it fell (Hick *et al*, 2022). This is illustrated in Table 12.2, which is based on EU-SILC data on Eurostat's website. While the market renter cost overburden rate *increased* in seven of these countries between 2012 and 2020, it *fell* by more than three percentage points (pp) in five countries, and was *stable* in Germany (-0.2 pp) and Norway (+1.1 pp).

Table 12.2 suggests that the depth and extent of the new private rental affordability crisis varies across the AEs. However, the data is averaged across *all* market rate renters in each country; and, of course, *low-income* renters typically pay much larger shares of their income on rent. In fact, Dewilde (2015) shows that rental affordability for low-income private tenants significantly worsened in Western Europe following the GFC. And indeed, the authors of the country chapters in this volume report that rental affordability among low-income renters is a policy concern in their country. Moreover, as Chapter 5 shows, in London and elsewhere in the South-East of England, low-income tenants were on average paying very high shares of their income on rent in 2019/20. Moreover, in those regions even middle-income private renters were on average facing very high rent-to-income ratios. Both Hulse in Chapter 2 and Schwartz in Chapter 3 show that the stock of rental housing available and affordable to low-income households has fallen in Australia and the United States respectively.

Rent control

The data on rents in household surveys is generally the rent that tenants were paying at the time of the interview, which in most cases is not the prevailing *market* rent. Rents paid on new leases are invariably higher than those paid on existing leases; and in rapidly rising markets, they are likely to be much higher. Rental affordability pressures will therefore tend to be more acute on new and recent leases than on long-standing ones. Hence, the demand for something to be done about affordability problems seems more likely to come from recent and prospective movers in the rental market. For tenant

Table 12.2: Cost overburden rate for market renters in 14 European countries, 2012 and 2020

Country	2012	2020	Change
	%	%	
Austria	17.3	12.7	−4.6
Belgium	37.2	29.4	−7.8
Denmark	34.7	25.2	−9.5
Finland	11.8	14.2	+2.4
France	16.2	20.1	+3.9
Germany	23.7	23.5	−0.2
Greece	53.0	79.2	+26.2
Italy	34.2	28.1	−6.1
Ireland	21.3	16.7	−4.6
Norway	29.8	30.9	+1.1
Portugal	35.8	19.7	−16.1
Spain	44.7	35.9	−8.8
Switzerland	16.6	20.0	+3.4
UK	23.8	37.7	+13.9

Notes: The latest EU-SILC data is for UK 2018. Hick *et al* (2022) suggest that the exceptionally high overburden rate and increase in Greece is likely due to the austerity measures demanded by the EU as a pre-condition for the provision of bank bailouts in the wake of the GFC.

Source: Eurostat.

rights advocacy groups, that 'something' is very often the introduction, extension, strengthening or stricter application of rent controls.

Six of the countries covered in this book have regulations that limit the extent to which rents may be increased on existing tenancies. Some of these regulations are long-standing, as is the case in Denmark, Germany and the Netherlands. New York City and several other US cities and states have rent controls in one form or another, but the great majority of rental homes in America are not subject to rent controls (Whitehead and Williams, 2018). Private rents are not regulated in Australia or England, but in Ireland 'Rent Pressure Zones' in high-demand areas have been introduced. It is perhaps a measure of just how acute the affordability crisis is in Ireland that, as Byrne notes in Chapter 4, Rent Pressure Zones now cover around half of all private rental homes. In Germany, rent regulation was tightened considerably in 2015 with the introduction of the Rent Brake. Kofner explains in Chapter 7 that, in a major departure from soft regulation in place over recent decades, the Rent Brake extended regulation from *existing* tenancies to include *newly* agreed ones. The Berlin state government subsequently went even further and introduced a Rent Price Cap in 2020, which set maximum rents that could be charged on new and existing tenancies, though newly built housing was exempt. However, the German constitutional court subsequently ruled that the Berlin state government had overstepped its legal powers in introducing the Rent Price Cap.

Rent controls are highly contentious politically. Landlords and other critics argue that (among other things) they reduce the supply of private rental homes, thereby making the affordability problem even worse (Marsh *et al*, 2022). The impact of rent controls depends, of course, on their design, the housing market and institutional context within which they are introduced, the nature and availability of tax expenditures and housing subsidies, and the extent to which they are enforced, among other things (Whitehead and Williams, 2018; Marsh *et al*, 2022). As Marsh *et al* (2022) explain, attempts to undertake empirical analysis of their impact are fraught with methodological difficulties. However, these nuances and difficulties tend to get lost in public discourse about the desirability or otherwise of rent controls.

For politicians seeking to win votes in forthcoming elections, rent controls may be a tempting prospect. First, they appear to be popular with the public. A representative survey in Britain in 2021, for example, found that three out of five respondents were in favour of the introduction of rent controls. Second, in some AEs, welfare rights activists and groups representing tenants are campaigning for the introduction of (or stricter) rent controls (Marsh *et al*, 2022). This helps ensure that concerns about the lack of affordability of rental housing regularly make headlines in newspapers and on news websites; and often feature on national and local television and radio. It raises the public profile of rental affordability concerns and that makes it harder for policy makers to ignore.

Third, an attraction of rent controls for politicians is that, unlike means-tested housing allowances for tenants, and supply-side subsidies for social housing, they do not require public expenditure to implement. Therefore, policy makers do not have to raise taxes, or shift spending from other government programmes, to pay for rent controls. On the contrary, as rent controls lower rents or limit rent increases, they may reduce public expenditure on housing allowances and rent supplements in social assistance programmes. To politicians focused on seeking votes, therefore, rent controls may appear to be costless to the taxpayer.

Fourth, while the introduction of new government programmes often encounters implementation problems, rent controls can be introduced simply via legislation. All that is needed is a date on which the rent restrictions will be introduced. Fifth, while the benefits of government programmes may take years to become apparent, the impact of rent controls (depending on their design) can become apparent relatively quickly, thereby ensuring that the political payoff from introducing them is likewise rapid. And sixth, the immediate losers from rent controls are landlords, a group that is viewed unsympathetically by the public in some countries, including England (Roberts and Satsani, 2021; Jones and Mostafab, 2022) and Denmark (Scanlon, Chapter 8, this volume).

Airbnb

As noted in Chapter 1, the rise of Airbnb since 2008 has generated concerns about the impact it is having on rents, house prices and the supply of homes for residents in city centres and popular tourist destinations. Moreover, locals complain about the noise and disruption created by anti-social Airbnb guests and Airbnb parties. Not surprisingly, therefore, local authorities are beginning to introduce measures that aim to limit the harm that it is doing to in the areas most affected by Airbnb (Cocola-Gant and Gago, 2021).

One of the attractions of Airbnb for tourist and business customers is that it is often cheaper than the cost of hotel rooms. To that extent, Airbnb has the potential to *dampen* hotel room rates. In contrast, by competing with owner-occupiers and rental landlords for properties in the residential market, Airbnb potentially acts to *increase* home prices and rents. It is therefore a disruptive force for both the hotel trade and the housing market (Guttentag, 2015; Dolnicare and Zare, 2020) and one that has generated a rapidly growing literature in both tourism and housing studies journals. As well as higher rental income from Airbnb than from letting to long-term residents, another advantage for hosts is that it enables them to disinvest from the property market at very short notice because the guests are very transient (Cocola-Gant and Gago, 2021. Meanwhile, the short-term lettings that are common in liberal market economies like Australia and England enable BTL landlords to switch properties from the private rental sector to the Airbnb short-stay market (and vice versa) relatively quickly (Kemp, 2020).

The COVID-19 pandemic

The GFC, of course, is not the only major economic shock to have hit the advanced and developing economies since the turn of the century. The COVID-19 pandemic led to the biggest global economic turndown in living memory. Unlike the GFC, it was an *exogenous* shock resulting from the response by governments and households around the world to the rapid, global transmission of the COVID-19 virus. Much of the world economy came to a rapid halt or slowdown on a scale never seen before (Tooze, 2021).

It is hardly surprising, therefore, that COVID-19 had an impact on housing markets including private rental housing.

Each of the nine country chapters in this book summarise the short-run impact on COVID-19 on the PRS and the measures taken by governments to minimise the spread of the virus and limit its consequences for health and social care provision (see also Pawson *et al*, 2022). And in Chapter 11 Crook compares the impact on private rental housing markets in the case study countries. He argues that the ways in which countries responded to COVID-19 was shaped by their pre-existing housing and social safety net institutional configurations. Denmark, Germany and Norway had in place laws that provided renters with strong security of tenure and relatively comprehensive social safety nets. Their governments, therefore, had less need to introduce new measures to limit the impact of the pandemic on tenants and workers.

In contrast, in Australia, England, Ireland and the United States, pre-pandemic security of tenure for tenants was less strong and social safety nets were either less generous, or less comprehensive in scope and reach. As Crook argues in Chapter 11, governments in these liberal market economies consequently had to introduce an array of new measures, or enhance the support provided by existing schemes, to limit rent arrears and evictions in the private rental market and to give workers better income support. For the most part, these new COVID-19 measures were ad hoc in nature; they were invariably temporary and terminated as the lockdowns were phased out. As a result, the most serious 'Covid rent arrears' are likely to be translated in the medium term into evictions and homelessness to a greater or lesser degree. For example, as Crook notes in Chapter 11, in England court actions for eviction have been rising since 2021.

In Australia, the United States, England and elsewhere, private rents have been rapidly rising since 2021. There appear to be both demand and supply-side reasons for this surge in rents. The demand for private rental housing has increased because of the return to city centre living among some of tenants who moved to suburban and exurban locations, or returned to the parental home, during the COVID-19 pandemic. Increased rental demand also reflects the bounce-back in new domestic and international students resulting from applications that deferred during the pandemic. On the supply-side, many Airbnb hosts that switched into residental lettings during the pandemic have now returned to the more lucrative holiday and business traveller over-night stay market. In England, reports in the trade press suggest that private landlords have disinvested, or switched to Airbnb, in response to tax increases on rental homes and/or the increase in mortgage interest rates in the wake of the Russian invasion of Ukraine. Beyond these short-term factors, as the chapters on Australia, England and the United States highlight, is a long-term under-supply of rental homes.

The Russian invasion of Ukraine

It remains to be seen what the long-term effects of the COVID-19 pandemic will be on private rental housing in the AEs. To some extent, though, that is now a moot question because of the Russian invasion of Ukraine in February 2022, which has created the third major economic shock to the world economy since the turn of the century.

The economic recovery from COVID-19 brought with it a largely unexpected, sharp rise in inflation due to the post-lockdown surge in consumer demand, slower than anticipated recovery of supply chains, and labour shortages resulting from what newspapers called the 'great resignation' among older workers below the official pension age in the wake of the pandemic. In England, labour shortages were further exacerbated by Brexit, which choked off economic immigration from the EU27. The rise in inflation produced a fierce debate about whether it would be only transitory, or more enduring as workers responded to rising prices by demanding higher wages.

However, this debate was transformed overnight when Russian armed forces invaded Ukraine in February 2022. The invasion resulted in even higher levels of inflation, particularly in energy and food prices. Central banks responded to rising inflation by raising interest rates. This generated a debate, not only about how *long* this new surge in inflation would be, but also about how *high* inflation might get; and about whether the rise in interest rates would push some economies into recession or even stagflation. In short, the economic recovery from the pandemic was superseded by a new global economic shock caused by the Russian invasion of Ukraine.

The toxic combination of rapidly rising inflation, falling real incomes as wages fail to fully keep up with consumer prices, and higher mortgage interest rates, created a cost-of-living crisis on a scale not seen for many years. That will inevitably have consequences for private rental housing. Rent arrears, for example, are very likely to rise among low-income tenants struggling to afford food and pay energy bills. And that in turn may well result in evictions, especially among those households that already have outstanding arrears accrued during the COVID-19 pandemic. In Scotland, the government introduced an across-the-board rent freeze in both private and the social housing in response to the cost-of-living crisis (Marsh *et al*, 2022). Meanwhile, tenant advocacy groups campaigned for rent freezes to be introduced in England and Wales.

The cost-of-living crisis will in the short term reduce the ability of some households at the rent/buy margin to move from renting to owner-occupation. The uncertainty caused by the war may lead to increased investment flows into private rental housing and away from stocks and shares for the duration of the hostilities. On the other hand, the rise in interest rates will make government and corporate bonds more attractive to risk-averse investors. In Germany, the influx of well over a million refugees seems likely to stress rental housing markets and put upward pressure on rents; and that in turn may increase the demand for stricter rent controls. For these and other reasons, the Russian invasion of Ukraine, and the cost-of-living crisis it exacerbated, may well have a significant impact on private rental housing. However, that is a subject for future scholarship on private renting to examine and debate.

References

Aalbors, M.B. (2016) *The Financialisation of Housing: A Political Economy Approach*, New York, Routledge.

Andrews, M. (2010) 'The changing route to owner occupation: the impact of student debt', *Housing Studies*, 25(1), 39–62.

Cocola-Gant, A. and Gago, A. (2021) 'Airbnb, buy-to-let investment and tourism-driven displacement: a case study in Lisbon', *Environment & Planning A*, 53(7), 1671–1688.

Christophers, B. (2022) 'Mind the rent gap: Blackstone, housing investment and the reordering of urban rent surfaces', *Urban Studies*, 59(4), 698–716.

Crook, A.D.H. and Kemp, P.A. (2011) *Transforming Private Landlords*, Oxford, Wiley.

Dewilde, C. (2015) 'Explaining the declined affordability of housing for low-income private renters across Europe', *Urban Studies*, 55(12), 2618–2639.

Dolnicare, S. and Zare, S. (2020) 'Covid-19 and Airbnb: disrupting the disruptor', *Annals of Tourism Research*, 83, 1–3.

Fields, D. (2018) 'Constructing a new asset class: property-led financial accumulation after the crisis', *Economic Geography*, 94, 118–140.

Fields, D. and Uffer, S. (2016) 'The financialisation of rental housing: a comparative analysis of New York City and Berlin', *Urban Studies*, 53(7), 1486–1502.

Fields, D. and Rogers, D. (2021) 'Towards a critical housing studies research agenda on platform real estate', *Housing, Theory & Society*, 38(1), 72–94.

Fields, D. (2022) 'Automated landlord: digital technologies and post-crisis financial accumulation', *EPA: Economy and Space*, 54(1), 160–181.

Fuller, G.W. (2021) 'The financialization of rented homes: continuity and change in housing financialization', *Review of Revolutionary Political Economy*, 2, 551–570.

Gallent, N. (2019) *Whose Housing Crisis? Assets and Homes in a Changing Economy*, Bristol, Policy Press.

Guttentag, D. (2015) 'Airbnb: disruptive innovation and the rise of an informal accommodation sector', *Current Issues in Tourism*, 18(12), 1192–1217.

Hick, R., Pomati, M. and Stephens, M. (2022) *Housing and Poverty in Europe*, Cardiff, Cardiff University.

Immergluck, D. (2015) *Preventing the Next Mortgage Crisis*, London: Rowman & Littlefield.

Jones, C. and Mostafab, A. (2022) 'The revival of private residential landlordism in Britain through the prism of changing returns', *Journal of Property Research*, 39(1), 56–76.

Kemp, P.A. (2015) 'Private renting after the global financial crisis', *Housing Studies*, 30, 601–620.

Kemp, P.A. (2020) 'Commentary on multiple property ownership', *International Journal of Housing Policy*, 20(1), 144–155.

Kofner, S. (2006) 'Private equity investment in housing: the case of Germany', paper for the European Network of Housing Research International Housing Conference, Ljubljana, Slovenia, 2–5 July.

Kofner, S. (2014) *The Private Rented Sector in Germany*, CreateSpace Independent Publishing Platform.

Krippner, G.R. (2011) *Capitalizing on Crisis*, Cambridge, MA, Harvard University Press.

Marsh, A., Gibb, K. and Soaita, A.M. (2022) 'Rent regulation: unpacking the debates', *International Journal of Housing Policy*, DOI: 10.1080/ 19491247.2022.2089079

Martin, C., Hulse, K. and Pawson, H. (2018) *The Changing Institutions of Private Rental Housing: An International Review*, Melbourne, Australian Housing and Urban Research.

Martin, C., Hulse, K., Ghasri, M., Ralston, L., Crommelin, and Goodall, Z. et al (2022) *Regulation of Residential Tenancies and Impacts on Investment*, Melbourne, Australian Housing and Urban Research Institute.

Martin, I.W. and Niedt, C. (2015) *Foreclosed America*, Stanford, Stanford Briefs.

Mian, A. and Sufi, A. (2014) *House of Debt: How They (and You) Caused the Great Recession, and How We Can Prevent It From Happening Again*, Chicago, University of Chicago Press.

Mills, J., Molloy, R. and Zarutskie, R. (2019) 'Large-scale buy-to-rent investors in the single-family housing market: the emergence of a new asset class', *Real Estate Economics*, 47(2), 399–430.

Morris, A., Hulse, K. and Pawson, H. (2021) *The Private Rental Sector in Australia: Living with Uncertainty*, Singapore, Springer.

Murie, A. (2022) 'Right to buy: the long view of a key aspect of UK housing policy', in Stephens, M., Perry, J., Williams, P. and Young, G. (eds) *UK Housing Review 2022*, London, Chartered Institute of Housing, pp 45–54.

North, D.C. (1990) *Institutions, Institutional Change and Economic Performance*, Cambridge, Cambridge University Press.

Pawson, H., Martin, C., Aminpour, F., Gibb, K. and Foye, C. (2022) *COVID-19: Housing Market Impacts and Housing Policy Responses – An International Review*, Sydney, COSS and UNSW.

Pierson, P. (2004) *Politics in Time*, Princeton, Princeton University Press.

Resolution Foundation (2021) *Hope to Buy: The Decline of Youth Homeownership*, Resolution Foundation Briefing.

Roberts, S. and Satangi, M. (2021) 'The bad landlord: origins and significance in contemporary housing policy and practice', *Housing, Theory and Society*, 38(4), 496–511.

Rogers, D. (2017) *Geopolitics of Real Estate: Reconfiguring Property, Capital, and Rights*, London, Rowman & Littlefield.

Ronald, R. and Kadi, J. (2018) 'The revival of private landlords in Britain's post-homeownership society', *New Political Economy*, 23(6), 786–803.

Steinmo, S., Thelen, K. and Longstreth, F. (1992) Structuring Politics, Cambridge, Cambridge University Press.

Sprigings, N. and Smith, D.H. (2012) 'Unintended consequences: local housing allowance meets the right to buy', *People, Place and Policy Online*, 6(2), 58–75.

Stephens, M. (2011) 'Comparative housing research: a system-embedded approach', *International Journal of Housing Policy*, 11(4), 337–355.

Streeck, W. and Thelen, K. (2005) 'Introduction: institutional change in advanced political economies', in W. Streeck and K. Thelen (eds) *Beyond Continuity*, Oxford, Oxford University Press, pp 1–39.

Tooze, A. (2018) *Crashed,* London, Penguin.

Tooze, A. (2021) *Shutdown*, London, Viking.

Turner, A. (2016) *Between the Debt and the Devil*, Princeton, Princeton University Press.

van Loon, J. and Aalbers, M.B. (2017) 'How real estate became "just another asset class": the financialization of the investment strategies of Dutch institutional investors', *European Planning Studies*, 25, 221–240.

Wetzstein, S. (2017) 'The global urban housing affordability crisis', *Urban Studies*, 54(14), 3159–3177.

Whitehead, C. and Williams, P. (2017) *Changes in the Regulation and Control of Mortgage Markets and Access to Owner-occupation Among Younger Households*, Working Paper 196, Paris, OECD.

Whitehead, C. and Williams, P. (2018) *Assessing the Evidence on Rent Control from an International Perspective*, London, LSE.

Wijburg, G. and Aalbers, M.B. (2017) 'The alternative financialisation of the German housing marketss', *Housing Studies*, 32(7), 968–989.

Wijburg, G., Aalbors, M.B. and Heeg, S. (2018) 'The financialisation of rental housing 2.0', *Antipode*, 50(4), 1098–1119.

Wood, G. and Ong, R. (2015) 'The facts on Australian housing affordability', *The Conversation*, 11 June.

Index

References to figures appear in *italic* type; those in **bold** type refer to tables.